Shadow Play

Shadow Play

The Murder of Robert F. Kennedy,
the Trial of Sirhan Sirhan,
and the Failure of
American Justice

✸ ✸ ✸

WILLIAM KLABER
AND
PHILIP H. MELANSON

ST. MARTIN'S PRESS

NEW YORK

Design by Ellen R. Sasahara

Library of Congress Cataloging-in-Publication Data

Klaber, William.
     Shadow play : the murder of Robert F. Kennedy, the trial of Sirhan Sirhan, and the failure of American justice / William Klaber, Philip H. Melanson.
          p.   cm.
     ISBN 0-312-15398-8
     1. Kennedy, Robert F., 1925–1968—Assassination. 2. Sirhan, Sirhan Bishara, 1944-   . I. Melanson, Philip.   II. Title.
E840.8.K4K58   1997
364.1'524'0973—dc21   97-5670
                                                                              CIP

First Edition: May 1997

10 9 8 7 6 5 4 3 2 1

*This book is dedicated to the memory of
Allard K. Lowenstein and Gregory Stone.*

In our sleep, pain which cannot forget falls drop by drop upon the heart until, in our despair, against our will, comes wisdom through the awful grace of God.

—Robert Kennedy, quoting Aeschylus following the murder of Dr. Martin Luther King, Jr. (1968)

Contents

✳   ✳   ✳

Foreword

✻　✻　✻

Sirhan Sirhan was captured red-handed in the crowded pantry of the Ambassador Hotel in Los Angeles where Senator Robert F. Kennedy had just been fatally shot and where witnesses saw him firing a pistol. So what is the justification for this book and its charge of a "failure of American justice"? The answer becomes clear in the following pages: a close-minded police investigation that was at times shockingly incompetent and a defense that ignored evidentiary defects.

It is in the celebrated murder case that the public has an opportunity to observe how the criminal justice system works. Repeatedly, such prominent cases have revealed unprofessional police investigations that have left disturbing doubts for the public of the validity of the outcome in these cases and of the effectiveness of American criminal justice. The widely publicized investigation of President John F. Kennedy's assassination and the recent spate of high profile trials are examples of why the public has such a poor impression of our system.

In *Shadow Play*, William Klaber and Philip Melanson's insightful portrayal of the police investigation of Senator Robert F. Kennedy's murder and the prosecution and trial of Sirhan Sirhan, the authors raise even more serious doubts about the integrity of criminal justice. If these showcase investigations reveal so much incompetence, how much worse can we expect the handling of the ordinary criminal case to be?

With regard to crime generally in America, the criminal justice system appears to be mostly irrelevant. The bureaucratic and hierarchical system of police, prosecutors, and judges affects only a tiny percentage of dangerous crime—3 million out of the 34 million serious felonies reported annually by the Department of Justice's crime victim survey. Most crime is unreported or unsolved. Moreover, the 3 million felonies that do enter the criminal justice system through police arrest suffer serious erosion in the screening and adversary process that leaves only little more than 10 percent of them ending up in convictions and sentences of more than one year. This huge "mortality" of criminal cases is largely caused by incompetent police investigative work, legal defects in the quality or quantity of evidence obtained, and the inability of prosecutors and courts, because of starved resources, to effectively handle even this number of criminal cases.

The murder of Senator Robert F. Kennedy in the midst of his campaign for the Democratic nomination for the Presidency of the United States was not crime generally. It was an extraordinary and horrendous crime. Yet authors Klaber and Melanson demonstrate credibly that RFK's murder was handled by the Los Angeles police and the FBI, at best, as clumsily and incompetently as the run of the mill crimes are handled. At worst, their story shows police concealment and destruction of evidence and intimidation of witnesses to cover up any evidence that would contradict the conclusions they immediately drew at the time of the killing, or that would question the good faith of the LAPD's determination that Sirhan Sirhan acted alone and was the sole gunman in the shooting of Robert Kennedy.

Even so, Klaber and Melanson have not succumbed to the temptation to spin a tale of dark conspiracy. To the contrary, they have presented a sober but dramatic analysis of the investigation of the murder of RFK and the prosecution of Sirhan Sirhan. What makes their analysis different from earlier accounts of this national tragedy, and therefore more compelling, is that they were able to inspect the voluminous LAPD files on the case that had been kept from the public by the police and Los Angeles officials for twenty years after the assassination. These once-secret files are as significant for what they do not show as for what they do. Astonishingly, vital physical evidence taken from the scene of the murder, such as doorframes and ceiling tiles containing bullet holes, possibly indicating a second gun, were destroyed by the police and were not available for Sirhan Sirhan's trial.

Even at the time of Sirhan Sirhan's trial there were conspiracy theories circulating about more than one person firing a gun when Kennedy was shot and about a beautiful young woman wearing a polka-dot dress running out of the death scene shouting "We killed him!" But there was no publicly known substantiating evidence, and the police could dismiss these claims as attempts to replay the JFK conspiracy theories. However, Klaber and Melanson plumb the LAPD files to reveal shocking details from police-recorded witness statements that undeniably show that shortly after the assassination, the police were receiving eyewitness accounts from clearly reliable individuals providing support for the claim that others besides Sirhan Sirhan were involved in the killing. At the least, this information should have prompted the police to open up their investigation to pursue these new leads. Instead, the authors provide graphic evidence that police interviewers intimidated some of these witnesses to change their stories and to support the official theory of only one gunman, Sirhan Sirhan.

Why? Were the police so convinced they had the real killer that they were willing to ignore other evidence that could jeopardize their case against Sirhan Sirhan? Were the police just lazy and satisfied they had enough to make a case against Sirhan Sirhan? These questions are inescapable from the evidence revealed by Klaber and Melanson. They don't prove a dark conspiracy. But they certainly provide fertile ground for the growth of such a theory.

In addition to raising these questions, the flawed police investigation and the lead defense lawyer's lack of attention to it leave the justice of Sirhan Sirhan's conviction also in question. Although even a sloppy investigation can result in a correct trial verdict, the omissions and ambiguities pervading this investigation and trial do not permit this conclusion. It was crucial for the trial to resolve the questions of whether others were involved in Senator Kennedy's murder and whether the fatal bullet was fired from Sirhan Sirhan's gun. By themselves the answers to these questions would not absolve Sirhan Sirhan if he were a co-conspirator, but whether he was or not was an issue raised by other evidence emphasized by the authors, which may have been able to prove he did not engage in a voluntary or conscious act.

Sirhan Sirhan's prominent defense lawyer never argued any of this evidence to the jury. Instead, he conceded Sirhan Sirhan's guilt and rested his entire strategy on saving Sirhan Sirhan's life by attempting to prove that he acted under diminished capacity, and, therefore, was guilty of a homicide lesser than first-degree murder. Whatever strategic or professional judgments motivated this decision by defense counsel, it nevertheless resulted in the trial failing to cure the evidentiary defects caused by the police conduct in the case, and leaving the reader of this book with the uncomfortable feeling that there may have been a failure of American justice as claimed in the subtitle. That is, Sirhan Sirhan may have been wrongly convicted of the murder of Robert Kennedy.

That Sirhan Sirhan's guilt still may by a legitimate question is a shame on the administration of criminal justice in Los Angeles. There can be no tolerance for unprofessional or incompetent law enforcement investigation or prosecution. It must be the rule in a criminal investigation that it be conducted thoroughly, objectively, and fairly. Only such an investigation can result in a trial that will produce a verdict recognized as fair even by the accused, and that will have the confidence of the general public. Klaber and Melanson make a good case that the investigation of Robert Kennedy's murder and the trial of Sirhan Sirhan failed this rule. As a consequence, the doubts about Sirhan Sirhan's guilt cannot finally be put to rest solely on the verdict of the jury.

—Samuel Dash,
Georgetown University Law Center,
Washington, D.C., February 10, 1997

Preface

✢ ✢ ✢

*Robert Kennedy's death, like the president's, was mourned as an
extension of the evils of senseless violence . . . a whimsical fate
inconveniently interfering in the workings of democracy.
What is odd is not that some people thought it was all random,
but that so many intelligent people refused to believe that it might be
anything else. Nothing can measure more graphically how limited
was the general understanding of what is possible in America.*

—Former New York congressman Allard Lowenstein (1977)[1]

IT WAS PRIMARY night in California, June 4, 1968. As Robert Kennedy addressed his cheering supporters in the Embassy Room of the Ambassador Hotel, Paul Schrade looked on with pride and admiration. An hour earlier Schrade had been upstairs with the senator, working on the details of his speech. Now from the stage of the Los Angeles hotel he watched as Kennedy declared victory and assumed his place as a frontrunner for the Democratic presidential nomination.

When he had finished speaking, Robert Kennedy stepped off the stage into a dimly lit hallway en route to another press conference. He spotted Schrade and called out for him to follow. Kennedy then passed through a set of swinging doors into a narrow food-preparation area, where he paused to shake hands with several busboys. "Finally," Schrade thought as he observed the scene, "a real president."

Just then Schrade experienced what felt like a severe electric shock—the thought raced through his mind that he had stepped in some water with live television wires. Schrade's body began to convulse uncontrollably. As he fell to the floor he was certain he was being electrocuted.

When he regained consciousness a short while later, Paul Schrade felt bruises on his chest where he had been stepped upon by a panicking crowd. There was a sharper pain in his forehead where a bullet lodged in his skull. A short distance away Robert Kennedy lay mortally wounded.

Years later, the pain of that awakening still scarred Schrade deeply. Sirhan Bishara Sirhan, to everyone's satisfaction, had been convicted of Robert Kennedy's murder, but Schrade was troubled because the wound in his own head made no sense, given the explanation offered for it by the Los Angeles police. When he tried to find out more, Schrade discovered that the police files on the crime were sealed.

In 1974, at the urging of former New York congressman Allard Lowenstein, Paul Schrade joined a small group of citizens trying to open the secret police files. A year later he became a plaintiff in an unsuccessful lawsuit seeking to force disclosure. In the decade that followed, Schrade took the fight to Mayor Thomas Bradley and the Los Angeles Police Commission.

Finally public pressure prevailed. In 1988 the police files in the Robert Kennedy assassination were made available for inspection by the California State Archives in Sacramento. Schrade and a small group of researchers (including this book's coauthor Philip Melanson) then began to sift slowly through the more than fifty thousand pages of released documents.

On April 2, 1992, almost twenty-four years after the assassination, a silver-haired Paul Schrade, accompanied by several colleagues, walked down the polished corridors of the Los Angeles County Courthouse pulling a small wagon carrying five heavy boxes. In the boxes were copies of a "request," a formal petition asking the Los Angeles County Grand Jury to appoint a special prosecutor to investigate the Los Angeles Police Department for "willfull and corrupt misconduct" in the investigation of the murder of Robert Kennedy. Accompanying the request were eight hundred pages of exhibits offered to back up claims of the LAPD's "destruction of evidence, falsification of evidence and coercion of witnesses."

In addition to that of Paul Schrade, the petition to the grand jury bore the signatures of over fifty prominent citizens, including historian Arthur Schlesinger, Jr., former RFK press secretary Frank Mankiewicz, former Watergate prosecutor Sam Dash, author Norman Mailer, farm workers' leader Cesar Chavez, and Harvard law professor Gary Bellow.

The request was also signed by several men who played a direct role in the events surrounding the assassination. One of these was William Bailey. On the night of the murder, Bailey was an agent for the FBI stationed in Los Angeles. He inspected the crime scene and interviewed witnesses a few hours after the shooting. Over time Bailey became convinced that the official version of the murder was a fabrication.

William Bailey now teaches criminal justice at a small college in New Jersey. Each year he puts on a mock trial of Sirhan in which the class sits as jury. "First I present the prosecution case in the best way I know," he told the authors, "then the defense. I have never been able to convict Sirhan." As Bailey explains it, his trial of Sirhan is a tutorial in the suspension of judgment. "I want to show them," he says, speaking of his students, "that in criminal investigations, things are not always what they seem."

Dr. Cyril Wecht also signed the grand jury petition. Wecht is a lawyer, a medical doctor, and a former president of the American Academy of Forensic Sciences. In days following the death of Robert Kennedy, Wecht worked with Los Angeles County coroner Dr. Thomas Noguchi on the autopsy report. What he discovered disturbed him greatly. To Wecht, the evidence strongly suggested that Sirhan Sirhan was not the source of the bullets that struck Robert Kennedy.

Several weeks after the murder Dr. Wecht was contacted by the mother of Sirhan Sirhan. She asked if he would represent her son in court. Wecht was stunned and flattered, but after several days' consideration he declined, in part because he was not an active criminal lawyer. Wecht felt justified in this decision when Sirhan secured the services of several highly respected attorneys. A year later he would be dismayed when these men did not introduce at Sirhan's trial any of the potentially exonerating evidence.

"There's no question that Sirhan deserves a new trial," Wecht said recently. "This case has never been as simple as it looked. Forensically speaking, it's a puzzle."

Though Schrade, Bailey, and Wecht, among others, have struggled with the facts of this murder for more than a quarter century, the assassination of Robert Kennedy was not regarded as a puzzle by those who investigated the crime. The case against Sirhan Sirhan, in the public mind, could hardly have been more open and shut. Robert Kennedy was shot and killed, and Sirhan Sirhan, firing a pistol, was apprehended only a few feet away. In time, the accused assassin would admit to the crime, offer a motive, and assert that he acted alone—a prosecutor's dream. Rumors of conspiracy seemed, for once, not only unfounded, but easily refuted.

But this seemingly most apparent of the 1960s political assassinations turns out to be, in many ways, the most complex; certainly, the most bizarre. For example, while the accused assassin insisted he acted alone, reliable witnesses saw him being led to the crime by a beautiful woman, who, shortly thereafter, was seen running from the hotel laughing. She then vanished. More disturbing, ballistic evidence collected by the police and the coroner strongly suggested that a second gun was fired during the murder, and that Sirhan Sirhan may not have shot Robert Kennedy at all. Some of the most important pieces of this evidence also vanished. Most strange is that, despite his admission of guilt, the confessed assassin seemed, genuinely, to have no memory of the crime. What did this mean? Normally, one would expect a murder trial to sort through these circumstances to separate fact from fiction. Not in this case.

The trial of Sirhan Sirhan was, from the beginning, a self-conscious event. "We are aware that this is not just another criminal case," Los Angeles district attorney Evelle Younger announced. "We are aware the whole nation, even the whole world, is watching." So many newsmen, in fact, attended the trial, that a second courtroom had to be outfitted with video monitors to accommodate the overflow. Those in attendance spoke about the trial in reverential terms.

Time magazine labeled it "a classic of criminal jurisprudence." Others called it "the trial Lee Harvey Oswald never had," "the trial of the century," or "a showcase of American justice." Anticipating, incorrectly, a parallel proceeding against the accused assassin of Dr. Martin Luther King, the *New York Times* asserted, "both will represent trials of the American system of justice as much as they will trials of the men in the dock."

In the late 1960s, the image of legal authority in America badly needed reaffirmation. The country, it seemed, was fracturing along racial and generational lines. Each week hundreds of young men died in an unpopular Asian war, riots were increasingly common on university campuses and in the streets of the nation's cities, and political murders were occurring with unprecedented frequency.

For its part, the government appeared powerless to stop the political violence, and the American judicial system seemed unable to cope with these events after the fact. Lee Oswald, the accused assassin of President John Kennedy, forcefully asserted during his brief public moment that he was a patsy. He was then shot to death on TV by a local hoodlum before any legal proceedings could begin. James Earl Ray, the accused assassin of Dr. Martin Luther King, alleged in his brief public moment that he was a victim of a conspiracy. He was also quickly hustled off the stage without a trial.

It then fell to the prosecutors and defenders of Sirhan Sirhan to reassert the authority and integrity of American justice. It is clear that those involved understood and accepted this mandate, but, in so doing, they became careless with the truth. There were some who were guilty of worse. Destruction of evidence, coercion of witnesses—these were acts of volition.

Far more common were sins born of vanity and ignorance in otherwise honorable men. Each act of neglect, each deceit in pursuit of an adjudicated truth, seemed small given the assumed certainty of the defendant's guilt and the greater good of the nation's honor. But the secrecy, the negligence, and the deceit accumulated, until what was acted out in that small Los Angeles courtroom was not a glowing tribute to American jurisprudence, but rather a farcical shadow play in which historical truth and the rights of the defendant were sacrificed at the altar of public justice.

Acknowledgments

✻　✻　✻

The authors owe a special debt to Jean Klaber and Judith Melanson for their patience, advice, and support throughout this five-year project. We gratefully acknowledge the numerous other persons whose assistance helped bring this endeavor to fruition.

The late congressman Allard K. Lowenstein, in the face of official recalcitrance, courageously pursued unanswered questions about the assassination until his tragic murder in 1980. His associate, the late Gregory Stone, dedicated his life to the continuance of Congressman Lowenstein's work, forming the link between the early researchers and the modern historians of the case.

The late Lillian Castellano was the driving force behind the Los Angeles–based Kennedy Assassination Truth Committee. Her tenacious efforts to bring light into the case record was a model of citizenship. Floyd Nelson, also a founder of the Truth Committee, continued Ms. Castellano's work after her death. His selfless contribution stretches over three decades.

Paul Schrade was a friend of Senator Kennedy. He was also seriously wounded during the assassination. His vigorous pursuit of the truth regarding Kennedy's death while constantly upholding the senator's living political legacy is a true profile in courage. Attorney Marilyn Barrett played a central role in converting Gregory Stone's research into the 1992 petition to the Los Angeles Grand Jury.

Author and former Sirhan defense investigator Robert Blair Kaiser generously shared his recollections of the Sirhan trial. His brilliant 1971 book *"RFK Must Die!"* remains indispensable to any serious student of the case, and without his insights into the behavior and motivations of Sirhan Sirhan any attempt to approach this central mystery would be incomplete.

Attorney Phyllis Cooper was kind enough to share her memories of her late husband Grant Cooper. Through her grace and intelligence the authors gained a fuller understanding of the man who was lead attorney for the Sirhan defense team.

Sirhan Sirhan granted two rare extended interviews that greatly enhanced the authors' understanding of the protagonist of this legal drama. Adel Sirhan, brother of Sirhan Sirhan, and researcher Rose Lynn Mangan were instrumental in helping arrange these interviews. They were also most generous with their knowledge of the trial and the case.

Michael Caruso, then of *Vanity Fair,* had the courage to commission this story as a magazine article when others feared to do so. Terry Moran of Court TV had the vision to present material contained in this book during his coverage of Sirhan's previous parole hearing. Gretchen Young of HarperCollins was the first to believe that the story of Sirhan's trial should be a book. Our agent Stuart Krichevsky and editor George Witte of St. Martin's Press showed skill and determination in bringing this project to completion.

Our researchers Doria Alfiero, David DeSousa, and Laura Speanburg spent many hours pursuing the arcane.

The expertise, advice, and assistance of the following people also played an important role in bringing this book into being: Howard Bean, Malcolm Brown, Mike Clark, Dennis Cotton, Michael DeMelo, Terry Dumont, Judy Ferrar, Amity Gaige, Winifred Gallagher, Rick Hornung, Walter Keller, Helen Koss, Mara Lurie, Deborah McDonald, Brett Melanson, Jess Melanson, Betty Popovich, Lisa Porto, Tom Rumpf, Michael Segell, Tina Skerritt, Liz Tucker, Jennifer Walsh, and Eric Weisberg.

While not necessarily sharing the authors' viewpoints or objectives, the following people connected to the Robert Kennedy case were kind enough to share their experiences and insights: Al Albergate, LADA's office; William Bailey, former FBI special agent; Andy Boehm, journalist; Sheldon Brown, LADA's office; William R. Burnett, LADA's office; Frank Burns, Ambassador Hotel witness; Jonn Christian, journalist; William Cowden, L.A. Police Commission; David Cross, attorney, case researcher; Angelo DiPierro, Ambassador Hotel witness; Vincent DiPierro, Ambassador Hotel witness; Steve DuBoss, Ambassador Hotel witness; Scott Enyart, Ambassador Hotel witness; Edmund Fimbres, assistant city attorney, Los Angeles; Evan Freed, Ambassador Hotel witness; Brent Gold, Ambassador Hotel witness; Maria Gomez, Superior Court of Los Angeles; Alvin Greenwald, attorney for Scott Enyart; Brooker Griffin, Ambassador Hotel witness; Margaret Hahn, Ambassador Hotel witness; Christine Harwell, attorney for Scott Enyart; Frank Hendrix, president, Ace Guard Service; Robert Houghton, LAPD, former chief of detectives; Godfrey Isaac, attorney for Sirhan Sirhan; Dr. Robert Joling, forensic expert; Roger LaJeunesse, FBI liaison with LAPD; Betsy Langman, journalist and case researcher; James H. Lesar, attorney, FOIA (FBI) action; Luke McKissack, attorney for Sirhan Sirhan; David Mendelsohn, journalist; Skip Miller, attorney representing the city of Los Angeles; Judy Mitchell, Ambassador Hotel witness; Dan E. Moldea, journalist; Paul Nellen, journalist; Manuel Pena, LAPD, member of SUS; Robert Pinger, jury foreman, Enyart trial; George Plimpton, journalist, Ambassador Hotel witness; Lt. Robert Priola, Corcoran State Prison;

Nina Rhodes, Ambassador Hotel witness; Amadee O. Richards, RFK case supervisor, FBI; Paul Scharaga, LAPD, Ambassador Hotel witness; Barabara Schlei, L.A. Police Commission; Dr. Martin Schorr, defense psychologist, Sirhan trial; Steven Sowders, LADA's office; Dr. Herbert Speigel, expert on hypnosis; Robert Talcott, L.A. Police Commission; Theodore Taylor, coauthor *Special Unit Senator*; Lawrence Teeter, attorney for Sirhan Sirhan; Jack Thomas, journalist; William Turner, journalist; Karl Uecker, Ambassador Hotel witness; Lisa Urso, Ambassador Hotel witness; Dr. Cyril Wecht, forensic expert; Robert Weidrich, journalist; Nancy Zimmelman, and California State Archives.

PART I

The Trial

✵ ✵ ✵

ONE

The Ambassador Hotel

✳ ✳ ✳

Like all people at all times, they were confronted . . . by the present,
which always arrives in a promiscuous rush, with the significant, the
trivial, the profound and the fatuous all tangled together. The . . .
kings, prelates and nobles of the times sorted through the snarl, and
being typical men in power, chose to believe what they wanted to
believe, accepting whatever justified their policies and convictions,
and ignoring the rest.

—William Manchester, *In a World Lit Only by Fire*

JOHN HOWARD STEPPED through the door of the interrogation room and stared at the man seated in the chair. The prisoner, now showered, looked considerably better than he had before. Still, nobody knew his name.

An hour earlier Howard had told the prisoner, who had not been saying anything, that he had the right to stay silent. The slightly built, dark young man responded politely that he wished to "abide" by that "admonishment." Well, that settled one thing; he could speak English. The deputy district attorney then offered a card with his telephone number: "If you want to talk to someone."

Upon learning that the husky man in a suit was with the Los Angeles County DA's office, the prisoner brightened and made his first nonperfunctory utterance since being in custody.

"Remember Kirschke?"

"I've known Jack for a long time," answered a surprised Howard. "Why? Why did you ask that?"

"Interested," the young man replied.

When John Howard got word a little later that the prisoner was asking to speak with him, he had forgotten all about Jack Kirschke. But the mysterious young man had not. To Howard's chagrin, that is what he wanted to talk about.

"Yeah, we were talking about Kirschke." Howard sighed, thinking that if they could get going about one thing it might lead to something else. "How come you followed that? I was interested to ask you."

"No, I didn't follow it. I was hoping you'd clue me in on it, brief me on it, you might say."

"It was a tough lawsuit. You'd have to know Jack. He was a deputy; I worked with him."

"No, I mean—I mean the substance of the case."

Jack Kirschke, like Howard, had been a deputy district attorney in Los Angeles. Several years earlier, he had been charged with the bedroom murder of his wife and her lover. The story made headlines for months.

"The substance," Howard found himself saying, "actually was whether or not he was the guy that—there is no question his wife and a friend of hers got shot. There is no question about that. The question was who did it."

But the prisoner wanted to talk about things more subtle than guilt or innocence. Had Jack Kirschke sown the seeds of his own destruction? In prosecuting others did he feel he was above the law?

Suddenly the absurdity of the situation overwhelmed John Howard. Only hours before, the unidentified man in front of him had gunned down a United States senator, a presidential candidate. Now the two of them were having a friendly philosophical discussion. Either this guy was one cool customer, or something was wrong. Howard's instincts took over.

"Do you know where we are now?" he asked. "I've told you you've been booked."

"I don't know," replied the prisoner.

"You are in custody. You've been booked. You understand what I've been—"

"I have been before a magistrate, have I or have I not?"

"No, you have not. You will be taken before a magistrate as soon as possible. . . . You're downtown Los Angeles in the central jail. Now when I say this, if you know, you know—you know—I'm not saying this because I don't know. We're not communicating very well up to now, but you are downtown Los Angeles, okay? This is the main jail for the L.A. Police Department. You'll be booked into a cell . . . do you understand that? Do you understand where you are?"[1]

Like the prisoner, John Howard had not had any sleep that night. Normally on a Tuesday he would have been home in bed early, but this was primary night in California. Howard had been out at the Plush Horse Inn in Redondo Beach, which served as campaign headquarters for his friend Lynne

Frantz, who was running, unsuccessfully as it turned out, for Congress in the Seventeenth District.

Political gatherings were happening all over Los Angeles. There were three in the Ambassador Hotel alone, the largest of these in support of the presidential campaign of Robert F. Kennedy.

June 4, 1968, was arguably the most important day in the political career of the young senator from New York. A week earlier, in losing the Oregon presidential primary to Senator Eugene McCarthy, he had suffered the painful distinction of being the first Kennedy to be defeated in an election of any kind. California, however, was the big test. The winner would take its 174 delegates into the Chicago Democratic convention, now only weeks away.

Even with a victory in California, Robert Kennedy would still trail Vice President Hubert Humphrey in the crucial delegate count. But the momentum gained would be impressive, and there were many who thought Kennedy would swoop down upon the Humphrey delegates like a cattle rustler. Kennedy was a proven master at managing a convention floor, and there were still favors owed to the family that could be called in. In addition, Kennedy could leverage the feeling within the party that he was the man best suited to defeat Richard Nixon in the general election, as his brother had eight years before. But for any of this to happen, Robert Kennedy had to win in California, and the polls had predicted a tight contest.

As the first results of the evening came in, Senator McCarthy took the lead. But the vote from Los Angeles County, where Kennedy expected to do well, was locked up in an electronic purgatory, condemned by a foul-up in the new computerized vote-counting system. Eager for some solution to the drama, CBS projected a win for Kennedy just after 9 P.M. A little later, NBC did the same. But the vote from Los Angeles was still not in, and McCarthy, despite the network predictions, was still leading in the vote that was.

In the Royal Suite on the fifth floor of the Ambassador Hotel, Robert Kennedy huddled with what amounted to his shadow cabinet. Pierre Salinger, Richard Goodwin, Ted Sorenson, Fred Dutton, Frank Mankiewicz, Larry O'Brien—all these men had worked closely with President Kennedy. Also nearby were supporters such as United Farm Workers leader Dolores Huerta, pro football lineman Roosevelt Grier, Olympic decathlon champion Rafer Johnson, writer George Plimpton, labor activist Paul Schrade, and astronaut John Glenn. These were friends the senator had made on his own and, in a sense, they represented the new energy that was igniting the campaign.

Downstairs in the Embassy Room more than 1,800 jubilant campaign workers and admirers filled the hall beyond capacity. The Secret Service, however, was not there: they would protect presidential candidates only after the events of this night. Also absent were the Los Angeles police, even though three political functions were going on with thousands of participants. Safety and order depended on less than a score of hotel security personnel and hired guards from the Ace Guard Service.

By 11:30 a Kennedy victory seemed certain. Aides begged the candidate to move quickly to salvage some small portion of the national TV audience that could have been his only two hours ago. As Kennedy prepared to go downstairs, he paced back and forth rehearsing his remarks and the list of people he would thank. On a nearby couch his wife Ethel rested, three months pregnant with their eleventh child. Kennedy asked if she was ready. Ethel rose from the couch and the two of them headed toward the service elevator that would take them to the kitchen on the second floor. Once there, Kennedy flagged down a waiter, popped an olive into his mouth, and then made a triumphant entrance onto the ballroom stage.

The night before in San Diego, Robert Kennedy had nearly collapsed while making his final speech. The campaign had left him physically and emotionally drained. Now, in victory before his followers, he seemed rejuvenated. He thanked by name many of those who had helped him in California. Then, feeling a little giddy, he also thanked his dog Freckles "who has been much maligned in this campaign," jokingly attacked his brother-in-law Stephen Smith for being "ruthless," and, to great applause, invoked Don Drysdale's sixth straight shutout as though he had been watching the Los Angeles Dodger pitch that evening. When the cheering died down, Kennedy spoke about healing a divided country.

"What I think is quite clear is that we can work together in the last analysis [to overcome] the division, the violence, the disenchantment with our society, the division between black and white, between the poor and the more affluent, or between age groups or over the war in Vietnam. We are a great country, an unselfish country, a compassionate country. And I intend to make that my basis for running."

Kennedy's words were engulfed by cheers. After a long wait in the intense heat, his supporters were finally getting satisfaction. The candidate asked their indulgence for a minute or two more.

"What I think all of the primaries have indicated, whether they occurred in Colorado, or Idaho, or Iowa, wherever they occurred, is that the people in the Democratic Party and the people in the United States want change. . . . The country wants to move in a different direction. We want to deal with our own problems in our own country and we want peace in Vietnam."

In seeking to end his remarks Kennedy made a playful swipe at an old political enemy. "Mayor Yorty has just sent us a message that we've been here too long already," he said to the glee of those listening. "So my thanks to all of you and now on to Chicago and let's win there."

Once again the room erupted. "We want Bobby! We want Bobby!"

As Kennedy stepped away from the podium he seemed to be heading toward the campaign workers who had formed an escort phalanx off the right front of the stage. "This way, Senator," said someone in his entourage, and Kennedy moved instead to the back of the stage and toward the food-preparation area which has become known as the pantry—the route that would take him to a scheduled press conference in the Colonial Room. It was 12:15 A.M.

Bill Barry, the ex-FBI man who functioned as Kennedy's bodyguard, attempted to help Ethel down from the stage.

"I'm all right," she said. "Stay with the senator."

Barry left her and tried to catch up. He pushed his way through the crowd, but he was too late to assume his usual position in front of Kennedy, who was being led down the narrow hallway behind the stage by hotel maître d' Karl Uecker.

As Kennedy passed through the doorway that led into the pantry, he was joined by twenty-six-year-old security guard Eugene Cesar. Cesar wore the uniform of Ace Guard Service and had a holstered revolver on his hip. He took hold of the senator's right arm at the elbow and moved along with him.

The room was crowded and a bit chaotic as Kennedy and his entourage made their way through. Balloons popped underfoot. TV cameramen carried their bulky equipment. The splicing of events filmed before the shooting and the chaos captured afterward has led many people to believe, erroneously, that they saw the murder replayed on television, but all the television cameras were shut down as they passed from the dramatic speech to the upcoming press conference. Nothing was expected here except the usual dispensing of greetings by the candidate.

By official count there were seventy-seven persons in the pantry when Robert Kennedy was shot. But it was not as though the senator were on-stage with a roomful of people looking on.

It would be more useful to imagine seventy-seven people stuffed into a subway car. Taller people see more than shorter people, but even their view is obstructed. One of the tallest men in the pantry was Jesse Unruh, the chairman of Kennedy's campaign and the powerful speaker of the California legislature. When asked later if he had seen Kennedy fall Unruh said, "I would not say he was in my view, but I could tell approximately where he was. There were several larger people behind him, including Paul Schrade. . . . I saw glimpses of him."[2]

The sound in the room was also a confusing montage. There were greetings and cheers, balloons popping, some pushing, more cheers, some more popping sounds, a few screams, cheers, cursing, some shoving, people falling down, screams, more shoving, and then general chaos. Most people in the pantry saw only bits and pieces of things that happened right around them. What we know of the event is derived from their accounts and the physical evidence. It is a mosaic.

As Kennedy made his way through the pantry, he stopped to shake hands with Jesus Perez and Juan Romero, both busboys at the hotel. Karl Uecker, the maître d' who had been leading the procession, was eager to keep moving. "Let's go, Senator," he said in his thick German accent. He took the senator's arm and began to lead him forward again.

Lisa Urso, a San Diego high school student, stood near the pantry exit. As Kennedy moved toward her, she was rudely shoved from behind. A young man considerably shorter than she stepped in front of her and moved to her right.

"I thought it was gonna be a waiter and it looked like he was trying to get in there and shake the senator's hand," she recalled.[3] But then the young man's arm made an odd movement across his body, and Urso sensed something was wrong. She froze and watched helplessly.

Vincent DiPierro, a waiter at the Ambassador, saw the short dark man push past Urso and advance on Kennedy. The man had a strange smile on his face. It seemed to several others that the man moving toward Kennedy was going to shake hands, but his words and gun showed otherwise. TV producer Richard Lubic thought he heard the man say, "Kennedy, you son of a bitch!" Lisa Urso saw a flash from the gun. She saw Paul Schrade fall, then Robert Kennedy.

Karl Uecker also saw the gun. He felt it fire very close to his face—twice. After the second shot Uecker said he grabbed the man's gun hand and slammed it onto the steam table—leftward and downward, away from Kennedy. Several men, including Roosevelt Grier and Rafer Johnson, joined the struggle for the weapon, but after a short pause it began firing again. Down went seventeen-year-old Irwin Stroll, shot in the knee. Down went William Weisel, an ABC-TV director, hit in the stomach. Several more shots. Reporter Ira Goldstein was wounded in the hip and Elizabeth Evans, an artist and close friend of Kennedy aide Pierre Salinger, was struck in the head.

Radio reporter Andrew West turned on his tape recorder and began to narrate over the screams and the sound of gunfire:

"Senator Kennedy has been shot. Is that possible? It is possible, ladies and gentlemen. It is possible. He has. Not only Senator Ken-

nedy but . . . Oh my God! Senator Kennedy has been shot and another man, a Kennedy campaign manager, and possibly shot in the head."

The struggle for the gun went on and on. Andrew West fearfully described it:

"Rafer Johnson has ahold of the man who apparently fired the shot. . . . He has fired the shot. He still has the gun. The gun is pointed at me this moment. I hope they can get the gun out of his hand. Be very careful. Get the gun! Get the gun! Get the gun! Get away from the barrel. Get away from the barrel, man. Look out for the gun!"

As soon as he heard shots fired, writer George Plimpton joined the struggle for the gun. Just inches from the assailant's face, Plimpton noticed something odd. The man with the gun had "enormously peaceful eyes," an almost beatific expression on his face. "In the middle of a hurricane of sound and feeling," Plimpton recalled, "he seemed peaceful."[4]

Peaceful or not, the small man had great strength. It took over forty seconds to separate him from the gun. Once disarmed, the gunman began to feel the kicks and punches of angry onlookers. "Keep people away from him!" yelled Andrew West. "We don't want another Oswald."

Jesse Unruh tried to stop people from attacking the gunman. The physically imposing politician started pulling people away. Finally he jumped up onto a steam table to try and calm the situation. "We don't want another Dallas," he shouted. "If the system works at all we are going to try this one."

Robert Kennedy lay on his back, limbs spread, bleeding from behind the ear. Juan Romero knelt down beside the fallen senator. "Come on, Mr. Kennedy," he exhorted. "You can make it." Young Daniel Curtin took rosary beads from his pocket and handed them to Romero. The busboy wrapped them in Kennedy's left hand.

"Is everybody all right?" Kennedy asked in a barely audible voice.

Dr. Stanley Abo, a Los Angeles radiologist, was the first medical doctor to reach Robert Kennedy. He put his ear to the senator's chest and heard very shallow breathing. He took a pulse. Abo then stuck a finger into Kennedy's head wound to relieve the pressure that had built up. The wound bled profusely. "You're doing good," the doctor told Kennedy. "The ambulance is on the way."

Ethel Kennedy arrived. She begged, with little effect, for the crowd and newsmen to move away. Then she began to comfort her husband. Robert Kennedy was aware of her presence.

"Oh, Ethel, Ethel," he said softly.

Police Sergeant Paul Scharaga had just stopped to buy cigarettes. As he climbed back into his patrol car he heard a radio call about a shooting at 3400 Wilshire Boulevard. Scharaga knew that was the Ambassador; he was less than a block away. He swung his car around and drove quickly to the rear of the hotel.

As Scharaga moved through the parking lot he encountered an older couple in a state of near hysteria. The woman, in her mid- to late fifties, did most of the talking. She claimed that they had been near the exit stairs when a young woman and man ran past shouting gleefully, "We shot him! We shot him!" In response to the question "Who did you shoot?" the woman, who was wearing a polka-dot dress, replied, "Senator Kennedy. We shot him! We killed him!" The young woman and her companion then disappeared into the parking lot, laughing as they went.

Scharaga immediately went back to his car and put out an all points bulletin on the two reported suspects.

While Sergeant Scharaga was in the parking lot behind the Ambassador, LAPD patrolmen Travis White and Arthur Placencia arrived at the hotel's front entrance on Wilshire Boulevard. Both were rookies. White had been active on the force for about a year, Placencia for two weeks. The officers jumped out of their black-and-white squad car and followed the motions of various hotel employees and other bystanders who were shouting, "He's up here. He's up here."

White and Placencia entered the hotel pantry and were directed to a pile of bodies at the far end of the room. Several large men had a small man pinned to a table and were warding off people who were trying to get at him. "Kill the bastard! Kill him!" Placencia heard someone shout.

Another police officer who had just rushed in, Randolph Adair, noticed something odd about the man being held. "The guy was real confused," recalled Adair. "It was like it didn't exactly hit him what he had done. He had a blank, glassed-over look on his face—like he wasn't in complete control of his mind at the time."[5]

The officers then began to peel people away trying to take the man into custody. They had to pry the man from Jesse Unruh's grip. "I charge you with responsibility for this man," Unruh ordered. Neither White nor Placencia recognized Unruh, but they handcuffed the prisoner, and then, with Unruh escorting them, made their way out into the lobby and then down to the first floor, where the patrol car was waiting. The crowd on the way out was ugly and threatening.

When they got to the car Placencia stuffed the prisoner into the back-seat, then sat next to him. Unruh jumped into the front seat with Officer White. Normally any unauthorized person would have been ejected immediately, but there was no time. Angry people were already surrounding the vehicle and pounding upon it. White turned on the siren and gunned the engine. The crowd stepped back for an instant and the police car pulled away.

In the backseat Officer Placencia reached for his field officer's handbook. In it was the admonishment he would read to his dazed-looking prisoner. "You have a right to remain silent," he said, reading with the aid of his flashlight, "and if you give up the right to remain silent, anything you say can and will be used against you in a court of law." Placencia asked the prisoner if he understood. There was no reply. The officer then read the prisoner his rights a second time. After that Placencia asked the suspect his name. He asked again, and then a third time. He got no reply.

Placencia then turned his attention to the man in the front of the car. "Who are you?" he asked.

"I'm Jesse Unruh."

"Oh," said Placencia, wondering why one of the most powerful men in California was riding in his patrol car. "Who did he shoot?"

"Bobby Kennedy," replied Unruh.

As Officers White and Placencia were hurriedly escorting their prisoner from the hotel, two medical attendants arrived in the pantry. They lifted Robert Kennedy onto a stretcher and rolled him outside to a tan-colored ambulance, unit G–18 of the Central Receiving Hospital. Ethel Kennedy and several close aides rode with the wounded senator. The ambulance quickly covered the eighteen blocks to the hospital, where treatment room 2 was already being prepared.

According to Dr. Faustin Bazilauskas, Robert Kennedy arrived at Central Receiving "lifeless"—no blood pressure, no pulse. Bazilauskas forcefully massaged Kennedy's heart by pressing on his chest while Nurse Supervisor Bette Eby readied a heart-lung machine. In three minutes Kennedy was hooked up. He was then given a shot of Adrenalin, and the senator's breathing and heartbeat began again.

Once his condition was stabilized, Nurse Eby inspected the senator. Behind the ear she saw a gunshot wound with powder burns around it. It was obvious the wound was severe and the nurse suggested an immediate transfer to nearby Good Samaritan Hospital, where Kennedy could receive the attentions of a neurosurgeon. Calls were made and the transfer took place quickly.

When Robert Kennedy was wheeled into Good Samaritan at 1 A.M., he came under the care of Dr. Henry Cuneo, an experienced brain surgeon. Cuneo examined the senator and found two gunshot wounds to the armpit area and another to the back of the head behind the ear. As the other attending doctors continued to prepare Kennedy for the expected surgery, Dr. Cuneo walked over to Ethel Kennedy.

"Extremely critical," he told her bluntly. Then to give her what little good news there was he added, "His blood pressure has gone down, his heart is beating strongly, his airway is free of obstructions, and his color is good."

Despite the doctor's attempt to brighten the news, Ethel Kennedy understood exactly what he had said. She almost fainted and then got ahold of herself. She was offered a sedative. "No, thank you," she replied. "I want to be awake and alert."

A little before three in the morning Robert Kennedy's press secretary, Frank Mankiewicz, held a news conference from the hood of a police car in front of Good Samaritan. Mankiewicz told reporters that Robert Kennedy was about to undergo surgery for a bullet lodged in his brain. "His breathing is good; his heart is good," said Mankiewicz. "He's unconscious and the doctors describe his condition as very critical."

Officer Frank Foster sat in Parker Center's interrogation room 1 facing the prisoner. The two men were alone, and the similarity in their ages seemed to create a small bond of trust. The prisoner asked Foster if he had children.

"I have two," Foster replied, "a little girl and a little boy. . . . The little girl, she's three; she was three in February. The boy, he'll be—let's see—eight months old the ninth of this month. He crawls around a lot, gets into everything. He sure wants to move about."

"You know," said the prisoner, "it—it happens about that time you know—you know that—that age."

"I think—I think in another month he'll probably—"

"Start," offered the prisoner.

"Yeah."

"Creeping."

"Of course, he's pretty big for his age," Foster continued. "He's kind of heavy, but he gets around pretty good."

"How much did he weigh when he was born?" the prisoner inquired.

"Well, let's see. I think it was eight pounds something . . . but afterward he grew like a little weed—he'd gained and gained, and now his hands—fantastic. They're big and strong. He gets ahold of something, you can hardly pull him off, you know—"

"About eight months or so," agreed the prisoner, "he will still be wanting to try to walk, but as soon as maybe the third month, he—his hands, you know, the grip."

"Yeah, fantastic," said Foster.

"Wonderful, little kids," replied the prisoner.[6]

Down the hall in room 318, Sergeants Frank Patchett and Adolph Melendres were interviewing Thomas Vincent DiPierro. DiPierro was a college student employed part-time as a waiter at the Ambassador where his father, Angelo, was one of the maître d's. DiPierro told the police that he had entered the hotel pantry closely behind Senator Kennedy. As Kennedy stopped to shake hands with busboys Perez and Romero, DiPierro's eye had been caught by a young man hanging on to a tray stand. He watched as the young man moved toward Kennedy as if to shake his hand. Then he saw the man pull a revolver and fire; blood spattered DiPierro's eyeglasses, and Kennedy aide Paul Schrade fell against him, wounded in the head.

Because his account of the murder was clear and detailed, and because he was watching the assailant before the shooting began, Vincent DiPierro was perhaps the best eyewitness the police now had. There was only one problem: DiPierro had seen the assailant with an attractive woman. Sergeant Patchett asked the young man what made him think that the girl was with Sirhan.

"Well she was following him," answered DiPierro. ". . . She was holding on to the other end of the tray table and she—like—it looked like she was almost holding him."

"Did you see him get off the tray stand?"

"Yes, I did."

"And then he walked toward the senator?"

"Yes."

"This girl—"

"She stayed there."

"At the tray stand?"

"Right. I glanced over once in a while. She was good-looking so I looked at her."

Patchett, perhaps not entirely convinced that DiPierro understood the seriousness of what he was saying, asked once again: "What is in your mind that makes you think they were together, the fact that they were standing together?"

At that point Deputy District Attorney John Howard, who had just come in from interviewing the assailant, broke into the conversation: "Did you see him speak to her?"

"He turned as though he did say something. . . ."

"Did she move her mouth like she was speaking to him?"

"No, she just smiled."

"And would it seem to you that she smiled at something that had been said?"

"Yeah."

DiPierro was again asked to describe the girl. She was "very good-looking," he said almost apologetically. She had brown hair and "wore a white dress with black or purple polka dots" and had a peculiar "pudgy" nose.

"Okay," said Patchett, looking to conclude. "Just to sum this up, what's the thing that sticks out in your mind?"

"The stupid smile on his face."

"Smile on his face?"

"It was kind of like an envious smile, like, ah you know, villainous. I don't know how to describe it."[7]

Back over at Rampart Station the police were interviewing another witness who, like DiPierro, reported the movements of a mysterious woman.

Sandra Serrano was a twenty-year-old keypunch operator who had co-chaired the Youth for Kennedy Committee in the Pasadena-Altadena area. She had come to the Ambassador Hotel to celebrate with several of her friends. While waiting for the final election results she sought relief from the hot, crowded ballroom and went outside to sit on an exit stairway. At about 11:30, according to Serrano, three people pushed by her on the stairway going up—a woman in a polka-dot dress and two men, one of whom she would later recognize as the accused assassin. She remained on the stairs for "about a half hour" and saw no one else. Suddenly two of the trio she had previously encountered rushed by down the stairs. The woman seemed exuberant, and she and Serrano had a bizarre exchange of words.

"We shot him! We shot him!" the woman exclaimed.

"Who did you shoot?" asked the bewildered Serrano.

"Senator Kennedy," came the reply.

In shock, Serrano went inside where she ran into her friend Irene Chavez. Tearful, nearly hysterical, she described her strange encounter, only to discover that Robert Kennedy had indeed been attacked. Word of the shooting had begun to spread. Soon Serrano found herself being interviewed by NBC correspondent Sander Vanocur on national television. A stunned, blurry-eyed audience heard a dramatic account given by a shaken but coherent young woman:

"This girl came running down the stairs in the back, came running down the stairs and said, 'We shot him. We shot him.' And I said, 'Who did you shoot?' and she said, 'We shot Senator Kennedy.' . . . She was Caucasian. She had on a white dress with polka dots. She was light skinned, dark hair. She had on black shoes, and she had a funny nose."

At about 4 A.M. Officer Foster was relieved by George Murphy of the DA's office and Sergeant Bill Jordan of the Los Angeles police. The prisoner still had not revealed his identity, nor had there been any talk about what had happened earlier that night. The conversations that did occur were the kind one might have in a bus-terminal waiting room. The officers asked the prisoner if he had an extensive education.

"No," he replied. "I read a lot."

"I gathered that," said Jordan. "You like to read?"

"I enjoy it."

"What do you like to read?" asked Murphy.

The prisoner tried to engage the officers in a discussion of *To Kill a Mockingbird,* Harper Lee's depression-era novel about a white attorney in rural Alabama who defends a black man unjustly accused of rape. The novel won a Pulitzer Prize in 1960 and touched the conscience of the nation. Now, in the basement of police headquarters, it was being offered as a topic of conversation by the captured assailant of a United States senator. Neither Murphy nor Jordan, however, had read the book.

The men found common ground for conversation when the prisoner confessed that he didn't understand the stock market and asked the officers what they knew about it.

"A lot of money changes hands on stocks," said Jordan. "It's kind of a legalized gambling is about what it boils down to."

"If you wanted to buy stock, you'd do it just the same way I would," said Murphy.

"How?" asked the prisoner.

"Call up a broker and say, 'I'd like to buy some stock.' "

"But, hell," the prisoner replied, "if you want to gamble, you can call up any old bookie and say, 'Play such and such a bet.' "

"No," answered Jordan, "it's accepted, no stigma attached to it; even in church they accept the stock market."

"I never had any money to fool around with stocks," Murphy added. "Policemen don't make that much money."

"I wish I had," replied the prisoner. "I wish I had some. Really, that would be a good adventure to—to experiment with."

From money the conversation got philosophical once again.

"What is justice?" asked the prisoner.

"Fair play," replied Murphy.

"What is fair play?" asked the prisoner.

"Well," said Murphy, "fair play is only that you don't take advantage of anybody."

"Right," agreed the prisoner. "Treat others as you would want them to treat you, that's what Jesus said. Beautiful thing."

"Do you go along with that?" Murphy asked the man who had just shot and wounded six people he had never met.

"Very much so, sir. Very much."[8]

In the middle of the night Robert Kennedy was moved to the ninth floor of Good Samaritan. There he was operated upon by Dr. Cuneo, Dr. Maxwell Andler, and Dr. Nat Downs Reid. The doctors opened the back of the senator's head, removed a large blood clot that had formed, and then retrieved as many small fragments of metal and bone as they could. The operation took three hours.

At sunrise Frank Mankiewicz informed the press that the operation was over and Robert Kennedy had been returned to intensive care. He reported some small improvement—the senator could now breathe unassisted. But Mankiewicz also told the reporters that Robert Kennedy may have suffered an impairment of blood to the midbrain. "The next twelve to thirty-six hours," said the press secretary, "will be a very critical period."

As the new day began, the Los Angeles police still didn't know the identity of the man they had in custody. They had his fingerprints, which were being sent around the country. They had a key that was now being tried in every car door in the neighborhood of the Ambassador Hotel. They also had the pistol recovered from the scene of the shooting. Using the weapon's serial number, the police quickly discovered that the gun had been originally purchased by one Albert L. Hertz in 1965. It had changed hands several times since then, and detectives were tracking the line of possession.

When young Munir Sirhan reported early for work at Nash's Department Store in downtown Pasadena, he saw a knot of coworkers gathered around a television set. Robert Kennedy, he was told, had been shot. Munir paused to watch and saw the image of the unidentified gunman flashed on the screen. It was his brother Sirhan. Munir immediately drove home to wake up his older brother Adel and tell him the awful news. Munir then drove Adel to the headquarters of the Pasadena police.

At around 9:30 Adel entered the police station alone, carrying a newspaper with a photograph of Robert Kennedy's assailant. "I think this is my brother," he said softly to the desk sergeant as he held up the paper. Soon he was upstairs talking to a collection of men from the LAPD and the FBI.

After convincing investigators that he was not part of any conspiracy, Adel returned home with a contingent of police led by Sergeant William Brandt. Several hundred people were already in front of the Sirhan home, sent there, in effect, by Los Angeles mayor Sam Yorty, who had just gone on television and announced that the attacker of Robert Kennedy was one Sirhan Sirhan of 696 East Howard Street.

"Can we come in, or do you have something to hide?" asked Brandt.

"No," answered Adel, looking at the crowd and then the police, "you can come in."

Once inside, the police were shown to Sirhan's room in the back of the house. There they found literature pertaining to a mystic group called the Rosicrucians as well as many other books on the occult. They also found two spiral notebooks, one right on top of a dressing table, the other on the floor by the bed. The books were filled with very odd repetitive writing, but Sergeant Brandt soon found several passages which seemed to target Robert Kennedy for murder. Brandt filled several boxes with material from Sirhan's room and returned to Rampart Station.

That evening President Lyndon Johnson went on television to speak to the nation.

"Tonight," he intoned solemnly, "this nation faces once again the consequences of lawlessness, hatred, and unreason in its midst. It would be wrong, it would be self-deceptive, to ignore the connection between lawlessness, hatred, and this act of violence.

"It would be just as wrong," Johnson continued, now playing the other side of the court, "just as self-deceptive to conclude from this act that our country is sick, that it has lost its sense of balance, its sense of direction and common decency. Two hundred million Americans did not strike Robert Kennedy last night no more than they struck John Kennedy in 1963 or Martin Luther King in April of this year. But those awful events give us ample warning that in a climate of extremism, of disrespect for law, of contempt for the rights of others, violence may bring down the very best among us. A nation that tolerates violence in any form cannot expect to be able to confine it to just minor outbursts."

Johnson told the nation that he was appointing a special presidential commission. Serving on the commission would be Archbishop Terrence Cook of New York, Senators Roman Hruska of Nebraska and Philip Hart of Michigan, university president Dr. Milton Eisenhower, attorney Albert Jenner, law professor Patricia Harris, workingman philosopher Eric Hoffer, U.S. district judge Leon Higgenbotham, and Representatives William McCulloch of Ohio and Hale Boggs of Louisiana. Boggs had been a member of the Warren Commission five years earlier; Jenner had been on its staff. The purpose of this new commission, Johnson declared, would be to discover "what in the nature of our people and the environment of our society makes possible such murder and violence" and to propose ways to prevent it in the future.

California governor Ronald Reagan was also quick to go on national television to ease the conscience of the nation. "Two hundred million Americans did not do this," he said. "One young man did it, and for not even an American reason."

A little later Reagan had more to say at a press conference in Sacramento. He attributed the shooting of Robert Kennedy to a growing permissiveness in society and in the courts in particular. Reagan scorned the attitude "that says a man can choose the laws he must obey, that he can take the law into his own hands for a cause, that crime does not necessarily mean punishment." He continued:

"This attitude has been spurred by demagogic and irresponsible words of so-called leaders in and out of public office, and it has been helped along by some in places of authority who are fearful of the wrong but timid about standing up for what is right.

"In so doing they have thrown our nation into chaos and confusion and have bred a climate that permits this ultimate tragedy. This nation can no longer tolerate the spirit of permissiveness that pervades our courts and other institutions."

Governor Reagan, whose presidential ambitions were already public knowledge, left the press conference without taking any questions from the stunned newsmen. Robert Kennedy was in the hospital fighting for his life, and Reagan had pointed a finger at some number of "so-called leaders." Who were these men the governor was attacking, the reporters wanted to know? Reagan's communications director, Lyn Nofziger, tried to answer.

"We're just not going to get into a position," said Nofziger, "of calling names or making accusations against certain people in this country."

"You've already done that," called out one reporter.

"All right, then, we'll stand on the statement."

Another newsman asked if the governor's statement wasn't pointed at Senator Kennedy himself.

"You'll have to draw your own conclusions," replied Nofziger, speaking as though he were defending a moral principle, "because the statement is there and we do not intend to go beyond it."[9]

The record for public pronouncements on June 5 belonged to Los Angeles mayor Sam Yorty. He seemed to be everywhere there were reporters or TV cameras. Shortly after Sirhan Sirhan's identity became known, Yorty was in front of network television cameras. With Chief of Police Thomas

Reddin at his side, Yorty revealed that the police had "learned his car was seen outside meetings where Communist organizations or Communist front organizations were in session. From that circumstance we probably can deduce he was in contact with Communists."

The so-called front organization that Yorty was referring to was the W. E. B. Du Bois Club on Hollywood Boulevard, a left-wing political group named after the black American civil rights leader. What Yorty failed to mention was that the car belonged to Sirhan's brother Adel, who frequently played music at an Arab nightclub a few doors away.

Yorty's next stop for the day was Rampart Station, which was serving as the police command post for the Robert Kennedy investigation. The police had scheduled a press conference for a little after noon. Once at the station Mayor Yorty began to paw through the box of belongings the detectives had just brought in from their search of Sirhan's home. He examined the two spiral notebooks. A little while later, as the police press conference in the basement was ending, Mayor Yorty just happened to wander in.

"What can you tell us about Sirhan Sirhan?" asked Robert Blair Kaiser, then a reporter stringing for *Life* magazine.

"Well," said the mayor, "he was a member of numerous Communist organizations, including the Rosicrucians."

"The Rosicrucians aren't a Communist organization," the reporter pointed out.

"Well . . . ," the mayor huffed. Yorty then waited for all the reporters to set their mikes and reposition their cameras.

"It appears," he said, "that Sirhan Sirhan was sort of a loner who harbored Communist inclinations, favored Communists of all types. He said the U.S. must fall. Indicated that RFK must be assassinated before June 5, 1968. It was a May 18 notation in a ringed notebook."[10]

Yorty was hardly done for the day. There would be an interview by Radio News International and another session with the press in front of television cameras. Yorty was now thumping Sirhan's notebooks like they were the Old Testament, warning the congregation that an "evil Communist organization has played a part in inflaming the assassination of President [sic] Kennedy."

Yorty's behavior, to almost everyone's dismay, was a gross breach of legal ethics and procedure. The evidence he was touting on television had been secured from Sirhan's home without a warrant. It had yet to be determined if the notebooks were Sirhan's, or whether he had done all the writing in them. They had not yet been ruled admissible in a court of law, and the mayor's antics were increasing greatly the possibility that they would be barred as evidence.

State attorney general Thomas C. Lynch telephoned the mayor to express his concern, citing court rulings that "evidence may be ruled out and a trial severely hampered by such public statements."[11] Other calls came in from prominent members of the legal community, including U.S. attorney general Ramsey Clark and Los Angeles district attorney Evelle Younger, who appealed to Yorty to end his public posturing. The American Civil Liberties Union also protested Yorty's behavior as did the *New York Times*, who characterized the mayor as "a man uninhibited by considerations of propriety when these get in the way of an opportunity for national publicity."[12]

The mayor's immediate response to the criticism was to call it "political nonsense." "If they haven't got enough evidence to convict this man," he said, "then we need to get someone else to prosecute."[13]

The next day, during arraignment proceedings, superior court judge Arthur Alarcon issued an order banning public officials and all persons connected with the case from engaging in indiscreet talk that might prejudice a fair trial. The order promised "swift contempt-of-court action" for violators. Just to make sure it was understood to whom it applied, a copy of Judge Alarcon's order was personally served upon the mayor of Los Angeles.

Yorty immediately called a press conference. "I was not accorded due process," he complained. The mayor then went on to defend his actions, saying that he made his statements about Sirhan to "get the facts to the public and prevent rumors and violence."[14]

As Robert Kennedy lay unconscious in the intensive-care ward of Good Samaritan, Dr. James Poppen of Boston's Lahey Clinic arrived in Los Angeles, brought there by an air force transport. Poppen was a skilled neurosurgeon who had attended to President John Kennedy at various times and to Senator Edward Kennedy when he had been severely injured in a plane crash. At about 10 A.M. Poppen examined Robert Kennedy and knew right away that the outlook was nearly hopeless. Kennedy's life depended upon the abatement of the swelling and bleeding in his head. If the trauma continued, the blood circulation to the brain would be cut off.

At about noon, the doctors hooked Robert Kennedy up to an electroencephalograph, a device which monitored the senator's brain waves. Initially the readings were good. "Just slightly below normal," noted Dr. Cuneo. But by late afternoon the signals began to diminish. The damage in Robert Kennedy's head was now compounding. The senator's heart, however, still beat strongly.

Outside Good Samaritan Hospital hundreds of people, many of them young, waited together. They had been there all day, they would stay the night. Some held signs saying "Pray for Bobby." Except for a brief statement at 5:30 in the afternoon which said that Robert Kennedy's condition continued to be "extremely critical," there had been no official word for seventeen hours since the operation.

Then at 2 A.M. Frank Mankiewicz came walking slowing down the emergency ramp of the hospital. He crossed the street to an auditorium that was now serving as press headquarters. Mankiewicz stood before the newsmen, bit his lip, then began to speak. "Senator Robert Francis Kennedy died at 1:44 A.M. today, June 6, 1968. With the senator at the time of his death was his wife, Ethel, his sisters, Mrs. Patricia Lawford and Mrs. Stephen Smith, and his sister-in-law, Mrs. John F. Kennedy. He was forty-two years old."

Robert Kennedy's death initiated a week of national mourning. In New York, schools closed, taxis displayed black ribbons, and WPIX-TV broadcast the single word "SHAME" for two and a half hours. Hundreds of thousands of people lined the railway tracks from New York to Washington, an unofficial honor guard for Kennedy's funeral train. In a week Ethel Kennedy received more than 325,000 letters of sympathy.

Newspaper columns and commencement addresses were common forums for dismay. "There is something in the air of the modern world," said James Reston in the *New York Times*. "The fantasy violence of American literature, television and the movies provides a contemporary gallery of dark and ghastly crime, which undoubtedly adds to the atmosphere in which weak and deranged minds flourish."[15]

There were many variations on this theme: Robert Kennedy was murdered because the violence America was perpetrating abroad in places such as Vietnam was finally coming home; or Robert Kennedy was murdered because disrespect for law (fostered by those opposing the war) had become epidemic.

In a ceremony at Tufts University, Harvard professor and Kennedy family friend John Kenneth Galbraith expressed his disgust at this repeated analysis. He noted that all across the country, "men of well-padded intellect with a genius for platitude have been warning against violence." Galbraith had even greater contempt for the commission just appointed by President Johnson, citing "the effort to sweep problems under the rug by asking elderly men of great repute and inertia to study them."[16]

Few Americans, however, were waiting for the conclusions of President Johnson's commission. A Gallup Poll taken the day after Kennedy was shot showed that the public believed, by a margin of 4 to 3, that the attack was the product of a conspiracy.[17] There were even a few people of note who spoke plainly about these beliefs.

On NBC's *Tonight Show* Truman Capote suggested to a nationwide audience that the murders of President Kennedy, Dr. Martin Luther King, and Senator Kennedy were part of one large conspiracy. The author of *In Cold Blood* said that the paradigm for the murders might be found in Richard Condon's *The Manchurian Candidate,* a novel (and then movie) in which the president of the United States is to be killed by a hypno-programmed robot assassin.

In a review in the *New York Times,* Jack Gould labeled what occurred on the *Tonight Show* as "not within the acceptable province of entertainment television shows." Gould reprimanded Johnny Carson for an interview that was "far from adequate," and scorched Capote for indulging in "an orgy of rampant conjecture."[18]

The *Times,* however, took a less judgmental position when it reported the reaction of Yevgeny Yevtushenko, whose perception of the crime was not very different from Capote's. The Soviet poet had met Robert Kennedy in 1966, felt a fondness for him, and, following the murder, he wrote a long poem titled "Freedom to Kill." The *Times* printed it in full.

In the poem Yevtushenko pictured the United States as a nation going "dangerously insane," a place where "ears of grain filled with bullets wave in the fields of Texas," and "murderers attend funerals dressed in mourning." The poem begins:

> *The color of the Statue of Liberty*
> *Grows ever more deathly pale*
> *As, loving freedom with bullets*
> *You shoot at yourself, America.*[19]

The prisoner, nursing a sprained knee and sitting in a wheelchair, was rolled into the prison chapel, now devoid of religious insignia as it had been converted into a makeshift courtroom, for security reasons. Clad in blue dungarees and a white shirt with the sleeves rolled up, the accused was lifted in his chair by four deputy sheriffs to a raised platform, where he faced superior court judge Arthur Alarcon at the altar. Robert Kennedy had been dead a day.

Earlier, the Los Angeles County Grand Jury had convened in the chapel to hear twenty-three witnesses before handing down an indictment for murder. Now the prisoner was to be arraigned. The proceeding took about a half hour. The prisoner's court-appointed lawyers, Richard Buckley and Wilbur Littlefield, did most of the talking. Could they postpone the plea until psychiatric tests could be completed? The judge consented.

During the proceedings Judge Alarcon pronounced the defendant's name: "SEER-han Bishara SEER-han." The defendant, who, two days before, would not reveal his identity to anyone, now made his first public statement. "It's not SEER-han," he said in a voice heard throughout the room. "It's pronounced Sir-han."

TWO

The Summer of '68

✳   ✳   ✳

They came pinwheeling into history out of some dim, Dostoevskian underground, one of them a stir-smart fugitive con with no known ambition higher than making the FBI's "Ten Most Wanted" list, the other a damaged little Jordanian immigrant burning to avenge the six-day Arab-Israeli war all by himself.

—*Newsweek,* describing James Earl Ray and Sirhan Sirhan

A T THE JUNE 7 chapel arraignment there was, in addition to the public defenders, another attorney looking after the defendant's interests. This was Abraham Lincoln Wirin, chief counsel of the local office of the American Civil Liberties Union. Wirin, who was formally known by his initials A. L. but was called "Al" by almost everyone, was introduced during the proceedings when Judge Alarcon announced that the civil liberties lawyer had been invited by the court to observe "the manner in which the constitutional and procedural rights of the defendant have been obeyed and preserved."

Actually Wirin had been invited into the case earlier by the defendant, the morning after the shooting. Sirhan, while still the anonymous assailant, requested to see an attorney from the ACLU. Wirin, who had been attempting to get in to see the prisoner, was immediately available. When the two met under heavy security, the prisoner whispered his name into Wirin's ear. Then, with the imperfect knowledge that the ACLU sometimes championed the rights of minorities, Sirhan asked if Wirin would represent him. The attorney responded that he could not: the ACLU only took cases with constitutional issues at stake. But he was interested in seeing that the accused received a fair trial, and, toward that end, Wirin offered to help Sirhan find suitable representation.

The Los Angeles County Public Defender's Office, which provided Sirhan with Buckley and Littlefield, was perhaps the best operation of its kind in the country. It was well funded and had 208 full-time attorneys on staff.

Still, the prevailing opinion was that a case of this importance required an experienced, well-respected, private defense attorney.

Although it would not be a pleasant job to defend, without compensation, the man who allegedly shot Robert Kennedy, Wirin thought he might be able to find a qualified lawyer to volunteer. Indeed, inquiries soon came in from nationally known criminal attorneys F. Lee Bailey and Melvin Belli. But Wirin was focusing on local talent. He commissioned journalist Robert Blair Kaiser, who had contacted him in hopes of getting an interview with Sirhan, to approach the well-known criminal attorney Grant Cooper. When Wirin returned to Sirhan with a list of possible attorneys, Sirhan recognized Cooper's name and selected him as his first choice. At about the same time, after talking to Kaiser, Cooper made up his mind to offer his services to Sirhan.

Grant Cooper was at the top of his profession. The sixty-five-year-old attorney had recently served as president of the Los Angeles County Bar Association. He had also been president of the American College of Trial Lawyers and vice president of the State Bar of California. Colleagues often spoke of Cooper's "unquestioned integrity."

Cooper had practiced law since 1927. He earned a reputation as a tough prosecutor while serving in the Los Angeles County DA's office from 1929 to 1935. He returned to that office in 1940 for a two-year tour as chief deputy district attorney. During that time Cooper played a key role in the fight against the powerful crime and gambling interests that had corrupted the mayor's office and large segments of the police force. The campaign was successful. Mayor Frank Shaw was forced to step down, a new commission was empowered to oversee the police department, and the gambling interests looked to the desert of Nevada for a new home.

After he left the prosecutor's office, Grant Cooper devoted himself full-time to criminal defense. His most famous case was that of Dr. Bernard Finch and his girlfriend, Carole Tregoff, who were accused of murdering Finch's wife. Cooper defended Finch and Tregoff twice and came away with two hung juries. The pair were convicted in 1961, defended a third time by another lawyer.

For Wirin and the penniless Sirhan, securing the voluntary services of such a well-respected attorney was an enormous coup. There was just one hitch. Cooper was already engaged.

Earlier in the year, Maurice Friedman, a Las Vegas developer, retained Cooper to defend him in federal court. Friedman, along with four others, was charged with rigging gin rummy games at the Beverly Hills Friars Club. The defendants had installed several "peekholes" in the ceiling over the game tables, and information had been relayed to certain players by way of electronic signals. The scam reportedly cost several businessmen over

$400,000 in losses, and celebrities Phil Silvers, Tony Martin, and Zeppo Marx had also been cheated out of substantial sums. The case had been given great attention in the media, and the start of the trial was only days away.

Thus Cooper's ability to represent Sirhan was complicated. He could head the Sirhan defense only if another attorney could be found to handle the initial phases of the case, and only if his future participation could be kept secret so as not to prejudice a jury against his present client. When his first two choices declined to serve as cocounsel, Cooper suggested an experienced California appeals lawyer named Russell Parsons.

On June 19, at 6 A.M., Al Wirin telephoned Russell Parsons in his room at the Elks Club, a place Parsons frequently called home. The two met an hour later, and over breakfast Wirin proposed that Parsons handle the Sirhan case while Cooper was busy with the Friars Club trial. Parsons immediately accepted and by noontime he was on his way to visit Sirhan in his cell. Sirhan seemed delighted to finally have an attorney of his own, and Parsons's feisty talkative style appeared to put the young prisoner at ease.

Immediately after the visit Parsons held a press conference in his office. He told the collected newsmen that he would represent Sirhan without fee as a public service. "There's a poor devil in trouble," said the attorney, finessing the fact that this particular poor devil was also notorious, "and that's enough for me."

Parsons also said that he would be joined by another attorney: "He's a prominent lawyer who has tried many cases. But he is now representing a client who has paid him a large fee to represent him. If it is known that he plans to be Sirhan's lawyer, it might damage the case of the client he is now representing. For that reason if it is even hinted that he might be planning to represent Sirhan . . . he will withdraw from the Sirhan case."[1]

As he would on other occasions, Parsons had said more than he needed to say. If only a hint would ruin the deal, why hint? Grant Cooper was prominent indeed. So prominent that he had been featured on the front page of the *Los Angeles Times* only the day before. Cooper, the paper reported, had been playing gin rummy while federal court was in session. Actually, the defense attorney had agreed to play a hand of rummy with card expert Oswald Jacoby to demonstrate to the Friars Club jury how the game is played. Cooper beat Jacoby by fifty-nine points and then announced, "I'll quit while I'm ahead."

Astute observers didn't need more clues. They soon focused their suspicions upon Cooper. A week later the beleaguered defense attorney was forced to answer the rising speculation about his assuming the Sirhan defense by saying, "Definitely, positively, unequivocally *no*." If that didn't convince everyone, those who knew better stayed politely silent from that point forward.

Russell Parsons had been practicing law since 1917. When asked his age at the initial press conference the seventy-five-year-old attorney replied, "In the late sixties, that good enough? Who are you going to tell? Some girl?" The *Los Angeles Times* dutifully reported Parsons's age as sixty-nine.[2]

Like Cooper, Parsons had worked in the Los Angeles County DA's office as a prosecutor in the late 1930s. Before that he had gained some notoriety defending one "Rattlesnake" James, a villain who murdered his wife by forcing her foot into a box of poison snakes. By filing numerous appeals, Parsons managed to keep the convicted James alive for seven years, that at a time when appeals were not easily strung together.

In the modern era, Parsons was best known for his appeal on behalf of Charles Cahan, a convicted bookmaker who was tried on evidence secured by placing hidden microphones in his home without a search warrant. In 1955, the California Supreme Court overturned Cahan's conviction, saying that such evidence was illegally seized. Six years later, in *Mapp v. Ohio,* the U.S. Supreme Court made this prohibition against unreasonable search and seizure applicable in all states. "It used to be a question of 'Have you got the evidence?'" Parsons told reporters eager for some color; "now it's 'How did you get the evidence?'"

The *Los Angeles Times* described Parsons as "peppery." Most everyone else referred to him as "the well-known California appeals lawyer." But not all the reviews on Parsons were favorable. Journalist Robert Kaiser, who himself would join the defense team, characterized Parsons to the authors as "garrulous, funny, senile, and a fool."

"Cooper wanted an attorney that wasn't going to take over the case," Kaiser elaborated, "somebody who would do what he was told, and not be a problem later on. So he got harmless old Russell Parsons, way over the hill Russell Parsons. And Parsons enjoyed his few months basking in the publicity and giving interviews to the *Toronto Sun,* the *London Daily Mail,* and the *Bombay News,* all of this, seeing his face on television and enjoying it. Until Cooper came into the case and then he was decidedly a fifth wheel."

As the team to defend Sirhan was being assembled, District Attorney Evelle Younger was deciding who would present the state's evidence at the trial. On June 14, Younger announced that the prosecution would be led by Chief Deputy DA Lynn D. "Buck" Compton.

Compton had been born in Southern California in 1921. He attended UCLA, and in his senior year he played guard for the Bruins in the 1943 Rose Bowl. Two years later, as an infantry platoon leader in the 101st Airborne, Compton took part in the desperate defense of the Belgian town of Bastogne against a furious onslaught by German forces. For heroic service Compton received the Silver Star, the Bronze Star, and a Purple Heart.

Upon returning from Europe, Compton joined the LAPD. While a police detective he attended Loyola University Law School at night, passing his bar exam in 1949. Two years later he joined the district attorney's office. He was elevated to the position of chief deputy DA in 1966. Upon being chosen to lead the Sirhan prosecution Compton informed the press that one of the purposes of the trial would be to "restore public faith in law enforcement."

Joining Compton on the prosecution team were Deputy DA John Howard and Deputy DA David Fitts. Howard was chief of the DA's special investigations division and had presented the case at the Sirhan grand jury hearing. He had been with the district attorney's office for sixteen years, having, like Compton, studied law at Loyola University. David Fitts was considered one of Evelle Younger's ablest prosecutors. He had been a deputy DA for fourteen years, having joined the prosecutor's office upon completing his law studies at Stanford University.

On June 28, Russell Parsons appeared in the temporary courtroom set up in the prison chapel. Presiding was Judge Richard Schauer, administrating judge of the superior court, criminal division. The prosecution was represented by John Howard and David Fitts. Unlike his previous appearance, when he had entered in a wheelchair, this time Sirhan, dressed in dark slacks, a light blue shirt, and black leather shoes, strode briskly into the courtroom and stood when addressed by the judge.

Parsons told Judge Schauer that he would not be able to enter a plea for the defendant unless he received a report from the court-appointed psychiatrist, Dr. Eric Marcus.

"Do you desire this to be a confidential report?" asked Judge Schauer. Parsons answered in the affirmative, and Schauer ordered the doctor's report to be for the benefit of defense counsel only.

After the seven-minute court session Parsons told the attending press that he had "strong doubts" that his client was in full possession of his faculties when he shot Senator Kennedy, hinting heavily that the defense for Sirhan would be psychiatric. The DA's office had already come to that conclusion. In a front-row seat that day, observing Sirhan, was Dr. Seymour Pollack, an experienced psychiatrist who had been brought in to advise the prosecutors.

On July 19, preliminary trial proceedings were moved to a sheriff's briefing room on the thirteenth floor of the Hall of Justice, a downtown edifice that held a strange mix of courtrooms, county offices, and jail facilities. Sirhan was placed in a windowless cell on the same floor, a cell which would be his home for the next nine months. Security was tight. New shades on the improvised courtroom's windows were made out of quarter-inch steel plate. Overhead, a sheriff's helicopter kept watch.

As the first order of business Judge Schauer consented to Russell Parsons's request for another two weeks to enter a plea for Sirhan. Then District Attorney Evelle Younger entered a motion to vacate Judge Alarcon's order limiting public discussion of the case by those connected to it. "We feel strongly about it," said Younger, "and would like to be heard on it as soon as possible." Judge Schauer set the hearing date on the motion for August 2.

On that date Sirhan Sirhan would plead "Not guilty" to the charges against him. This provided the following day's headlines, but it was a minor moment in the day's proceedings: expected, and without much meaning. "Not guilty" left open the most options for the defense, and it could be changed later if conditions warranted.

During the court session Sirhan was seen holding Russell Parsons's hand as a little boy would hold the hand of his father. Later Parsons explained to newsmen, "He relies on me . . . looks at me as an advisor." Then he added, "Sometimes he even gets on his knees and talks to me."[3]

The real action of the day centered around Evelle Younger's motion to override Judge Alarcon's order. Younger himself argued the motion before Judge Schauer, citing "the fundamental concept that appears throughout our Constitution and our entire system of government, where, if possible, you let the people know as much as possible about the way your government is performing."

In this forum Younger argued heartily for the free flow of information in a democratic society. After the trial, however, the district attorney and the LAPD would decide that the police files in the Robert Kennedy murder would be kept secret indefinitely.

Younger may have had personal reasons for wanting Judge Alarcon's order lifted. It was no secret that he coveted higher office. Just days earlier he had been appointed by Richard Nixon to head the presidential candidate's Advisory Council on Crime and Law Enforcement, a symbolic post. Now, in Sirhan's trial, Younger had the perfect vehicle to enhance his reputation, yet Judge Alarcon's order stood in the way of any public statements that could give him additional recognition and stature.

"We certainly don't want any prejudicial material to disseminate," argued Younger to Judge Schauer, "but we are not for one minute agreeing to the proposition that you can determine prejudice by weighing or measuring the amount of space given to a matter."

"I hesitate to interrupt," said Schauer. ". . . Who is to judge whether a certain comment is prejudicial?"

"I think you, at the moment," answered Younger; "ultimately there may be others."

"But under the position that you are asserting," responded Schauer, "I would make that judgment after the statement was made. . . ."

"I think that is true," agreed Younger, "and I think it is important to recognize that the court does not have alone the responsibility to see that a defendant gets a fair trial, free of prejudice."

Evelle Younger then went on to hypothesize certain questions in which it would be in the public interest to have comments from involved authorities.

"For example: Was there a conspiracy to assassinate Senator Kennedy? Is there any foreign government connected or involved, directly or indirectly? . . . Is there any evidence that more than one gun was fired in the pantry of the Ambassador Hotel? . . . I think those are important issues where not only the public interest but also the defendant's interest requires that we be able to answer the question."

Younger was trying hard to conjure threats to the public well-being, but, at the time, conspiracy was not being seriously considered by the media or anyone else. The newspapers had printed some details about the woman in the polka-dot dress, after witness Vincent DiPierro described her to the grand jury on June 7. But when on June 21 the LAPD canceled their "wanted-for-questioning" bulletin concerning this woman, there was no public outcry. There also was no serious speculation about the involvement of foreign governments. Perhaps most significant, Younger's statement was the very first to raise the issue of a second gun in the pantry. The first public speculation on the matter would not occur until the following year, when Sirhan's trial was already over.

Judge Schauer was not moved by Younger's argument. "It seems to me," he said, "that nothing could be more clear in the law than that this case demands an order restricting publicity. The motion to vacate [Judge Alarcon's] order restricting publicity in its entirety is hereby denied."

Evelle Younger wasn't finished. He brought his case to the Second Appellate District Court of Appeals. When he lost there, he went to the Supreme Court of California, which, like both lower courts, affirmed the right of Judge Alarcon to restrict public statements about the Sirhan trial.

Accompanying Russell Parsons into the case was a private detective in his mid-thirties named Michael McCowan. McCowan had worked for the LAPD for ten years while putting himself through law school. His ambition to be an attorney, however, came to an end when he became involved in what police termed "a land swindle scheme." According to police documents, McCowan "resigned from LAPD in 1965 in lieu of disciplinary action after being arrested for theft and tampering with the United States mail."[4]

During his legal difficulties McCowan had retained Russell Parsons to represent him. Later, when McCowan set himself up as a private detective,

Parsons availed himself of his services, using McCowan primarily as a process server and routine investigator. When Parsons returned to his office after having visited Sirhan in jail, the news of his entry into the case had already spread. McCowan was inside the office waiting. "You need help," he said to Parsons. "I'm here to help. I'll drop everything I'm doing."[5]

Another investigator would come into the case by a more circuitous route. In the weeks following the murder of Robert Kennedy, journalist Robert Blair Kaiser followed events closely. He had initially contacted Al Wirin requesting an interview with Sirhan. Although Wirin was in no position to grant such a request, he reported back that Sirhan seemed open to the idea. Next, under Wirin's direction, the journalist had played a pivotal role in bringing Grant Cooper into the case. Kaiser sensed that he had created for himself an inside track to a very big story.

Robert Kaiser had begun his career in journalism in the late 1950s as a reporter for the *Arizona Republic* after having spent ten years studying for the Jesuit priesthood. In 1961 he went to work for *Time* magazine, where in 1963 he won the Overseas Press Club's award for the best magazine reporting on foreign affairs for his reports from Rome. In that same year he wrote *Pope, Council and World* (Macmillan), a best-selling book on Pope John's effort to modernize the Catholic Church.

By 1968 Kaiser was writing freelance in Los Angeles. Although he had written successfully on a variety of subjects, his high-profile work in Rome had given him a reputation as a reporter of religious news. Now the journalist saw an opportunity to demonstrate the full range of his skills. Kaiser proposed to Cooper that in exchange for exclusive rights to the Sirhan story, he would contribute a percentage of his take to the defense effort. Cooper and Parsons were donating their time, but money was still badly needed to meet the many expenses of litigation.

Cooper agreed to Kaiser's idea, but told the journalist that the mechanics would have to be worked out. After all, how could they conveniently gain access to Sirhan for the writer? What assurance did they have that Kaiser wouldn't write something that would damage the defense? How could they be sure that Kaiser wouldn't end up as a witness for the prosecution?

Cooper's idea was that Kaiser could sign on as a defense investigator. This would give the writer access to the defendant. At the same time he would be prohibited from writing about the substance of the case before trial, and he would be out of reach of the prosecution.

In early August, using his new status as defense investigator, Robert Kaiser first gained access to Sirhan. Kaiser had two projects in mind. The first would be a background story on Sirhan for a national magazine; the second would be a book on the case. Both projects would bring much-needed money into the defense effort, but there was another benefit. In doing his research the writer quickly gained a familiarity with the case beyond that held by the defense attorneys themselves. Thus equipped, Robert Kaiser soon became a valued member of the Sirhan Sirhan defense team.

On August 8, six days after Sirhan pleaded not guilty, Richard Nixon was nominated in Miami Beach to be the Republican Party's presidential candidate. Nixon promised the cheering GOP delegates that he would "bring an honorable end to the war in Vietnam." He also promised "a militant crusade against crime," saying, "the right to be free from domestic violence has become the forgotten civil right."

Three weeks later startling images of such violence would be featured on the nightly news as the Democratic Party gathered in Chicago to nominate its candidate for president. During the week preceding the nomination, confrontations between protestors and police had escalated. Initially the disturbances were confined to Lincoln and Grant Parks, but by nomination night the violence had engulfed several miles of downtown Chicago.

With Hubert Humphrey's nomination assured by the murder of Robert Kennedy, debate over the party's Vietnam policy plank became the chief dramatic focus. Party regulars put forward a plank supporting the present administration's policies in Vietnam. A minority plank called for a swift end to American participation in the war. When former JFK press secretary Pierre Salinger addressed the delegates he declared, "If Robert Kennedy were alive today, he would be on the platform speaking for the minority plank." The majority position carried by a margin of 3 to 2.

Outside the convention center a horrific scene was unfolding. In front of reporters and delegate spouses looking out the windows of the Conrad Hilton Hotel, police seemed to be attacking everyone in sight, focusing particular violence upon newsmen and their equipment. One account, printed on the front page of the *New York Times,* told how the police, without warning, attacked onlookers standing quietly behind a police barrier in front of the hotel. According to reporter Anthony Lukas, the police pushed the screaming bystanders, including middle-aged women and children, through a plate-glass window of a street-level restaurant and then ran into the restaurant to beat and arrest the bleeding victims.

A few months later President Johnson's Commission on Violence, brought into being by the murder of Robert Kennedy, issued a report describing what happened in the streets of Chicago as a "police riot." Not everyone saw it that way. But whether one saw irresponsible youths desecrating the political process, or a police apparatus gone beserk, the televised images from Chicago were profoundly disturbing.

★　　★　　★

On October 4, Judge Schauer announced that he was assigning the Sirhan trial to Judge Herbert V. Walker. It was an obvious choice. Walker was at the end of a distinguished career and was well thought of by those in the legal profession. In 1964 the Criminal Courts Bar Association, an organization of criminal defense attorneys, gave him an award that praised his standards of fairness and justice. The *Los Angeles Times* applauded Walker as "the dean of the criminal court judges."

Herbert Walker was born in 1899. He spent most of his childhood in central California. By age fourteen he was alone, his father dead and his mother in a mental institution. At the first opportunity Walker joined the U.S. Navy and served two years on the battleship *Kentucky* during the First World War. Following the war Walker worked various jobs in the Louisiana oil fields and got bit parts in silent films after he moved back to California.

Walker graduated from the USC Law School in 1928. Fifteen years later he would succeed Grant Cooper as chief deputy district attorney for Los Angeles County. Thus the chief prosecutor (Lynn Compton), the lead defense attorney, and the judge had all held the same high position of chief deputy of the Los Angeles DA's office.

In 1953 Herbert Walker was appointed judge of the state superior court by then-governor Earl Warren. During his sixteen years on the bench, Walker had sentenced nineteen men to die in the gas chamber. Only one was ever executed: Walker's most famous defendant, Caryl Chessman, convicted of robbery and rape in 1948. Walker was the eighth and final judge to condemn Chessman to death, a sentence that was carried out in 1960.

Herbert Walker lived in a modest house in the suburbs. He was a registered Republican and a practicing Episcopalian, and he wore a large Stetson hat when he wasn't indoors. He was considered "old school" by his peers, one of whom described him as "a period piece." "He has a very good, strong code of morality and believes in a fair trial," reported another colleague. "But he believes in the dry words of the law and doesn't consider the courtroom an appropriate place for the humanities."[6]

This last assessment might have given Sirhan's attorneys some pause, for the defense of Sirhan was to be constructed on a foundation of new ideas. Yet neither Parsons nor Cooper was concerned. Walker's reputation was "firm, but fair." So long as he was fair, it would be the jury and not the judge who would make the important decisions.

Herbert Walker brought the Sirhan court to order for the first time on October 14. "This is a petition of Sirhan Bishara Sirhan for an order of discovery," the judge announced as the session began.

Under California law the defense was entitled to petition the prosecution to reveal certain evidence they might have which would shed light on the case. "Any orders I make are directed to the district attorney only," cautioned Walker, making sure everyone understood the limits of discovery, "and can only affect those documents and other things that he, the district attorney, has in his possession."

The motion for discovery had been primarily drawn up by investigators Michael McCowan and Robert Kaiser. There were thirty-seven groups of requested materials. At one point prosecutor David Fitts approached the defense table and dropped upon it a large pile of papers representing witness interviews, transcripts, and summaries for sixty-seven witnesses who had been in the Ambassador Hotel the night of the murder. Then Fitts deposited another pile representing fifteen witnesses who had seen Sirhan at a local gun range.

In remarks to the court, Deputy DA Compton characterized the surrendered witness interviews as "negative" in regards to the question of a possible conspiracy. Russell Parsons would parrot those words later in the afternoon when he talked to reporters. "We have seen," said the attorney who had not yet had time to review the material gained in discovery, "no evidence of conspiracy." The following morning the *Los Angeles Times* ran with the large-type, front-page headline "Both Sides Agree Sirhan Was Alone."

The same day Judge Walker was overseeing the mechanics of discovery, the Summer Olympic Games were getting under way in Mexico City. There would be several stunning performances by U.S. athletes. Bob Beamon would leap 29 feet 2.5 inches to break the world long jump record by an astounding 2 feet. High jumper Dick Fosbury would win a gold medal by employing the "Fosbury Flop," a previously unknown technique of jumping over the crossbar backward and landing safely on the back.

The most lasting image from the games, however, came when American sprinters Tommy Smith and John Carlos rose to accept their gold and bronze medals in the two-hundred-meter dash. As the American national anthem played, Smith and Carlos raised clenched, gloved fists in a black power salute protesting the treatment of blacks in the United States. The two were suspended from the games and expelled from the Olympic village for misusing the Olympic forum.

On October 22, Judge Walker once again called court into session. This time the issue to be decided was whether or not the notebooks taken from

Sirhan's bedroom the morning of the murder had been obtained legally by the police.

Russell Parsons opened with a question for prosecutor Lynn Compton.

"Counsel, may I inquire whether or not in this case there was in your possession or had you obtained a search warrant granting the officers permission to search the premises in Pasadena where Mr. Sirhan had resided?"

"We will stipulate at the time of the search in question the officers were not armed with a search warrant."

"Thank you very much. The validity of the search now shifts to the prosecution."

"Are you ready to proceed?" asked Judge Walker.

"Yes, Your Honor," replied David Fitts. "Sergeant William Brandt."

Under Fitts's direction Brandt told the story of how he came to interview Adel Sirhan the morning of the murder on the second floor of the Pasadena Police Department and how he and several other officers accompanied Adel back to the family home on Howard Street Fitts asked if the police had asked for permission to enter and search the home.

"I asked him if we could search the home," Brandt replied. "He said as far as he was concerned we could; however, it was his mother's house."

"All right, did he say anything further about his mother at this time?"

"We asked him if he would call his mother for permission and he indicated he would prefer that we did not talk to his mother at that time."

When Sirhan's older brother Adel took the witness stand he told a very similar story when Fitts asked if he had consented to a search.

"I told him I had nothing to hide," said Adel; "those are my exact words. He asked me, 'Do you mind if we search the house?' and I said, 'I have nothing to hide, but the house isn't mine, I do not own the house.' "

"Did you ever tell him that you had no objection to their searching?"

"I said my mother owns the house, but I do not want her disturbed."

"Was that all you said?"

"Yes, that is all I said."

Other witnesses were introduced, including Sirhan's mother Mary and brother Munir, but the facts remained stable. Judge Walker asked for any final argument.

"I think the officers are entitled to rely on ostensible rather than actual authority . . ." offered Lynn Compton. "The boy [actually thirty-year-old Adel] had a key and he did reside in the home. I think the officers were perfectly reasonable in relying on the apparent authority to consent to their entry."

"There was no reasonable indication for their visiting this house . . . ," countered Russell Parsons. "They would have great difficulty in obtaining a search warrant from a magistrate, from any judge of the court."

In making his decision Judge Walker reminded counsel that he was not ruling on the admissibility of the evidence, only on the issue of whether it was legally obtained. "I don't think there is anything in the law that requires an owner's consent," he said. "I think under the circumstances, in light of all the testimony, the officers did have reasonable authority. . . . The motion to suppress will be denied."

Two days later it was revealed that District Attorney Evelle J. Younger had petitioned the Supreme Court of the United States to overturn the Supreme Court of California and do away with Judge Alarcon's order restricting public comment on the Sirhan trial. "The only feasible way to meet the danger of false charges and rumors," said Younger in Washington, "is to allow responsible public officials to indicate on occasion, why certain witnesses have not been used, or how certain leads have proven false or irrelevant."[7] It would be several months before the Supreme Court would be able to consider Younger's petition, but there would be time: the set date for the start of the Sirhan trial kept receding.

When Grant Cooper agreed to assume direction of Sirhan's defense he believed the Friars Club affair would be over by September. In that expectation Russell Parsons had gotten a November 1 trial date. When the card-cheating trial dragged on, Parsons asked for another continuance, and the trial was put off until December 9.

On November 5, Richard Nixon defeated Humbert Humphrey to become the thirty-seventh president of the United States. Nixon won a comfortable victory in the electoral college, but his margin in the popular vote was only one half of one percent. The televised street violence during the Chicago convention had clearly injured Humphrey's chances, and early political forecasts had him losing to Nixon by thirty percentage points. In the final weeks of the campaign, however, Humphrey steadily closed the gap, only to lose the election in a near dead heat.

On December 2, the Friars Club verdict came in. All five defendants were found guilty. That same day Grant Cooper announced that he was going to head the Sirhan defense team. A few days later Cooper made his first appearance in court.

"Your Honor please," said Cooper addressing the court, "at this time the defendant moves for a continuance to January 7, 1969, for the following reason: As Your Honor is undoubtedly aware, I have been engaged in a trial of a case in the federal court which began June eleventh and continued from June 11 to just last week."

Cooper told the court that he had met Sirhan for the first time a few days earlier for a short get-acquainted visit. "I have discussed the case from time to time with Mr. Parsons while I was trying the case in the federal court but, obviously, I did not have an opportunity, if Your Honor please, to get into any of the facts, and, obviously, I am now familiar with the facts in a general way, have read about them in the press and discussed them generally with Mr. Parsons, but I have not had an opportunity to do the type of preparation that is so essential."

In his remarks Cooper implied that a month really wouldn't be enough time to properly prepare, but then he acknowledged the patience and courtesy that had been extended to the defense over the last months. "Having some appreciation of the Court's position I would only ask for continuance to January seventh." Judge Walker agreed.

Cooper had a particular reason for asking for the January 7 trial date. "I realize the sixth is a Monday," he told the court, "but there is another attorney going to assist us in the case, Mr. Emile Zola Berman of New York. . . . He has commitments that will prevent him from being here earlier than the seventh."

The final member of the Sirhan defense team had been announced. He would be joining the case the day before the trial began.

Emile Zola Berman had been born on New York's Lower East Side to Russian Jewish immigrants. He was named after the famous French author whose book *J'accuse!* had excoriated the French military for bringing false charges of treason against Captain Alfred Dreyfus. Zola had helped Berman's mother emigrate from Russia and looked out for her while she was in Paris.

Emile Berman grew up on New York's Lower East Side, where he acquired the nickname "Zuke," a name that would carry over into in his future professional life. In 1925 Berman graduated from NYU Law School. He then practiced law in New York. During the Second World War, Berman flew bombers in the China-Burma theater for the Army Air Corps and was discharged a lieutenant colonel with a Distinguished Flying Cross, an Air Medal, and a Bronze Star.

After the war Berman worked primarily as a negligence lawyer, with some criminal work mixed in. In 1956 he represented Staff Sergeant Matthew McKeon, a drill instructor at the marine boot camp on South Carolina's Parris Island. McKeon had led his training platoon into a coastal swamp, where they were overtaken by a fast-rising tide. Six members of his platoon drowned. A military court charged McKeon with murder and dereliction of duty, but after a stiff defense by Berman, McKeon was found guilty of drinking while on duty and simple negligence.

Emile Berman was highly thought of in New York legal circles. On several occasions he was appointed by the state appellate division to conduct investigations of attorneys suspected of misconduct. In 1962 Berman ran and lost as the Democratic candidate for district attorney of Nassau County.

Although Berman's skills in criminal law had been amply demonstrated, it was his experience in negligence litigation that most interested Grant Cooper. Berman was an acknowledged expert in handling medical witnesses: he lectured on the subject at various universities. Since it was already decided that Sirhan's defense was going to be psychiatric, Cooper wanted a man on the team who was skillful in presenting medical evidence. Moreover, Berman was a Jew, and Cooper thought that might help in defending an Arab in a case with political overtones.

Although Berman's commitments kept him occupied until January 7, he did manage to come to Los Angeles for a handful of days in the middle of December to meet with the defense team. While the New York attorney was in Los Angeles, it was announced that the U.S. Supreme Court refused to hear District Attorney Evelle Younger's third and final appeal, leaving in place Judge Alarcon's order forbidding public comment on the Sirhan trial from those connected with the case.

On December 10, Grant Cooper visited the offices of the district attorney to meet meet with Deputy DA John Howard and Deputy DA David Fitts. Cooper wanted to obtain the results of tests done upon blood reportedly taken from Sirhan the night of the murder. (The test results would come back negative for syphilis, but, remarkably, according to the police, no tests were conducted to detect the presence of drugs or alcohol in Sirhan's system.) Cooper was also eager to view photocopies of pages from Sirhan's notebooks, which until this time had not been provided to the defense.

The prosecutors were looking for something as well. According to a memorandum by David Fitts:

> Mr. Cooper was asked whether his client might consent to the administration of a lie detector test to be performed by an acknowledged and totally impartial expert with a view to determining whether Sirhan acted alone or in concert with others. Mr. Cooper was advised that the results of such tests would be for their ultimate historical significance and would not be available to the parties. Mr. Cooper was receptive in principle, but with this proviso: In the event that something beneficial to the defendant was developed in the course of the test, [he would be allowed] to make use of it after a final judgement was obtained in the case, presumably at an executive clemency hearing.

The proposal offered by Howard and Fitts is remarkable for several reasons. It appears to transgress the proper boundary between the prosecution and the defense. One might wonder why the results of the examination were to be kept secret and why, if something exculpatory were found, it would not be used until after the case had been decided. Most strange is the prosecution's desire to probe Sirhan's affiliations for their "ultimate historical significance." The question of whether Sirhan acted alone or in concert with others should have been of interest to the district attorney as a prosecutorial matter, not an historical one. That the prosecutors were speaking in these terms indicates the answer to the polygraph exam was presupposed.

The opening of the Sirhan trial was still weeks away, but the prosecutors were already seeking to make peace with history, and, toward this end, looking to enlist the aid of the chief defense attorney. They met with some success. Although a polygraph session with the defendant did not take place, there would be other joint-venture examinations of Sirhan, to be described, to which Cooper would consent—examinations that would stretch the boundaries of normally accepted criminal procedure.

Grant Cooper's first extensive interview with Sirhan had occurred just days before his meeting with Fitts and Howard. The session, which took place in Sirhan's windowless cell in the Hall of Justice, had been Cooper's introduction into the complexities of what he had thought was a tragic but simple case. Prior to this, as Cooper had admitted, what he knew of the murder he had learned from the newspapers, a few brief meetings with Russell Parsons, and a summary report written by Michael McCowan.

To Cooper's pleasant surprise, he found his client to be cooperative, intelligent, and well-spoken. But, as will be discussed later, the attorney was positively baffled by a number of Sirhan's statements. "I just can't figure this kid out," Cooper would confess to Robert Kaiser.[8]

The chief defense counsel wouldn't have a lot of time to apply himself to this problem. His focus was about to be split again. On January 3, just four days before the Sirhan trial was scheduled to begin, Grant Cooper was called to testify before a closed-door session of a federal grand jury on a matter unrelated to Robert Kennedy's death. Cooper was in front of the grand jury for over three hours. At the end of the day rumors began to circulate that the well-respected attorney was about to be on the receiving end of a criminal indictment.

THREE

Voir Dire

✳ ✳ ✳

*I want to find out why it happened. I didn't understand the other
two killings [President Kennedy and Dr. King]. I want to understand
this one. This time I want to know why. I want to be spared the
hangover of doubts.*

—Sirhan trial spectator to *New York Times* reporter Lacey Fosburgh

O N JAUNARY 7, 1969, the trial of
Sirhan Sirhan began as scheduled
in a small seventy-five-seat courtroom on the eighth floor of the Hall of
Justice. Only a dozen members of the general public and less than a third
of the more than one hundred credentialed newsmen were given seats in
the courtroom. Journalists who didn't work for a major news outlet were
sent to an auxiliary courtroom several floors below, where for three months
they would watch the proceedings on closed-circuit TV.

Guarding the eighth-floor corridor was a set of newly installed armored
doors, through which entrance was gained by display of the proper color-
coded plastic badge. Beyond the doors, newsmen, witnesses, and court
officers were searched and then scanned by a hand-held metal detector
before being allowed to pass another line of police officers in front of the
courtroom itself. Inside, sheriff's deputies, both in and out of uniform, were
strategically placed around the room. Heavy beige curtains hid steel plates
covering the windows, and the remote TV camera was concealed in an air-
conditioning unit in an attempt to maintain a normal courtroom atmosphere.

Five floors above, Sirhan Sirhan was led from his six-by-eight-foot windowless cell, where he had spent most of the last six months. He was taken
by elevator to the ninth floor and then down a secured staircase and into
the courtroom. The defendant was dressed in a crisp gray suit. He appeared
nervous and kept touching his mouth with his fingers as the proceedings
began. On occasion his gaze would stray to his mother and his younger
brother Munir, who were seated in the back of the room.

The mood in court was expectant. The day before, in a front-page article, *New York Times* reporter Douglas Kneeland spoke of the historical importance of the trial by recounting the murder of Robert Kennedy. "With his death," Kneeland said of the fallen senator, ". . . politics lost its bright edge for countless thousands of Americans." In *Newsday,* reporter Bob Greene predicted that the Sirhan trial would become "one of the most celebrated in American judicial history."

But there was little to celebrate this day. As soon as Judge Walker called the court to order, Sirhan's attorney, Grant Cooper, approached the bench and, to the audible disappointment of those in attendance, requested that the proceedings be adjourned to the privacy of Judge Walker's chambers. Once all were assembled inside, Cooper was the first to speak.

"If Your Honor please, the defendant moves the Court for a continuance of at least thirty days for the reason that there has been certain adverse publicity that will materially affect the defendant's right to a fair trial at this time, publicity . . . with respect to the personal problems of Grant Cooper."

Sirhan's chief attorney was, indeed, having problems. On December 3, the very day it was reported that Cooper would represent Sirhan, another article about the defense attorney appeared on the front page of the *Los Angeles Times.* This story reported that Cooper was the object of a federal investigation concerning irregularities in the Friars Club trial.

The difficulties for Cooper had begun on July 24 of the previous year, when Assistant U.S. Attorney David R. Nissen spotted a transcript of a secret grand jury proceeding on the defense attorney's table. It was a document the Friars Club lawyers were not entitled to possess. Nissen immediately called for a conference in Judge William P. Gray's chambers, where he asked how the secret transcript came to be in Grant Cooper's possession.

"The only documents I have are the ones I got from you," said Cooper.

"Well, Mr. Cooper," replied Nissen, "that document did not come from me. It did not come from any of my associates."

After a brief recess during which the defense attorney was given the opportunity to examine the document, Judge Gray asked Cooper if he had ever seen it before.

"I have it," Cooper said. "I had it in my file, Your Honor."

"You don't know how you got it?" Judge Gray asked.

"I didn't get it from any other source," answered Cooper, implying, once again, that the document had come from the prosecution.

Two days later U.S. Attorney Matthew Byrne again asked Cooper in Judge Gray's chambers how he came to possess the transcript.

"I found it on the table in the courtroom," replied Cooper, now contradicting his earlier statement.[1]

A subsequent investigation by the U.S. attorney revealed that the transcript on Cooper's desk had been secured by bribing a clerk at the office which photocopied the documents for the grand jury. In addition it was discovered that other transcripts had been obtained in the same manner and that Cooper and several other attorneys in the case were aware of this repeated illegal penetration of the grand jury process. Action against the suspected offenders, who were still litigating for their clients, was delayed until the Friars Club trial was concluded.

With the verdict now in, Grant Cooper was being called upon by the U.S. attorney to account for his actions. He had not only participated, to some degree, in illegally obtaining secret grand jury transcripts, he had lied on two occasions to a federal judge. The Friars Club card-cheating scandal had now become the Friars Club bribery and perjury scandal.

The question of who was behind the stolen transcripts was never publicly resolved, although by most indications it was Friars Club defendant Johnny Roselli, who was represented by attorney James P. Cantillon. Indeed, one of the questions put to Grant Cooper during the bribery probe was "Did your numerous phone calls to Mr Cantillon . . . pertain to the then and continuing possession of the illegally obtained federal grand jury transcripts?"[2] Cooper refused to answer this question.

Johnny Roselli described himself as a businessman, but the *Los Angeles Times* made note of Roselli's long-term relationship with the Chicago mob, labeling him a "one-time lieutenant of Chicago gangster Al Capone." In 1944 Roselli had been convicted of attempting to extort millions from motion picture companies by manipulating their unions. After serving three years of a ten-year sentence, he was paroled in 1948.[3] In more recent years it was said that Roselli had looked after the West Coast interests of Chicago crime boss Sam Giancana.

Johnny Roselli had not dreamed up the Friars Club scam, nor had he participated in the card cheating itself. Several years after the operation was up and running, Roselli found out about it, and, because he was Johnny Roselli, he demanded and received a cut. Along with the others he was implicated when the FBI closed in.

There may have been moments when the authorities had wished they hadn't bagged Roselli. His very presence as a defendant created difficulties. Out of apparent fear two of the alleged peekhole operators, Edwin N. Gebhard and Albert K. Snyder, both of whom the FBI was courting as potential witnesses, refused to cooperate with the investigation, even though they were offered immunity from prosecution. Later, Assistant U.S. Attorney David Nissen said that certain witnesses "pleaded to the point of tears that they not be required to testify against [Roselli] for fear they would be killed."[4]

Gebhard and Snyder's fear of retribution was apparently well founded, and Grant Cooper came close to being unwittingly involved in something more serious than bribery. With Gebhard and Snyder absent, the government's card-cheating case rested primarily upon one witness, George Emerson Seach. Seach had put in time as a peekhole operator at the Friars Club and then moved on. When he got into trouble elsewhere he became an informant for the FBI and triggered the Friars Club investigation.

When the Friars Club indictments were handed down, Roselli met with his friend Jimmy (the Weasel) Fratianno. According to Fratianno (in a detailed confession published in Ovid Demaris's book *The Last Mafiosi*), Roselli proposed that Fratianno murder Seach. Roselli then handed Fratianno an envelope with several thousand dollars "for expenses." According to Fratianno, the cash had come from Grant Cooper's client and Roselli's friend, Maurice H. Friedman. As the story goes, Fratianno and several cohorts then went out to Las Vegas, where Seach was living, but before the hit could be made the FBI put the witness under federal protection.[5] Thus, Seach testified, and all the defendants were convicted.

At a closed-door session on January 3, Grant Cooper attempted to satisfy the grand jury's bribery investigation by making a limited confession. The transcript reveals this colloquy:

> COOPER: Well to begin with I knew that transcripts of the federal grand jury were not available to defense counsel. That I knew. And I also knew that at some place in the chain of events somebody had to come in possession of these illegally; that I knew as a lawyer. . . .
> QUESTION: So at the time . . . you were aware that if a federal grand jury's transcripts were available, they had been obtained illegally?
> COOPER: I assumed that somewhere at some time they had been obtained in some improper fashion, that is right.
> QUESTION: An illegal fashion?
> COOPER: Yes, I would say that is true.

A little later there was this exchange:

> QUESTION: Were you ever in the state of mind, Mr. Cooper, that you were going to get all the grand jury transcripts?
> COOPER: I thought at one time I would.
> QUESTION: Did you anticipate at that time that they would be delivered to you?
> COOPER: I did.

Cooper's antiseptic mea culpa did not end the matter. It only suggested more questions: forty-six of them to be exact. These were drawn up by presiding U.S. District Judge Francis C. Whelan, who posed them for Cooper to answer. Realizing that there would be no satisfactory end to the probe if he continued to blindly cooperate, Cooper changed strategy. Invoking the right of attorney-client privilege, he refused to answer any further questions. Whelan threatened to hold Cooper in contempt and send him to jail if he did not answer, but Cooper responded that he was willing to go to jail and fight the issue of attorney-client privilege in court.

On January 7, the set starting date of the Sirhan trial, Grant Cooper would be photographed at nine in the morning walking down the corridors of the Hall of Justice with Emile Berman, his cocounsel in the defense of the alleged murderer of Robert F. Kennedy. At one in the afternoon the same day, Cooper would be photographed walking down the corridors of the Federal Court Building across the street with Herman F. Selvin, the criminal defense attorney representing him in the grand jury probe of the Friars Club bribery allegations. For six months Cooper had delayed public knowledge that he would represent Sirhan so as not to prejudice a jury against his client in the Friars Club trial. Now it was the Friars Club trial that was threatening to prejudice a jury against Sirhan.

This is what Cooper argued on January 7, when he petitioned Judge Walker for another thirty-day "cooling off" postponement. Cooper offered to submit evidence of the extent to which his legal difficulties had been played up in the media. Cocounsel Emile Berman tried to support Cooper's position. "Nobody," argued Berman, "in the role of principal counsel here can persuade a jury about anything if his sincerity [i.e., credibility] has been destroyed. . . . There isn't a place in the country today if this case were sent there that would not be aware of the fact that the chief counsel in this case has been labeled a liar."

"If Your Honor please," responded prosecutor Lynn Compton, "it strikes me if we follow Mr. Berman's statements to their logical conclusion we could never try this case. . . . Mr Cooper might be indicted and be prosecuted for criminal conduct; and certainly that would be much more devastating in terms of its effect on this case than the articles which have heretofore appeared."

Judge Walker was in no mood for another delay. He denied the motion for a postponement, but ruled that the defense could submit for the record whatever evidence they had concerning potentially prejudicial press reports. Court was then adjourned so that attorney Cooper could attend his own inquest in federal court.

As the day's session had illustrated, the grand jury proceedings against Grant Cooper and the trial of Sirhan Sirhan were on a collision course. The U.S. attorney had evidence on Cooper, but Cooper was doing the entire legal establishment a tremendous favor by representing Sirhan Sirhan. Cooper could certainly not defend Sirhan while he was in jail, and further discrediting the attorney seemed counterproductive.

Something had to give way, and the trial of Sirhan Sirhan was clearly the more important of the two. Thus the grand jury proceeding against Grant Cooper was put off to some future time when the attorney could again be held accountable for his participation in the bribery scandal. Eight months later the matter was concluded when Cooper pled guilty to two counts of contempt and was fined one thousand dollars.*

Despite the stated fears of the defense attorneys, the most damaging effect of the new Friars investigation was not its propensity to prejudice a jury against Sirhan Sirhan or compromise Grant Cooper, but its consumption of so much of the chief defense attorney's time and attention. When he spoke to the court in early December, Cooper had admitted that a month was not enough time to familiarize himself with the case and prepare for trial. Now, a great deal of that precious month had been spent contemplating not Sirhan's legal defense, but his own.

The remainder of the first week of Sirhan's trial was spent dealing with various motions put forward by the defense. To the dismay of the assembled reporters, much of this took place in Judge Walker's chambers.

Grant Cooper moved that the potential jurors be questioned in writing to save time. Walker denied the motion, saying he thought that would only complicate the process.

Cooper next moved that there be one jury for the guilt or innocence phase of the trial and a separate jury to decide the penalty if the result was a conviction of first-degree murder. Under California law a separate hearing would be held to determine penalty in the event of a first-degree verdict; but, in the past, the jury had usually been the same panel that had tried the case. Walker denied the motion.

Cooper's most ambitious motion was to quash the indictment against Sirhan because, as he asserted, the grand jury handing down the indictment had been improperly constituted. Under the system in place each judge in the Los Angeles County Superior Court nominated two prospective jurors, the final panel then being selected at random from this list of nominees. Cooper contended that this process resulted in "blue ribbonism," that minority groups and the economically disadvantaged were not properly represented. He asked Judge Walker for a thirty-day continuance while the

---

*That Grant Cooper was under criminal investigation while he was representing Sirhan Sirhan is open to the interpretation that, in some way, he was on a leash—unable or unwilling to investigate aggressively those who were about to investigate him. The authors have heard this theory informally advanced on several occasions. As will be demonstrated, the authors believe that Grant Cooper's conduct toward the prosecution throughout the trial was overly cooperative and conciliatory, this relaxed posture contributing to Cooper's misunderstanding of a number of important evidentiary issues to the severe detriment of his client. This said, however, the authors are aware of nothing in Grant Cooper's words or actions that would indicate that his conduct sprang from anything other than his judgment as to the best interests of his client, however wrong he may have been.

defense readied its challenge. Walker, again, denied Cooper's motion for a delay, but agreed that the challenge could take place after the jury had been selected, thus giving the defense lawyers time to prepare.

On the following Monday, twenty-five candidate jurors, called veniremen, were escorted into the courtroom. After they took an oath of truth, Judge Walker spoke to them as a group.

"Under our system of jurisprudence," he said, "it is the function of the jury to determine the issues of fact. In performance of that function you have as much authority and as much responsibility as any other judge . . . Now you also understand under the law of this state a person charged with a crime is presumed to be innocent . . . [and] that presumption remains with the defendant until the People by good and sufficient evidence have proved him guilty beyond a reasonable doubt."

Walker informed the jurors that as soon as he was finished they would be questioned about their qualifications to serve on the jury by attorneys from both sides in an examination process known as *voir dire*, derived from the French "to speak the truth." He told them that the trial might last several months and during that time those who served would be sequestered in a hotel with conjugal visits by "spouses of record" permitted only on weekends. Walker then nodded at Grant Cooper to proceed.

The first prospective juror to undergo voir dire was Mr. George Doudle. After a few perfunctory questions about Mr. Doudle's occupation and prior jury experience, Cooper went for the heart of the matter as he saw it.

"Now at the outset," he said in a voice loud enough so all the candidate jurors could hear, "there will be no denial of the fact that our client, Sirhan Sirhan, fired the shot or shots that killed Senator Kennedy." This was the first time since the trial began a week earlier that Robert Kennedy's name had been spoken in court.

Grant Cooper's statement had a simple objective: to forestall resentment toward the defense. Cooper wanted the jurors to understand that there would be no denial of the fact that Sirhan killed Senator Kennedy. He also wanted them to know that for a killing to be a murder, in addition to an act, there had to be a requisite state of mind: an intent or premeditation.

What Cooper wanted to find out in return was whether the knowledge that the defendant pulled the trigger would so influence the juror that he could not fairly decide the issue of the assailant's state of mind.

"Now you have been told," Cooper said to Mr. Doudle, "that this defendant will admit committing the act, to wit, the shooting, and would that cause you to be prejudiced against him so you couldn't try the issue of intent?"

"Yes, I believe so," answered Doudle.

"It would cause you to be prejudiced?" Cooper said, a little surprised. "Yes."

"All right. I will challenge the juror for cause."

Any potential juror who voiced or exhibited prejudice during voir dire could be excluded from service "for cause" by way of a challenge from attorneys on either side. There is no limit in number to such challenges, though each must be approved by the judge. Later, from the pool of already-questioned "unprejudiced" candidates, each side could eliminate up to twenty veniremen with peremptory challenges, which require no rationale other than an attorney's belief that a juror would not look favorably upon his client.

Besides culling the unsuitable and the unwanted, voir dire also eliminated any juror who simply did not care to serve. A venireman could always claim, usually with justification, that a prolonged jury service would cause economic hardship. If the hardship claim was not accepted by the judge, any unwilling venireman could then excuse himself by saying that he harbored prejudice. The practical result of these procedures was that all the juror candidates meriting serious consideration *wanted* to serve on the jury, and were inclined to provide the "correct" responses to questions they were being asked by the attorneys.

Since the jurors were interviewed in each other's presence, the right answers quickly became common knowledge. Thus, over and over, the attorneys questioned potential jurors who, yes, had heard that Robert Kennedy had been murdered, but really hadn't thought much about it or discussed it with their friends and certainly had no feelings at all about what kind of punishment should be delivered to his assailant if convicted, and so forth. The attorneys expected this, so the questions they asked were geared not so much to elicit information as to impart a certain mind-set about the juror's duties that the attorney wanted to reinforce. This process became obvious the first day during the questioning of Rosa Molina.

"Mrs. Molina," began Grant Cooper in a fashion that would be regarded as sexist today, "is there a Mr. Molina?"

"No, sir."

"I take it he passed on?"

"Yes."

"What was his business or occupation?"

"He was with U.S. Rubber. U.S. Rubber Tire."

Cooper asked Mrs. Molina whether she had any objections to the death penalty. Molina said she did not. Cooper asked if his asking this very question made her think his client was guilty of murder in the first degree. She said it did not. So far she had given the "right" answers. Cooper then asked whether, if a verdict of first-degree murder was rendered, Molina would favor a sentence of life or death.

"I would, according to the law and the evidence," responded Molina, trying to give the appropriate answer. "I would follow according to what the law is."

"Well, the law doesn't tell you," Cooper responded.

"The law doesn't tell me," repeated Molina, searching for some direction.

"The law doesn't favor one punishment over the other," said Cooper. "That is something you have to search your conscience; there are no guidelines."

"You want me to tell you just what?" asked Molina candidly.

"Do you favor one punishment over the other?"

"I have no prejudice of any kind now," said Molina, seeking the magic words.

Cooper was still not satisfied. "Do you at the present time with that background of knowledge, have a leaning one way or the other toward life or death as a proper punishment?"

"No, I don't."

"All right."

Cooper went on with his didactic questions. He explained briefly the defense of diminished capacity (sometimes called "diminished responsibility"), whereby a defendant without the requisite premeditation might be found guilty of a lesser crime. Did Mrs. Molina, he asked, have a prejudice against such a defense? She did not. Cooper explained that the defense might be presenting the testimony of a number of psychiatrists. Some people, Cooper asserted, called psychiatrists "headshrinkers" and thought they were "crazy." Did Mrs. Molina have any such feelings? She did not. Some of these doctors, Cooper said, employ certain psychological tests such as inkblots which some people regard as "silly." Did Mrs. Molina feel this way about those tests? She did not. Cooper then appeared to refer to his Friars Club difficulties. Would Mrs. Molina hold any "misconduct" on the part of an attorney against his client? She would not. Was Mrs. Molina the kind of person that believes there are two sides to every story? She was.

When it was his turn to question Molina, Prosecutor David Fitts had his own set of instructive questions. Just because a witness had a professional title that ended in "-iatry" or "-ology," he wanted to know, would the juror still feel free to make up her own mind about what was being discussed? Molina said she would. Just because the issue at stake is something difficult to prove, like a state of mind, asked Fitts, the juror wouldn't let that in itself constitute reasonable doubt, would she? Molina said she wouldn't.

Fitts was also interested in countering the most dramatic moment of the day. He referred to Cooper's concession that Sirhan Sirhan fired the shot that killed Senator Kennedy as a "strategy" to win credibility points with the jury.

"Your Honor, please," interrupted Cooper. "I would strike 'strategy' from the question. It isn't a question of strategy."

"Well, let us not be so naive," answered Fitts.

Judge Walker upheld Cooper's objection and Fitts had to rephrase.

"Merely by virtue of the concession which Mr. Cooper suggested to you," said Fitts carefully, "are you at this time disposed to believe that whatever defense the defendant may offer in this case must necessarily be worthy of credence?"

"What?" responded Molina. "Worthy of what?"

"Credence. Belief," said Fitts.

"Counsel," interrupted Judge Walker. "Get into the habit of using certain words that are normally understood by everybody in the community. I suggest that you eliminate words such as 'credence.' "

"Well," answered Fitts, a little put off, "if the Court please, one of the things I like to find out is whether a juror understands the word 'credence.' " A short while later Fitts would use the word "vicissitudes," peevishly adding, "if I may use the expression."

Fitts had a final warning to Mrs. Molina. He asked if she ever watched courtroom dramas on TV like *Perry Mason*. Molina said she did.

"These dramatizations," cautioned Fitts, "are generally speaking for the purpose of entertaining you and promoting a product. They may or may not show just what happens in court. . . . You understand we probably won't be as entertaining as the courtroom dramas on TV, but that isn't going to disappoint you too much, is it?"

Mrs. Molina said it wouldn't.

By the end of the first day Rosa Molina was the only venireman to have made it onto the panel from which the trial jury would be selected. Two had been challenged for cause, two had claimed hardship, and two had been sent to speak to their employers to see if they would still have a job after a three-month absence. By the end of the second day Molina had been joined by only two others, and it began to appear that jury selection, as some had predicted, would consume an entire month.

On Wednesday the attorneys were back in court, asking potential jurors questions that had already been asked numerous times before. During the afternoon Deputy District Attorney David Fitts was questioning Lawrence Morgan, a systems analyst for IBM. Fitts asked Morgan whether in a few months he would "have the courage to come down and look at Mr. Sirhan and say he should die in the gas chamber?"

Two days earlier, when Fitts had first asked that question, Sirhan had doubled over in his chair as though he were nauseous. Now he leaned forward and smiled directly at Morgan. Fitts noticed immediately.

"You can see him now," the prosecutor said, "and he smiles at you, and for all I know he will smile at you throughout the trial."

"I smile at you, too, Mr. Fitts," answered Sirhan in a loud but good-natured voice.

"That is true," replied Fitts. "You smile a lot."

Judge Walker quickly jumped in: "Confine yourself to the questioning, Mr. Fitts."

Later that afternoon Mrs. Alvina Alvidrez, a woman who had worked for the Robert Kennedy campaign, revealed that "under no circumstances whatsoever" would she be able to vote for the death penalty. Prosecutor Fitts subsequently challenged for cause. Grant Cooper immediately objected.

"Your Honor, please," he said, "we resist that challenge on the ground that we have a right to this juror on the issue of guilt or innocence."

Judge Walker sided with the defense attorney and disallowed the challenge. This brought a vehement protest from prosecutor Fitts, and a furious discussion of law. But the relevant law was quite new and hardly clear, and the hour was late. Judge Walker agreed to consider the matter again the next day. "It may be that I am wrong," he said, "and if it can be shown that I am, I am willing to change my mind."

Alvina Alvidrez and her objection to the death penalty was a no-lose situation for the defense. There was no question of her actually sitting on the jury; if Judge Walker allowed her to stay, then the prosecution would have to spend a peremptory challenge to see her gone. If Judge Walker forced her off the jury, then Cooper had established grounds for appeal.

The prosecution's position was also clear. They were not particularly concerned with reversal on appeal. They simply didn't want to waste their peremptory challenges on panelists who, in their view, shouldn't be on the jury to begin with.

The next morning the matter of Alvina Alvidrez was the first order of business.

"We renew our challenge for cause," announced David Fitts, "based on her assertion that under no conceivable circumstances could she ever impose the death penalty."

Prosecutor John Howard then cited a California Supreme Court decision, *People v. Beivelman,* which had been handed down only a week before. In that case a murderer had unsuccessfully challenged his conviction on the premise that his jury was biased because objectors to the death penalty had been excluded.

In countering Howard, Grant Cooper cited *People v. Witherspoon,* a U.S. Supreme Court case decided only six months earlier. "Under the view of the *Witherspoon* majority," said Cooper, "a jury from which all prospective jurors opposed to the death penalty have been excluded is not an impartial

jury but rather constitutes a 'hanging jury'—one that is 'uncommonly willing to condemn a man to die.' "

But, as the prosecution was willing to point out, the actual precedent
from the *Witherspoon* decision was unclear. In making its decision the high
court seemed to argue both sides of the case. It affirmed the right to challenge a juror who was unalterably opposed to the death penalty, while at
the same time it prohibited the systematic exclusion of conscientious objectors, leaving it for others to define what forms of exclusion would be
deemed systematic. Despite this confusion, Judge Walker ruled once again
that Alvidrez could stay on the jury, at least for the guilt or innocence phase
of the trial. If a penalty hearing were necessary, he added, the prosecution
could challenge and an alternate juror be substituted.

But the next morning, Judge Walker changed his mind. Overnight he
had apparently found refuge in the *Beivelman* decision, which he quoted as
he spoke from the bench. The prosecution challenge would stand, Walker
ruled, and Alvina Alvidrez would not serve as a juror.

Later, in the corridor outside the courtroom, defense attorney Emile
Berman seemed almost pleased. "We believe that the ruling on conscientious objection," he said, "affords a constitutional issue."[6]

On January 13 Emile Berman made a secret journey to the prosecutor's
office. In a memorandum to District Attorney Evelle Younger, Lynn D.
Compton captured the bizarre nature of the visit.

> Emile Zola Berman, one of the defense counsel in [*sic*] Sirhan,
> came to see me this afternoon in a very hush-hush fashion. He did
> not want either co-counsel or anybody else to know that he con-
> tacted me. He wants to make sure that the fact that he came down
> here is kept completely confidential by you and me; nobody is to
> know of his visit.

Berman told Compton that while he was recently vacationing in the
Caribbean, he had received a telegram requesting that he call a certain
person in the United States. When Berman made the call, the person, whom
Berman would not identify, gave him a message, supposedly from Evelle
Younger, saying the district attorney was anxious speak to him "very con-
fidentially." Berman was now attempting to make that connection. Compton told Berman that he had no idea what it might be about, and the visit
ended. There is no further record of whether Berman actually met with
Younger, and, if so, the purpose of their meeting.

★   ★   ★

On January 17, *Life* magazine published a portrait of Sirhan Sirhan written by defense investigator Robert Blair Kaiser, who, by this time, had a contract with the publishing firm E. P. Dutton to write a book about Senator Kennedy's assassination.

As someone connected to the case, Kaiser could not discuss anything that might become a legal issue in the trial. As a result, the article was a personality profile, nothing more. Still, for many Americans, it was the first look at the alleged assassin of Robert Kennedy. They learned that Sirhan read books on logic and philosophy, that he smoked ten cigars a day and wore forty-nine-cent plastic Japanese sandals. They learned that his chest was hairy, his teeth white, and his handshake firm. They also learned that Sirhan was interested in public affairs. Recently, however, he had stopped ordering the *Los Angeles Times*. Sirhan was becoming depressed by world events.

"It's all violence, chaos, unrest," Sirhan told Kaiser. "Whatever happened to the good old days, peace and quiet?"

Kaiser described Sirhan's reaction to an article in *Esquire* in which William F. Buckley, Jr., said that Sirhan was not an American, but someone whose "loyalties were clearly to Jordan."

"What does he mean?" Sirhan protested to Kaiser. "Not American. I *feel* like an American. If I went back to Jordan I would be a foreigner."

But Sirhan recognized that he would not be looked upon as American by those who did not know him. "My name! My name!" he cried to Kaiser. "As soon as anyone heard it, everything else stopped."

Kaiser portrayed Sirhan's mother Mary as a very religious woman who read her Bible daily and prayed that her son would somehow be exonerated. He described the coffee table in the living room of her modest house, where there were several magazines that featured stories on Robert Kennedy.

"She picks up the magazines now and then," Kaiser wrote, "and talks to the face of Robert Kennedy on the *Time* cover, telling him how sorry she is. Kennedy, moreover, talks to her. 'It's O.K., Mary,' she says he says. 'I forgive you, it's O.K.' "[7]

Judge Alarcon's order to limit pretrial discussion was designed to protect the defendant's right to an unprejudiced trial. Its coincident effect was to limit public understanding of any lurking complexities. Thus, although Robert Kaiser was aware of a number of important unresolved issues, one would never know by reading his article that there were any unanswered questions in the case, much less ones bearing on the guilt or innocence of the alleged murderer.

On January 24, after the questioning of fifty-nine veniremen, a jury was selected to try the case against Sirhan Sirhan. Agreement came early Friday afternoon, the last day of the third week of the trial. The prosecution had used only seven of its peremptory challenges, the defense five. The jury contained eight men and four women, seven Republicans and five Democrats, four Mexican Americans, eleven Christians and one Jew. Unlike high-profile trials of the present day, the names, places of residence, and occupations of the jurors were published in the newspapers. The jurors were

Albert N. Frederico, a plumber for the city of Los Angeles,
Mary Lou Busby, a high school math teacher,
Lawrence K. Morgan, a systems analyst for IBM,
Gilbert F. Grace, a Los Angeles Department of Water and Power employee,
George Broomis, also a Los Angeles Department of Water and Power employee,
Ronald G. Evans, a switchboard installer for Pacific Telephone,
Susan J. Brumm, a service supervisor for Pacific Telephone,
Benjamin Glick, a retail clothier,
Alphonse Galindo, a civilian mechanic employed by the navy,
Irma Q. Martinez, an employee of Southern California Gas,
Bruce D. Elliot, a computer specialist for TRW Systems, and
Nell Bortells, a business representative for Pacific Telephone.

The jury would not be sworn in for another two weeks. There were additional motions to be heard and alternate jurors to be selected. In the intervening time they would be sent home with Judge Walker's admonition not to discuss the case with anyone and to avoid friends and others who "might try to advise you." Walker then recessed court until the following Wednesday, when the attorneys were to have their final arguments ready regarding Grant Cooper's motion to quash the indictment against Sirhan Sirhan.

The mood in the hallway after the day's proceedings was upbeat. Both sides appeared to be satisfied.

"I think we've got people from all walks of life," said Grant Cooper, ". . . and that's America. I just don't know what kind of juror I would have looked for in this particular case, but I think we got a good conglomeration."[8]

"They are nice people," said fifty-five-year-old Mary Sirhan hopefully. "They stand up and say they are sure of themselves. To consider taking a life you have to be sure of yourself. It's up to their conscience. They are nice people. I am satisfied."

Mrs. Sirhan was then asked if her feelings toward the jury would make the trial easier to endure. "Through this, we learn," she said, answering the question with a homily. "Before everything else we get our power from God above. I get my power from Him daily."[9]

On February 3, the defendants in the Friars Club card-cheating case were sentenced by U.S. District Judge William P. Gray. Grant Cooper's client, Maurice H. Friedman, received the stiffest penalty: six years and $100,000 fine. Johnny Roselli was sentenced to five years and a $55,000 fine.

Judge Gray castigated Friedman for the "cynical cheating of people—many of whom were your friends." Gray took note of Roselli's long criminal record but also credited him for not manufacturing a defense—"at least not on the stand." (Roselli didn't testify at the trial.) "I'm not sure what you did otherwise," said the judge, apparently suspicious of some of Roselli's extracurricular activities.

The Friars Club defendants had protested U.S. Attorney Matthew Byrne's presentencing memorandum, which had not spoken favorably of any of them. They had demanded that the judge withdraw from the case because he had been influenced by the document. Judge Gray denied the motion but did allow the defendants to submit their own affidavits in opposition to the government memo. Attorney James P. Cantillon then announced that Johnny Roselli's affidavit would have to be kept secret because it "involves national security."★

As jury selection continued for the Palestinian immigrant accused of murdering an American presidential candidate, tensions were once again on the rise in the Middle East.

On January 26 in Iraq, fourteen men, including nine Jews, were hung by the neck for alleged espionage. Shops, offices, and schools were ordered closed for the day and an estimated three hundred thousand Iraqis gathered in Baghdad's Liberation Square. There they were encouraged by government officials to sing and dance while the bodies of those executed were on display.

On February 2 in Israel, club-wielding government security forces sent ninety-three Palestinian schoolgirls to the hospital with injuries as they broke up a demonstration in Gaza by some four thousand girls aged eleven

---

★Johnny Roselli had apparently been involved in the CIA-sponsored assassination plots against Cuban premier Fidel Castro in the early sixties. He was presumably trying to use that fact in his sentencing affidavit to put some of his present troubles at bay. In 1976 Roselli would be called before the Senate Intelligence Committee to testify in secret about the joint mob-CIA activities. He was due to appear again when his dismembered body was discovered floating in a barrel off the coast of Florida in July of that year.

to eighteen. Three young women were jailed on charges of spying and aiding guerrillas.

Two days later in Egypt, which at the time did not have diplomatic relations with the United States, Mohammed Yasser Arafat was elected chairman of the PLO. Immediately upon taking office Arafat promised to escalate "armed struggle" in all parts of "occupied Palestine."[10]

Closer to home, riots and disturbances on California's college campuses were making daily headlines. On January 23, 380 students were arrested at a rally at San Francisco State College. A week later the California Highway Patrol had to be called in to restore order at the University of California, Berkeley. In speaking out against the growing unrest, Governor Ronald Reagan declared that the dissenters were engaging in "guerrilla warfare," the purpose of which was "to create launching pads for insurrection against the social order."[11]

Grant Cooper's motion to quash the indictment of Sirhan Sirhan was a major undertaking. Cooper not only intended to argue his case, he planned to present elaborate evidence to demonstrate that the grand jury selection process was inherently prejudicial.

On Tuesday, January 28, the attorneys for both sides gathered in Judge Walker's chambers. There Cooper revealed that he intended to subpoena all 130 judges of the Los Angeles County Superior Court to have them testify about their nominations for the grand jury. At the time each judge was entitled to nominate two candidates, although not every judge did so. In 1968 this resulted in 170 nominees, from which the 23 grand jurors were selected by chance.

So that the judges would not have to suspend their own court calendars, Cooper proposed enclosing with the subpoena a questionnaire that the judges could fill out and return in lieu of appearing in court. On the form the judges were to be asked about the age and the racial, educational, and economic status of their nominees and whether they had made any affirmative efforts to nominate individuals from groups who were traditionally underrepresented.

"Our position," contended Grant Cooper when it was time to argue the motion, "is that the very system itself, as it has existed over the past ten years, has the result of being discriminatory." Cooper wasn't exactly blaming the judges. "They tried to get persons of outstanding ability," he said, "persons of outstanding integrity, but they made no effort to get persons from the lower economic groups or from younger persons in the community. . . . I don't believe there were any poor persons, and a very high percentage—I have been given over seventy percent—were college graduates."

Lynn Compton argued that Grant Cooper's entire contention, even if proved, was irrelevant. The grand jury, he said, did not decide the issue of guilt or innocence, only the question of whether there was sufficient evidence to warrant a trial. The defense, Compton pointed out, had already conceded in court on numerous occasions that the defendant was the one who fired the shot that killed Senator Kennedy.

"So it seems to me," said Compton, "that the defense must, as a primary condition precedent, make some allegation that had the grand jury been differently constituted than it was, that there was some different result that might have occurred in the grand jury proceedings—to wit that he might not be indicted . . . which to me seems rather specious on the state of this record."

Judge Walker was in sympathy with Compton's arguments. Nevertheless, perhaps out of an abundance of caution, he ruled that Grant Cooper could present the evidence on his motion to quash the indictment. The frantic process of printing and serving subpoenas and questionnaires began.

Three of the subpoenaed judges chose to testify in person rather than submit a questionnaire. One of these was Judge Arthur Alarcon, in whose court the legal proceedings against Sirhan had begun seven months before. When Alarcon assumed the witness stand, Grant Cooper asked the judge whether he had attempted to find grand jury nominees from minority groups. Alarcon, who was of Mexican-American heritage, said that he had tried, but that sometimes these efforts were frustrated because persons in lower economic groups were unable to make the financial sacrifice necessary to serve on the grand jury.

Judge Edward R. Brand was next to take the stand. He was noticeably unsympathetic to Cooper's questions.

"Judge Brand," asked Grant Cooper, "in determining whom you were going to approach or solicit as a grand jury nominee, did you attach any importance whatsoever to the racial, ethnic, geographic, economic, or age groupings?"

"Well," replied Judge Brand, "that's one of those questions like, 'Have you stopped beating your wife?' I don't know how you can answer that question. . . . I have never concerned myself, Mr. Cooper, with hyphenated Americans. I only know one kind of American and I am not concerned with whether their ancestors were Polish or Japanese or Scandinavian or what."

Judge Brand wanted it understood that the grand jury did more than just hand down criminal indictments.

"You see, Mr. Cooper, as you know the function of the grand jury is multiple . . . to act as watchdog over many departments of the county; over the budget, which, by the way, is approximately one-point-five billion dollars, and to examine many penal facilities, juvenile facilities, hospital facilities, facilities for the elderly, to determine whether they are properly operated."

Judge Brand's point was that the duties of the grand jury required an intelligent and educated person, and that its heavy work schedule and ten-dollars-a-day compensation were not attractive to everyone. That grand jurors tended to be people retired from professions from which they brought insight and expertise was simply an efficient use of society's human resources.

By the following week Cooper had received over one hundred questionnaires back from the superior court judges. He then brought to the witness stand Raymond G. Schultz, a professor of business administration at California State College, Long Beach. Using the information from the questionnaires, Schultz had analyzed the grand jury nominees by race, occupation, economic status, and age. The conclusion: the 1968 Los Angeles Grand Jury was older, whiter, more affluent, and better educated than the population at large.

Many of Schultz's findings were not the kind that would cause great concern. For example, Schulz reported that, according to the 1960 census, 26 percent of the people in Los Angeles had not completed high school, whereas only 2 percent of those nominated for the grand jury were in that category. At another point Cooper had Schultz introduce a large map upon which the prospective grand jurors and the nominating judges were located geographically with dots. The conclusion: judges tend to nominate people who live relatively near to them.

Cooper's marquee witness in the motion to quash was the defendant, Sirhan Sirhan. Other than a few monosyllabic words uttered in previous hearings, this would be Sirhan's first public performance. Though it had been made clear that the defendant would only testify as to his financial situation, the press, with little else to do, played it up. "Sirhan to Testify," the headlines ran.

When he was called, the defendant strode confidently up to the witness stand. Then, as court clerk Alice Nishikawa administered the oath, Sirhan raised his right arm over his head, fist clenched, mimicking the black power salute given by sprinters Carlos and Smith at the Olympics several months earlier. This gesture was not likely to please many people in the courtroom, and it overshadowed his uneventful eight-minute testimony, during which it was established that for the five previous years he had an income that averaged about $1,100 per year.

It was February 4 before Grant Cooper was done making his presentation on the motion to quash. Judge Walker then ruled that the entire matter was irrelevant and deficient on its merits. Eleven days had been consumed in preparing and arguing this motion. It was a colossal waste of time and energy by a defense team that still lacked a full understanding of the physical evidence.

Did Grant Cooper really think that Judge Walker would throw out the murder indictment against Sirhan while simultaneously consigning the entire grand jury process to constitutional limbo? It wasn't going to happen. Cooper knew it. At best he was trying to establish grounds for appeal, but in so doing he was most likely indulging his desire to be seen arguing constitutional issues. New law is rarely made in high-profile cases, and Cooper's arguments, as Compton and Judge Brand had demonstrated, were seriously flawed.

The effort to quash the indictment was, simply stated, bad law. It was also bad politics. The shortcut interpretation of Cooper's motion was that the defendant should not be held accountable for murdering another man because he was young and poor. This was not an idea that was going to warm many hearts. Its most likely effect was to inspire emotions against the defendant. The jury was not sequestered during this time, and while they were instructed not to read about the case, it would be the unusual juror who would not discover why the trial was being delayed.

The person most noticeably humiliated by Grant Cooper's motion was Mary Sirhan, who followed her son on the witness stand. Under Cooper's direction Mrs. Sirhan testified that since 1966 she had worked in a church nursery school making a yearly income of between $1,500 and $1,800. She also revealed that she was paying off a mortgage on a house she had bought for $12,000.

Mary Sirhan had not wanted to testify, not about how poor she was. But she did what was expected of her. Even so, her commonsense revulsion for the point being made was evident. When Judge Walker told Mrs. Sirhan she could step down from the witness stand, the diminutive woman rose from her chair and spoke extemporaneously. "I thank God that He gave me the strength," she said in her thickly accented voice, "and I also thank the United States, that I never got hungry and I have a roof over my head."

Later she would explain herself to newsmen in the hallway.

"I have God's blessing," she said. "They say I make little money. That is not what is poor."

After Judge Alarcon and Judge Brand had testified on Cooper's motion, the attorneys for both sides and the defendant entered Judge Walker's chambers for a private session. David Fitts was the first to speak.

"I want to go into the subject of the sodium Pentothal or sodium Amytal interview of this defendant," he said.

"I thought it was Pentothal,"* replied Judge Walker.

"Amytal is what they have in mind, Judge," Fitts answered

Fitts explained to Judge Walker that both he and defense attorney Grant Cooper had spoken to prosecution psychiatrist Dr. Seymour Pollack and defense psychiatrist Dr. Bernard Diamond, and that both doctors had requested examinations using the drug.

"There has been some disappointment in the result of the interview[s] under hypnosis," added Fitts, "and the general feeling of the psychiatrists in now requesting this sort of sodium Amytal interview is that which they failed to discover under the hypnotic examination might well be brought out."

"If I might interrupt," said Cooper. "I've talked to my client and he is willing to undergo an examination under sodium Amytal or sodium Pentothal and that is correct is it not?"

"Yes, sir," replied Sirhan.

In the preceding weeks, either on days when the court was not in session or sometimes after court was over, Sirhan Sirhan had been undergoing a series of extraordinary interviews with Drs. Diamond and Pollack. In several of these sessions Sirhan had been put under hypnosis. Judge Walker was told by prosecutor David Fitts that the defendant "was a susceptible subject and did actually fall into a deep hypnotic state."

All of this was unusual in the extreme. Why was anybody hypnotizing Sirhan in his cell? What were they looking for? What was the thing they "failed to discover" under hypnosis? Why did they now need a truth serum?

It had not been spoken about in open court; it had only been alluded to in Judge Walker's chambers. It had not been written about in any newspapers or magazines. But in the winter of 1969 the best-kept secret in America was that Grant Cooper's client, Sirhan Sirhan, apparently, and with many reasons to believe his representations, had no recollection of murdering Robert Kennedy. Equally baffling was that, although he had been cooperating in his interrogations (submitting to hypnosis and agreeing to be drugged), during his seven months in custody the defendant had been hard pressed to come up with a coherent explanation as to why he would commit such a crime.

---

*Note: Sodium Pentothal (like Amytal) is a drug that can be injected into a subject, producing a hypnotic effect and lowering inhibitions. It is sometimes referred to as "truth serum."

FOUR

The Judge's Chambers

✻   ✻   ✻

*If you strip everything away, it looks like a guy went in there with
a gun, shot a guy, shot five other people. . . . You arrest him
and he says, "I shot the son of a bitch."
That's as cold turkey a lawsuit as I've seen in twenty-eight years.
We have a lot of guys up for life with a lot less evidence. . . .
Sirhan is guilty. Sirhan said he was guilty. If he isn't guilty,
it's the sweetest frame in the world.*

—Sirhan prosecutor John Howard, 1975[1]

O N THE MORNING of February 13,
an atmosphere of anticipation
filled the Hall of Justice. This was the day each side was to make its opening
arguments, welcome news for those who had suffered through five tedious
weeks of defense motions and jury selection. The mood quickly dissipated,
however, as defense and prosecution attorneys disappeared, once again, into
the chambers of Judge Walker.

Waiting newsmen and spectators milled about; some read the morning
paper. "Israel Downs Syrian Mig" read the front page of the *Los Angeles
Times.* In other stories: elements of the First Air Cavalry were involved in
a sharp engagement along the Cambodian border; nine hundred National
Guard troops were deployed in Madison to quell disturbances at the University of Wisconsin; and in New York, the residents of Queens jeered
Mayor John Lindsay as he inspected a borough still paralyzed three days
after a snowstorm that would come to bear his name. But it was a story in
the previous day's *Los Angeles Times* that would set the course for the morning's proceedings. Judge Walker brought down the gavel at around 10 A.M.
Grant Cooper was the first to speak.

"If Your Honor please," he said in measured tone, "the defendant Sirhan Sirhan moves for a mistrial."

Cooper argued that an article by *Times* staff writer Dave Smith, concerning the rumor that Sirhan would now plead guilty to the charge of first-degree murder, had "prejudiced the defendant's case to the point where he cannot get a fair trial."

Judge Walker appeared to share Cooper's concern. "Everybody knows it has been on the radio every hour," he stated. "It has been in the newspapers, certainly in the *Times* yesterday morning, in the most important spot in the daily newspaper."

"The front page," said defense attorney Berman.

"The front page, right-hand column," replied Judge Walker.

"And big headlines," added Berman.

The story read:

SIRHAN CHANGE OF PLEA SEEN LIKELY. ADMISSION OF GUILT MAY SHORTEN TRIAL AND BRING LIFE SENTENCE

Sirhan Bishara Sirhan probably will plead guilty to first-degree murder in the slaying of Sen. Robert F. Kennedy, it was learned Tuesday.

The switch from an earlier plea of innocence could come when the trial reconvenes Thursday morning, and would result from either an understanding or a firm belief that a life term would be the maximum penalty.

The *Times* story went on to speculate that if the plea change took place, the trial which had been expected to run two or three months might last only a handful of days. It also asserted that Sirhan's lawyers were willing to make the deal, despite their conviction that the psychiatric evidence was in their client's favor, because "they could not hope for a jury verdict of less than first-degree murder."

Negotiations for a plea bargain are normally conducted in strict secrecy for fear of prejudicing a jury if the process fails. In this case, the Sirhan jurors, who were not yet sequestered, had ample opportunity to be exposed to the story, despite Judge Walker's admonition to avoid publicity about the trial. What person sitting in judgment, Grant Cooper would argue, would be inclined to bring in a lesser verdict once he or she had learned the defendant had been willing to plead guilty to murder in the first degree?

The *Los Angeles Times* story was not the first to appear on the plea negotiations. A similar article by Bob Greene had appeared in Long Island's *Newsday* a day earlier, but that story was of less concern, because of the small likelihood of its influencing the jury.

In the privacy of Judge Walker's chambers the various parties in the case tried to sort out the issues. Deputy District Attorney Lynn Compton suggested that Smith's story was merely "surmise" or "speculation." Judge Walker replied that there was "too much detail" in the article for it not to have had a source. But who?

At different moments each party took a turn at declaring innocence.

"I'm sure none of my staff told it," said Judge Walker. "I'm sure of it."

"None of the information contained in this article was given to Mr. Smith," said Grant Cooper. ". . . I mean none by the defense."

"I want to assure the Court that nothing that is contained in that *Times* article or any newspaper article that carried that story came from anybody in the district attorney's office," said Mr. Compton.

"That remains to be seen," said Judge Walker, responding to Compton. "If it becomes important we'll find out where all the information came from, but . . . someone, some way . . . has revealed everything that went on in these chambers, in spite of the fact that I sealed the records."

Very early in the case, Grant Cooper had decided upon a psychiatric defense for Sirhan. To lead the team of doctors in support of this defense, he had engaged the services of Dr. Bernard Diamond of the University of California, a man who had extensive experience in the field of legal psychiatry. Cooper had served with Dr. Diamond on a special California commission appointed by Governor Edmund Brown to modernize California's insanity laws.

Realizing the direction Sirhan's lawyers were going, the prosecution hired its own psychiatrist, Dr. Seymour Pollack of the University of Southern California. Under California law, the prosecution psychiatrist would normally not be allowed to examine the defendant in person, but could only observe him in court and comment on the defense psychiatrist's presentations.

But Grant Cooper had another idea. Believing his client to be unquestionably ill, he decided to allow the prosecution psychiatrist access to Sirhan. It was a gamble. If Pollack did not agree that Sirhan was mentally impaired, he could greatly damage Cooper's case by being able to speak with authority from the witness stand based upon his own tests and observations. Conversely, if the prosecution doctor held that Sirhan was ill, then some sort of deal with the district attorney would seem unavoidable.

Dr. Pollack made full use of this offer. Between January 19 and February 1 he visited Sirhan eight times, spending a total of twenty-three hours with the prisoner. On two of these occasions he put Sirhan under hypnosis and attempted to probe his mind. Grant Cooper, understandably, was eager to see some profit from this investment. In another unprecedented move, Cooper decided that all the doctors should gather at his office to compare notes to see if some sort of consensus on Sirhan's state of mind could be reached.

Thus on February 2, Dr. Orville Roderick Richardson, Dr. Eric Marcus, Dr. Martin Schorr, and Dr. Bernard Diamond sat down with the prosecution adviser, Dr. Seymour Pollack, in the library of Grant Cooper's office.[2] Cooper and Berman would join the group later. A roundtable discussion of Sirhan's mental state ensued, with each doctor sharing with the others his diagnosis of the defendant. But the crucial opinion belonged to Dr. Pollack, and to everyone's dismay he was evasive.

"I don't have any firm opinions," he told the group. An increasingly vexed Dr. Diamond pressed Dr. Pollack to take some position on the case. "I haven't decided yet," Pollack said at one point, still retreating. "I have raised questions—"

"Seymour," interrupted Diamond. "To hear you say 'questions are raised' communicates no information to me that I didn't already have. I'm thoroughly familiar with the questions. You're not saying anything."

Diamond was angry. Pollack had been given extended access to Sirhan, and was now saying he didn't have a professional opinion about the defendant. "I do not feel, Seymour, that you have played fair. I think you have sat and listened to each one of us give an opinion, but whenever it comes to expressing your opinion, you have quibbled, you have evaded, you have said, 'The question is raised,' but not in one significant detail that has been relevant to the trial did you make any kind of commitment. Now, either this means that this particular conference was held prematurely, or you are misusing this conference."

"I told you honestly," Pollack pleaded, "I don't have—and I can't disclose what I don't have."

"You do not have any opinions?"

"I haven't any firm opinions. . . ."

Diamond sought a clarification as to what Pollack thought was still missing. "Can you imagine an additional test, or is it one of those situations where you can't ever make up your mind? . . . You give me the impression, Seymour, that nothing would get you off the fence."[3]

Diamond left the meeting early, and what followed was an elaborate presentation on Sirhan's mental state by Dr. Schorr. Whether it was Schorr's graphs, diagrams, and chrome-plated, telescopic pointer or, more probably, the delayed effect of Dr. Diamond's disdain, by the end of the session Pollack was making noises to the effect that he saw Sirhan as "more disturbed than less." When he left the meeting Pollack phoned the district attorney's office and told them that he thought Sirhan was psychotic.

Only three days after Pollack had represented to the defense doctors that he held no firm opinions, the prosecution psychiatrist would submit to

District Attorney Evelle Younger a seventeen-page memorandum packed with opinions. Pollack's memo was wordy and seemed to argue all sides of the case, but in the end he stated, "I have no doubt that substantial mental illness was present and still exists in Sirhan and merits consideration in this case." Cooper's gamble had paid off, or so it appeared, for now there seemed nothing in the way of a deal with the prosecution.

On the afternoon of February 4, Chief Deputy DA Compton entered Judge Walker's chambers and informed the judge that the prosecution and defense had come to an agreement. The deal was this: Sirhan would plead guilty to first-degree murder in exchange for the assurance of a life sentence. Normally in a situation where both the prosecution and the defense agree on the disposition of a case, that disposition is accepted by the presiding judge. But not here. To the surprise of everyone, Judge Walker declined to accept the deal.

Since a plea bargain scuttled by a judge was outside the experience of both the prosecution and the defense, each side scrambled to examine the options. District Attorney Evelle Younger flew to Washington. Six months earlier Younger had been appointed head of Richard Nixon's Advisory Council on Crime and Law Enforcement. Now, apparently, it was he who was seeking the advice, but who he saw and what they said has never been revealed. Younger, however, did allude to this trip upon his return when he made reference to the "international" implications of the case. "I have made it convenient for appropriate persons in the government to express an opinion to me. They declined and made no comment or recommendation."[4]

While it is hard to believe that Younger went all the way to Washington to receive no comment at all from the Nixon Justice Department, it was certainly the politic thing to say. The federal government had no right to make any comments or recommendations in a case prosecuted under the laws of California. Whatever was or wasn't discussed in Washington, when Younger returned it was agreed that the next step would be another, more forceful attempt to get Judge Walker's cooperation. This attempt featured the presence of the district attorney himself, his first such appearance at the trial.

A little after nine the morning of Monday, February 10, the district attorney, his deputies, and the defense attorneys entered the chambers of Judge Walker. Younger opened the proceedings. "I understand that the defendant is prepared to plead guilty and accept a life sentence," he declared, asking Grant Cooper to confirm this to the judge. Then Younger delivered a remarkable speech.

"We favor it, Judge," he said, alluding to the plea bargain, "and the law requires your approval. . . . We have known generally what the testimony of the psychiatrists that have been appointed at the request of the defense would be, and now that we have gotten our psychiatrist's report, a man whom we have great confidence in, we are in a position where we can't conscientiously urge the death penalty, number one. Number two, we don't think under any circumstances we would get the death penalty even if we urged it. And number three, we don't think we can justify the trial under those circumstances.

"It appears that the result is a foregone conclusion. Our psychiatrist, in effect, says that the defendant is psychotic, and his report would support the position of the defense because of diminished capacity and the death penalty wouldn't be imposed. So . . . are we justified in going through the motions of a trial, a very traumatic and expensive trial, when we can't conscientiously ask for the death penalty anyway? We don't think we are."

Judge Walker then asked Grant Cooper for his thoughts. Cooper responded by saying that he believed the psychiatrists' reports would merit no more than a verdict of guilty to second-degree murder. But that, conceded Cooper, would mean little to the defendant. The chief difference between the two in terms of punishment (excluding the death sentence) was the length of the minimum sentence. In this case, Cooper reasoned, "by virtue of the prominence of the deceased and the great deal of publicity . . . the minimum would mean nothing . . . so we have concluded that the wise thing to do, assuming we have the opportunity, would be to enter a plea of guilty to first-degree murder with life imprisonment."

Evelle Younger immediately rejoined the battle, trying to address the concern voiced by Walker the week before by referring to "the public's interest." The DA assured Walker that he recognized the need that "whatever is done not only be the just and proper thing to do, but appear to be the just and proper thing too. Your Honor, I am sure, doesn't want anybody to think that there was any hanky-panky going on if we do this."

Younger had a proposal: between the time when the plea bargain would be accepted and the sentence imposed, the defense, the prosecution, and the police would work out the mechanics by which they could "put into the record all pertinent materials including statements of witnesses and that sort of thing and the psychiatrists' reports, so that the second-guessers, and they will be legion, who write books and magazines, serials and so forth, wondering why it was done or why this wasn't done, we will at least have it in the record."

In reply Judge Walker began by assuring the parties that he held them in deep respect. "I have given this a great deal of thought," he said, "because I know it has been talked of, but the ramifications of this thing I think should be thoroughly given to the public. I appreciate the cost. I appreciate the sensation, but I am sure it would just be opening us up to a lot of criticism and criticism by the people who think the jury should determine this question. I think you have a very interested public," Walker said, then quickly added, "but I don't let the public influence me. But, at the same time, there are a lot of ramifications and they continually point to the Oswald matter and they have us wonder what is going on because the fellow wasn't tried."

Judge Walker then made an informal proposal. "Obviously, in open court if there was a plea of murder, then you could have a trial to determine degree and the penalty; that would be all right with me."

Lynn Compton had a suggestion of his own. "If the defendant were to plead guilty to first-degree murder, there wouldn't be any evidence to put on, we simply would offer no evidence on the penalty and there would be no trial." Compton's idea seemed to be a subtle warning to Walker. If the judge wanted to keep making up new rules, the prosecution could, in a sense, take the ball and go home. Walker held firm.

Grant Cooper had a different idea. "Of course, another way it could be done, if we had first-degree [plea], we could put on a very skeleton outline of the case at the time of plea instead of submitting reports, and we could put witnesses on to testify."

"Well then they would say that it was all fixed, it was greased," replied Walker, more determined than ever, "so we will go through with the trial. . . . I am not going to argue it any further, gentlemen. My mind is made up."

Cooper's suggestion of a "skeleton outline" of a trial seemed at the time to be a spontaneous idea, yet it revealed something deeper in the chief defense counsel's outlook, and ultimately his entire handling of the case. Something approaching that thought had been on his mind from the beginning. In early January, in a meeting with defense investigator Robert Kaiser and Dr. Bernard Diamond, Cooper revealed that he envisioned a contest in which many of the punches would be pulled. "I'd let them stage anything they want," said Cooper.

"When would you make the plea?" asked Diamond.

"When the evidence was in," Cooper responded. "We'd have a conference with the judge. But it would all be worked out ahead of time."

"You wouldn't need a jury then."

"Well, I wouldn't say that. . . . The verdict—of first-degree murder with life imprisonment—would just be predetermined, that's all."[5]

Cooper's mind-set disturbed Kaiser. A week or two later he would hand the chief defense counsel a memorandum expressing "profound reservations about some kind of prearrangement between you and the DA whereby you would agree in advance to the penalty, and then *stage* [emphasis Kaiser's] some kind of trial. I don't know enough about the ways of the law here, but as a layman . . . either you have your client plead guilty, or you engage in a genuine, if friendly, adversary proceeding, where supposed truth is given a good test according to the rules of evidence as evolved through centuries of good Anglo-Saxon jurisprudence. I don't see how you can combine the two."[6]

Kaiser's memo appears not to have greatly influenced Cooper, but it hardly mattered since Cooper was not the person making the key decisions. Judge Walker was, and his pronouncement on the plea bargain seemed final. Yet the prosecution and the defense were still in the mood to make a deal. After Judge Walker had turned them away, Cooper, Parsons, and Berman, accompanied by Lynn Compton, hurried over to the district attorney's office, where yet another alternative was proposed. In this variation Sirhan would plead guilty to first-degree murder and then let the jury decide the issue of penalty. In return, the prosecution would make a positive recommendation of life in prison. After lunch, the attorneys were back in front of Judge Walker asking for a delay in the trial so that they might explore this option.

Walker was sympathetic but worried. "Here's another very practical thing you fellows have to be thinking about, and maybe you have—the district attorney shows up this morning and everybody outside is saying, 'Why was the district attorney up there?' . . . I said he came to show me his respect, but they know that isn't the truth." The judge correctly saw the danger. "If we start dragging our feet, I think it would damage the case tremendously," he told the attorneys. "We've got a lot of smart people out there."

"They've already asked," said Cooper. "Their antennae are up."

"So let's move," commanded Walker. "You've got two days."

In the two days he was given, Cooper and his cocounsel would meet with Sirhan twice. Cooper had these meetings recorded. On February 13, he would try to have them entered into the court record, justifying his attempt with this explanation: "We had a full and frank discussion with the defendant in the presence of his mother; and the presence of his brother; and his three counsel. . . . We taped the interview so there would be no question as to the advice that we gave him." During these meetings, however, Cooper was almost alone in his inclination to accept the prosecution offer of a positive recommendation of life in prison in exchange for a guilty plea. In the meeting of February 11, Mary Sirhan expressed the seemingly unrealistic hope that the trial might still result in Sirhan's acquittal. Sirhan's brother Munir was also opposed to the deal. Munir, who had recently spent a short time in jail on a vagrancy charge, announced that he'd rather die than spend even ten years in prison. Sirhan asked for a day to think about it.

The next day's deliberations, however, would be complicated by the plea bargain story on the front page of the *Los Angeles Times*. It made

Cooper all the more sure that a verdict of first-degree murder was unavoidable, and he wanted to grab what they could get from the prosecution while offers were still being made. But he was the only one. Emile Berman was adamant, telling Cooper that if a plea were entered, he would return to New York and not participate. "If we plead this kid guilty," he said, "we're destroying his right to a fair trial, and he'll never have the possibility of an appeal."[7] Russell Parsons concurred. He told Cooper that he was in favor of a full trial, and would make that recommendation to Sirhan when they met again.

Dr. Bernard Diamond called Cooper as soon as he saw the reports about the plea in the news. "He was quite upset about it," Cooper reported later, "because he said that he felt that [Sirhan] definitely and positively . . . had diminished capacity, and it should definitely be nothing worse than second degree; . . . he did not want to compromise his principles in testifying on the penalty phase. No amount of argument could change him."

Because of the story in the morning paper, it was difficult for the attorneys to confer with Sirhan unnoticed. A considerable group of reporters waited for them at the foot of the marble stairs leading to the Hall of Justice. Charles Arlington, a reporter from radio station KFWB, recorded the chaos:

"Speculation arose this morning when the *Los Angeles Times* said Sirhan would probably change his plea, putting himself on the mercy of the jury," said Arlington into his microphone. He then recorded another newsman's question directed at Grant Cooper, who was trying to navigate through the group.

"No comment," said Cooper tersely.

"I have no comment," said Russell Parsons to a similar inquiry. "I just told you that and I've told the five newspapers all over the world since six o'clock this morning."

"This is something that somebody made up then?"

"I never said that," replied Parsons.

"No comment," said Cooper again.

Once inside, Cooper sat down with Parsons, Berman, Kaiser, and Sirhan. Also at the meeting was a young lawyer named Abdeen Jabara. Jabara represented a group of moneyed Arab Americans from Detroit. The group had been horrified at the murder of Robert Kennedy and its public relations consequences for the Arab American community. But they had also seen in the trial of Sirhan Sirhan a way to tell the Arab side of the Arab-Israeli conflict.

In October of 1968, Jabara had held a confidential meeting in Chicago with Russell Parsons and defense investigator Mike McCowan. At that meeting Jabara reportedly promised monetary support for the defense of Sirhan. In exchange he requested a role in presenting at the trial the historical context of the war with the Jews in Palestine. Parsons saw no problem with this and agreed. Jabara then became what was called a "defense consultant." Being an Arab he quickly gained the confidence of the defendant and his family, something that Grant Cooper had only done in a tenuous way. Thus when the lawyers met with Sirhan to discuss the plea bargain, Jabara was there and his opinion carried weight.

Cooper began the meeting by informing Sirhan of Dr. Diamond's sentiments opposing a plea bargain. Berman and Parsons then counseled against making the plea. Abdeen Jabara weighed in with them. Jabara pointed out that the story in the *Los Angeles Times* would be "beautiful grounds" for reversible error. He thought Sirhan had an excellent chance of getting second degree on the merits, and he was aware that a full-blown trial might help focus world attention on the plight of the Palestinians.

Jabara also knew that the Arab American community was becoming impatient with Sirhan's representation. In the *Los Angeles Times,* Dr. M. T. Mehdi, chairman of the Action Committee on American-Arab Relations, had already commented on the report that Sirhan might plead guilty. The defense attorneys, Mehdi said, "failed to understand that the Sirhan case is an historic political event and not an ordinary legal problem."

Alone in his position, Cooper would argue his case. "You can't overlook the fact that the man that was shot and killed was a candidate for the office of president and was a U.S. senator and a very popular individual. Second degree would be an empty victory. We as lawyers would be big heroes, but what's it going to help Sirhan? It's still life imprisonment. The minimum doesn't mean a damn thing."

Sirhan had his own ideas of what a deal should look like. "I would [plead] to the first degree," he told the group, "with a guarantee of life and having a chance to tell my story on the witness stand, plus another guarantee of parole after seven years. I absolutely want a guarantee of that."

At this Sirhan's attorneys got upset.

"The parole board," said Berman, exasperated, "has nothing to do with the deal here."

"No power at all," added Cooper. "Nor would a judge make such a recommendation."

"Well hell," said Sirhan when all the arguments were heard, "I might as well fight it out."[8]

In chambers the next day Cooper explained Sirhan's position to Judge Walker. "Following a full discussion of the matter, the defendant agreed with his counsel that he would plead guilty to first-degree murder to the Court, with the assurance that he would get life . . . but that he definitely would not plead guilty and submit the matter to the jury."

What followed was yet another effort by both sides to get the judge to accept the original deal, including hints of judicial reversal if Walker didn't comply.

"We would respectfully request an opportunity," said Deputy DA Compton, ". . . to try to ask Your Honor to take another look at this proposal and let us give you some thoughts that we may have overlooked in our discussions last Tuesday."

Both attorneys made subtle references to the action they thought Walker should take—"as the law requires." "I want to make certain that we have made a record, Your Honor," said Cooper, "that shows that there is no question but that the defendant would plead guilty provided there was life imprisonment."

"The statute which requires the Court's approval in that particular instance," added Compton, "envisions more the Court's analysis of the proposal from the light of whether it does essential justice to both sides of the case and that the question of the format or the public exposure of the evidence is really not relevant. . . . It is our analysis of the case that this plea would do essential justice to both sides of the case."

But Walker would not be moved. "As far as I'm concerned," he answered, "this matter of a plea of first degree with life imprisonment has been disposed of. You had ample opportunity the other day to make all the arguments you wanted to. . . . As I said before, I think the jury should determine the penalty. That's my decision. Let's go ahead and try the lawsuit."

In open court with the jury absent Cooper made his motion for a mistrial. He cited a number of legal precedents but focused his greatest attention upon *Marshall v. United States,* a case where a newspaper had printed potentially prejudicial evidence about a defendant. Speaking of the case Cooper said, "Despite the fact that each juror swore he would not be influenced by the newspaper reports and felt no prejudice, the Supreme Court reversed the conviction and called for a new trial. . . . The court held that the jury's learning of the prohibited evidence through newspaper articles was prejudicial per se."

But Judge Walker made it clear that "prejudice per se" would not be a concept favored in his court this day. "As I see it," Walker said, "the mistrial hangs solely on what they have heard and beyond that whatever consideration they have given to it . . . [whether] they can set whatever they have heard aside and determine the case on the evidence and the law given by me." Walker proposed questioning each juror about the story.

Cooper was skeptical. "Frankly, I don't think it's going to do any good," he said, "because I don't believe that any juror, with the admonition that Your Honor has properly given [about avoiding trial publicity], is going to admit that he is in contempt of court; and I don't think any of them, if they have read this article—and I believe some of them must have, human nature being what it is—I don't believe any of them would be willing to admit that they violated Your Honor's order."

"I think jurors are fair-minded and as honest as any people who walk around," Walker responded, "and I think that their answers should be given full credence; and I will tell you, this Court intends to do so."

Cooper was wrong. In the questioning of jurors that followed almost all of them admitted to having heard or read some version of the Sirhan plea bargain story. Mr. Morgan had read something about it in the newspaper. Mr. Glick had heard the news on the radio. Mr. Broomis got the news from his wife. And so on. The real question, which Cooper had in the back of his mind but didn't articulate, was would a juror who had heard the news admit to being prejudiced by it? Prejudice, by its nature, is difficult to see in oneself and easy to deny. At this point the jurors present were there because they wanted to be. Only one juror, Ronald Evans, admitted under Cooper's questioning that it would be difficult to bring in a verdict of second-degree murder or manslaughter under the circumstances. But even this did not affect Judge Walker. After recess he decided that the jury had not been compromised, and he overruled Cooper's motion. The trial would begin immediately.

On February 20, after the trial had been under way for a few days, another front-page story on Sirhan's plea bargain appeared in the *Los Angeles Times*. It became the focus of another discussion in Judge Walker's chambers. Cooper was the first to speak. "If it please the Court, what I'm about to say is said without rancor . . . [but] I must now quarrel that an article appeared in the Thursday morning, February 20, issue of the *Los Angeles Times* which I now offer in evidence only in part, only in support of the original motion for a mistrial and, second, I move for a mistrial again on this ground."

Cooper was angry about the article's content. "It reflects quite accurately everything that was said in chambers," he said. Cooper then pointed an accusing eye at the DA's office: "I have had the greatest cooperation from the office of the district attorney and these particular deputies here throughout the trial. They have acted as gentlemen. We have tried to reciprocate in kind. They have been most generous in anything about this case, but, notwithstanding . . ."

Judge Walker quickly jumped in. "Well let me say that I gave some of that information out myself. . . . I called Mr. Ron Einstoss and gave him that story and that is how it got out. . . . It was my feeling that if they got the other part, the whole story should be out."

Cooper responded that he thought such action was "misconduct" on the part of the judge. Walker responded that he already checked with the bailiff and that the jury had had no access to this story.

"That's correct," affirmed court bailiff William Polhemus. "They have not passed a newsstand or any news rack or anything."

Prosecutor Lynn Compton then joined the discussion. "There was an inference made," he said, "that these *Times* articles came from the district attorney's office. I am not sure upon what it was predicated, unless it was the simple fact that the *Times* newspaper has a staff reporter that occupies a pressroom in the district attorney's office and, admittedly, has a closer contact with us than any of the other news media that are covering this trial."

Compton then went on the offensive, reminding those present "there's an outfit called *Newsday* in the East which broke the story about the plea and a lot of details that are in the *Times* article before the *Times* ever ran it. . . . The eastern press apparently has some source of information that is better or equal to the *Los Angeles Times,* and we . . . resent the implication that has been made in some of the comments here that the *Times* article had to originate with the DA's office when it didn't."

"I will say very frankly," Cooper replied, "that I did believe from a reading of the article that I thought that it emanated from the DA's office, and my impression from a reading of the article was that it came from Evelle Younger himself." Indeed, earlier in the week, Younger had demonstrated incaution by stating on television that Sirhan's trial could take "three months or three days."

Judge Walker then weighed in with a rumor of his own. "The story was given to me that your man, your investigator-writer, was the one that did it."

"Kaiser?" Cooper responded incredulously.

But it wasn't Kaiser. As one who was working on a book about the trial, Kaiser had the least incentive to leak anything to anyone.

After the trial a friend of the Sirhan family, Rose Lynn Mangan, approached Cooper to ask if Kaiser had really been the one to leak the story. "No," Cooper said with disgust, "it was Berman!"

That Emile Berman had been talking off the record to the press was evident a week before the plea bargain story broke when, in another *Newsday* article, Bob Greene cited the concern of "defense sources" that Sirhan's "pose of a would-be nationalist hero" would interfere with his defense of diminished capacity. This was Berman's primary worry, and he was most certainly Greene's source.

Berman had quickly become disenchanted with defense strategy, particularly with the political overtones that were beginning to creep in. Nevertheless, once committed, he found it difficult to leave. "He stayed on with great reluctance," Robert Kaiser told the authors. "He was there in name and body only; his spirit wasn't there."

According to Kaiser, it was this disenchantment that led to the leaks to the press. "He wasn't in town very long before he started drinking heavily, and the worse things got the more he drank. And the reporters quickly learned that they could ply him with drinks and then pump him. They were all staying at the Ambassador [as was Berman], many of them were."

The chain of accusations and denials had now come full circle. Everyone had denied leaking information to the press, yet everyone had done so. Judge Walker, by his own admission, had provided the impetus for the most recent story. The district attorney's office had clearly provided some material to the *Los Angeles Times*. And one of Sirhan's own lawyers was the source of the original leak.

The failed plea bargain negotiations offer a unique window onto the interior landscape of the trial of Sirhan Sirhan. From the conversations in the judge's chambers, the underlying suppositions and motivations of the various participants can be considered.

For example, why did Judge Walker so adamantly refuse to allow the plea bargain? Was it, as he claimed, because of the historical significance of the case? Walker may certainly have had such feelings, but the solution he was willing to accept, a plea of guilty on the facts and a hearing only on the penalty, was hardly a scenario that would bring any historical or factual clarity as to what took place the night of the murder. When the district attorney offered to place into the record witness statements and other evidence, Walker shifted his stance and declared this case to be one where only the jury could pass sentence. Walker claimed that he was not influenced by what "the public" wanted, yet clearly he was very sensitive to what was being said about the trial and how he was being perceived, as his leaking the plea bargain story demonstrates. Could it be that a desire to end a distinguished career presiding over a trial of great importance played a major role in Walker's rulings?

Judge Walker's motivation probably derived from an amalgamation of sentiments—a strong personal desire to preside at the trial, coupled with a belief that the case shouldn't be put in a box too neatly and tucked away. From an historical point of view Walker's insistence on a trial was laudable. Still, if his motivation was heavily colored by his own personal desires, then Walker's obstinacy came very close to costing Sirhan his life.

And what of Grant Cooper? Why was he so in step with the wishes of the prosecution, so eager to plead Sirhan guilty to first-degree murder when he himself believed Sirhan guilty of no more than second-degree?

Cooper was surrounded by people who did not want Sirhan to make the plea. His co-attorneys wanted to fight on to preserve the option of appeal. The doctors wanted to explore the new frontiers of legal psychiatry. Others wanted to proceed for political reasons. At times it seemed as though Cooper was the only one thinking primarily of Sirhan.

From his conversations it is evident that Cooper, although baffled by his client, believed that Sirhan was a sick man, innocent of the charge of first-degree murder. But, as Cooper saw it, the only differences between first-degree murder and second-degree were the possibility of the death sentence for the more serious crime and a shorter minimum sentence for the lesser. Cooper reasoned that since Sirhan was not likely to be paroled quickly for murdering a presidential candidate even if he were found guilty of second-degree murder, why not grab the sure thing, life in prison, and eliminate the risk of being sentenced to death.

But although Cooper appeared to hold his client's interests at heart (and his calculations in the equation of justice would prove correct), the plea bargain negotiations exposed the defense attorney's chief flaw: he saw the trial of Sirhan as a staged event with a foregone conclusion. Perhaps he believed Evelle Younger's words when Younger said, "We can't conscientiously urge the death penalty." Perhaps he relied on Compton's idea of the prosecution recommending a life sentence during the penalty phase of the trial in return for a guilty plea. Even though Cooper could not deliver the guilty plea from Sirhan, he seemed to go out of his way to cause the prosecution no grief. By his words and actions it appears that Cooper believed he had forged some sort of gentleman's agreement: if he helped move things along, the prosecution would reciprocate when it came to deciding the penalty. Since Cooper saw no serious evidentiary conflicts, he was betraying no one.

But Grant Cooper would come to feel betrayed. Several years after the trial, he would tell journalist Betsy Langman that the prosecution "reneged" on their promise not to ask for the death penalty.[9] Thus, perhaps believing that he had such a promise, Cooper during the trial would journey off into a landscape of psychological constructions and political rationalizations that bore little relation to Sirhan and ultimately rang false to the jury.

It is, however, the prosecution's actions which are the most difficult to understand. Why were they so eager for a plea bargain? The prosecutors not only acceded; they pursued the idea with vigor. Are we to believe they cared so ferociously about the taxpayers' money? Was District Attorney Younger's professed conscience their driving force? If we accept the stated reason that as a matter of conscience they couldn't seek a sentence of death, why, when the trial was over, did the prosecutors ask for that very penalty?

And why did Younger go to Washington? Whom did he see? Did they really offer no comment or recommendation? Or did they decide that the country needed no further reminders of political murder, and that another assassin hustled off the stage would be the safest, and therefore the wisest, course to take?

John Seigenthaler, who had served under Attorney General Robert

Kennedy at the U.S. Department of Justice, questioned the propriety of Younger's Washington trip in his book *A Search for Justice*:

> The admission by [DA Younger] that he had contacted officials of the federal government to make it "convenient . . . to express an opinion to me," once again will cause some to wonder what the administration of justice is all about. Younger's discovery that "they"—the appropriate officials of government—declined to make a "recommendation" only elevates the idea that somehow the U.S. State Department could have an effect on the case.[10]

A more shadowed view of the prosecution's zeal in pursuing a plea bargain would be that within the DA's office, and certainly within the Los Angeles Police Department, there were some few men who were aware that there were severe problems with the physical evidence, a nasty little secret kept from the defense attorneys and the public at large. Although Grant Cooper had already chosen a psychiatric defense for his client—a defense which shouldn't have exposed any of the difficulties in the eye-witness accounts, the ballistics, or the autopsy—there was no guarantee that these anomalies would not surface at the trial. What if Cooper just stumbled over something that caused him to view the murder from a different per-spective? What if he felt cornered and came out fighting—demanding that the prosecution prove the most basic elements of the crime, such as, did the bullets that struck Robert Kennedy really come from Sirhan's gun?

FIVE

Doorframes and Dish Trays

✳ ✳ ✳

*Despite all the obstacles, new facts have come out about what FBI
agents, policemen, and other reputable persons said about the matter
of bullets in doorframes, and it seems fair in view of these facts to
say that there is now a rebuttable presumption that more than one
assassin was involved. But what is even clearer is that nobody is
making a serious effort to rebut that presumption. The notion seems
to be that the presumption can be waited out, that unanswered
questions will fade, given time, and that the best way to deal with
awkward new facts is to ignore them until they can be denounced as
"nothing new" and then dismissed.*[1]

—Former New York congressman Allard Lowenstein (1977)

THE PEOPLE OF the State of California
versus Sirhan Bishara Sirhan."

Court clerk Alice Nishikawa, with the jury present, opened the trial's
formal proceedings on Thursday, February 13, 1969, by reading the articles
of indictment. The primary article charged that "on or about the fifth day
of June 1968, the said defendant, Sirhan Bishara Sirhan, did wilfully, un-
lawfully, feloniously and with malice aforethought murder Robert Francis
Kennedy, a human being."

Judge Walker admonished the jury that they were not to accept as evidence anything said by either side in an opening statement. He then nodded to David Fitts, who stood and stepped to the lectern.

Though he was not the man in charge, it was generally agreed that
Deputy District Attorney Fitts was the class act of the prosecutor's office.
In contrast to his more burly, crew-cut associates, the Stanford-educated
Fitts was slim, erect, with a full head of graying hair. He had been compared
in the press to the late screen actor Montgomery Clift—the idealized image
of the thoughtful American man.

Fitts opened the case against Sirhan Sirhan by offering a factual recapitulation of the crime. He did so in great detail. The prosecutor first described

the line of possession of the alleged murder weapon, then Sirhan's movements in the week preceding the shooting. After that, he reviewed the movements of Robert Kennedy on primary night, culminating in his entrance into the hotel pantry.

According to David Fitts, Sirhan Sirhan approached Robert Kennedy in the pantry and "brought his right hand with the .22 caliber revolver in it to the very vicinity of the senator's head and at point-blank range in rapid succession fired eight shots." Fitts promised to demonstrate "that these shots that were recovered from [victims] Goldstein and Weisel and the one recovered from the body of the senator were all fired by the same gun, that is the gun recovered by Roosevelt Grier and Rafer Johnson."

The prosecutor then spoke to an issue that was not being adjudicated, but was on the agenda nonetheless. "The evidence in this case will show," he said in conclusion, "that defendant Sirhan Sirhan was alone responsible for the tragic incidents at the Ambassador Hotel in the early morning hours of the fifth of June; that he acted alone and without the concert of others. I thank you very much."

The next morning Emile Berman rose for the defense. As expected, he avoided a direct challenge to the prosecution. "One thing I'd like to fasten down with you and that is that the evidence in this case will disclose that this defendant, Sirhan, is immature, emotionally disturbed, and mentally ill. . . . This is not Berman talking now," he said, oddly referring to himself in the third person; "this is what you will hear from great doctors in psychiatry, psychology, and other social sciences."

Berman went on to recount a list of gruesome atrocities Sirhan was said to have witnessed as a small boy in war-torn Palestine—his home "bombed," a man "torn apart" by an explosion, and "a little girl's leg blown off, and the blood spurting from below her knee as though from a faucet." These stories represented the awkward marriage of the psychiatric and political motive, a relationship which would eventually come to burden the defense.

"There is no doubt," Berman told the jury, "that he did, in fact, fire the shot that killed Senator Kennedy. The killing was unplanned and undeliberate, impulsive and without premeditation or malice, totally a product of a sick, obsessed mind and personality."

Berman went on to explain to the jury that at the time of the shooting Sirhan was not himself. "He was out of contact with reality, in a trance in which he had no voluntary control over his will, his judgment, his feelings or actions. I do not expect you to accept my statement as evidence. I tell you these matters because we will prove them through great men in the fields of psychiatry and psychology." Though Berman didn't elaborate, this was the first public indication that the defense would argue that Sirhan had been in an altered state when he had committed the crime.

"We ask you to listen to the evidence," concluded the defense attorney, "to adopt what science has to offer, to consult with your conscience. In short, we ask you to let justice be done."

During the following recess Berman told reporters out in the corridor that Sirhan had probably not liked his opening statement. "Sirhan was saying to himself, 'That S.O.B. Berman, speaking of me like that, the dirty so and so'—but it's the truth. I tell it just like it was. This is a fantasy kid who went overboard on mysticism and went crazy with power when he saw himself in a mirror. Strictly unbalanced. In short, a nut."[2]

After recess the prosecution began to call the first of its sixty witnesses. Many of these would be people who were in the pantry and who could relate some portion of what happened when Robert Kennedy was shot. On the second day, Arthur Placencia, the young police officer who took Sirhan into custody, was called to testify. Under John Howard's direction Placencia recounted how he came upon the defendant, read him his rights in the squad car, and delivered him to detectives at Rampart Station. The only unexpected testimony occurred when Howard inquired about a statement Sirhan was said to have made in the patrol car.

"Did you hear Mr. Sirhan say," asked Howard, " 'I did it for my country?' "

"No, sir."

"You didn't hear that?" asked a surprised prosecutor. The alleged comment had been widely reported in the newspapers.

"No, sir."

When Grant Cooper began the cross-examination, he asked Officer Placencia whether he had inspected the prisoner's eyes while they were in the squad car. Placencia conceded that he had done so with a flashlight. Cooper asked why.

"Pupil reaction," replied the officer, "to see if anybody you have in custody might be under the influence of a drug or alcohol."

"And how did his pupils react?" asked Cooper.

"I can't recall, sir."

"You can't recall?"

"No, sir."

Grant Cooper then pulled out several sheets of paper. They were a transcript of an inquiry Placencia had undergone in early September. Cooper read from the transcript.

Q: Did you check him to determine if he was under the influence of anything such as drugs?
A: Oh, yes. I checked his pupils.
Q: How did you check his pupils?

A: With the flashlight. Put it up to his face and sort of looked to
see if his pupils react.

Q: How did they react?

A: They didn't.

Q: They didn't react to light at all?

A: No. His pupils were real wide.

Having read from the transcript, Grant Cooper again put his question.
"Now did his pupils react to the light?"

"Yes, sir, according to the report. That's what I said."

"In other words then, his pupils did not react to the light, did they?"

"No, sir."

"Now what did that mean to you as an officer?"

"That he was under the influence of something."

Had Officer Placencia really forgotten what had happened when he
flashed the light in Sirhan's eyes? The memory had certainly been clear only
several months earlier. Perhaps the young policeman had been made to
understand by his colleagues or superiors that this testimony might help a
murderer escape punishment, and that, as a patrolman with only two weeks'
experience, he was poorly qualified to make such a test.

Placencia's loss of memory was a small example of how evidence over
time begins to bend to the purposes of those presenting it. Grant Cooper's
use of a previous statement to impeach a witness, or in this case, refresh his
memory, was an elementary tactic of cross-examination. Unfortunately, this
minor skirmish with Officer Placencia very early in the proceedings would
represent Cooper's brightest moment of the entire trial. Had he used the
same skepticism toward the state's physical evidence, the trial transcript
might read quite differently. But Cooper was content to accept as factual
most everything offered by the prosecution.

A month earlier, as the defense was making preparations for jury selection, Grant Cooper received a telephone call from a man named William
W. Harper. Harper was a respected criminalist who had been a consultant
in over three hundred homicide cases during a thirty-five-year career. He
was a qualified expert witness in seven states, including California.

Harper had called Cooper to give some serious advice. "Beware of Wolfer," he said, speaking of the LAPD's criminalist assigned to the RFK investigation; "he gives them what they want." Harper had come up against
the police investigator's forensic work on several occasions, work Harper
regarded as unscientific and self-serving. "Wolfer's not competent," Harper
cautioned. "He will do what's expected of him."[3]

Cooper expressed his appreciation to Harper for the notice, but he told
the criminalist that he was not concerned. After all, Cooper reasoned, there

was no question about what had happened. Harper was less certain of this than Cooper, but the criminalist had delivered his message, and he let the matter drop—for the time being. Cooper, however, had been warned.

In June of 1968 DeWayne Wolfer was a criminalist assigned to the crime laboratory of the LAPD's Scientific Investigation Division (SID). He had been on the force for fifteen years. Within two hours of the shooting Wolfer was at the Ambassador Hotel directing the collection of evidence, the taking of photographs, and conducting bullet flight-path analysis. In a 1971 deposition he described his work that night:

> I went to the scene of the crime and I explored the trajectory of all the holes in the wall and the walls of victims [*sic*]. . . . I was there immediately after the death of the Senator. I retrieved and was in charge of the crime scene and I recovered the bullets that were recovered.[4]

Wolfer's description here contains several significant slips of the tongue. He speaks of exploring the trajectory of "holes in the wall" and of recovering "the bullets that were recovered." At other times Wolfer would absolutely deny that there were any bullet holes in the walls or that he recovered any bullets from the crime scene. The sharp conflict between Wolfer's assertions and the surviving evidence forms one of the central mysteries of the murder of Robert Kennedy. As will be explained, if there were bullet holes in the walls or bullets recovered in the pantry, then a second gun had to have been fired during the murder. Wolfer asserts that there were no bullets or bullet holes. The evidence suggests otherwise.

There are, for example, a number of photographs (see photo insert herein) that appear to contradict the police criminalist. In one of these Wolfer himself is posing in front of the pantry doorway, pointing to an apparent bullet mark. In another, the chief medical examiner for Los Angeles County, Dr. Thomas Noguchi, is also pointing at the doorframes. Later, when asked to describe how the photograph came about, Noguchi said that he asked DeWayne Wolfer for the location of any bullet holes. "He pointed, as I recall . . . to several holes in the doorframes of the swinging doors leading into the pantry. I directed that photographs be taken of me pointing to these holes."[5]

Los Angeles police officers Robert Rozzi and Charles Wright were also shown in an AP photo kneeling by a doorway, pointing to a hole and illuminating it with flashlights. The caption reads: "Police technician inspects a bullet hole discovered in a door frame. . . . Bullet is still in the wood." In 1975, Rozzi elaborated:

"Sometime during the evening when we were looking for evidence, someone discovered what appeared to be a bullet a foot and a half or so from the bottom of the floor [*sic*] in a doorjamb on the door behind the stage. I also personally observed what I believed to be a bullet in the place just mentioned. What I observed was a hole in the doorjamb, and the base of what appeared to be a small-caliber bullet was lodged in the hole."[6]

Rozzi's partner, patrolman Charles Wright, confirmed the observation twenty years after the murder when he was asked by journalist Dan Moldea how certain he was, on a scale of one to ten, that it was a bullet he observed in the hole. "You can never be 100 per cent sure," responded Wright. "But I would say it would be as close to a ten as I'd ever want to go without pulling it out."[7]

On the morning of June 5, only hours after the murder, two amateur photographers, John Shirley and John R. Clemente, took pictures of the pantry and the doorframes. In March 1969, Shirley provided a statement to Lillian Castellano of the Kennedy Assassination Truth Committee, a small group of citizens seeking answers to the questions and conflicts in the official account of the murder.

Said Shirley:

> In the wooden jamb of the center divider were two bullet holes surrounded by inked circles which contained some numbers and letters. I remember a manager pointing out those particular marked bullet holes to another person who appeared to be a press photographer.
>
> It appeared that an attempt had been made to dig the bullets out from the surface. However, the center divider jamb was loose, and it appeared to have been removed from the framework so that the bullets might be extracted from behind.

The man who helped authorities remove the wood was Dale Poore, a carpenter employed by the hotel. In a 1975 interview conducted by the DA's office, Poore described what he saw. "It looked like the bullet had went [*sic*] in at sort of an angle as it was traveling this way. So it made a bit of an oblong hole and the fiber of the board had closed in some after it went in."

Shortly after Poore did his work, a veteran crime reporter for the *Chicago Tribune*, Robert Weidrich, entered the hotel pantry. Weidrich spoke to several police officers, who pointed out maître d' Karl Uecker as a crime-scene witness. Weidrich interviewed Uecker and filed his story, "Felt Him

Fire His Gun, Hotel Worker Says." The article contained the following corroborating revelation:

> On a low table lay an 8-foot strip of molding, torn by police from the center post of the double doors leading from the ballroom. These were the doors through which Sen. Kennedy had walked, smiling in his moment of victory.
>
> Now the molding bore the scars of a crime laboratory technician's probe as it had removed two .22-caliber bullets that had gone wild.[8]

When Philip Melanson contacted Weidrich in 1988, the reporter still remembered the name of the police officer he had spoken to that night as Detective Sergeant J. R. MacArthur. He remembered MacArthur because he was "amazingly cooperative," and Weidrich had written him a note of thanks when he got back home. Regarding the two bullets referred to in his article, Weidrich did not witness the actual removal, but he stated, "I would have asked, 'What did you find?' [MacArthur would have replied] 'Oh, we found these two slugs.'

"The molding had obviously been removed from the wall," Weidrich asserted; "they had recovered the two slugs."

Apparent bullet holes in the hotel pantry were also observed by crime-scene witnesses Lisa Urso, Martin Patrusky, Vincent DiPierro, Angelo DiPierro, and Karl Uecker. All of them testified at the trial of Sirhan. None of them were asked about the bullet holes by the prosecution or the defense.

It could be argued that these witnesses were not qualified to identify a bullet hole, but such could not be said about William Bailey. An agent with the FBI stationed in Los Angeles, Bailey was in the pantry within hours of the shooting, inspecting the crime scene in preparation for witness interviews. In 1993 Bailey described to the authors what he saw that night: "As I toured the pantry area I noticed in a wood doorframe, a center divider between the two swinging doors, two bullet holes. I've inspected quite a few crime scenes in my day. These were clearly bullet holes; the wood around them was freshly broken away and I could see the base of a bullet in each one."

Because the Los Angeles police were not providing security in the Ambassador Hotel, they arrived too late to seal off the crime scene. They failed to do so, even belatedly. People ran in and out of the pantry. There was no systematic search for guns. Evidence was up for grabs. One detective reported seeing a man in a tuxedo trying to pry a bullet out of a wall with a penknife.

Whatever evidence escaped Los Angeles law enforcement during those chaotic early moments will never be known. Evidence that was gathered by the police, however, seems too often to have fared no better than it would have in the hands of souvenir hunters. The doorframes and the alleged bullets contained in them are an important example.

On the night of the murder the holes in the doorframes were regarded as prized evidence, as demonstrated by the photographs taken of DeWayne Wolfer and others pointing to them. Here were the LAPD crime solvers hard at work. What Wolfer and the others didn't know until the next day was that five bullets would be recovered from the five wounded bystanders, and that Kennedy had been wounded three times, two bullets remaining within him and a third, by police accounts, passing through his shoulder and penetrating the ceiling. A fourth bullet passed harmlessly through Kennedy's suit jacket.

The arithmetic here is devastatingly simple: the gun taken from Sirhan Sirhan held a maximum of eight bullets; thus, with at least eight bullets already accounted for, there could be no bullets in the walls or doorframe, if only one gun was firing. Any bullets or bullet holes in the walls would be irrefutable proof of a second gun.

With the recovery of the bullets from the wounded victims, the apparent bullet holes by the door, which had been trophies the night before, now became unwelcome evidence. The doorframes were subsequently removed by the police. Under the heading "Work Requested," the police property report for the frames called for "trajectory analysis." The two pieces of wood molding were never seen again by anyone on the outside, including any member of the Sirhan defense team.

Coming, as he did, late into the case, Grant Cooper had a very poor understanding of the physical evidence. Police secrecy regarding the doorframes abetted his ignorance. At no point in the trial was the issue of extra bullets, in the doorframes or elsewhere, ever mentioned.

It is not clear from the accounts of William Harper's cautionary conversation with Cooper whether or not the criminalist was calling to offer his services. Greater interest by Cooper might have been the entrée Harper was looking for before volunteering. The defense was top-heavy with psychiatrists and psychologists, but they had no forensic expertise. The two investigators they had, McCowan and Kaiser, were overmatched by the workload and were not forensic experts in any case. No one was focusing on ballistics.

In not inviting Harper to join the defense, Cooper was most likely playing it safe. In his own mind he was certain of the facts, and probably saw no advantage to making trouble for the prosecution, even if it could be demonstrated that DeWayne Wolfer's work was flawed. In addition, the defense lawyer had little incentive to look in the direction of extra bullets.

Evidence of a second gun, in any usual circumstance, would not exonerate gunman number one, and would settle conclusively, and adversely for the defendant, the issue of premeditation. The circumstances under which this would not be so would have to be bizarre: for example, gunman number one acting without awareness or volition. But in his opening statement Emile Berman had maintained that his client "was out of contact with reality, in a trance in which he had no voluntary control over his will." If this was the case, then the defense attorneys should have been more vigilant in their examination of the physical evidence.

The first public notice of any problems with the bullet count occurred on May 23, 1969, a full month after Sirhan's trial had concluded. An article by Lillian Castellano and Floyd Nelson titled "Ten Shots from an Eight-Shot Revolver" appeared in the *LA Free Press*. Basing their analysis on the Shirley/Clemente photograph of the two bullet holes in the center divider and the AP photo of Officers Rozzi and Wright, Castellano and Nelson made a prima facie case that at least ten bullets had been fired during the murder. "This means," the authors concluded, "that the police have not told us the truth—the District Attorney has not told us the truth—the news media have not reported the truth. . . . It is a very frightening thought."

The Castellano/Nelson article received little attention, though the LAPD was certainly aware of the allegations. The following Wednesday, perhaps in an effort to forestall concern raised by the article, District Attorney Evelle Younger promised to release the case files held by the police. "The Los Angeles Police Department," Younger said, "has agreed without reservation that the interests of the public and law enforcement are best served by full disclosure of the results of the comprehensive investigation which they have conducted." Younger made no mention of the issue of extra bullets. Three weeks later the doorframes and the ceiling tiles would be destroyed by the police.

Even after the publication of the Castellano/Nelson story, most people who had seen the bullet holes continued to have no idea that what they saw represented any problem to the case. It is a tribute to how well the bullet-count secret was kept that years would go by, many years in some case, before the significance of witness and police observation would be understood.

In the mid-1970s Los Angeles attorney (and former Charles Manson prosecutor) Vincent Bugliosi gathered affidavits from witnesses (including law enforcement investigators Rozzi, Wright, and Bailey) who had not been questioned on this point by the police or trial lawyers. In the 1980s RFK researchers Gregory Stone and Philip Melanson tracked down witnesses (including Urso, DiPierro, and Weidrich) who had unrecorded bullet-count information.

In the spring of 1990, investigative journalist Dan Moldea conducted an extensive probe into the question of extra bullets. He interviewed scores of LAPD officers and sheriff's deputies who had been involved in the case. His May 13, 1990, article in the *Washington Post,* "RFK's Murder: A Second

Gun?" provided strong new evidence of extra bullets, based on statements of some of the law enforcement officers:

—Patrolman Al Lamoreaux recalled "seeing one or two holes in the door around wherever he had just shot him . . . it was obvious. Just being a dumb cop you look and see where the bullets went."

—Sergeant Raymond Rolon told Moldea, "One of the investigators pointed to a hole in the doorframe and said, 'We just pulled a bullet out of there.'"

—LAPD photographer Charles Collier, upon being asked whether he was sure that he took pictures of bullet holes in the pantry, said: "A bullet hole looks like a bullet hole if you've photographed enough of them."

—Detective Sergeant J. R. MacArthur, the senior police detective at the crime scene, said he had seen "quite a few" bullet holes.

—Deputy Sheriff Thomas Beringer reported seeing a bystander trying to take a bullet out of a doorframe with a penknife. Asked if it might not have been a nail in the hole instead of a bullet, Berringer replied, "It wasn't a nail. It was a definite bullet hole."

LAPD property reports confirm that ceiling tiles and wood from the doorframe were removed from the crime scene. This evidence remained in police possession until June 27, 1969, one month following the publication of the Castellano/Nelson article raising the issue of extra bullets. On this date police records indicate that the doorframes and the ceiling tiles were destroyed. This destruction of evidence occurred while Sirhan's case was still under appeal in the courts.

In 1993 the authors interviewed former police detective Emmanuel Pena. In charge of preparing the case for trial and investigating any conspiracy-related leads, Pena had held an important position in Special Unit Senator, the police task force set up to investigate Robert Kennedy's murder. Pena actively defended the police handling of the case, but seemed surprised by the timing of the doorframes' destruction. He was asked whether he had ordered the wood moldings destroyed.

"No," replied Pena.

"Did you know that they were destroyed?"

"No."

"Do you think their destruction was proper?"

"No," said Pena, after a thoughtful pause, "evidence should never be destroyed until a case is finished in the courts."

The destruction of the doorframes and the ceiling tiles in 1969 was not revealed until 1975, during hearings conducted by the Los Angeles City Council. "There was no place to keep them," asserted an attorney representing the police. "You can't fit ceiling panels into a card file."[9] This raises the question of whether the LAPD also trashed all of the assorted rifles, bales of marijuana, or vehicles that constituted bulky evidence in all of its cases on appeal in 1969, or was there some special reason they wished this particular evidence to disappear?

The LAPD's subsequent position, articulated by then assistant chief Daryl Gates, was that the destruction didn't matter: the artifacts contained no bullet holes; they were not evidence. One would expect that any department whose publicly and privately pronounced goal was to avoid "another Dallas" should have been overjoyed to preserve and release evidence that would refute critics.

But Gates's explanation made no sense for another reason. The destroyed artifacts included the ceiling tiles, which the LAPD admitted had contained bullet holes—critical evidence if one were trying to substantiate the rather tortured trajectories of the bullets put forth by DeWayne Wolfer. So critical, in fact, that in 1975, California attorney general Evelle Younger, Sirhan's former prosecutor, used the police-ordered destruction as an argument in front of superior court judge Robert A. Wenke, to forestall an investigation into the question of extra bullets through flight-path analysis:

> The Court has already been informed in this proceeding that the crucial ceiling panels and door jambs from the pantry have been destroyed in a routine manner by the Los Angeles Police Department. Without these items, it will be impossible to compute angles of flight for a number of bullets.

Younger went on to offer a self-serving explanation for why this evidence never saw the light of day at Sirhan's trial.

> One reason this evidence probably was never introduced at trial when it was a subject of speculation [was] because there is no empirical evidence that bullet flight paths can ever be accurately reproduced.[10]

A police property report, curiously dated twenty-two days after the items were booked into evidence, describes "two" ceiling tiles removed and in possession of the Los Angeles police. But there may have been more. FBI and LAPD crime-scene photographs show that numerous ceiling tiles were removed, including several outside of Sirhan's officially defined range of fire.

Crime-scene witness Lisa Urso was wandering around the hotel and was not discovered by authorities until later in the morning. She described to Philip Melanson what she saw in the pantry when she returned three hours after the crime.

Urso recalled that just after the shooting, before she left the pantry and went upstairs, she looked up at the ceiling and was surprised to see what appeared to be "bullet holes." She doesn't remember how many. When she returned several hours later, she noticed that tiles had been "removed from the ceiling" and placed on the floor—five or six, she estimates. A uniformed police officer stood guard while another was kneeling, "poking around"—poking for bullets, she thought. Said Urso: "I don't know how many rounds a gun holds, but it sounded like there were more people shot than there were bullets to go around. And they [the police] kept saying about ricochets."

According to the official bullet count as constructed by DeWayne Wolfer, one bullet penetrated a ceiling tile and became lost in the ceiling after having passed through Senator Kennedy's shoulder. Another bullet was said to have penetrated the ceiling, bounced off the cement underflooring, and reentered the pantry through a ceiling tile "and then struck victim Evans in the head." This scenario seems less likely after an inspection of Mrs. Elizabeth Evans's medical report, which describes the bullet as entering "just below the hairline" and traveling "upward." A closer inspection of the ceiling tiles in police custody could have substantiated whether this ricochet scenario was based in fact or was just a convenient way for the LAPD to account for more bullet holes in the ceiling than they knew what to do with. The destruction of the tiles ended any possibility of examination.

Another avenue of inquiry closed off by the quick disposal of evidence relates to the two bullets allegedly discovered on the front seat of Sirhan's car (parked near the crime scene). In 1975 an independent panel of court-appointed firearms experts discovered traces of wood on the base and tip of both bullets. Did Sirhan fire them into wood, dig them out, and then drive around with them on the front seat? Were they really found in his car? Could they have come from wood in the hotel pantry? Without the doorframes, a microscopic comparison of wood from those frames with the wood tracings on the bullets was not possible.

In the official audit of bullets, the item most in conflict with common sense and Newtonian physics was Wolfer's explanation of the bullet that struck Paul Schrade. With four bullets in Evans, Stroll, Weisel, and Goldstein, two bullets in Robert Kennedy, and one lost in the ceiling, Wolfer now had only one bullet left to account for Schrade's wound. This was the bullet that penetrated Kennedy's suit jacket. Wolfer's report said that this bullet "passed through the right shoulder pad of Senator Kennedy's suit coat (never entered his body) and traveled upward striking victim Schrade in the middle of the forehead."

This analysis sounds plausible until one inspects the senator's suit jacket and police reconstructions (see photo insert herein), which reveal that this bullet was traveling upward at an eighty-degree angle (almost vertical) and was moving slightly back to front and, thus, away from Paul Schrade, who was reliably placed by witnesses four to five feet behind Robert Kennedy.

When he testified at the trial, Schrade was unaware that the bullet that struck him represented any problem to the police account of the murder. Seventeen years later he was no longer being polite about the matter. "I want you to explain to me," he shouted at a stone-faced Daryl Gates at a police commission hearing, "how a bullet traveling up and away from me can make a ninety-degree turn and end up in my head?"

The doorframes and the ceiling tiles were not the only evidence of extra bullets to disappear. Police "logs of work performed" describe tests done on the doorframes and ceiling tiles. According to the police, chemical, microscopic, X-ray, and fluoroscope tests were conducted. None of the results of these examinations are anywhere to be found in police files. Yet such results were certainly small enough to fit in a filing cabinet, and evidence that there was no second gun involved would presumably be valued currency in an investigation that knew it would eventually face skeptical journalists and conspiracy buffs.

Other evidence relating to the doorframes appears to be missing or altered. The police files released in 1988 contained detailed personal statements by LAPD officers describing what they did the night of the shooting: gathering evidence, providing security for the senator at the hospital, crowd control, finding witnesses. The statements of the officers seen in photos pointing to the holes in the doorframe are silent about this and related activities. They are also the only statements not written in the first person. The removal of the ceiling tiles and the doorframes, or their probing (verbally described by police officers and witnesses), do not show up in any of the officers' statements—as if these activities never occurred.

For years researchers noted that on photos of the alleged bullet holes in the doorframe there was a circle drawn in pencil around one hole. Inside the circle was scrawled, "723 LASO, W. Tew." This seemed to indicate that Los Angeles Sheriff's Office (LASO) deputy W. Tew, badge number 723, had examined this hole.

In 1990 journalist Dan Moldea discovered that retired deputy Walter Tew had died a year earlier. One of his former colleagues who was at the RFK crime scene confirmed that Tew had found what he thought was a bullet. "That would be a typical way a deputy would mark evidence," he stated.[11] But Deputy Tew would also disappear into the LAPD's evidentiary black hole: there is not one mention of his name in any document, roster, or log.

In his interviews with LAPD personnel, Dan Moldea talked to several men who had a direct relationship with DeWayne Wolfer. One was Lieutenant Donald W. Mann, who was the LAPD's chief criminalist and Wolfer's direct superior.

"[Wolfer] was hard to supervise," Mann reported to Moldea. "He would go off by himself, and sometimes he would get himself in trouble, and us too. He would work with them [other LAPD divisions] without me even knowing it. It kind of burned me up at times. To keep the paperwork straight, I would sign off on some of the stuff."[12]

Moldea then asked Mann if he had signed off on any reports concerning bullets recovered from the crime scene. Mann replied that he would only "hear talk" and that it was "secret stuff."

"No, I didn't okay those reports," said Mann. "The Chief told me, 'It's perfectly all right. You are relieved of responsibility.' . . . It was just kind of taken out of my hands."[13]

Moldea's interview with Wolfer's subordinate, Officer David Butler, yielded a startling eyewitness account of evidence recovery in the hotel pantry. Moldea asked Butler who might have removed bullets from the wall the night of the shooting.

"DeWayne Wolfer took two bullets out of the wall," Butler answered.

"Were you there when he took those bullets out?" Moldea asked a few moments later.

"Yes."

Moldea then asked how the bullets were removed from the center divider.

"Tear it out," responded Butler. "We had to disassemble it to find the bullets."

"So you disassembled it to find the bullets?"

"Right."[14]

In a subsequent interview with Moldea, Butler would qualify his story only after he realized that it was a potential embarrassment to the police and his mentor, DeWayne Wolfer. Then his rather vivid account of extracting bullets from the doorframes faded into a more vague story of having seen what he thought were bullets in small evidence packages labeled "bullet evidence" or "firearms evidence." Since, according to Wolfer, no bullets or bullet fragments were recovered at the crime scene, Butler's second story is just about as damaging as his first. Moreover, Butler's second story, coming as it did after the officer realized that his first account was a potential embarrassment, makes it seem likely that the first account was the more reliable.

That Butler, as well as other police officers, could have had knowledge of crime-scene bullets without understanding their significance as proof of a second gun is a measure of how insulated and compartmentalized the LAPD's murder investigation became. Butler's initial story would seem to confirm the crime-scene photographs and the numerous civilian and police accounts of bullets recovered from the pantry doorframes. It stands in direct contrast to DeWayne Wolfer's somewhat less than scientific explanation for the holes given in a 1971 deposition:

> I found no bullet holes in the doorframe. I found many holes, but none containing or caused by bullets. . . . They were caused by some object poking the wood—a ramrod, a tray, a dish tray. There was [*sic*] many of those portable carts and that had a round area on it. That could have certainly caused it [the holes].[15]

DeWayne Wolfer could make such a statement in 1971 without the threat of contradiction: the doorframes no longer existed, most witnesses who could challenge him were unaware of the controversy, and the most compromising photographs would remain locked away in police files for another seventeen years. Even so, the dish-tray analysis stands naked.

Compare Wolfer's explanation with the account of maître d' Karl Uecker. After being interviewed by police the morning of June 5, Uecker returned to the crime scene. He noticed two holes in the center divider that he is positive were not there prior to the shooting. He passed through the doors dozens of times each night and is sure that he would have noticed them if they had existed previously. Uecker pointed the holes out to a man in plain clothes whom he took to be a detective. The man responded that everything would be checked out. "These holes were never there before," Uecker said steadfastly many years later, "and I knew where the shots were going to. I saw him [Sirhan] shooting, and I know it must have been this way."[16]

In 1975 there was an unexpected confirmation of Uecker's observation and a stunning refutation of Wolfer's casual hypothesis. In response to a Freedom of Information Act initiative by Washington attorney Bernard Fensterwald, the FBI released certain documents from its files on the RFK murder. Fensterwald and his colleagues were startled by what they received. Among the bureau documents was a series of photographs of the pantry interior, including several close-ups of the missing doorframes. Four of these photographs showed what were labeled as "bullet holes." Photograph "E-3" was labeled "Close up view of two bullet holes which is [*sic*] located in the center door frame inside kitchen serving area and looking towards direction of back of stage." Thus, the holes in the doorframes, which were identified by the LAPD's forensic expert as being caused by portable dish trays, were sufficiently sinister in appearance to attract the attention of not only numerous police officers and hotel employees, but also crime scene photographers from the Federal Bureau of Investigation.

★　　★　　★

In 1971 Los Angeles County district attorney Joseph Busch wrote a report on the various allegations of impropriety then surfacing about the police handling of the Robert Kennedy murder. Busch wrote the report "because I felt it incumbent on my office to conduct an independent investigation so there would be no loss of confidence on the part of the public as to whether the facts as presented in the courtroom were correct."

One of Busch's targets was Lillian Castellano and her allegation about a second gun.

> Mrs. Castellano suggests that there is evidence that there were more than eight bullets recovered after the shooting. Sirhan's gun was an eight shot revolver. Her evidence consists of an Associated Press photograph of two police officers pointing to a hole in a door frame, a caption under the picture that says, "bullet still in the wood" and a photographs of two holes in a wooden door jamb. These holes were circled and had numbers and letters around them. When added to the eight bullets accounted for in Mr. Wolfer's ballistic report, there are supposedly eleven bullets in the pantry. However, no support is given to the caption or photographs by anyone who actually saw bullets in the holes, or removed bullets from the holes. Mrs. Castellano has no responsible evidence to show that more than eight shots were fired in the Ambassador Hotel on June 5, 1968.[17]

District Attorney Busch cites a lack of supporting evidence in attempting to refute Castellano's claims of extra bullets. As has been demonstrated, this corroborating evidence in the form of pantry witnesses, hotel employees, police officers, FBI agents, and crime scene photographs was within easy reach of the district attorney. Where the lack of responsibility occurred was in destroying the doorframes and then offering an unlikely and unproven explanation for the apparent bullet holes observed in them.

Because the Los Angeles police destroyed the doorframes and the ceiling tiles and mislaid or destroyed whatever scientific tests were done upon them, and because DeWayne Wolfer's dish-tray theory is without substantiation and contrary to all eyewitness and photographic accounts, there comes a point when one is justified in concluding that a second gun in the Robert Kennedy murder is a very real possibility. Moreover, it would appear that the LAPD and DeWayne Wolfer were not being honest with this evidence.

The specter of a second gun changes most everything. It forces one to look anew at the evidence that supposedly linked Sirhan's gun to the bullets that struck Robert Kennedy. It calls into question the exact nature of Sirhan's role in the murder. It lends new importance to Sirhan's alleged lack of memory of the event. Now the serious flaws in the prosecution's evidence are not just curiosities. Did any bullets from Sirhan's gun actually strike Robert Kennedy? Who was the woman seen running from the pantry? And who, exactly, is Sirhan Sirhan?

Unaware of a bullet-count problem or a second-gun possibility, Grant Cooper moved without suspicion into the ballistics phase of the trial. William Harper's words had been forgotten, and the chief defense attorney was concerned with being as cooperative as possible. Several days before the prosecution was to summon DeWayne Wolfer, Cooper had a conversation with Deputy DA Fitts.

"It is our intention to call DeWayne Wolfer to testify with respect to his ballistics comparison," said Fitts. ". . . It is our understanding that there will be a stipulation that these objects came from the persons whom I say they came from. Is that right?"

"So long as you make that avowal," answered Cooper, "there will be no question about that."

"Fine," replied Fitts. "We have discussed the matter with Mr. Wolfer as to those envelopes containing those bullets and bullet fragments; he knows where they came from."[18]

SIX

The Criminalist

✳ ✳ ✳

*Because DeWayne Wolfer's testimony under oath corroborated the
facts learned through my investigation and preparation, I did not
retain an independent ballistics expert to analyze the slugs removed
from the deceased's body. Had I any feeling that, in a case of this
importance, Mr. Wolfer either willfully falsified his ballistics analysis
or negligently, improperly or otherwise arrived at his conclusions,
I would have had an independent ballistics expert or experts
study the bullets.*

—Sirhan defense attorney Grant Cooper, 1972

A S DEWAYNE WOLFER strode to
the witness stand he seemed at
ease. Wolfer's dark hair was slicked back to frame a full, forty-three-year-
old face. He was dressed in a business suit, which, as a police criminalist,
was his working attire.

"Your occupation, sir?" asked David Fitts, who would direct the questioning for the prosecution.

"Police officer for the City of Los Angeles," replied Wolfer, "assigned
to the Scientific Investigation Division, Crime Laboratory, where I act as
a criminalist—the study of firearms—and as a ballistics expert."

"What is that science?"

"Ballistics is the science, a study of the flight patterns of projectiles, and
we have internal ballistics and external, and that is from the time the bullet
is fired or leaves the muzzle of the gun and flies through the air until it
terminates."

"What education and experience have you had or undergone to prepare
yourself for this particular field?"

"In this particular field, in the field of formal education I have my bach-
elor's degree from the University of Southern California, where I was a
premed student there with a background in the field of chemistry, physics
and different types of laboratory technique courses, photography and the
like."

At the time of the trial, there was no specific major or grade point average required for the position of LAPD criminalist, and Wolfer's studies at USC seemed to relate tangentially at best to his chosen profession. As a zoology major he received more C's than all other grades combined, and he received five D's, including one in his major and two in chemistry. He also had a history of offering inflated credentials to bolster his perceived expertise, something that would come to haunt him in a few years.

Wolfer's primary purpose for the prosecution was to connect the gun taken from Sirhan Sirhan to the bullets removed from the shooting victims. David Fitts held up envelopes that contained several spent bullets.

"I now ask you to examine the contents of the envelopes which are before you in evidence, and when you have examined them all, would you tell me if you have examined them before?"

Before the witness could answer, Grant Cooper jumped up. "I will stipulate he has seen them all before," he said. "Pardon me. Maybe I shouldn't have done that."

"I think the stipulation in this instance might save a little time," said Fitts. "I take it, sir, that those bullets came to you in the due course of police procedure at the laboratory, is that correct, sir?"

"That's correct."

In addition to the bullets, the prosecution was intent on introducing into evidence several photographs of Robert Kennedy's wounded head. The photographs would help establish, by way of the "tattooing" in the vicinity of the fatal wound, the muzzle distance of the gun at the time the shots were fired. Fitts asked Wolfer to explain tattooing.

"Basically at the time a gun is fired," responded Wolfer, "there is expelled from the muzzle of the gun, in addition to the projectile, unburned fragments. . . . Tattooing is where the powder particles are actually hurled or thrown into the wound itself and tattoo the skin."

Grant Cooper strongly opposed the introduction of the head-wound photographs, believing they would illustrate the horror of the crime and make the jury less inclined to look leniently upon Sirhan. Cooper thought if he could agree in advance to what the prosecution was trying to prove, he might get the photos excluded.

"These photographs are highly inflammatory," he said to Judge Walker. "We will stipulate that there was powder tattooing on the ear of Senator Kennedy; that the gun was held as close as the witness wants to testify that it was held. . . . We will stipulate that these fragments did come from Senator Kennedy; we will further stipulate they came from the gun."

"With reference to the circumstances of the shooting, Your Honor," replied Fitts, determined to have the photographs introduced, "Your Honor has heard Karl Uecker and any number of witnesses who attempted to describe what happened; one witness has put the muzzle of the revolver some three or four feet from the senator's head, others have had it at varying range. The only way we can clear up whatever ambiguity there may be there and to show the truth is by the testimony of this witness. . . . Now I think the prosecution is entitled to present that."

"We don't quarrel that it was held within one inch," said Cooper, again.

"Well," responded Judge Walker, "I think the prosecution has a right to present its case, whatever they think should be presented. The objection will be overruled."

A concession, as Fitts had just made, that the scientific evidence did not match the witness accounts, might ordinarily signal a problem for the prosecution. Not here. Grant Cooper had no intention of exploiting this conflict. He was only dimly aware of it. But the contradictions were more serious than Fitts's casual allusion would indicate. Not one witness to the shooting placed Sirhan's gun in a position to duplicate the tattooing seen in the photographs the prosecution was trying to introduce. This discrepancy was not lost on medical examiner Dr. Thomas Noguchi, who described the realization in his 1983 memoir *Coroner*: "Eyewitnesses are notoriously unreliable, but this time the sheer unanimity was too phenomenal to dismiss. Not a single witness in that crowded kitchen had seen him [Sirhan] fire behind Kennedy's ear at point-blank range."[1]

To the prosecution none of this mattered. They possessed the scientific data: Kennedy had been shot at point-blank range. Recollections which failed to place Sirhan in a position to do this would not be solicited, and if they came out they would be ignored. Since the defense was not challenging, this would be easy to do.

With the photographs of Kennedy's wounded head in the hands of the jury and Wolfer's description of his own powder-burn tests to determine firing distance, Fitts was now set to lay down his version of the facts.

"Did you form an opinion," he asked Wolfer, "as to the muzzle range of the pistol at the time the shot was fired in the senator's head?"

"The weapon," asserted Wolfer, "was held approximately one inch away from the senator's ear at the time it was fired."

As Fitts had conceded, this assessment did not agree with the account of the prosecution's "star witness" (as they called him), Karl Uecker, who described to the court the week before how he had blocked the assailant from getting point-blank access to Kennedy. But Uecker wasn't asked about the gun's distance from Kennedy's head. Not by the prosecution; not by the defense.

Uecker, however, was emphatic about the distance problem in a statement made six years later:

> I have told the police and testified during the trial [he meant the grand jury proceeding] that there was a distance of at least one and

one-half feet between the muzzle of Sirhan's gun and Senator Kennedy's head. The revolver was directly in front of my nose. After Sirhan's second shot, I pushed his hand that held the revolver down, and pushed him onto the steam table. There is no way that the shots described in the autopsy could have come from Sirhan's gun. When I told this to the authorities, they told me that I was wrong. But I repeat now what I told them then: Sirhan never got close enough for a point-blank shot, never.[2]

However certain he might be, if Uecker alone had made this observation about the firing distance, one might justifiably assume he was mistaken, perhaps due to the trauma of a discharging pistol held next to his face. But Uecker was not alone. In fact, almost all the witnesses confirmed his recollection, including those who, along with Uecker, had made the LAPD's list of "five best" witnesses: Frank Burns, Martin Patrusky, Juan Romero, and Jesus Perez.

Frank Burns is now a successful Los Angeles attorney. He worked for the Robert Kennedy campaign in 1968 and was an aide to Jesse Unruh, Speaker of the California Assembly. Burns was within several feet of Kennedy when the shots were fired. In a 1987 interview with the authors, he vividly recalled the tragedy that was still painful for him to talk about.

Burns was adamant that Sirhan's gun was never anywhere near contact with Kennedy's head. "We're talking several . . . several feet," he asserted. Burns said it might have been as many as six feet. The crime was reenacted in his spacious office using the authors and chairs as stand-ins for the principals. Burns positioned "the gun" three to four feet from "Kennedy's head." He was extremely confident that his positioning of the stand-ins and the distance it created was accurate.

Waiter Martin Patrusky was three to four feet from Kennedy. He asserted that the gun never got closer than three feet. Busboy Juan Romero told authorities the weapon was "approximately one yard from the senator's head." Jesus Perez, who spoke at the trial through an interpreter, was never asked about firing distance.

Beyond the "five best" witnesses, newspaper reporter Pete Hamill placed the gun at least two feet from the senator. Kennedy volunteer Valerie Shulte said it was six feet away. Assistant maître d' Edward Minasian placed the barrel three feet from Kennedy. Vincent DiPierro told the grand jury the gun was four to six feet away. Lisa Urso told the authors that the gun was "three to six feet" from Kennedy.

TV producer Richard Lubic was walking behind and to the right of Uecker. "Sirhan's gun was two to three feet from Kennedy's head," Lubic insisted in a 1975 interview. "It is nonsense to say that he fired bullets into

Senator Kennedy from a distance of one to two inches, since his gun was never anywhere that near to Senator Kennedy."[3]

The only witness to place the gun within a foot of Kennedy was *Los Angeles Times* photographer Boris Yaro. Yaro, however, had observed the shooting through his camera lens—although not taking pictures. "The senator and the assailant," Yaro told the FBI two days after the shooting, "were little more than silhouettes."

This fundamental conflict between the eyewitness accounts and the physical evidence was not addressed at the Sirhan grand jury proceeding or the trial. Los Angeles officials would later try to make it disappear by misrepresenting the eyewitness evidence to an unsuspecting public which had no access to the case files. In December of 1974, Los Angeles district attorney Joseph P. Busch was interviewed by Tom Snyder on NBC-TV's *Tomorrow* show, along with former congressman Allard K. Lowenstein:

> SNYDER: The eyewitness testimony does not seem to match up with the coroner's report that the gun that fired the shot was an inch or maybe two inches away from Kennedy's head but no eyewitness can place it closer than eighteen. How would you account for that seeming discrepancy?
>
> BUSCH: Well, that's not true. It was point-blank, right into the right ear of the senator. The gun was right there. The bullet that killed him entered right there, and we can show it.
>
> LOWENSTEIN: Now who has said that they saw it? Just name one witness that said they saw a gun, point-blank, fired into Senator Kennedy's ear? Tell us one.
>
> BUSCH: Would you like Mr. Uecker, the man that grabbed his arm? Would you like any of the fifty-five witnesses?
>
> LOWENSTEIN: Yes, Mr. Busch, I would, because Mr. Uecker swears that it was two feet.
>
> BUSCH: Oh, come on, Mr. Lowenstein.

In addition to the problem of distance there are three ancillary discrepancies. One has to do with Kennedy's position in relation to Sirhan, another with the angle of the shots that struck him, and a third with the sequence of shots as reported by the witnesses.

A year after Sirhan's trial, criminalist William W. Harper, on behalf of the Sirhan appeals lawyers, made his own review of the ballistic evidence. After examining the evidence bullets, the autopsy report, and the police trajectory diagrams, Harper swore to an affidavit containing his conclusions. Harper's principal finding was that Robert Kennedy "was fired upon from two distinct firing positions":

Firing Position A, the position of Sirhan, was located directly in front of the Senator, with Sirhan face to face with the Senator. This position is established by more than a dozen eyewitnesses. A second firing position, Firing Position B, is clearly established by the autopsy report. It was located in close proximity to the Senator, immediately to his right and rear. It was from this position that 4 (four) shots were fired, three of which entered the Senator's body. . . . It is extremely unlikely that any of the bullets fired by Sirhan's gun ever struck the body of Robert Kennedy.

The body orientation of Robert Kennedy in relation to Sirhan at the time of the shooting is not as certain as either the police or their critics would like. The autopsy revealed that Robert Kennedy was wounded in the right back. According to the witnesses Kennedy was either walking toward Sirhan when he was shot or was turned leftward shaking hands when the shooting began. The police maintain that Kennedy turned more than 90 degrees when he stopped to shake hands and was thus presenting his back to Sirhan. Many witnesses disagree with this positioning. One clear description is contained in a 1975 statement by Martin Patrusky, who was only feet away from Kennedy when he was shot: "I saw the man, who turned out to be Sirhan, firing at Kennedy. Kennedy's back was not facing Sirhan. Sirhan was slightly to the right front of Kennedy."[4]

If the witnesses who place Kennedy facing Sirhan or turned at a much milder angle are correct, then a significant front/back problem compounds the already described distance riddle. There are other problems.

According to the autopsy all the wound tracks were upward: the Kennedy head wound was at a mild 15 degrees off the horizontal, but the three back shots were described as at steep 59, 67, and 80 degrees, as though a gun had been pressed to the senator's back and pointed up so as not to protrude. In contrast, Sirhan was said to have fired with his gun parallel to the floor. Even if one were to attempt to solve the distance problem by imagining an unperceived lunge at the senator, it would be difficult to then simulate the steep upward track of these bullets.

Just how difficult was described by criminalist William Harper. In 1971 Harper visited Dr. Thomas Noguchi in the presence of an unnamed investigator from the DA's office. Harper asked the investigator to reproduce Sirhan's firing stance to achieve the recorded wounds in Robert Kennedy.

"Using Dr. Noguchi as a model," Harper reported, "the DA's investigator placed himself in a position almost beyond belief. The position reminded me of something between Rudolf Nureyev performing the *pas de deux* and the shooting stance of a left-handed detective friend of mine when shooting right-handed around the front left corner of a simulated building in the FBI Combat Course."[5]

The sequence of shots poses a more difficult problem. Recall that Kennedy was wounded three times from behind, with a fourth bullet passing through his coat—all of these shots at very close range. Yet, Uecker told the grand jury he grabbed Sirhan's gun hand after the second shot and deflected it away from Senator Kennedy. This was corroborated by Edward Minasian's grand jury testimony. He described how Uecker had slammed Sirhan's hand down onto the steam table. He was asked about the shots from Sirhan's gun that were fired after his arm was deflected:

> Q: Were those shots fired in the general direction of the senator?
> A: I doubt it because the senator at that time was—well, the suspect was shooting from this approximately this point . . . at the end of the table. And when the senator fell, he fell in this area right here on an angle. . . . [W]e had him and his arm was somewhere on this steam table here. And I doubt if it was in the same direction as the first two shots.

Even if the distance, position, and angle discrepancies are magically solved or ignored, if Sirhan's gun were deflected away from Robert Kennedy after the second shot, then the weapon could not have inflicted four "point-blank" hits on the senator from behind. Is it possible that Uecker and Minasian are mistaken about the shot sequence? Consider the relevant testimony at Sirhan's trial by the crime-scene witnesses:

> JACK GALLIVAN: I heard a series of shots, maybe two, then a pause and the rest. . . .
> MARTIN PATRUSKY: All of a sudden there was like a firecracker going off; then there was another; then there was a pause. Then all of a sudden there was rapid fire.
> RAFER JOHNSON: I thought it was a balloon going off, two poppings and then I looked in that direction and I heard some other popping. . . .
> ANGELO DIPIERRO: I heard the shot. . . . I thought it was a prank or something . . . then a volley of shots . . .
> VINCENT DIPIERRO: [In response to question about when Uecker grabbed gun] I believe it was the second or third shot.
> JUAN ROMERO: He [Sirhan] put his arm like that and he shot two shots . . .
> IRWIN STROLL: The procession stopped and then there was one pop . . .
> IRA GOLDSTEIN: There were about two of them at first . . .
> BORIS YARO [to the FBI]: I heard what I thought were two explosions.

This collective testimony stands in stark contrast to prosecutor Fitts's opening statement, that Sirhan had put a gun "to the very vicinity of the senator's head and at point-blank range in rapid succession fired eight shots." Despite this conflict, which casts serious doubt on whether his client had actually fired the bullets into Robert Kennedy, Grant Cooper made no move to try to justify these accounts with the police version of the crime.

Anticipating possible questions at the trial, however, the Los Angeles police did make a number of attempts at filmed reconstruction of the crime, using actual participants. Over the years, law enforcement officials referred to their filmed reenactments of the assassination, stating or implying that these validated the official version by showing how Sirhan inflicted Kennedy's wounds as described by the autopsy report.

In 1973 former congressman Allard K. Lowenstein raised questions with Los Angeles authorities concerning Karl Uecker's testimony that he had blocked Sirhan from getting his gun point-blank to Kennedy. Lowenstein was shown a photograph said to be of the official reconstruction of the crime. In it, Uecker was standing like a department-store mannequin instead of wrestling with Sirhan, and the gun was so close it almost touched the head of the officer portraying Kennedy. This, Lowenstein was told, proved that Uecker's account supported the official version. Later, when Lowenstein tracked down Uecker, the former maître d' called the reenactment "phony," saying that the authorities told him specifically to pose in this manner even though he protested that his positioning and that of Sirhan's gun were inaccurate.

Despite repeated requests for their release by researchers, the filmed police reenactments were never made public. Then in 1986 they were accidentally made available to researcher Gregory Stone. They had been recorded at the Ambassador Hotel crime scene on November 12 to 15, 1968. Some takes used the actual witnesses and shooting victims. Other versions used law enforcement personnel in all of the roles. The film is poor quality: the motion is jerky and shadows obscure the second series of takes.

When the authors analyzed these long-suppressed films, it was very obvious why they were never released. In spite of the creative efforts of the officials, the reenactments failed to re-create the crime as described by the best evidence. To validate the official version, Sirhan must get the gun point-blank behind the senator's right ear. He must inflict three wounds and a suit-coat shot at an upward, leftward angle. This must be done before Uecker deflects his gun away from Kennedy.

In the series in which Uecker participates, he acts out his consistent account well. He blocks Sirhan against the steam table and prevents him from getting behind Kennedy. The front/rear problem is well illustrated. Before Uecker's intervention, Sirhan fires at the senator's right temple, holding the gun level. The weapon is never behind the ear at an upward angle. RFK's shoulder wounds are never simulated. Three to four shots are fired at the head.

In the second series, without Uecker, more liberties are taken. Sirhan is allowed to push aside the Uecker stand-in as if the maître d' was not actively resisting. The gun gets very close to Kennedy while the senator turns his back to Sirhan—something disputed by many witnesses. With all this creative license the actors are able to solve the distance and orientation problems, but the angle and sequence problems remain.

A third series of takes has Sirhan five feet in front of Kennedy, again firing shoulder level parallel to the floor. It simulates nothing relating to the known data.

In terms of evidence preservation, it would seem that official reenactments would be an important part of the case record, even if not introduced at the trial. Not so. The films have disappeared from official files. When the LAPD released its file in 1988 there were no copies of the film. Repeated requests to the DA's office brought the response that it too had no such films. Fortunately, the bootleg second-and third-generation copies reside at the California State Archives, the University of Massachusetts RFK Assassination Archives, and the authors' basements.

Despite the many discrepancies between the physical evidence and the witness statements, none of it would be anything more than curiosity if it could be scientifically proven, beyond all reasonable doubt, that all the bullets recovered from the victims came from Sirhan's gun. Under the direction of Deputy District Attorney David Fitts, this is exactly what Wolfer tried to do from the witness stand.

"I direct your attention to this envelope which is People's 55," said Fitts, "and it bears certain writing, perhaps from your hand. What does it contain?"

"It contains three of the test shots that I took from People's 6, the weapon," replied Wolfer, "and this was from the water recovery tank, and that would be three test shots I used for comparison purposes. . . . Looking at the scratches under the comparison microscope and the lands and grooves of this test bullet, I can say that they were fired from this gun and no other gun, and that is what I attempted to do with each of the exhibits."

"In other words, it is somewhat analogous to fingerprints. No individual or two individuals have identical fingerprints, no two guns leave the same striations on the projectiles that are being expelled by them."

"That is correct."

Fitts's analogy is a good first step in understanding bullet striation analysis, but striations differ from fingerprints in that they are not quite so unique. They are also difficult to read, even with a comparison microscope, as Sir Gerald Burrard contends in his book, *The Identification of Firearms and Forensic Ballistics.* Burrard warns his readers not to trust unsupported ballistic comparison testimony:

> Mere assertions by some investigator, no matter how great his reputation as an expert, should be regarded with extreme caution. . . . The most ridiculous claims have been put forward on behalf of the comparison microscope, and there is a danger that the mere fact of its possession may endow a witness with all sorts of imaginary skill and knowledge, at least in the eyes of the jury and public. . . . If, therefore, the evidence is unsupported by photographs which clearly tell their own story, that evidence should be regarded with suspicion.[6]

At Sirhan's trial DeWayne Wolfer claimed that he made a match between all the victim's bullets and those test-fired from Sirhan's gun. The bullets, Wolfer claimed, "were placed under a comparison microscope, and based upon the striation comparison of the bullets from my test to those of the evidence bullets, . . . I am able to say [they were] fired from that gun."

Wolfer's testimony, however, was conspicuously lacking in any supporting documentation. According to Burrard, this should have kindled suspicion in the defense attorneys. It did not. The lack of supporting evidence did attract the notice of independent firearms expert Lowell Bradford, who, a few years later in a court petition, would attack Wolfer for his naked presentation at Sirhan's trial. Bradford charged that Wolfer offered "no examiner's notes, no pretrial discovery information, no demonstrative exhibits, no explanation of exact examination methodology used in the case, no statement of the basis for the opinions rendered that give an indication of identification."[7]

Uncontested at the trial, Wolfer's testimony would close the case against Sirhan, as far as any doubt about who fired the bullets that struck Robert Kennedy. But Wolfer's analysis would be challenged in a series of hearings and official investigations which would occur during the next decade.

In 1971, two years after his testimony at the Sirhan trial, DeWayne Wolfer became a candidate for appointment as chief forensic chemist of the Los Angeles Police Department, the director of the entire crime laboratory. Learning of this development, Los Angeles attorney Barbara Warner Blehr filed a civil-service action to block Wolfer's appointment, on the grounds that he was "completely unqualified for the position."

Blehr's suit not only faulted Wolfer's work on the Sirhan case, but cited two other cases as well, relying on evidence developed by William Harper and other criminalists (including a former head of the LAPD crime laboratory). Listing a number of basic precepts of firearms identification, Blehr then documented instances in which Wolfer had not adhered to them, concluding that "these violations were made in response to an overzealous desire to help the cause of the prosecution."

In Board of Inquiry hearings that followed Blehr's challenge, Wolfer angrily defended himself. "I have never in my life been approached to change opinions or go for the prosecution" he said. "I call them as I see them." Chief of Police Ed Davis agreed with the besieged criminalist, calling Blehr's charges a "vendetta." "In my estimation," said Davis, "Mr. Wolfer is the top expert in the country."[8]

The action by Blehr precipitated considerable controversy, both about Wolfer and about the official conclusions in the Sirhan case. Investigations were launched by both LAPD and the district attorney's office. A grand jury investigation probed the integrity of the exhibits in the Sirhan case. And Wolfer sued Blehr for $2 million. The court dismissed the suit, ruling that Blehr's letter was a public document and thus immune from libel action.

An example of how one of Wolfer's professional peers viewed his credibility is contained in a 1971 letter written by Marshall Houts, a former FBI agent and expert in legal medicine, who served as editor in chief of *Trauma* magazine, which dealt with issues of forensic science. On June 26, Houts wrote to his friend Evelle Younger, who had prosecuted Sirhan and had since become attorney general for the state of California, to warn him about Wolfer's impending promotion:

> Dear Ev,
>
> This is an elaboration of our discussion last night at Bob Fullerton's.
>
> As I indicated then I have no personal interest in this matter, but do have a deep academic and professional concern over Wolfer's horrendous blunders in the past and those he will commit in the future if he continues on his present assignment. I am also concerned that you and the present District Attorney stand a strong chance of getting burned by Wolfer's misdirected hyperenthusiastic procedures and testimony. . . .
>
> Wolfer suffers from a great inferiority complex for which he compensates by giving the police exactly what they need to obtain a conviction. He casts objectivity to the winds and violates every basic tenet of forensic science and proof by becoming a crusading advocate. This is rationalized as being entirely legitimate since the accused is guilty anyway which makes the social objective worthy of the means to obtain it. . . .
>
> Unfortunately, there are many Wolfers in this broad area of fo-

rensic science. There are no minimum standards for employment (except in a comparatively few of the larger crime laboratories in the country) which means that a poorly trained man without experience or integrity can set himself up as an "expert" and he is off and running. There is also no denying one of the basic facts of life in the law enforcement field: the pressures on the criminalist by the police arm to give them what they need to make their cases is substantial.

I will not elaborate on the details of the three cases under consideration by the civil service board (Sirhan, Kirschke, and Terry) other than to say that the real experts of integrity who have examined portions or all of the evidence are appalled at what Wolfer did. . . .

Sincerely yours,

Marshall Houts

In October 1971, the results of the police and district attorney's investigations were made public almost simultaneously. Both endorsed Wolfer's expertise, attributing certain key discrepancies to "clerical errors," thereby clearing the way for his appointment. Despite Houts's scathing indictment and others like it, DeWayne Wolfer was given his appointment as forensic czar of the LAPD. But Marshall Houts's prediction that Wolfer would become an embarrassment would prove accurate. Four years later, in 1975, two separate legal battles would produce a resounding rejection of Wolfer's methods and a refutation of his key testimony at the Sirhan trial.

In the summer of 1975, shooting victim Paul Schrade filed several legal actions relating to the assassination. He had firm legal status as an injured party in the shooting that took his friend's life. In one of these actions Godfrey Isaac, representing Sirhan, got to question DeWayne Wolfer in front of superior court judge Robert Wenke.

Isaac was interested in Wolfer's account of his test bullets. Under his questioning Wolfer admitted that he had stored the bullets in an unmarked envelope in his desk drawer for nine months. Isaac asked why. Wolfer responded that he did it for security reasons, "because under the circumstances I knew which was Sirhan's and no one else did."

"Was it common procedure," asked Isaac, "for you to put test bullets into your desk drawer rather than somewhere else within the LAPD?"

"Oh, I would say probably not," replied Wolfer, "it would not be common procedure. . . ."

"May I see the evidence envelope that has your handwriting on it?" asked Isaac. He was handed the very same envelope that Fitts had introduced into evidence at Sirhan's trial. "Were bullets #55 in that envelope?"

"I would assume they were," replied Wolfer with hesitation. "I have no way of telling you positively if they were in the trial in this envelope. I would assume they were. I don't know. I can't tell you."

"Do you recognize the handwriting on this envelope?"

"Yes, this is probably my handwriting. Looks like it. It appears to be."

"Showing you down where it has 'Make: I and J.' That stands for Iver and Johnson?"

"That is correct."

"And below that the number H 18602. Is that number in your handwriting?"

"Yes, it is, but that is an incorrect number."

Incorrect indeed. The revolver taken from Sirhan had the serial number H 53725, but the bullets that were used for comparison and which established that the victims were shot "by this gun and no other" were marked as being from H 18602, another Iver Johnson Cadet model that the police were using for other test purposes. This discrepancy went unnoticed at Sirhan's trial. William Harper discovered it after the trial was over.

"When you put the H 18602 on that envelope," asked Isaac, "did you believe that was the number of the gun from which the bullets contained therein were fired?"

"Well now, I don't know what you mean by that particular statement."

"Why did you put H 18602 on the envelope?"

"Because I asked a person for the number of the gun in the case of Sirhan; that was the number he repeated to me. I assumed that was the Sirhan gun and wrote those numbers down. . . ."

"From whom did you ask the number?"

"Here, today, I wouldn't recall."

H 18602, like Sirhan's gun, was an Iver Johnson Cadet model .22 caliber revolver. According to Wolfer's reports, it was used for muzzle-distance tests on June 11, 1968, and for sound-level tests at the Ambassador Hotel on June 20. If H 18602 were really the source the bullets in the envelope, Wolfer's test results would have to be a complete fabrication. If Wolfer mislabeled the envelope, as he maintained, other questions arise. According to a 1974 DA's office memo assessing the incident,

> It is difficult to rely upon an individual's microscopic comparison of bullets, an obviously sophisticated task, if that same person erroneously marks an evidence envelope in a matter of historical significance.[9]

Test-firing H 18602 and comparing the recovered bullets with the test bullets in People's exhibit number 55 would have been one way to determine what had occurred here. Was that possible? During his testimony DeWayne Wolfer would assert that the test gun was still available, but an official police record indicated that it had been destroyed in July 1968—seven months before Sirhan's trial. In 1971, the record was "corrected" to show that the gun had been destroyed not in July of 1968, but in July of 1969.

During the hearing in front of Judge Wenke, Wolfer was also questioned by attorney Howard J. Privett, who was representing CBS (a copetitioner with Schrade). Privett asked Wolfer if he had taken any photographs of bullets durings his ballistic work.

"The record so indicates," answered Wolfer, "that there is an indication that there was one set of photographs taken, that could well have been taken by me. . . ."

"Will you tell us, then, when and under what circumstances two photomicrographs, that you believe were taken, were taken?"

"Well, I have to go back a ways. It wasn't—these photographs did not come to my attention until approximately a year ago when certain records were brought to me in the laboratory, and asked did I want these records. In these records, there was two photomicrographs of comparison of two bullets, under comparison microscope. Approximately a year ago this was brought to my attention, and I went to Jimmy Watson and he identified the two bullets, and he said that I was the one that photographed these to the best of my recollection today."

The photomicrograph, as it was called, represented one of the few pieces of documentation of Wolfer's scientific analysis, but it had not been introduced at Sirhan's trial. Wolfer's story here was not one to inspire confidence. According to the LAPD criminalist, he was not aware of the photograph until certain evidence in the Sirhan case was presumably about to be disposed of in 1974. At that time he went to another officer and that officer told him what the bullets were and told him that he had taken the photograph.

"Were those photographs that you have just identified," asked Privett, "are those marked either by exhibit number or item number, the bullets of which they represent?"

"No," answered Wolfer, "they merely indicate the fact that they are Kennedy bullets. So this would indicate to me by the fact that they are Kennedy bullets, one is Kennedy and one is one of my test shots."

"Does the photomicrograph indicate which one is the Kennedy and which is the test shot?"

"No, it does not."

"And so by looking at either the negatives or the prints or the jacket in which they are contained it is not possible to determine which photomicrograph represents a picture of the Kennedy bullet and which represents a test bullet?"

"That is correct."

The admission that the bullets photographed were not even labeled as to which was which was another indictment of Wolfer's supposed scientific method. But this was only the first of several damaging revelations regarding this particular evidence.

When the police files were opened in 1988 there was discovered a curious undated, unsigned memo concerning the photomicrograph in question. The document stated:

> There exists a photograph of the Kennedy bullet and a test bullet taken through a comparison microscope. . . . The existence of this photograph is believed to be unknown by anyone outside of this Department. It should be effective rebuttal evidence should this case ever be retried. However, the release of this information at this time would be susceptible to criticism because lay people would in all probability have difficulty deciphering the photograph. The issue of its not being revealed at an earlier time may further make its authenticity suspect, particularly to the avid, exact assassination buff.

The siege mentality in this document is all too apparent. The reasons why the police were not eager to have the photomicrograph released would become manifest only later. In October of 1975 a panel of seven forensic experts concluded that the photo was not as represented: that is, it was not of the Kennedy neck bullet (exhibit 47) and one of the test bullets (exhibit 55), as Wolfer and the memo contended, but of the Kennedy bullet and the bullet from victim Goldstein (exhibit 52).

Was this mistake another example of "clerical error"? Was it deliberate? What, if anything, among the ballistic evidence could be relied upon?

In 1974 Deputy DA Dinko Bozanich wrote a forty-page memorandum to District Attorney Joseph Busch regarding the proposed examination of the Sirhan ballistic evidence by a panel of independent experts. The purpose of the memo was to evaluate "the present integrity or utility of the Sirhan firearms exhibits" and what risks there might be in having them examined. "The focal point of such an evaluation," stated Bozanich, "is predominantly the image of this office which is projected to the public, rather than any concern for the efficacy of Sirhan's conviction or the proved conclusion that one man acted alone in killing Kennedy."[10]

The Bozanich memo claimed that the allegation that the ballistic evidence suggests two guns "coincides with the precise area where this office is at a disadvantage because of doubts regarding the present integrity of the Sirhan exhibits and the lack of secondary evidence in the form of police photographs."[11] "Wolfer never had any photographic reproductions prepared of the evidence and test bullets used in his microscopic comparisons during the Sirhan investigation."[12]

Toward the end of the memo Bozanich concluded:

> As this office knows a refiring of Sirhan's gun at this date would not necessarily produce bullets with the same individual characteristics as those actually used by Wolfer during the Sirhan investigation. . . . Rather, the likelihood of inconclusive results is substantial, aside from the realistic possibility that a refiring of Sirhan's gun would produce sufficient differences in striations to conclude that the Sirhan bullet exhibits were not fired by Sirhan's gun.[13]

As part of its defensive posture in this matter, the district attorney's office would assert that some of the Sirhan ballistic evidence had been tampered with, or bullets substituted, when certain outside parties had gained access to it in 1971. One internal DA's office memo marked "CONFIDENTIAL" and titled "Theory Behind Present Attempt to Discredit Wolfer" claimed:

> The tampering of the Sirhan evidence could have resulted in three possible ways. First, [journalist Theodore] CHARACH, who had access to the exhibits 17 times, could have tampered with it. . . . Second, [criminalist William] HARPER could have done it, since he saw the exhibits 7 times. He is also a representative for HYCON, which is developing a new type of camera for ballistics work. If HARPER could utilize this camera to prove the two-gun theory, it would personally enhance him and promote sales of the HYCON COMPANY. Third, people who had a vested interest in the Black Panther cases could have tampered with the evidence, knowing there was a movement to discredit Wolfer, which of course could affect coming cases of Panthers.[14]

As if the offered range of possible motives for switching bullets was not broad enough, in the following paragraph of the memo an additional motive for tampering with the Sirhan evidence was put forward:

> If the American public was satisfied that there was a grand design to eliminate the Kennedy family, there would be great public sympathy towards Ted Kennedy and the liberal Democrats.

On May 27, 1996, the present attorney for Sirhan Sirhan, Lawrence Teeter, wrote a letter to LAPD chief Willie Williams. In the letter Teeter maintained that he (in connection with Sirhan case researcher Rose Lynn Mangan) had "unearthed substantial evidence concerning the substitution of and tampering with bullets in the Sirhan case." One of Teeter's citations read:

> Dr. Noguchi's autopsy report states that when a bullet was removed from the vicinity of Robert Kennedy's sixth cervical vertebrae, Dr. Noguchi inscribed "TN31" on the base of that bullet. That bullet later became People's Exhibit 47. However, the bullets were later examined by a court-appointed panel of seven firearms experts in 1975. At that time, the examiner who looked at the bases of the bullets noted that People's 47 contained the designation "DWTN" on the base. The fact that LAPD firearms expert DeWayne Wolfer ("DW") confirmed in 1975 that the bullets in the court's custody were the same ones he had examined in 1968 strongly suggests that the substitution of a stand-in neck bullet in place of the original took place prior to the trial.

The claims of evidence tampering and bullet switching have come full circle. Both sides in the Sirhan case have made serious charges against the other. As a result, what should be the most reliable evidence in the case, the bullets themselves, are now of very diminished value. The careful handling and documenting of this evidence by a trained and diligent forensic expert could have served to prove or disprove subsequent claims of tampering. Absent such demonstrated competence, the authors must agree with Deputy DA Bozanich that "there is substantial question as to whether or not the Sirhan exhibits have been effectively preserved."[15]

In 1975, despite the opposition of the district attorney, as part of the action initiated by Paul Schrade, CBS News, and four other plaintiffs, Judge Robert Wenke ordered an independent panel to examine the Sirhan firearms evidence. The seven experts were jointly agreed upon by the plaintiffs and the defendants (the DA's office and the California State attorney general's office). The court issued a narrow mandate for the panel: it would examine the gun and bullets, but it was not to investigate bullet trajectories, eyewitness data, or the issue of possible extra bullets in the pantry ceiling and doorframe.

After two weeks of analysis, the forensic panel delivered its report to Judge Wenke. In one of its key findings the panel reported: "It cannot be concluded that Exhibits 47 [nonfatal Kennedy], 52 [Goldstein], and 54 [Weisel] were fired from the Sirhan revolver. The reasons for this are that there are insufficient corresponding individual characteristics to make an identification."

★   ★   ★

The panel also found that they were unable to conclude that a second gun was involved. The issue, in other words, was still very much open. But DeWayne Wolfer had testified at Sirhan's trial that with his microscope he had managed to do what the seven forensic experts had been unable to do—conclude scientifically that the Goldstein, Weisel, and Kennedy bullets all came from Sirhan's gun and no other. Panelist Lowell Bradford stated:

> The examination results contradict the original identification made at the trial of Sirhan B. Sirhan in that there is no basis for an identification of any of the victim bullets through the classical process of microscopically comparing them with test bullets. . . .

Judge Wenke's forensic panel delivered their findings in a courtroom packed with reporters. What should have been a landmark event in the pursuit of historical truth in the Robert Kennedy case turned out to be an example of the media's unwillingness or inability to get beyond superficial impressions and the official spin.

The distortion resulted partly from the order in which the panel presented its findings. First up was the announcement that there was no evidence that a second gun was fired. The media had their headline, and the race was on to be the first to report it, not to discover its context or its more complex meaning. They rushed from the courtroom to call in their stories:

"7 Experts Say RFK Slain by Single Firearm" (Associated Press)

"RFK Second-Gun Theory Ruled Out" (United Press International)

"No Second Gun in Kennedy Assassination, Panel Says" (*Los Angeles Times*)

"One Gun Killed Bobby: Experts" (*New York Daily News*)

This wave of case-closed headlines created the perception that, finally, the issues in the RFK case were settled—one gun, once and for all. Neither the public nor the media would perceive the gross inaccuracy. In reality, not one of the seven experts ruled out the possibility of a second gun (each wrote an individual report accompanying the collective one).

In response to the media coverage of the firearms panel, panelist Lowell Bradford issued the following statement:

The findings of the firearms examiners is being improperly interpreted by the news media.

1. The examiners found that the Sirhan gun *cannot* [emphasis Bradford's] be identified with the bullets from the crime scene.

2. The firearms evidence does not in and of itself establish a basis for a two gun proposition; likewise, this same proposition, on a basis of other evidence, is not precluded either.

Bradford would go on to recommend the examination of other evidence including "witnesses' statements that another gun was fired," "bullet pathways," and "evidence of more than eight bullets fired." This evidence, Bradford contended, deserved "the same kind of consideration and systematic analysis" as had been given the bullets.

Brushing aside Bradford's statement, Los Angeles authorities were quick to claim victory. "After years of unwarranted attacks on Criminalist DeWayne Wolfer," said LAPD chief Ed Davis, "his integrity and professional excellence have been vindicated."[16] "It will be gratifying to LAPD criminalist DeWayne Wolfer," crowed city attorney Dion Morrow, "that his professional judgment and the quality of his work have been upheld." Morrow termed the panel report "a complete vindication of LAPD's ballistic work in the RFK case."[17]

The reprieve granted to DeWayne Wolfer's professional reputation following the firearms panel report would last only a few months. In December of the same year, the Jack Kirschke murder case came up for review by the California State Court of Appeal. (Ironically, this was the case Sirhan had discussed with his captors hours after the assassination.) During these proceedings, a three-judge panel censured the police criminalist for his testimony in the original trial. Wolfer had testified that enlarged photographs of bullets backed up his ballistic opinion, but the three-judge panel found that they didn't.

The appellate court, however, was most upset about Wolfer's other findings. "Unquestionably, Wolfer's opinion testimony on acoustics and anatomy was negligently false," wrote Justice Robert S. Thompson. "His testimony of his educational qualifications borders on perjury and is, at least, given with reckless disregard for the truth."[18]

In 1977 Wolfer would receive another rebuke by way of a reinvestigation of the assassination sponsored by the district attorney's office. The probe, run by special counsel Thomas Kranz, tried very hard to minimize the evidentiary discrepancies in the case and to praise the police work done in the investigation. Still, the *Kranz Report* was forced to admit to what it termed "the woeful lack of evidence reports and documentation concerning previous ballistics examination and trajectory studies, which had become evident during the examination of DeWayne Wolfer."[19] The report would continue:

> In light of the inability of Wolfer or other LAPD officials to produce substantial written documents, analyzed evidence reports or pertinent information regarding Wolfer's 1968 ballistics tests, his log report and laboratory work, it must be concluded that Wolfer is responsible for the sketchy and insufficient analysis or, if extensive reports and documents were prepared, Wolfer was negligent in permitting such reports and documents to be destroyed.[20]

The *Kranz Report* then went on to discuss missing tests reportedly performed upon the destroyed ceiling tiles.

> It appears that even in discussion between the LAPD Crime Laboratory and the District Attorney's Office prior to the trial, the reports of these x-rays and photographs were not given to the prosecution team. The explanation by the LAPD that these photographs and analysis "proved nothing," reflects the lack of judgment by the LAPD in fully co-operating with the prosecuting office. Even though it was anticipated that defense counsels' argument would center on diminished capacity at the trial, the fact that the actual murder bullet, People's #48, had been so badly damaged and fragmented and could not be linked to the murder weapon, necessitated a much more thorough, definitive, and complete documentation of ballistics, firearms and trajectory studies. The failure to do so reflects on the entire prosecution.[21]

In May 1980, DeWayne Wolfer would be back in the news again. "LAPD Suspends Forensic Chemist" was the headline in the *Los Angeles Times*. The story by Myrna Oliver read:

> The Los Angeles Police Department has suspended its chief forensic chemist and one subordinate, reprimanded another, and ordered six more to face a Board of Rights hearing concerning their work for the Department's Scientific Investigation Division, the *Times* learned Friday.
> DeWayne Wolfer, head of the Scientific Investigation Division, was suspended by Police Chief Daryl Gates, May 23 for 30 working days without pay. Internal affairs investigators determined that Wolfer had failed to provide proper storage and analysis of bullets and other evidence and had improperly supervised firearms and explosives investigators. . . .

Oliver reported that Wolfer had become "widely known for his forensic work," but that he had also become a figure of controversy. She noted that a district attorney's inquiry in 1971 had "cleared him of any wrongdoing" in the Sirhan case, but that in 1975, the California Court of Appeals "concluded that Wolfer gave false testimony bordering on perjury in the 1967 murder trial of former Deputy District Attorney Jack Kirschke."[22] Had Grant Cooper been brave and inquisitive, his questioning of Wolfer might have begun to unravel the knot of mysteries at the core of the case.

In the testimony of DeWayne Wolfer at the trial of Sirhan Sirhan, Grant Cooper had the makings of a stunning cross-examination. Had Cooper been properly prudent, William Harper (or another private forensic expert) would have been seated at the defense table advising him.

Cooper might have asked Wolfer what caused him to be photographed pointing to bullet holes in the walls which he now said weren't genuine? What tests had Wolfer conducted to establish that the holes were caused by dish trays? Why were the doorframes removed and booked as evidence if they contained no bullet holes? Why were they to be subjected to trajectory analysis? How could Sirhan have shot Kennedy in the back when he was observed by many witnesses to be in front of the senator, and how could all four shots have been point-blank when most witnesses said the defendant fired only two shots before his gun was deflected? How could a bullet traveling at a sharp upward angle turn and enter Paul Schrade's head? How could bullets which were identified as having come from a pistol other than Sirhan's be used for firearms comparison purposes? And why was this evidence kept for nine months in Wolfer's desk drawer?

Cooper might also have demanded certain evidence. The doorframes and ceiling tiles were allegedly in existence at that time and should have been produced. Cooper could have demanded to see the results of the tests supposedly done upon them. The defense attorney could have run his own tests on the victims' bullets as well as on the enigmatic spent bullets allegedly found in Sirhan's car. He could have demanded to see the scientific backup for Wolfer's conclusion of a bullet match. He could have inspected the photomicrograph, and, with expertise of a forensic adviser, determined that it was not as the police represented.

But Grant Cooper was not in a combative mode when he rose to cross-examine DeWayne Wolfer. Quite the opposite.

"Officer Wolfer," began Cooper, "let me ask you what time are you leaving?" DeWayne Wolfer had an out-of-town professional commitment the following day, and Grant Cooper wanted to be sure not to inconvenience the criminalist.

"When we get through," replied Wolfer. "Then I will go over and make my reservation for the first flight I can get on."

"We won't keep you," reassured Cooper.

Cooper then went on to ask several questions with no apparent purpose. Was the revolver used for test purposes still available? Wolfer responded that it was (although police documents would indicate that it wasn't). Cooper then asked Wolfer about any margins of error he might have built into his calculations of firing distance. In a very tangled reply Wolfer asserted that he took his findings of distance and doubled them to create a tolerance for error.

But Grant Cooper had his own solution to the distance riddle. As will be seen later, the defense attorney seemed to have a recurring desire to clean up messy evidentiary situations as the trial progressed. Logically, these messes should have been the worry of the prosecution, but Cooper didn't like them. Sounding more like the prosecution on redirect than the defense on cross-examination, Cooper applied his own logic to dismiss the conflicts in the evidence concerning gun-muzzle distance.

"Let me ask you this," said Cooper, referring to Sirhan's .22 caliber revolver. "With your experience of firearms . . . a weapon like this can cause death, and it did cause death, is that true?"

"Yes," said Wolfer.

"And it can cause death from one inch, two inches, three inches, six inches, one foot, three feet, six feet. . . . It could cause death if it were in the right place?"

"Yes."

And that was the cross-examination of DeWayne Wolfer. According to Grant Cooper, any questions about firing distance were irrelevant: a .22 caliber revolver could kill if it were fired from a distance of one inch or six feet.

DeWayne Wolfer could have been on the witness stand for the rest of the week answering questions and defending his testimony. Instead, he made his flight that afternoon.

SEVEN

Missing Persons

✸ ✸ ✸

I am . . . perplexed as to why the police department and the District Attorney's Office "abstracted from the file" some materials pertaining to their assessments of various witnesses with whom they conducted interviews and why some items of investigation were regarded too secret that they were barred from anyone, except the District Attorney, the F.B.I. and the Los Angeles Police Department. . . . This appears to me as a colossal violation of the Constitutional and statutory rights of the accused.

—Sirhan defense attorney Grant Cooper, May 1969

O N T H E A F T E R N O O N following the shooting of Robert Kennedy the Los Angeles police found Sirhan's pink-and-white 1956 DeSoto Fireflight illegally parked on New Hampshire Street, just a few blocks from the Ambassador Hotel. In the glove compartment was Sirhan's wallet. Also in the car were some matchbooks from Shakey's Pizza Parlor, a raffle ticket, and a book titled *The Divine Art of Healing* by Manley Palmer Hall. Most ominous, though, was a sales receipt for $3.99 from the Lock, Stock 'n' Barrel for .22 caliber ammunition dated June 1, 1968.

The receipt had been issued by Larry Arnot, a retired Pasadena fireman who was working the shop's counter that day. When the police questioned Arnot, he told them that sometime in the afternoon of June 1 three men, including one whom he identified as Sirhan, walked into his store. Sirhan, he recalled, bought two boxes of .22 caliber hollow-point Mini-Mag ammunition. One of the other men bought two boxes of Super-X Westerns. The four boxes of bullets were put on the same receipt.

Perhaps disturbed by his story, the police asked Arnot to submit to a polygraph examination. Arnot consented and the test took place. Apparently satisfied that any open questions had been resolved, prosecutor David Fitts called Larry Arnot to testify at the trial.

"Mr. Arnot," began Fitts, "directing your attention to the first day of

June 1968, were you employed at a gun shop called the Lock, Stock 'n' Barrel in San Gabriel, California?"

Arnot answered in the affirmative. Fitts then asked his witness to describe the sale of bullets to Sirhan.

"You want me to relate the whole transaction?" Arnot replied, a little unsure. "The whole transaction?"

"Tell us what you know about it, sir," responded Fitts. "If you remember."

"Approximately three-thirty in the afternoon three individuals entered the store, walked to the portion of the store where the ammunition was stored. I approached them, asked them if I could be of assistance, and in turn was given the request for .22 ammunition—"

"If the Court please," interrupted Fitts. "I don't think I'm going to let this go any further. If I may take this witness in my own way.

"Mr. Arnot, do you recall having a conversation with Lieutenant Enrique Hernandez of the Los Angeles Police Department with reference to selling ammunition to three individuals?"

"Yes."

"Then he put you on the so-called polygraph, the lie detector, isn't that true?"

"Yes."

"And he indicated to you with reference to the sale of what is reflected on that slip that you were confused?"

"Yes."

"All right. And then you ultimately told Mr. Hernandez that so far as selling the ammunition which is reflected on People's 22, that you had it mixed up with a sale to three other people and were in your own mind trying to connect it with the sale to Sirhan. Isn't that right?"

"I don't remember those words."

"Did you ultimately tell Mr. Hernandez that so far as that particular transaction reflected in People's 22, that you didn't remember Sirhan and you didn't remember anything other than that you had filled out that sales slip with respect to a sale?"

"Yes."

"That's all I have."

The owners of the Lock, Stock 'n' Barrel, Ben and Donna Herrick, were angered by Arnot's treatment by the police and the prosecution. They knew Arnot to be an honest man and saw no reason for him to make up a story. In addition, Donna Herrick had seen Sirhan in the store previously with two companions, and she filed statements with both the police and the FBI to that effect. But Donna Herrick was not called as a witness.

"They didn't want her to testify, because she wouldn't change her story," asserted Ben Herrick after the trial. Herrick then came to the defense of Arnot: "The sales slip definitely proves the fact that he was telling the truth and then they say the lie detector says he was telling a lie and they throw him off the witness stand. It just discredited the man's testimony and made a fool out of him, and for no reason because he was a prosecution witness to begin with, and it was the prosecution that did it to him. I just don't like the smell of it."[1]

There was nothing necessarily conspiratorial about Sirhan shopping for .22 caliber ammunition with two others. Although no one has come forward and admitted to being with Sirhan (perhaps out of fear), his companions might have been his brothers or just friends with no relation to the Robert Kennedy murder. But to the police and the trial attorneys even the barest mention of possible accomplices had to be eliminated. The police had no evidence that Sirhan was not accompanied by two others; indeed, Donna Herrick's story tended to corroborate that of Arnot.

Prosecutor Fitts would have had the jury believe that Sergeant Hernandez's polygraph discovered that Arnot had confused two separate sales. But a polygraph, if it can detect anything at all, is unable to detect confusion—only the physiologic reactions supposedly associated with telling a lie. It is clear from Fitts's interjection that Arnot's testimony was unexpected. Fitts then had to present Arnot as a man who had failed a polygraph test and had no memory of the sale. But if the prosecution truly believed this, why did they bother to introduce him as a witness?

A more likely explanation is that Arnot did see Sirhan with two others on June 1. Then, under pressure from polygraph operator Enrique Hernandez, he acquiesced to the police contention that he was confused. But later, under oath at the trial, Arnot's original memories of the transaction came spilling out despite his coaching. At that point, he had to be impeached by the very prosecutor who had called him to the stand.

As strange as this sequence was, defense attorney Grant Cooper's cross-examination of Arnot was equally bizarre. As if by instinct, Cooper opened his questioning, as he should, trying to exploit the inconsistency in Arnot's testimony. "Why did you tell us on direct examination that you sold this to Mr. Sirhan and two others?"

David Fitts immediately jumped up and testified for the witness. "I don't believe he said that."

Cooper accepted this answer, though Arnot had clearly made the statement. The defense attorney then, for no apparent reason, pressured Arnot into the nonsensical admission that he could remember the sale, but not the individuals involved. He then closed with the kind of questions trial lawyers ask when they want to appear to be doing something.

"These two boxes that you sold, Mr. Arnot . . . how many cartridges would that be all together, sir?"

"One hundred."

"In other words, there are fifty in a box?"

"That's correct."

"And the two boxes of the other at ninety cents, is that also another one hundred?"

"Yes."

"In other words, all together there would be two hundred bullets?"

"That's correct."

"Thank you. I have no further questions."

Arnot's time in court was brief and barely noted by the press. Nevertheless, his appearance revealed much about the selective nature of the proceeding. Arnot's treatment at the hands of the LAPD was typical for witnesses with information relating to possible accomplices. Most of these witnesses would not appear at the trial.

One account of the assassination which should have at least provoked curiosity on the part of the police was that of Don Schulman, a runner for Los Angeles TV station KNXT. Immediately following the shooting, Jeff Brent of Continental News Service grabbed Schulman for a radio interview. Both men claimed to have been in the pantry. Schulman was out of breath.

> BRENT: I'm talking to Don Schulman. Can you give us a halfway decent report of what happened within all this chaos?
>
> SCHULMAN: [ellipsis points indicate pauses] Okay. I was . . . ah . . . standing behind . . . ah . . . Kennedy as he was taking his assigned route into the kitchen. A Caucasian gentleman stepped out and fired three times . . . the security guard . . . hitting Kennedy all three times. Mr. Kennedy slumped to the floor . . . they carried him away . . . the security guards fired back. . . . As I saw . . . they shot the . . . ah, man who shot Kennedy . . . in the leg. . . . He . . . before they could get him he shot a . . . it looked like to me . . . he shot a woman . . . and he shot two other men.
>
> BRENT: Right. I was about six or seven people behind the senator, I heard six or seven shots in succession. . . . Now . . . is this the security guard firing back?
>
> SCHULMAN: Yes . . . ah, the man who stepped out fired three times at Kennedy . . . hit him all three times . . . and the security guard fired back . . . hitting . . . hitting him, and he [presumably Sirhan] is in apprehension.

Despite the fact that Schulman reported that he saw a security guard behind Kennedy fire a gun back at the assailant, a story which appeared on radio and TV and in some newspapers, the LAPD demonstrated a lack of investigative interest. This is curious because Kennedy was killed by a bullet entering the back of his head fired at close range, and security guard Thane Eugene Cesar was standing right behind Kennedy. Moreover, Cesar had an unholstered gun; he was not a friend of Kennedy; he had been standing guard over the room where the ambush took place, and as Kennedy had passed by, Cesar had taken the senator by the arm.

Nevertheless, the Los Angeles police did not thoroughly examine Eugene Cesar. They failed to clear up even elementary contradictions in the security guard's story, inconsistencies regarding his actions during the shooting. They also failed to verify the accuracy of his account regarding his disposition of a .22 caliber handgun. (Cesar told police that he sold it prior to the day of the assassination but a receipt of this transaction subsequently recovered by journalist Theodore Charach listed the date of sale as four months after the assassination.) They failed to check Cesar's gun the night of the murder to see if it had been fired or even what caliber it was. (Cesar claimed he was carrying a .38 caliber pistol which was not fired.) And although he had been standing close to Robert Kennedy and had witnessed the assault, Cesar was not called as a witness at the trial of Sirhan.

An explanation as to why would be offered in a 1971 article in the *Los Angeles Times* entitled "Sirhan Case—Was There a 2nd Gunman?" In the piece reporter Dave Smith quoted an unnamed "official," who stated that the inconsistencies in Cesar's story were cause for dismissing him as a suspect or witness rather than investigating him further.

Said the official: "The guy's stories didn't jibe. He told conflicting accounts and it seemed obvious he hadn't really seen anything. He really had nothing to tell us."[2]

"Because of the variances in his story," wrote Smith, "the guard was dropped from any further questioning, his credibility questioned by officials who felt he was trying to inject himself into a sensational case he knew little about."[3]

The logic here, of course, is impoverished. How can the police expect to solve any but the most obvious crimes if questioning ceases because a person who was close to the shooting and who played a security guard role gives "conflicting accounts"? Contrary to the assertion, Cesar had not tried to inject himself into the case. He was there at the scene, and while there was no evidence of wrongdoing on his part, considering the fact that the fatal bullet entered the back of Kennedy's head at close range, Cesar was worthy of scrutiny.

There were, however, people—unlike the police—who found Cesar's presence in the pantry suspicious. In researching what would become a film documentary on the assassination, Theodore Charach gained an interview in 1971 with Eugene Cesar. Charach got the former security guard to speak candidly about his feelings on several subjects. When asked whom he would have voted for in 1968, Cesar revealed that he had no affection for the Kennedys.

"I definitely wouldn't have voted for Bobby Kennedy," Cesar said, "because he had the same ideas that John did and I think John sold the country down the road. He gave it to the commies, he gave it to whoever else he wanted. He literally gave it to the minority."

Cesar said he supported Alabama governor George Wallace. He then, gratuitously, offered his opinion on race relations in America.

"The black man now for the last four to eight years has been cramming this integrated idea down our throats, so you learn to hate him. And one of these days at the rate they're going, there's going to be civil war in this country. It's going to be white against the black and the only thing I can say is the black will never win. . . . I can't see any other way to go."[4]

Eugene Cesar's statements would appear in Ted Charach's documentary *The Second Gun.*★ With the advent of the documentary in 1973, witness Don Schulman was called down to the district attorney's office for his first properly documented interview with authorities since the murder. When the investigators asked the young man if he was certain that Cesar shot Kennedy, Schulman protested, correctly, that he had not said any such thing. "I never said I saw [the guard shoot Kennedy]. . . . Hell, I didn't even see Sirhan shoot Kennedy. I know what the newspapers and everybody say, but I didn't see him do it."

The men from the DA's office pressed Schulman some more. There was no talk about whether he was or wasn't in the pantry. The questions implied that he was there. Schulman was asked if he was "absolutely positive" about the security guard.

"I'm pretty doggone sure he fired his gun," Shulman answered.

What is most odd about the police treatment of Schulman is the lack of documentation of any police interview with him during their original 1968 investigation. There does exist an LAPD memorandum, dated three years later, which refers to an interview Schulman supposedly had with LAPD sergeant Paul E. O'Steen on August 9, 1968. The document reports that

---

★After 1975 there was no recorded contact with Eugene Cesar for fourteen years. Those interested in the assassination story were unable to locate him. Los Angeles authorities claimed that Cesar had died in Arkansas. In 1989, however, journalist Dan Moldea found Cesar working as a plumber in Southern California. After repeated requests Cesar consented to be interviewed by Moldea. During these sessions he steadfastly maintained that he did not shoot Robert Kennedy. Ultimately Cesar consented to Moldea's proposal that he take a polygraph exam concerning his guilt or innocence. According to Moldea's polygraph operator, Cesar passed the test. Moldea subsequently concluded that Cesar had not participated in the assassination.

Schulman . . . stated he was outside of the kitchen when he heard noises like firecrackers. He did not see the actual shooting or suspect due to the crowd. Mr. Schulman was reinterviewed on July 23, 1971. He stated during this interview that he was in the pantry about twelve feet from Senator Kennedy when the shots were fired. . . . Why Mr. Schulman has changed his mind or why his memory which he describes as poor, has improved since August 9, 1968, is subject to scrutiny.

The 1971 memo contains several odd leaps of logic.

The memo would have one believe that Schulman, over a three-year period, gradually misremembered himself into the pantry. This conveniently overlooks the fact that just moments after the shooting Schulman asserted he was in the pantry and gave Jeff Brent's radio audience a detailed account of what took place in that room. In addition, whether or not he was correct about Cesar firing his gun, Schulman accurately asserted that Cesar had displayed his gun, something admitted by Cesar but noticed by only a few others.

Over the years Schulman has been consistent in asserting that he did not see Sirhan shoot Kennedy, something the 1971 memo alludes to as if this diminishes his credibility. What the memo doesn't explain is how it makes sense to assert that a person "did not see the actual shooting due to the crowd" if that person is not even in the room.

Most strange is the apparent effort to make Don Schulman disappear altogether. Schulman, like other witnesses with disturbing observations, doesn't appear on the LAPD's list of those in the pantry when the murder took place. Moreover, there is no surviving record of his supposed interview with Sergeant O'Steen—no audiotape, interview transcript, or interview summary. And if the O'Steen interview did take place, why wasn't it reported in the LAPD *Summary Report,* which is supposed to summarize every police interview of consequence?[5]

In October 1975, Schulman had his last official interview with Special Counsel Tom Kranz. Kranz was working upon an independent report, commissioned by the district attorney's office, which would reaffirm the official conclusions about the Kennedy murder. During the lengthy audiotaped session, Schulman made the following, slightly modified, statement about a second gun:

"I thought I saw a security guard pull his gun and possibly fire."

Later he would assert: "I saw other guns pulled and possibly fired."

Schulman's statement here about "others guns" is potentially significant, and he would not be the only witness to make this observation. In the same year in an interview with journalist Betsy Langman, Schulman would say that he was less certain that the security guard fired his gun but was "absolutely positive" that he saw other men in plain clothes with guns drawn in the pantry. Since there were no Secret Service agents present, and Kennedy had no armed bodyguards, who were these men? The LAPD maintains that there were no other guns in the pantry.

The response to Schulman's assertion that he saw other guns drawn is representative of police reactions when confronted with difficult issues in this case. The normal investigative response might be: "What did these other men with guns look like? How were they dressed? What were they doing? Where did they go?" Instead, to Schulman's assertion that he saw others guns, the unidentified interviewer responded, "No, there was no other guns."

"I thought I saw 'em," answered Schulman.

"Nope, you didn't."

After Schulman's departure Kranz and his colleague have a revealing discussion, putting down critics of the police version of the crime while the audiotape is still recording. Kranz then changes the subject back to Schulman: "I never felt, particularly in light of the ballistics examination, that his statements about a security guard had much weight."

"Yeah," his colleague answers, "but he really has not changed his [story]; he's still sticking with . . . he still sees guns and this kind of shit. . . . I think if, if this thing is gonna go anyplace and he's gonna be a problem, I'd like to call him in and we'll interrogate him." Since Schulman had just been questioned for an hour and a half, the purpose of such "interrogation" would seem to be intimidation.

Don Schulman would not be the only witness to merit peculiar treatment by the police.

On May 20, about two weeks before the California primary, a campaign luncheon was held for Robert Kennedy at Robbie's Restaurant in Pomona. Because of the size of the affair (four hundred guests), the night manager, thirty-five-year-old Albert LeBeau, was called in to help. After the murder, LeBeau saw Sirhan's picture on television and recognized him as someone he had seen acting strangely at the luncheon for Senator Kennedy. On June 7, LeBeau contacted the FBI and told them what he had seen. Subsequently he signed a five-page statement to the Bureau describing his encounter with the man he believed to be Sirhan.

LeBeau's initial duty at the luncheon was to act as ticket taker on the staircase leading into the restaurant. While collecting tickets on the crowded staircase LeBeau heard a noise and turned to see a woman who "had to climb over the rail from a booth and over a brick flower casing in order to get behind me. I saw a man coming over the rail and dropping onto the stairs behind the girl."

LeBeau intercepted the couple. "Do you have tickets?" he asked.

"We are with the senator's party," the woman answered.

LeBeau told them that tickets were still necessary. The woman then claimed, "We are part of the senator's party. He just waved us to come upstairs."

The woman, as described by LeBeau, was Caucasian, twenty-five to thirty years old, with "medium blond" shoulder-length hair. She appeared to be five foot six, somewhat taller than the man she was with. She also had a "nice shape, built proportionately." Her companion, whom LeBeau later recognized as Sirhan, said nothing during this exchange, but LeBeau did notice a coat draped over his right hand and forearm, this on a very warm May afternoon.

LeBeau sent the couple back down the stairs away from the luncheon. Later, however, as Robert Kennedy was giving his speech, he saw the couple once more standing against the back wall of the dining room among the hundred or so standees.

Whether the man he encountered was actually Sirhan could not be independently proved or disproved, but the basic facts of LeBeau's story were corroborated. William Schneid, a police officer from Pomona who was on duty in the restaurant, reported to the FBI that he had seen the couple cross over the "brick facade adjacent to the stairs and over the stair railing behind persons apparently checking for tickets at the foot of the stairs." He witnessed LeBeau stop the couple.

Schneid told the FBI that the man he saw bore a likeness to Sirhan, a slim Latin or Mexican man with dark curly hair, five foot six to five foot seven. Despite this, Schneid's FBI summary strangely states, "He did not feel the man observed by him would have been Sirhan Sirhan." The woman Schneid observed on the stairs was described as a Caucasian in her mid-twenties, five foot four to five foot seven with medium to light brown hair, an "attractive" woman who was "proportionate [in figure]," and "officious." Schneid had encountered her earlier, just prior to the arrival of Senator Kennedy. She had been standing by the kitchen door of the restaurant, apparently trying to get in. When Schneid told her that entrance was closed, the woman asked the officer which way Senator Kennedy would enter the luncheon. Schneid replied that the senator "would probably go up the stairs to the second floor." Schneid was never taken to a police lineup to see if he could identify Sirhan. He was not even interviewed by the LAPD.

On June 12 Albert LeBeau picked Sirhan's mug shot for the FBI as a man "closely resembling" the man he saw on the stairs. Despite this LeBeau was never afforded the opportunity to view Sirhan in a lineup for positive identification. Moreover, there are disturbing irregularities in LeBeau's police file.

Albert LeBeau was interviewed by the LAPD on June 26. A transcript of this session has not survived in police files. Nor has a tape recording, if one was made. What does survive is a "summary" of the interview, a convenient device if one is intent on shaping or spinning information given by a witness. The June 26 summary states that LeBeau had been previously interviewed by "Officer Thompson," but no record of that session exists in the files.

The summary of LeBeau's interview is a lengthy three-page, single-spaced document. It is unusual in that it is peppered with frequent quotations from LeBeau, which would indicate that the session was recorded, then excerpted. During the interview LeBeau apparently successfully picked Sirhan from a batch of twenty-five photos of dark-skinned young males. The summary, however, makes special mention of the fact that LeBeau failed to pick out another picture of Sirhan, this a Racing Commission ID photo, as though this failure seriously injured the witness's credibility.

The final sentence of the interview summary is uncharacteristically dramatic: "Just before the conclusion of the interview LeBeau was asked, 'Could you under oath swear that Sirhan is the man involved in the incident on May the 20th?' LeBeau hung his head and stared at the floor for several long moments and replied, 'No.' "

The LAPD's *Summary Report,* the 1,500-page document that summarized the police investigation, but which was not released to the public until 1986, puts an entirely different spin on the LeBeau interview. The *Report* says LeBeau "initially stated the man was Sirhan, *but later admitted he lied.*" There is no record of any such admission in police files. If the synopsis in the *Summary Report* chose to portray the lack of absolute certainty under oath as a confession of falsehood, then the honesty of the entire investigation is called into question.

On July 19 the FBI would be informed of another incident in which Sirhan appeared to be stalking Robert Kennedy. This incident took place in the Kennedy campaign headquarters in Azusa, California. Laverne Botting, a forty-one-year-old volunteer, told the Bureau that on May 30 she observed two men and a woman enter the office. One of the men approached her desk. This man, whom she would later recognize as "Sirhan or a person who very closely resembles Sirhan," said he was from the RFK headquarters in Pasadena (Sirhan lived in Pasadena) and asked if Robert Kennedy would be visiting the area. Botting replied that he would not. While the other two remained at a distance, Botting was able to describe the woman as a twenty-two to twenty-five-year-old Caucasian, five feet seven inches tall, with an "excellent figure" and "dishwater blond hair."

The Los Angeles police interviewed Botting three weeks later. Though she had told the FBI she would be able to make a definite judgment on her sighting if she saw Sirhan in person, she was never given the opportunity. Botting picked out Sirhan from a photo lineup and then told Officer C. B. Thompson that the man she thought was Sirhan was five foot four, twenty to twenty-five years old, with dark eyes and kinky black hair (characteristics closely resembling Sirhan).

In the interview summary Officer Thompson reports that Botting claimed that she had received a strange phone call: "I hear you think you saw Sirhan," her anonymous caller said in a threatening manner. "You had better be sure of what you are saying." If this call actually took place it raises the question of who, besides the Los Angeles police, would have an interest in exerting pressure on Botting's degree of certainty. Who beyond the LAPD even knew of her sighting?

Despite Botting's having given a description of the man she saw as closely resembling Sirhan, Officer Thompson's summary makes special note of the fact that Botting described the man she saw as having a broad nose and shoulders. This leads Thompson to ultimately conclude: "Witness has obviously made an honest mistake." As with LeBeau there exists no transcript nor audiotape of this interview.

If there had been no corroboration of her story the police might be forgiven for dismissing Botting's story as "an honest mistake." But there was a witness to the events described by Botting. Another volunteer at Kennedy headquarters that day, forty-five-year-old Ethel Creehan, called the police on June 7 and told them of the incident. She told them she was "fairly certain" the man she saw was Sirhan, but that she would not want to "testify to the fact without first seeing Sirhan in person." Like Botting and LeBeau, she would not be given the opportunity.

Ethel Creehan would be reinterviewed a month later by Officer Thompson. At that time she picked out Sirhan's photograph as resembling the man she observed with her coworker, Laverne Botting. Creehan described the man as being five foot eight. She described the girl as perhaps nineteen, but with makeup that made her appear twenty-three to twenty-five. According to Creehan she had brown or blond shoulder-length hair. She also had a "prominent" nose. (Note: witness Sandra Serrano said that the woman in the polka-dot dress had a "funny nose"; witness Vincent DiPierro said that she had a "pudgy" nose.)

In his summary of Creehan's interview Officer Thompson reports that he checked with a woman from Kennedy headquarters in Pasadena who said there was no reason why they would have sent anyone to Azusa to inquire about the senator's schedule. Thompson states this as if it casts doubt upon the stories of Botting and Creehan, when in fact it makes the afternoon visitors to Azusa all the more suspicious.

Thompson's conclusion on Creehan is also quite remarkable: "The person described by Mrs. Creehan as possibly being Sirhan is 4 inches taller than Sirhan. It is doubtful if the person she observed was Sirhan." Botting, remember, was given no credence for describing the mystery man as five foot four, but Creehan is apparently discredited for misestimating by a few inches the height of a man she viewed only casually some weeks earlier. It is difficult to escape the conclusion that the interviewing officer in these cases was searching diligently for anything at all to dismiss the witnesses' testimony.

The Los Angeles police found it easy to dismiss or discredit witnesses who reported seeing Sirhan in the company of possible accomplices, even though, in many of these preassassination stories, the same image (a woman in her early twenties with a good figure) appeared with regularity. More alarming is the LAPD's conduct toward a number of other witnesses who reported suspicious activity in or near the pantry of the Ambassador Hotel the night of the shooting.

On the night of the murder, Nina Rhodes was at the Ambassador Hotel with her husband to celebrate Robert Kennedy's primary victory. She is now a partner in a small international public relations firm. In the summer of 1992 she wrote a statement in support of a petition to the Los Angeles County Grand Jury requesting that body to investigate the Los Angeles police for misconduct in its investigation of the murder of Robert Kennedy:

> On June 4th 1968, I, Nina Rhodes, was invited to the Ambassador Hotel to celebrate Senator Kennedy's California primary victory. We were to attend a private party in the Senator's suite following his speech and press conference.
>
> During the speech, I spent most of the time waiting for the Senator in the Press Room. . . . As the speech came to a close . . . I left the Press Room to wait for the Senator at the bottom of the ramp. . . . The entourage moved rather quickly. I chased after the Senator and as I did, I heard a series of popping noises which I first thought were flash bulbs but then realized were gunshots. There were 12–14 shots in all. I was 6–7 feet from the Senator when I saw him and a number of others fall. Rosie Grier and Rafer Johnson charged after someone ahead and to the left of me. This surprised me because it was my impression that some of the shots had come from ahead of me and to my right (the Senator's position) and my attention was focused there. I saw Rosie and Rafer wrestling with a dark complected man wearing a denim jacket. The man was at a long metal table and twisted and turned but was subdued. Seeing the Senator on the floor, I screamed "No! No! No!" and then blacked out for a few minutes. . . .
>
> In conclusion I would like to stress . . . I heard 12–14 shots, some

originating in the vicinity of the Senator not from where I saw Sirhan. . . .

On July 9, 1968, Nina Rhodes had been interviewed by an agent from the FBI. Her interview summary states:

> At approximately 8:30 pm on June 4, 1968 [Nina Rhodes] went to the Ambassador Hotel with her husband Michael Rhodes. . . . [S]he followed the election results with Pierre Salinger, Frank Mankiewicz and various other Kennedy staff members. . . . [Moving forward to the shooting itself] She had just left the entrance to the kitchen and noticed the Senator shaking hands with various kitchen employees . . . when she suddenly heard a sound like a firecracker. . . . She instantaneously realized that . . . shots were being fired. *She later recalled hearing eight distinct shots* [emphasis added]. Everything appeared to her like still frames in a stop-action movie. . . . [T]he individual who fired the shots at the Senator appeared to her to be wearing a powder blue jacket and he seemed to be framed against the walls which were also powder blue. When she saw him he seemed to be turned from her so that she saw part of his back and left side as he was in what she described as a semi-crouch position.

When shown her FBI interview summary in 1992, Nina Rhodes took issue with no fewer than fifteen items as stated in the report, some minor, some not. Most relevant, Rhodes claimed in writing: "I never said I heard 8 distinct shots. From the moment the tragedy began I knew that there was at least 10–14 shots and that there had to be more than one assailant. The shots were to the left *and* [emphasis added] right from where I was."

Nina Rhodes's perceptions that ten to fourteen shots were fired and that they came from two separate sources were the items of greatest forensic value in her testimony. Her observations would be supported a decade later by sonic analysis performed upon surviving audiotapes.* It is significant,

---

*At the time of the shooting ABC-TV was still broadcasting from the Embassy Room where Kennedy had made his victory speech. Jeff Brent of Continental News and Andrew West of Mutual Broadcasting were also recording, although both had turned on their microphones after the firing had begun. In *The Assassination of Robert Kennedy* (1993, Thunder's Mouth Press) authors Jonn Christian and William Turner reported upon an investigation the LAPD could have done but didn't—sonic analysis.

In 1982 the authors commissioned Dr. Michael Hecker of the Stanford Research Institute in Menlo Park, California, to make acoustic analysis in search of sounds of individual gunshots. Following the tests Dr. Hecker concluded: "On the basis of auditory, oscillographic and spectrographic analyses of these three recordings, it is my opinion, to a reasonable degree of scientific certainty, that no fewer than 10 (ten) gunshots are ascertainable following

then, that in the FBI summary of her interview she is portrayed as hearing "eight distinct shots." It is also significant that despite her rather detailed account of the murder given to the FBI, the Los Angeles police do not include Nina Rhodes on their list of witnesses who they say were in the pantry at the time of the murder.

One person definitely on the pantry list was Evan Freed, who was standing very near to Robert Kennedy when the shooting started. Freed was a part-time news photographer in 1968. He is now a deputy city attorney for the City of Los Angeles. In 1992 he, like Nina Rhodes, swore an affidavit in support of the petition to the Los Angeles County Grand Jury.

In his detailed, four-page declaration Freed said that in 1968 he had been assigned to cover the Robert Kennedy campaign. He described the events at the Ambassador Hotel leading up to the shooting.

Freed said that during the evening he had been on the fifth floor of the Ambassador Hotel where the Kennedy campaign had rented a suite of rooms. He said he accompanied Kennedy on the elevator that took the senator down to the second floor, where he would speak to the crowd gathered in the Embassy Room. Some minutes prior to the end of Kennedy's speech, Freed said he wandered into the pantry. There he noticed two men "very similar in appearance" moving around. One of these men would turn out to be Sirhan. The two men did not stand together, but seemed to look at each other every now and then. Freed thought they might be brothers.

When Senator Kennedy entered the pantry after his speech, Freed began to walk beside him. When the shooting started he was "about 4 feet away," facing Kennedy. "I saw the 2nd man (wearing darker clothing) who had been in the pantry with Sirhan during the speech pointing a gun in an upward angle at the Senator. Based on the sound I heard, I believe the first shot came from this man's gun. In the background I could see Sirhan firing a revolver held in his right hand in the direction of the Senator. People in the crowd were screaming and grabbing Sirhan. . . ."

In his affidavit Freed said that as the crowd rushed forward toward Sirhan, they passed by the second gunman who was backing away. Moments later he saw the second gunman running in his direction pursued by another man yelling "Stop that guy, stop him!" According to Freed, the pursuer made an attempt to grab the gunman but failed. Then both men ran out of the pantry.

When Freed met with police detectives he said he told them the story

---

the conclusion of the Senator's victory speech until after the time Sirhan Bishara Sirhan was disarmed." [p. xxvi] he had related in his affidavit. "I was asked whether or not the man pursuing the 2nd gunman could have been yelling, 'Get an ambulance' or 'Get a doctor.' I told them that was not correct, *but they insisted that I had been incorrect in what I heard.* [Emphasis added.]"

Freed said that although he had given a description of the man who was pursuing the second gunman, there was never a request from the police that he produce a drawing of the man or look for him in photographs.

"I made it very clear that the 2nd gunman looked very much like Sirhan, except that his clothing was darker in color and coordinated."

Freed related that he had also been contacted by the FBI, but that they "seemed to to be avoiding asking me questions about the 2nd gunman, although I told them the same things I have stated above." Freed ended his declaration saying that he had never desired any publicity in the case and had no opinion as to who fired the fatal shots into Robert Kennedy. "My purpose in making these statements now is to help insure that a fair investigation is conducted in this case. I declare under the penalty of perjury that the foregoing is true and correct."★

Evan Freed's first police interview dated June 14 asserts that Freed claimed to have seen two men and a woman leave the pantry in a hurry

---

★In the summer of 1996 Evan Freed was approached by attorneys representing Scott Enyart and asked to appear at the trial (*Enyart v. LAPD*) where Enyart was seeking damages for the loss or destruction of photos he claimed he took of the Kennedy shooting. The Enyart attorneys were familiar with Freed's affidavit to the L.A. County Grand Jury. As a second-gun witness, Freed would presumably help Enyart establish why photos of the actual shooting would be so valuable and important. Also Freed, in his original affidavit, had claimed that the police had accepted photographic negatives from him and not returned them. This, too, interested the Enyart attorneys.

Since signing his affidavit in 1992, Evan Freed had become a deputy city attorney in Los Angeles. It was the city attoney's office, which was representing the police in opposition to Scott Enyart. According to Enyart's lawyer, Freed responded to them by sending a copy of a letter addressed to Marilyn Barrett (the attorney for the grand jury petitioners) bearing the date May 15, 1992 (two days after the date on his affidavit that was submitted to the grand jury). The letter stated that Freed was sending a "corrected copy" of the original affidavit, which he now termed a "letter." Barrett was instructed to now "discard" the original affidavit "since it contains factual errors." Freed stated that he had "inadvertently sent [Barrett] the first draft without reading it first."

According to Barrett, the letter and the second affidavit were never received by her. The original affidavit, signed by Freed "under the penalty of perjury," was the only one submitted to the grand jury.

In Freed's second affidavit the paragraph formerly about the second gunman was recast as follows:

"At about the same time, I saw the 'second man' (wearing darker clothing) who I described as resembling Sirhan, standing about 8–10 feet east of me. It is possible he could have been holding a weapon, but I cannot be sure. I cannot say how many shots were fired by Sirhan Sirhan or whether any shots came from the 'second man.' "

He also added the statement, "It is very clear to me that Sirhan Sirhan WAS a gunman in the incident. I cannot say whether or not he acted alone." The attorneys for Scott Enyart decided not to subpoena Evan Freed to testify at the Enyart trial.

after the shooting. The woman was described as "possibly wearing a polka dot dress." In a "reinterview" dated August 1, Freed's pantry story is retold but with no mention at all of the suspicious trio he had reported before. On September 11 Freed would be interviewed by the FBI. The summary of this interview reports: "He [Freed] looked up and saw a man shooting a gun. . . . The man who was doing the shooting was subsequently identified as Sirhan Sirhan. *Sirhan was the only person Freed saw shooting* [emphasis added]."

The authors are aware of no other interview summary in the FBI files where it is asserted that the witness saw only one person shooting. Freed says that he tried to tell the FBI about a second gunman, but they were uninterested in his observation. Nevertheless, it is in Freed's interview summary that the unique assertion that there was only one gunman appears.

Private investigator Michael McCowan, in his report to defense attorney Grant Cooper, would describe Evan Freed's account of the murder: "He claims he saw Sirhan do the shooting. Then he observed three people running in his direction: a girl, a man and another man who was being chased. No one has been able to substantiate this story, and a good explanation is that they were people running to a phone or for police."

McCowan here appears to have passed on wholesale the police interpretation of Evan Freed's testimony. Recall that the police allegedly were trying to convince Freed, despite his objections, that the running people were shouting "Get an ambulance" or "Get a doctor." If McCowan or the police truly believed that no one was able to substantiate Freed's story, then they can't have been very diligent in their search.

On the night of the murder Dr. Marcus McBroom was standing right outside the kitchen in the Embassy Room. McBroom told his story in detail to researcher Greg Stone in 1986.

> The first inference that we had that anything was awry was that we heard the first one or two shots. And then a woman in a polka dot dress ran out of the kitchen shouting "We got him" or "We shot him." No one really was even certain as to what she had said because no one initially really comprehended what was really happening. Immediately after she ran out, a man with a gun under a newspaper ran out in a very menacing way and myself and a man by the name of Sam Strain and the man running the ABC camera we drew back instinctively when we saw the gun.

McBroom described the woman in the polka-dot dress as between twenty-two and twenty-four years of age, brunet, fairly attractive, between five foot three and five foot four, and "proportionate." The man with the gun he described as an "Arab looking person" in a blue suit (Freed described the man in blue "coordinated" clothing), perspiring profusely, with a newspaper draped over his arm and a pistol visible underneath it. When McBroom was asked by police to pick out from a series of mug shots someone who looked similar to the menacing man, McBroom picked a photograph of one of Sirhan's brothers, thus confirming Freed's description of the man bearing a familial resemblance to Sirhan.

Freed's and McBroom's accounts of seeing suspicious persons flee the pantry would be corroborated by a number of witnesses in or just outside the hotel kitchen.

George Green, a thirty-three-year-old real estate salesman, reported to the FBI that at about 11:15 to 11:30 he was at the Ambassador Hotel observing Kennedy press secretary Frank Mankiewicz talk with reporters in a corridor leading to the pantry area. At that time Green saw a man whom he would later identify as Sirhan standing at the edge of the crowd. He was standing near a tall thin man and a female Caucasian in her early twenties. Green told the FBI that the woman had "a good figure" and wore a white dress with black polka dots.

Green entered the pantry area just as the shooting began. At first he couldn't identify the popping noises he heard, but then he recognized them as gunfire. Before Green joined the struggle to subdue the apparent assailant, he noticed a man and a woman rush out of the pantry. Their actions were conspicuous because everyone else seemed to be trying to get into the room. The woman wore a polka-dot dress.

Jack J. Merrit, a uniformed security guard working for Ace Guard Service, reported to both the police and the FBI that he saw "two men and a woman leaving the kitchen." He described the woman as approximately five feet five inches tall, with "light colored" hair. The men who were leaving wore suits; the woman, a polka-dot dress. According to Merrit, "They seemed to be smiling."

Twenty-one-year-old Kennedy supporter Richard Houston was standing outside the pantry when the shots were fired. He told the police that shortly thereafter he saw a woman run out of the room. Houston said the woman wore a black-and-white polka-dot dress "with ruffles around the neck and front." As she hurried by, Houston heard her say, "We killed him," after which she "ran out onto a terrace area outside."

Kennedy campaign worker Darnell Johnson was in the pantry ahead of the senator's party. While there he noticed a group of five people standing near each other. One of these would turn out to be Sirhan. Near him Johnson saw a six-foot-one man in a light blue sports coat, and a white female. Johnson described the woman as twenty-three to twenty-five years old, with light brown hair, five foot eight, 145 pounds and "well built."

The woman wore a white dress with quarter-size black polka dots. Johnson noticed that the three men and the woman left the room as Sirhan was being subdued.

Booker Griffin, a twenty-nine-year-old Kennedy supporter and director of the Negro Industrial and Educational Union, told police he thought he saw Sirhan on three different times during the evening. On two of those occasions Sirhan was standing next to a woman, and although Griffin did not observe them talking it was his impression that they were together. He noticed the two because they seemed "out of place." The woman he recalled was wearing a "predominantly white dress that may have had another color on it."

When the first shots were fired Griffin was standing just outside the pantry. He noticed the woman and another man whom he had seen earlier with Sirhan run out of the pantry. Something in their motion and demeanor made Griffin blurt out, "They're getting away!"

There were also witnesses who had noticed the woman in a polka-dot dress earlier in the evening. Lonny Worthy, Margaret Hahn, Judith Groves, John Ludlow, Eve Hansen, Nina Ballantyne, Susan Locke, and Jeanette Prudhomme were witnesses who reported seeing such a woman, either with a man resembling Sirhan or in suspicious circumstances.

Kennedy volunteer Susan Locke reported to the FBI that she saw a suspicious woman in the Embassy Room just before Kennedy's speech. According to Locke the woman seemed "somewhat out of place" and stood "expressionless" amid the crowd celebrating the apparent victory. Locke also noticed that the woman did not have the yellow badge necessary for admission to the Embassy Room and she pointed the woman out to Carol Breshears, a woman in charge of the Kennedy support organization called the "Kennedy Girls." Breshears then alerted a security guard to the presence of the woman. There is no report of what, if anything, the guard did. The mystery woman, according to Locke, was in her early twenties, "well proportioned," and wore a white dress with blue polka dots.

Jeanette Prudhomme, a junior high school student and a Kennedy volunteer, reported to the police that she believed she saw Sirhan with a woman and another man in the Ambassador Hotel. She described the woman as a female Caucasian, twenty-eight to thirty years old, five foot six, 130 pounds, with brown shoulder-length hair. According to the police report, "She was wearing a white dress with black polka dots approximately one inch in size, black shoes with heels."

While the description of the mystery woman offered by these witnesses varies in some respects, especially regarding hair color, a fairly consistent image emerges of an attractive woman in her early to mid-twenties, with long hair, a good figure, wearing a long flowing dress (not a suit or a miniskirt) with polka dots that are similarly described in terms of color and size.

There is also a rough but significant symmetry to the sightings by witnesses at the Ambassador: earlier in the evening in the Embassy Room, then near the pantry, then in the pantry, then running from the pantry across the Embassy Room, then outside the hotel. With the exception of a report by Darnell Johnson that he saw the polka-dot-dress woman look back into the pantry area after the shooting, there are no major conflicts of time and place between these accounts.

The commanding officers of the LAPD were certainly aware that their work would be scrutinized. They were also aware that the image of the Dallas police had suffered in reaction to what was seen as a very poor handling of the murder of President Kennedy. Thus from the beginning great emphasis was placed on public declarations pledging a thorough and professional investigation.

"Only those officers whose personal traits indicated complete dependability, ability to work with little supervision and flair for analyzing facts were chosen," declared Chief of Detectives Robert Houghton.[6] Houghton would later describe the police investigation as "the most extensive search for truth ever launched by a local law enforcement agency."[7]

Houghton's praise for the police would be echoed by that of chief prosecutor Lynn Compton. "The FBI and the Los Angeles Police Department have interviewed literally thousands of people running out every suggestion, lead or possibility," said Compton during the trial, "and they have failed to find any connection between Sirhan and anyone else."[8]

The assertion by the police that in their thousands of interviews they discovered no evidence to support the story of the polka-dot woman or other murder accomplices is simply untrue. There were many such witnesses and the police did not have to search far to find them. But never were the accounts of these witnesses collated by the police into one file, to be compared, cross-referenced, and studied. Instead, the "flair for analyzing facts" consisted of passing this evidence through a series of filters, such as interview summaries and summary reports, whereby the unwanted material would be diluted, discredited, rephrased, screened, isolated, and ignored.

In the case of George Green, his story of seeing Sirhan standing near a polka-dot woman would strangely disappear between his FBI interview and his later LAPD interview. Lonny Worthy's story would also be lost somewhere between the FBI and the LAPD interviews, and the same would be true of the information given by Susan Locke—this is particularly odd since Locke's details on the polka-dot woman comprised about a third of the information she gave to the FBI. Jeanette Prudhomme's account of Sirhan with the polka-dot woman is discounted in the LAPD *Summary Report*. "She was shown photographs of Sirhan," it states, "but was unable to make an identification." Considering liberties taken elsewhere, one might wonder what "make an identification" meant to the police in this instance.

The account of Richard Houston was left out of the LAPD *Summary Report*. The polka-dot story of guard Jack Merrit is stated briefly, without comment. That of Judith Groves is not reported at all. A terse sentence in the *Summary Report* states that Darnell Johnson says he saw Sirhan and the polka-dot woman. The report then says: "Note: Investigators believe Johnson's statements unreliable and contrary to fact." The basis for this belief is not explained.

Marcus McBroom's polka-dot-dress story is also not mentioned in the *Summary Report*. After reporting that McBroom had noticed Sirhan because he looked "out of place," the *Report* states, "All additional statements made by McBroom were later retracted and are not reported here." McBroom denies any retractions.

The LAPD *Summary Report* would dismiss Booker Griffin by stating that Griffin confessed "that the story of the male and female escaping was a total fabrication on his part." This allegation has no basis whatsoever in any of the tapes, transcripts, or summaries of Griffin's law enforcement interviews. It is so transparent in its goal of discrediting a witness that it serves as further evidence of a hidden agenda on the part of those producing the final *Summary Report* on the assassination.

In June of 1987, the authors interviewed Griffin in the offices of the talent agency he ran on Sunset Boulevard in Hollywood. He repeated his account of seeing Sirhan and the woman. He was then shown the recently released *Summary Report* alleging he had admitted he had lied.

Griffin reacted with disbelief, then anger. "This is not true," he said forcefully. "This is totally untrue."

Griffin indignantly, but calmly, defended his credibility: "I am a trained newsperson and I had been taught to watch details. . . . I was not there with a lay eye. I had covered, you know, shooting stories and others, and I was raised in a neighborhood situation where seeing people shot and being around bullets was something I was used to, and I was always taught to keep a kind of cool head. I'm not blind. I'm not a dishonest person. I know what I saw."

Whether or not a witness's story made it into the *Summary Report,* altered or otherwise, the report itself was not made public until 1986, and the investigation files were not made public until 1988—twenty years after the murder. Thus no witness was in a position to know whether his statements had been accurately represented in the interview summaries or the *Summary Report*. Also, no witnesses, and no one else, were in a position to know exactly how many others had seen another man with a gun or Sirhan with possible accomplices. Each witness was isolated and made to feel that he or she was the only one reporting anomalous information.

Through careful manipulation of the press, the Los Angeles police successfully painted the story of the woman in the polka-dot dress as the hallucination of one "overwrought" young woman. The truth was that many apparently reliable witnesses saw this woman and reported their sightings to the police.

Evan Freed, Nina Rhodes, and Dr. Marcus McBroom are, presumably, responsible citizens. None of them has sought publicity or gain concerning what they saw the night of the murder. None could be considered an assassination buff or a conspiracy theorist. They merely reported to the police what they saw. It is, of course, possible, they were mistaken. But despite evidence which supported their testimony, these witnesses, and others like them, were systematically ignored by the police.

If there was a short-term payoff to the manipulation of unwanted witnesses, it came the day defense attorney Russell Parsons stood before Judge Walker and requested under the California rules of discovery the right to examine the police files of these witnesses and others who had contact with Sirhan or who otherwise had witnessed the events of the murder. Prosecutor David Fitts later revealed that the LAPD was extremely reluctant to let go of these documents, but there was really no choice. He walked over to Parsons and placed the daunting pile of reports in front of him. "Do you want to count them?" he asked.

When the prosecution was finished turning over what they had to the defense, prosecutor Lynn Compton approached Judge Walker.

"I wonder if I might state something for the record which may be of assistance to Court and counsel."

Compton went on to say that the material in possession of the district attorney's office had been put into three categories: information pertaining to witnesses they planned to use at the trial, witnesses who provided background information who would not be called at the trial, and third, "miscellaneous type of information which deals mainly with the subject of investigations that have been conducted concerning other possible suspects as to the existence of conspiracy and that sort of thing which I might indicate is all negative."

After his assertion that the witness interviews were conspiracy negative, Compton said, "We want to make perfectly clear to this Court and the record that there is nothing in our possession which we seek to conceal or withhold from the defense. . . . We believe that we have furnished the copies of statements of people who could possibly be of any value at this time."

Despite these assurances, the prosecution may not have been as forthcoming with the defense as they pretended to be. On May 16, 1969, a posttrial meeting was held in the chambers of Assistant Presiding Judge Charles A. Loring. There it was revealed that the prosecution had used some amount of discretion in deciding which files would be passed on to the defense. The purpose of the meeting was to discuss the appropriate resting place for evidence presented and not presented at the trial. Assistant District Attorney David Fitts and Deputy Chief Houghton had this exchange in front of Judge Herbert Walker:

> FITTS: [talking about the discovery motion] They had a lot of specific names so they got that stuff and let me assure you here and now that which was delivered on discovery and that which was filed with the court was *scaled* [emphasis added] to this extent. They asked for interviews and interviews they got, but when it came down to embodying conclusions of investigative personnel you know and we believed, after examining this, that and the other, that even this [particular witness with information relating to a possible Sirhan accomplice] is a self-seeking son of a bitch—let it stay in the record. *Material of that kind I abstracted from the file.* [Emphasis added.]
>
> HOUGHTON: We got a lot of actually what was summaries of interviews, not Q's and A's. . . .
>
> FITTS: *Where possible the stuff was not made a matter of record.* [Emphasis added.]

Fitts and Houghton here appear to admit to screening the evidence handed over to the defense, particularly in regard to witnesses with accomplice-related information—a serious violation of due process. They also appear to refer to the excluding of raw information from the case record by use of interview summaries.

Is our reading of this conversation too harsh? The normally mild-mannered defense attorney Grant Cooper did not think so. He presented a declaration to the court in late May 1969 where he claimed to be "astonished" by the meeting which included the police, the prosecution, and the trial judge, but which excluded representatives from the defense.

"I am, of course, disturbed that the question of how certain Exhibits, marked for identification, or received in evidence, were to be treated for purposes of appeal, was discussed in my absence. I am further perplexed as to why the police department and the District Attorney's Office 'abstracted from the file' some materials pertaining to their assessments of various witnesses with whom they conducted interviews and why some items of investigation were regarded too secret that they were barred from anyone, except the District Attorney, the F.B.I. and the Los Angeles Police Department." Cooper ended his affidavit by declaring this conduct "a colossal violation of the Constitutional and statutory rights of the accused."[9]

From their own statements in Judge Loring's chambers after the trial, one can fairly conclude that the prosecution was not entirely forthcoming when it handed over its files to the defense on October 14. If this conduct was designed to limit the scope of inquiry in the case, it was immensely successful. Prosecutor Compton's pronouncement in court that the witness interviews did not support a conclusion of conspiracy, and Russell Parsons's hasty reiteration of that view later in the day, provided the front-page headline in the following morning's *Los Angeles Times:* "Both Sides Agree, Sirhan Was Alone."

That headline would signal the end of public consideration given to any witness with accomplice-related information. Though numerous, apparently reliable, witnesses had seen Sirhan in suspicious circumstances before the shooting, most would be ignored from this point forward. But there were two witnesses who saw Sirhan with a woman in a polka-dot dress the night of the murder who could not be dispatched with a shuffling of papers, an interview summary, or a morning headline. The Los Angeles police would direct inordinate resources to handling these witnesses, and their resulting testimony would undergo an extraordinary and tortured transformation.

EIGHT

The Spotted Ghost

✶ ✶ ✶

*As long as Miss Serrano stuck to her story, no amount of
independent evidence would in itself, serve to dispel the "polka-dot-
dress girl" fever, which had by now, in the press and in the public
mind, reached a high point on the thermometer of intrigue. She
alone could put the spotted ghost to rest.*

—Chief of Detectives Robert Houghton in *Special Unit Senator*, 1971

ON FEBRUARY 17, Jesus Perez was
called as a witness for the prose-
cution. A busboy at the Ambassador, Perez had exchanged greetings with
Robert Kennedy in the hotel pantry only moments before the murder. The
young man also claimed to have exchanged words with the assailant before
the shooting. Perez, however, spoke broken English, so his testimony at
Sirhan's trial was given through a court interpreter.

"Mr. Perez," began John Howard, "I would like to direct your attention
to the defendant in this case, the gentleman seated to my left at the extreme
end of the counsel table. Did you see that individual in the pantry area
before the senator made his speech?"

"Yes."

"How long before?"

"About a half hour more or less. I don't remember very well."

"You talked to the defendant before the shooting?"

"Yes."

"What did you say?"

"That I didn't know anything whether he [Kennedy] would come
through there or not."

"Was there any further conversation between you and Mr. Sirhan?"

"Some boys spoke in Spanish and he asked me what they were saying.
I told him they weren't talking about him, they were talking about *some
pretty girls* [plural, emphasis added]."

Perez's testimony, as translated by the court interpreter, differed from
that which he gave to the Los Angeles County Grand Jury a few days after

the crime. At that time Perez recounted in his own words the brief conversation he had with Sirhan in the pantry before the shooting. According to Perez, Sirhan had apparently been bothered by glances and bits of conversation among the busboys that he felt were directed at him. Sirhan approached Perez and asked him what the boys were talking about.

"And I tell him," Perez testified, " 'he is talking about *the beautiful girl* [singular, emphasis added]. He no talking about you.' "[1]

The difference between Perez's grand jury and trial testimony is slight. It would be unworthy of mention if it didn't touch on one of the central mysteries of the assassination. Was Sirhan in the company of an attractive woman moments before he fired a gun at Robert Kennedy?

The same day that Perez testified, another hotel employee, Vincent DiPierro, would be called to the witness stand. DiPierro was a student at Santa Monica Community College, employed part-time as a waiter at the Ambassador Hotel, where his father, Angelo, was one of the maître d's. Like Perez, he was questioned by Assistant DA John Howard.

"Directing your attention to June 4, 1968," commanded Howard, "do you remember that day was Election Day in Southern California?"

"Yes."

"Did you have occasion to go to the Ambassador Hotel?"

"Yes, I did."

"Now, you weren't working on that—I believe as I recall, it was Tuesday evening?"

"That's correct."

"Did you go to the hotel for some reason?"

"Yes, my father called me and said if I'd like to see Senator Kennedy I could come down."

Howard's courtroom examination of DiPierro was not the first time the assistant DA had questioned the young man about the murder of Robert Kennedy. The night of the shooting Howard had participated in DiPierro's 4 A.M. debriefing, along with LAPD officers Patchett and Melendres.

That night, DiPierro told the police that as Kennedy stopped to shake hands with busboys Romero and Perez, he noticed a young man, who would turn out to be Sirhan, hanging on to a tray stand. DiPierro's eye had been drawn to the young man, he said, because he was standing next to an attractive woman. "It looked like she was almost holding him," DiPierro reported. DiPierro then watched as the young man got down from the tray stand, advanced on Senator Kennedy, and fired his gun. Blood hit the young hotel employee in the face, and Kennedy aide Paul Schrade fell wounded against him.

During the interrogation at the police station, John Howard asked DiPierro if he had seen the assailant and the woman talk to each other.

"He turned as though he did say something," DiPierro answered.

"Did she move her mouth like she was speaking to him?"

"No, she just smiled."

"And would it seem as though she smiled at something that had been said?"

"Yeah."

DiPierro then described the woman to Howard as being "good-looking" with "a pudgy nose" and wearing "a white dress with black or purple polka dots."

Two days later DiPierro would tell the same story in testimony before the Los Angeles County Grand Jury. "I noticed there was a girl and the accused person standing on what we call a tray stacker," DiPierro said. ". . . she had a very good-looking figure—and the dress was kind of lousy. It looked as though it was a white dress and it had either black or dark purple polka dots on it. . . .

"They were both standing together. He looked as though he either talked to her or flirted with her, because she smiled. Together they were both smiling, as he got down, he was smiling. In fact, the minute the first two shots were fired, he still had a sick-looking smile on his face. That's one thing—I can never forget that."

Because he was so close, and because he was watching the assailant before the shooting began, DiPierro was perhaps the best eyewitness the prosecution had. Seemingly impressed with DiPierro's clarity and sincerity, Sergeant Patchett praised him in the initial report as a "very very good witness." But during the trial of Sirhan, John Howard did not ask the same questions he asked the night of the murder. And Vincent DiPierro's testimony would undergo a startling transformation.

At 12:30 P.M. on June 5, the Los Angeles police put out the following Teletype bulletin to law enforcement agencies all across the country.

I RAM 6-5-68 APB EMERGENCY
ASSAULT WITH INTENT TO COMMIT MURDER. IN CUSTODY
SUSPECT SIRHAN BISHARA SIRHAN AKA SIRHAN SHARIF
BISHARA . . . PRIOR TO SHOOTING, SUSPECT OBSERVED
WITH A FEMALE CAUC. 23–27, 5–6, WEARING A WHITE
VOILE DRESS, ¾ INCH SLEEVES, WITH SMALL BLACK POLKA
DOTS, DARK SHOES, BOUFFANT TYPE HAIR. THIS FEMALE
NOT IDENTIFIED OR IN CUSTODY . . . ANY INFORMATION
ON SUSPECT AND DESCRIBED FEMALE CAUC. RUSH
RAMPART DETS.

This was not the first all points bulletin to describe a possible accomplice. Only minutes after the shooting an APB carrying a similar description went out over police radio. Its source was Sergeant Paul Scharaga.

At the time of the Robert Kennedy murder Scharaga was a forty-year-old police veteran with an excellent record. He was in his patrol car one block from the Ambassador when news of trouble at the hotel came over his radio. Scharaga drove quickly to the parking lot behind the hotel, where he encountered a distressed older couple who had seen a woman wearing a polka-dot dress and a young man run from the hotel laughing and shouting, "We shot him! We shot him!"

Scharaga immediately went to his car and put out an APB on the two suspects. Scharaga's APB apparently did not stand long. Scharaga asserts that a senior officer requested that he cancel it. Scharaga refused. It was canceled anyway.

Police radio communications tapes (released in LAPD files) show that at 1:41 A.M. a patrol car radioed the dispatcher and asked for clarification: "Is there still an outstanding suspect, and, if so, can I have the descriptions?" After some cross talk, the dispatcher responded: "Disregard that broadcast. We got Rafer Johnson and Jesse Unruh who were right next to him [Kennedy], and they only have one man and don't want them to get anything started on a big conspiracy."

After Sergeant Scharaga put out his APB, he set up a logistics and communication "command post" as required by departmental procedure. He took the name and address of the couple in the parking lot, whom he remembers as "the Bernsteins," and gave a handwritten memo with this information to a courier, who took it to headquarters. It subsequently disappeared, and Scharaga had no copy. There is no official record of anyone ever finding or talking to "the Bernsteins."

In the days that followed, Sergeant Scharaga wrote up a report of his encounter in the parking lot. Copies were filed with the watch commander and the sergeant's office. In a 1992 interview with the authors Scharaga described what happened next: "A few days later, I wanted to go back and refer to the reports for one reason or another, but they were all gone. I asked the day-watch sergeant if he knew anything about it, and he said the several agents from SUS [Special Unit Senator, the elite police task force set up to investigate the crime] had come that morning and cleaned out all the reports. I called SUS and they denied they'd even been there."

Unknown to Scharaga at the time, in place of his report would appear a summary report of an alleged interview of Scharaga by two SUS detectives. (Recall that many witnesses with accomplice-related information had summary reports of interviews in their files instead of transcripts of the actual interviews. The alleged misrepresentations in the report in Scharaga's file are typical of those experienced by these same witnesses.) According to this summary report, Scharaga is supposed to have said that he believed the older couple heard the woman cry, "They shot him" instead of "We shot him."

In 1988 Paul Scharaga was shown a copy of his reported interview with the SUS detectives. He was quite angry, and signed an affidavit saying that the document "contained false and deliberately misleading statements." Four years later his anger was still apparent. "That report is phony," he said from his home in Missouri. "No one ever interviewed me, and I never retracted my statement from 'We shot him' to 'They shot him.' This is just how things were done. If they couldn't get you to change your story, they'd ignore you. If they couldn't ignore you they'd discredit you, and if they couldn't do that, they'd just make something up."

If someone in the LAPD was trying to make the shouting woman on the stairs disappear by "losing" Sergeant Scharaga's report of the incident, they had a much thornier problem in the person of twenty-year-old Kennedy campaign worker Sandra Serrano. Serrano, recall, was on a fire staircase outside the Embassy Room when she was passed by a man and a young woman who was shouting exuberantly, "We shot him! We shot him!"

A little while later Serrano would be interviewed by Sander Vanocur on national TV, where she would tell her story and describe the woman as wearing a "white dress with polka dots" and having a "funny nose."

Vanocur was not the first person to whom Serrano told her story. She had first approached a guard, then a close friend, and then a man who seemed to be in authority, John Ambrose, who happened to be an assistant district attorney for Los Angeles. He calmed Serrano down, then listened to her account. On June 7, Deputy DA Ambrose would file with the FBI a report of this encounter with the distraught young witness. In the report Ambrose recalled Serrano's description of the mystery woman as "between 22 and 26 years of age, approximately 5'5", wearing a white dress with black polka dots and heels, with a good figure." "Serrano impressed me," Ambrose concluded, "as a sincere girl who was a dedicated Kennedy fan, not interested in publicity."

The Los Angeles police interviewed Serrano twice in the early morning hours of June 5. Two days later she returned to the hotel to reenact her story for police, FBI, and Secret Service investigators. The next day she was reinterviewed by FBI agents and taken to police headquarters to view Kathy Sue Fulmer, one of several women whom the LAPD would offer as a possible, nonsinsister polka-dot woman. Fulmer had told police she was at the Ambassador with an orange polka-dot scarf. Serrano immediately asserted that Fulmer was not the woman she had encountered. Then it was on to NBC studios in Burbank for a screening of television footage of the crowd at the Ambassador. Neither Sirhan nor the other two persons showed up on the screen. On June 10 Serrano was again interviewed by investigators from three agencies. She performed a filmed reenactment. Then she was taken to police headquarters to inspect eight polka-dot dresses assembled by the LAPD.

The handling of Sandra Serrano by the LAPD was a campaign within a campaign. Break Serrano and the polka-dot-dress woman would be banished. In pursuing their objective the police would attack Serrano's credibility on all fronts, until it had won this most crucial battle in the war to dispose of the mystery woman. Serrano's consistency, her going on record before any controversy was known, the sincerity perceived by Assistant DA Ambrose, and the corroborating accounts of other witnesses would count for nothing. She would become the case's most interviewed witness.

The LAPD's challenges to Serrano's credibility were immediate. Notations on interview summary documents dated June 6 and 7 indicate that, as far as the police were concerned, Serrano's story was not credible and the polka-dot mystery was solved: "Polka-dot story Serrano N. G."; "polka-dot story of Serrano phony."

In her original interview Serrano had said that she heard "backfires" just before she saw the fleeing couple. The LAPD investigators began referring to the sounds Serrano heard as "gunfire." The fact that this was their word, not hers, would be irrelevant: they would put the word in her mouth and then bludgeon her credibility with it.

In a burst of investigative zeal, the LAPD brought Serrano to the Ambassador Hotel and fired a .22 handgun (similar to Sirhan's) inside the pantry. At the same time they recorded the event with a tape recorder and decibel meter from the steps outside, where Serrano had rested. The verdict: it was impossible to hear shots from her position. During the experiment, audiotaped by the LAPD, Serrano protests (her voice choked with emotion): "It sounded like backfires of a car, and I never heard a gun. I don't know what a gun sounds like." No matter. From that time forward every police report on Serrano would begin with the litany that it was impossible for her to hear pantry gunshots, as though that fact alone was enough to discredit her story.

During the fire escape sound tests, FBI agent Richard Burris began pressing Serrano again.

"On television, with Sander Vanocur," Burris challenged, "you didn't say anything about seeing a girl and two men going up the fire stairs. You only said you saw a girl and a man coming down. And later you told the police you saw two men and a girl going up together and one of them was Sirhan Sirhan. That was the most significant thing you had to tell the police and yet you didn't say anything about this in your first interview, your interview on television."

"I can't explain why," a confused Serrano cried. "You're trying to trick me. You're lying and you're trying to trick me."

Although she wasn't thinking clearly enough to know the answer, Serrano's instincts were correct. It was a trick question. During her first accounts to Ambrose and Vanocur, Sirhan's face and identity were not known to her, and she had no way to know at that time that the man she saw on the stairs was the alleged assassin. The most important fact then was that the woman said, "We shot him."

On June 12, Serrano tried to defend herself. She phoned the FBI and informed Agent Burris that she was in the process of retaining legal counsel and would not talk to investigators again unless her lawyer could be there. But on June 20, without counsel, Serrano would be "scientifically" certified as a liar by the LAPD's instrument of choice for dealing with conspiracy witnesses—Sergeant Enrique Hernandez and his polygraph machine.

The device that has become known as the polygraph was first developed in the early part of this century. It was initially greeted with great skepticism, but after helping solve some of Chicago's notorious gangland killings in the 1930s, the "lie detector," as it became known, gained acceptance, gradually taking its place in the public mind as a legitimate weapon in the modern law enforcement arsenal.

Had the polygraph remained in the arena of law enforcement, it would command more respect than it does today. But by the mid 1980s the machine had descended upon mainstream America, with as many as 2 million exams performed each year, most of these done by employers on current or would-be employees. The question of whether the polygraph was a legitimate scientific device or merely a sophisticated carnival trick was now relevant to a growing constituency.

Accurate scientific data on the validity of the polygraph have always been difficult to come by, but in 1983, the U.S. Office of Technology Assessment declared the device "virtually useless" for preemployment interviews, and more opposition to its widespread use developed. Critics such as psychologist David Lykken of the University of Minnesota claimed that, for discovering truth, the polygraph is "little better than flipping a coin." In 1989 Congress responded by making it illegal to use the polygraph for screening potential employees. Yet, paradoxically, the polygraph has played a useful role in solving crimes. Over the years, perhaps due to the belief that the device really works, the "lie detector" has been quite effective in eliciting confessions.

The principle problem with the polygraph is that it does not measure lies but, instead, measures (through physiologic responses) the anxiety that telling a lie supposedly produces. The commonsense difficulty here is that many different factors can cause anxiety, among them being asked questions that might lead to the suspicion that one has committed a crime even if one hasn't.

The inability of the polygraph to detect liars successfully is not its chief liability—it is the propensity for false positives, that is, labeling people liars because they are nervous, or simply because the examiner has been careless or has misinterpreted the various squiggles on the graph paper. Moreover, the validity of a polygraph test depends not only upon whether the technology is valid, the subject is appropriate, or the examiner is properly trained, but also upon the examiner's integrity—for an improper test based upon an examiner's carelessness, prejudice, or malice is very difficult to prove.

Although dishonest polygraph exams in criminal investigations can lead to great injustice, the chances that an innocent person will confess to a serious crime when confronted with dishonest results are slight. An unfortunate side effect to this reality is that it may actually encourage zealous operators to habitually present suspects with "guilty" results, hoping to flush confessions from those who truly are. But when the same game is played with a witness to a crime, instead of a suspect, the equation is changed. With little in the way of a personal stake in the truth, the witness may well decide to end the aggravation and be done with the whole thing. In this circumstance overzealous application of the polygraph is tantamount to tampering with evidence.

As Chief Houghton described in *Special Unit Senator,* on June 20, Lieutenant Manny Pena suggested to Sergeant Hernandez that he might "like to take Sandra Serrano out for an SUS bought steak."[2] After what must have been a delightful dinner for Serrano, she was polygraphed between 9 and 10 P.M. Although many tapes of LAPD witness interviews have been either lost or destroyed, a tape of Serrano's session with Hernandez has somehow survived. That the tape contained information potentially embarrassing for the police is indicated by the embargo order placed upon it: "Do not play or have transcribed without the express permission of Capt. Brown [second in command of SUS]."

During the pre-interview phase of the polygraph session, Serrano's aunt is present (her parents lived in Ohio). After her aunt departs, Serrano expresses her displeasure at being polygraphed.

"The thing that I don't get is why a polygraph is administered if it will not even stand up in court," she protests, ". . . if the United States courts don't even recognize it."

"No, no, somebody has given you the wrong information on that," Hernandez assures her falsely. "Sandy, if that was the case we wouldn't have, we wouldn't have polygraphs."

After glowingly explaining the wonders and workings of the machine (with Serrano remaining unconvinced), Hernandez administers the test, asking Serrano numerous times if she was telling the truth about the girl in the polka-dot dress. Serrano answers that she was. But then the questions end.

"Sandy," says Hernandez in a confidential tone, "I'm not gonna ask you any more questions, not a single one. I do want to talk to you like a brother. Look, I presume, I don't know what religion you are, I'm Catholic. Are you Catholic?" And with that Hernandez launches into his own solo rendition of "good cop, bad cop," showing a patronizing concern for Serrano on the one hand, and hinting heavily on the other at unpleasant things to come if she doesn't change her story. What follows is a series of excerpts from this emotionally charged session.

Hernandez informs Serrano—with considerable editorial license, according to our reading of the case—that "nineteen girls" have come forward with stories, but only two "really loved Kennedy as a person." The rest were gold diggers or publicity hounds. He tells Serrano that she is one of the two who loved RFK, and she is honestly mistaken about what she saw. Then Hernandez becomes assertive.

"Nobody," he says, "told you, 'We have shot Kennedy.' "

"Yes," Serrano responds, "somebody told me that 'We have shot Kennedy.' "

"No, Sandy."

"I'm sorry," she asserts again, "but that's true. That is true."

Hernandez invokes a wide range of themes for his game of "truth or consequences": "One of these days, you're gonna be a mother," he tells Serrano. "You're gonna be a mother, you're gonna have kids, and you know that you can't live a life of shame, knowing what you're doing right now is wrong."

"But I seen those people," Serrano protests.

"Sandy, you know that this is wrong."

"I know what I saw. . . . I remember seeing the girl!"

"No, No. I'm talking about what you have told here about seeing a person tell you, 'We have shot Kennedy.' And that's wrong."

"That's what she said."

"No it isn't, Sandy. Please don't."

"No! That's what she said."

"Lookit, I love this man."

"So do I."

"And you're shaming, you're, he, if right now, if he can't even—"

"Don't shout at me."

Hernandez then tells Serrano of his personal affection for Kennedy "the man," how Kennedy allegedly gave him a commendation that he greatly cherished. He accuses Serrano of thwarting the investigation. He repeatedly mentions Robert Kennedy and his family.

"You don't know and I don't know if he's a witness right now in this room watching what we're doing in here," says Hernandez. ". . . Please, in the name of Kennedy . . . don't shame his death."

"Don't, don't come on with this sentiment business," responds Serrano, acting more professionally than her interviewer. "Let's just get this job done."

But Hernandez won't be deterred. He invokes history, the nation, the Kennedy family, the senator's ghost, the Catholic Church, law and order, good health, redemption, and Serrano's children-to-come in an effort to persuade the witness to change her story.

"The Kennedys have had nothing but tragedy," he says to Serrano, and then he sweetens the pot. ". . . And I'm sure—you mark my words—that one of these days, if you're woman enough, you will get a letter from Ethel Kennedy—*personal*—thanking you for at least letting her rest on this aspect of this investigation."

Serrano, one must remember, was merely a witness. She was not a person accused of a serious crime, clinging to a flimsy story in the hope of escaping punishment. She had no reason to make up such a story, but more important, other witnesses (the "Bernsteins" by way of Sergeant Paul Scharaga) described the very people and, word for word, the conversation Serrano was reporting. Nevertheless, Hernandez keeps attacking.

"This didn't happen," he says forcefully.

"It happened," Serrano replies.

"No, it didn't happen."

"Yes," she affirms, her voice fading.

At another point, when Hernandez again states flatly that she did not hear the phrase "We shot him," Serrano again disagrees and laughs nervously (sounding on the verge of breaking into tears).

"Don't you be laughing it off with a smirk on your face," Hernandez says in a menacing tone. He then implores Serrano to "redeem something that's a deep wound that will grow inside of you like cancer."

Serrano sighs and says in a low voice, "Damn cops, why don't you just leave me alone?"

"The only time you will be left alone," says Hernandez, "is when you tell me the truth about what happened outside on the staircase."

Hernandez keeps telling Serrano that he can fix this thing by himself if she will just change her story. But if not, he will be forced to tell the world that she is a liar, and the interrogations will continue because he'll have to turn her over to other investigators "upstairs" who are presumably not as nice or as understanding as he.

"Now you see what happens," he warns her; "there's two ways to approach this thing. The first is for me to appeal to you as a decent woman who campaigned for Senator Kennedy. The other way is for me to hold up the paper [the polygraph results], go out there and tell these people, and have them tell whoever they're going to tell upstairs . . . and they're gonna want to talk to you again and again."

"To tell you the truth," Serrano answers wearily, "I don't know anymore what happened. I just don't know. It's all such a big mess."

"Sandra, look. I don't know how we can do it to stop this thing. The easiest way for you, so we can stop it, nobody ask you anything else, you go home, be relieved of this thing. I don't know how we can do it. Possibly if I ask you right now and I get a report and we dictate it to someone, you and me, maybe we can stop it there."

Hernandez finally gets his way. After an hour of agonizing confrontation he wears Serrano down to the point where she agrees to having been "messed up." With the stenographer present Hernandez leads Serrano through a series of questions where she agrees that she had been confused and pressured by the expectations of the media and the investigators. Now that he had Serrano rolling downhill, Hernandez was eager to accelerate the process by finding scapegoats for her.

"The facts that you saw," he offered, "were apparently misquoted, or misprinted, or mistelevised to the actual true facts."

That was too much for Serrano even in her distraught state. "Well they can't have been mistelevised because I said that. I actually said that. . . . I really thought there was something behind it. I was scared. I tell you I've been scared all this time."

Hernandez tried to help Serrano reconstruct where she heard it. In his version Serrano was sitting on the staircase when someone came down and said something about Kennedy being shot. When she was down at the Rampart Street police station she spoke to Vincent DiPierro who told her his story of the girl in the polka-dot dress.

"So, that's where that thing about the polka-dot dress, that's where it started," said Hernandez, asserting more than asking.

"I guess," answered Serrano, seeming not to care anymore.

The very next day the LAPD called a press conference. At the meeting Inspector John Powers, assistant commander of the detective bureau, publicly canceled the all points bulletin for the girl in the polka-dot dress. "It was determined that the person who originally described the female in the white polka dot dress was erroneous," explained Powers, apparently referring to Sergeant Hernandez's session the day before. Powers explained that "the key witness, the one who caused the alert to be put out," had been "overwrought" after the slaying. He then dismissed other reports of a girl in a polka-dot dress at the Ambassador Hotel. "The room apparently was full of them," he said.[3]

According to Chief of Detectives Robert Houghton in his book *Special Unit Senator,* the breaking of Sandra Serrano was the "turning point" in the Robert Kennedy murder investigation. "SUS closed the vexing case of the polka-dot-dress girl," Houghton wrote proudly. "In police work, for lack of a better word, we say a witness was 'contaminated.' "[4] The congratulatory mood within the police investigation was contagious, and Sergeant Hernandez's work with Serrano would draw special praise from senior police officials. Several weeks later Enrique Hernandez would be promoted to the rank of lieutenant.

Twenty-five years after the fact, Sergeant Hernandez's superior Emmanuel Pena still defends Serrano's treatment at the hands of the polygraph operator. "It was a necessary move on my part," he told the authors. "We tried every way in the world to find this gal in the polka-dot dress to see if we could substantiate her [Serrano's] story. And we couldn't do it. I wasn't about to leave the case hanging there."

Pena's words illustrate quite clearly the police mind-set. First, they take their own inability to locate the girl in the polka-dot dress as evidence that Serrano is lying. Actually that fact should help confirm her story. If, as Pena asserts, Serrano misheard the woman who actually said, "They shot him," then one might have expected that woman to come forward after all the publicity. That she didn't would support Serrano's more sinister interpretation of events. But Pena and the police seemed unwilling to leave any questions unanswered. "We got to a point," he said, "where we had to establish something on an investigative basis that she was mistaken."*

By any measure, Serrano's recantation was a stunning accomplishment. In a little over an hour Sergeant Hernandez and his truth machine had managed to take what appeared to be a sincere and coherent witness (albeit fatigued by two weeks of adversarial attention) with a story that was corroborated by a number of independent sources and got her to recant, agreeing instead to Hernandez's version of events, which could not be true. Serrano could not have gotten the polka-dot dress story from Vincent DiPierro, because she told it to Assistant DA Ambrose before she ever met the young waiter.

---

*The police efforts in regards to Serrano were quite far reaching. On July 22, 1968, according to an August 2 police "progress report," the LAPD contacted the Internal Revenue Service and requested that they "run a financial background" check on Serrano and five other witnesses. The stated purpose of the check was "to eliminate any possible connection with suspect Sirhan regarding money matters."

While other witnesses with accomplice-related stories were dismissed or ignored, Serrano and DiPierro were given special attention by the Los Angeles police. They were both invited to fashion shows, where they viewed and compared a variety of white dresses with black polka dots. Sandra Serrano's special status came from the fact that many thousands of people had seen her on TV describing the girl in the polka-dot dress. DiPierro was important in that he had actually seen Sirhan fire his gun. Thus, while both witnesses, according to the LAPD, were telling stories that were untrue, Serrano, because of her high profile, would be discredited, while DiPierro, because he was needed as a witness, would be rehabilitated.

By July 1, when Vincent DiPierro was reinterviewed by police, polka-dot-dress stories were unwelcome, smoking gun or not. As a result, he earned, as did most witnesses with accomplice-related information, a session with Sergeant Enrique Hernandez. An audiotape of this interview has survived, but it is of such poor quality that little more than an occasional word can be understood. Nevertheless, it is known that DiPierro took the polygraph test and was then told by Hernandez that he failed the part about the woman with Sirhan. From all indications DiPierro seemed less inclined to fight the police than Serrano, and most likely Hernandez had to invoke a shorter list of deities to get DiPierro to do his duty and admit that he was confused. As with Serrano, Hernandez then called in a stenographer to record the postpolygraph session.

"As a matter of fact," said Hernandez once the notes were being taken, "you have told me now that there was no lady that you saw standing next to Sirhan."

"That's correct," responded DiPierro.

"Okay. Now, I can appreciate what you would have or could have been going through on that evening." Hernandez here seems to be fluffing up the bed for DiPierro's change of heart; but, here again, a polygraph does not detect confusion, if it detects anything at all. "But I think what you have told me," Hernandez continued, "is that you probably got this idea about a girl in a black-and-white polka-dot after you talked to Miss Sandra Serrano."

"Yes, sir, I did."

Hernandez had now pulled a coup of investigative logic: ten days earlier he had gotten Sandra Serrano to admit that she had originally cribbed the polka-dot-dress story from DiPierro; now Hernandez had DiPierro confess that he had gotten the story from Serrano. But as Hernandez tried to wrap up the session, DiPierro's words seemed to betray his eagerness to cooperate.

"You did not see a girl in a polka-dot dress," said Hernandez seeking to cement his victory. "You did not see a girl in a black-and-white polka-dot dress standing behind Sirhan on that evening?"

"No."

"Is there anything else that you have told me previously or that you have told Sergeant Patchett or anyone else that . . . is not the truth?"

"No. Nothing," he answer. "Only about the girl."

"Only about the girl?" repeated Hernandez.

"Yes, sir. That good enough?"

The problems the police had with witnesses who had seen the mysterious girl brought no comfort to the defense lawyers. They were as much a bother to the defense as they were to anyone else. Grant Cooper and Emile Berman had both entered the case late, and Russell Parsons, although he had been on the case from early on, spent most of his energies filing motions and worrying about how the defense was going to raise money. Only the two defense investigators, Mike McCowan and Robert Blair Kaiser, did any real work as far as reviewing witness statements.

Kaiser, in particular, was quite critical of what he perceived as a pattern of bullying by Hernandez, and of the LAPD's rush to dismiss witnesses who had seen things that didn't agree with the official version of events. One evening as Kaiser listened to a tape of Grant Cooper's long interview with Sirhan in his jail cell, he felt compelled to sit down and write Cooper a memo. "Before we do too much more research on the death penalty," he wrote, "or call in too many more experts, we ought to do a little suggesting of our own—that maybe Sirhan has been programmed to do something he now considers 'stupid'—possibly without his complete awareness that he was being so used."[5] This idea, however, was never seriously considered by the attorneys.

To reduce the crime to its essentials, one could say that Sirhan either acted alone or as part of a conspiracy, and that his actions were either willful or unwillful. Looked at this way there are four possibilities. The prosecution maintained that Sirhan acted willfully and alone. The defense argued that Sirhan acted alone but without the necessary volition to constitute legal premeditation. But to Sirhan's attorneys any evidence of accomplices only indicated willful concerted action, which would destroy the defense contention of an act committed without premeditation. Never did the lawyers consider the fourth possibility: that evidence of others involved might exonerate Sirhan if his participation were involuntary.

The defense attorneys' lack of curiosity in this direction may have been abetted by the report of defense investigator Michael McCowan. In his report to Cooper, McCowan asserted that DiPierro

stated that he saw Sirhan with a girl in a polka dot dress standing with him by some stairs prior to the shooting. He later admitted that he made up the story and that it was Sandy Serrano who had told him that she saw a girl in a polka dot dress running out of the kitchen yelling, "We shot him! We shot him!" Miss Serrano's testimony was also proven false.

McCowan, recall, was a former police officer turned private investigator who offered his services to the defense team. His propensity to accept and pass on to Sirhan's attorneys the shabby police interpretation of these witnesses' testimony is noteworthy for its brevity and lack of analysis.

Vincent DiPierro was called to the witness stand by the prosecution on February 17, to dramatically point to the defendant as the man he had seen shoot Kennedy, and under John Howard's direction he did just that.

"Now this person you observed on the tray rack," asked Howard, "would you describe him for us?"

"Yes," replied DiPierro, "he had dark hair and a white shirt or possibly a light blue shirt, with dungarees or dark blue pants."

"Do you see that person in court?"

"Yes, sir, I do."

"Would you indicate him, please?"

"This gentleman seated here."

"May the record indicate Mr. Sirhan, Your Honor?"

Under Howard's direction, DiPierro's story was told in great detail, but the girl he had originally seen with Sirhan was never mentioned. Normally, a witness who had failed a lie detector test concerning the second most important element of his story might have been scratched as a witness by the prosecution or savaged by the defense. Not here. Nevertheless, there were some surprises during cross-examination. Grant Cooper asked a routine question and, despite the lie detector and the apparent coaching, the story of Sirhan and the girl came spilling out.

"What was there that caused you to notice him [Sirhan]?" asked Cooper.

"At the time," replied DiPierro, "there was there, I believe, a girl standing within the area of Sirhan. . . ."

"Then you did see a girl standing there by him at that time?"

"Not definitely by him, in the area of him."

"Pardon me. Can you tell us where she was?"

"I would say around the area of the tray rack where he was, but I cannot say."

"And you observed the girl first, did you?"

"Yes, I did."

"And you observed this girl because she was pretty?"

"Correct . . ."

"Did you observe how the girl was dressed at that time?"

"Well, I can recall she was wearing a polka-dot dress. . . ."

"And what kind of polka dots were these, were they black or—"

"Black."

"What color was her hair?"

"I don't recall. It has been so long. I don't recall."

"Do you remember in a statement you said it was brown, and would you say brunet?"

"Brunet, possibly dark brown."

After having elicited from the witness the "girl-with-Sirhan" story, Cooper then referred DiPierro to the transcript of his July 1 interview with Sergeant Enrique Hernandez. Cooper then read to the court the entire transcript of Hernandez's recorded session with DiPierro where the witness confessed that the story he was telling about the girl was false. Cooper finished with Hernandez's assertive question:

> Q: You did not see a girl in a polka-dot dress, you did not see a girl in a back-and-white polka-dot dress standing beside Sirhan on that evening?
>
> A: No.

"Now let me ask you first," said Cooper when he was done reading, "was this statement that you gave to Sergeant Enrique Hernandez on July 1, 1968, the truth?"

"Yes it was," said DiPierro.

Only minutes before, DiPierro had testified that he first noticed Sirhan because of the pretty brown-haired girl in a dress with black polka dots standing beside him. Now he was saying once again that the story was false. On redirect examination by Prosecutor David Fitts, DiPierro's testimony would become nearly schizophrenic.

"Are you telling us in substance," questioned Fitts, "there was a girl standing near Sirhan at or near the time of the shooting, sir?"

"Yes, sir," answered DiPierro.

"With a polka-dot dress?"

"Yes."

"And the kind of girl that attracted your attention, is that right?"

"Yes, sir."

And there it was. After all the screening, summary reports, polygraph tests, supposed witness retractions, witness selections, and coaching, the story the police were most trying to kill, that of the woman in the polka-dot dress, was now part of the trial of Sirhan Sirhan. David Fitts, however, was ready for this eventuality.

"I have a photograph, Your Honor," he said, addressing Judge Walker, "three views of a girl in a polka-dot dress."

After the photographs were admitted into evidence, Fitts went back to Vincent DiPierro.

"Mr. DiPierro, first I direct your attention to the black-and-white photograph, 10A. . . . Do you recognize that individual as anyone you have ever seen before?"

"Yes, I believe I saw her that night."

"Are you telling us that this appears to be a picture of the girl that you saw in the pantry at or near the time of the shooting?"

"Yes, but I believe she had darker hair than that."

"I didn't hear the answer, Your Honor," Grant Cooper interjected.

"He said, 'But I believe she had darkened her hair,' " replied Judge Walker, giving a somewhat inaccurate account of what the witness had said.

Fitts was eager to glide over this point.

"In any event," he said to the witness, "she seems to be pretty blond in the picture, doesn't she?"

"Yes, she does."

"Other than the difference in the color of the hair that you noticed, does she seem to be the girl?"

"Yes, I would think she would be."

"If the Court please, I believe that Mr. Cooper will stipulate with me that the girl depicted in these photographs is one Valerie Schulte, I understand, a Santa Barbara girl.

"I have nothing further."

To any juror paying attention it must have appeared that the testimony of Thomas Vincent DiPierro had in a short period undergone a tortured odyssey. First he identified Sirhan as the murderer, without having his testimony crushed by his alleged failure of a lie detector test. Next he told his entire story without ever mentioning the girl with Sirhan. Then in dizzying succession, he admitted to defense counsel Cooper that there was indeed a pretty girl with Sirhan the night of the murder, then he admitted that this story was false. Finally, on redirect, DiPierro agreed with prosecutor Fitts that there *was* a girl with a polka-dot dress in the pantry standing near Sirhan, but it was Kennedy girl Valerie Schulte.

The following day Valerie Schulte would be called to the witness stand. The attractive, blond young woman stood up and then, using a crutch, limped slowly to the witness stand—one leg in a brace, the result of a nasty ski accident she had suffered *before* the assassination.

"Miss Schulte," said David Fitts, "Directing your attention to the fourth day of June 1968, which was Election Day, did you go to the Ambassador Hotel on that evening?"

"Yes I did."

Valerie Schulte had indeed been at the Ambassador Hotel. After Kennedy's speech she had followed some distance behind the senator into the pantry where the shots were fired. After Schulte described the shooting from her vantage point, prosecutor Fitts asked another question.

"Would you tell us what you were wearing on this evening in question?"

"Yes, I was wearing a green dress with yellow polka dots."

"Did you bring the dress you were wearing that evening to court with you?"

"Yes, I did."

The witness was then handed a plastic bag containing the green dress.

"Would you just hold it up so that everybody can see it?"

In a trial filled with odd moments, this would be one of the most bizarre—symbolic for the extreme disregard for the truth manifested by both the prosecution and the defense. By any measure, the claim that Valerie Schulte was the mysterious polka-dot-dress woman was silly. She was never standing near Sirhan, which contradicts DiPierro's detailed account given the night of the murder of seeing Sirhan and the woman apparently talking. But most important, Schulte had her leg in a cast and was using a crutch. Moreover, she was wearing a dark green dress with large yellow lemon-shaped splotches. (After she had been excused, Valerie Schulte explained to inquiring newsmen that she had not come forward sooner "because I have never thought of my dress as having polka dots.")[6]

At this point the prosecution's position on the polka-dot woman defied all logic. Recall that Enrique Hernandez and his polygraph had already determined that Vincent DiPierro had lied when he said he saw a woman in a polka-dot dress that night. Now, apparently, he had been telling the truth.

And what of the other mystery-woman witnesses who had already been branded as liars? Were they now to be brought back and told that they were merely confused, that the dress they saw as white was really green, the polka dots they saw as black were really yellow, and the woman they saw running from the scene was really on crutches? No, it wouldn't be done. The police had a woman, and they had something they called polka dots, and to most everyone involved, including the press, that would do.

On the following day a picture of Valerie Schulte dominated the front page of the *Los Angeles Times*. After eight months of byzantine investigation, the case of the woman in the polka-dot dress was now publicly solved.

★   ★   ★

Though he had tried his best to do what was expected of him, the constant pressure upon Vincent DiPierro apparently wounded his sense of self. Just a little over a month after Sirhan was convicted DiPierro wrote a letter to local radio (KHJ) reporter Art Kevin, who was broadcasting a series on the unanswered questions in the Robert Kennedy murder. It was Kevin's segment on the polka-dot-dress woman that DiPierro found most interesting. Kevin had reportedly resisted police pressure not to air this segment which raised, once again, despite the public resolution of the controversy at Sirhan's trial, the specter of the woman in the polka-dot dress. It was, said DiPierro, "the first 'real true' report" of the incident and he praised Kevin for "the extensive research and brilliant job of reporting a factual story."

DiPierro told Kevin that the polka-dot-dress story "concerned my character personally, [and] I was deeply interested in *hearing the facts straight for a change* [emphasis added]." DiPierro then offered to assist Kevin on the story in the future.

But when Art Kevin drove out to the DiPierro residence a few days later he discovered that someone had been there before him. The door was answered by Angelo DiPierro, Vincent's father and a maître d' at the Ambassador Hotel. Vincent stood nearby. Kevin reported that both men "looked all shook up." Angelo DiPierro then told Kevin that the FBI had come by and explained in great detail how hard the police had worked in reconstructing the events in the pantry. The father hinted that he had some reason to believe there was some threat to his son's life and pleaded with Kevin to forget the whole thing. The door was then shut.[7]

The shutting door would apparently be the last change of mind and heart on the matter for Vincent DiPierro. In 1988, when DiPierro was interviewed by the authors, he was effusive in his praise for the work of the Los Angeles police, saying that they had protected him when his "life was in danger." (The conjured threat to DiPierro's life would seem to be a police or FBI ploy, for if Sirhan alone had murdered Robert Kennedy, as they asserted, who was left to threaten DiPierro?)

Shortly after her dramatic session with Sergeant Enrique Hernandez, Sandra Serrano quit her job and moved back to Ohio. Later she returned to California, but she avoided comment on the Robert Kennedy case for twenty years. Then in 1988, a week after the LAPD files on the case were made public by the California State Archives, a forty-year-old Sandra Serrano Sewell talked briefly to radio interviewer Jack Thomas about her treatment as a witness at the hands of the Los Angeles police. "I don't ever want to have to go through that again," she said, "that kind of everyday harassment, you know, being put in a room for hours with polka-dot dresses all around you. It was a bad scene and one that as a young person I was totally unprepared to handle. . . . I was just twenty years old and I became unglued. I said what they wanted me to say."

NINE

Malice Aforethought

✻ ✻ ✻

*One of the curious things about this historic trial is that there is a
mystery. No one awaits a secret witness or the disclosure of the real
murderer, but gradually developing more each week is a mystery
about Sirhan.*
*Who is he? What is he? Why did he kill Robert Kennedy, a man
he saw for the first time only two days before the assassination and
thought was a saint?*

—Lacey Fosburgh, *New York Times*, March 9, 1969

F OR THE REPORTERS covering
the Sirhan trial, the first weeks of
testimony had been difficult to translate into exciting copy. There had been
no conflict. Grant Cooper hadn't challenged the prosecution's reconstruction of the crime; he had cooperated in the presentation of Valerie Schulte
as the girl in the polka-dot dress. Hope for real drama now centered on the
moment when Sirhan Sirhan would take the witness stand in his own defense. How would the accused assassin conduct himself? How would he
justify his actions? Why had he murdered Robert Kennedy?

Under California law, motive, unlike premeditation and malice, is not
an element of murder. "Presence of motive may tend to establish guilt,"
Judge Walker explained to the jury. "Absence of motive may tend to establish innocence." Nevertheless, the state does not carry the burden of
proving any motive at all. Still, whether it leads to unknown perpetrators
or satisfies a jury's curiosity, answering the question of motive is central to
any case.

Since the captured assailant of Robert Kennedy was not providing information to anyone directly after the shooting, the initial question of motive was up for grabs. As has been demonstrated, public officials, including
President Johnson, Governor Reagan, and Mayor Yorty, quickly stepped
in with their own explanations. These views were, of course, expressions
of personal agendas—expected and discounted by those who cared to think
about them. Sirhan had not confessed to the crime; the police had barely

begun their investigation. This, however, did not prevent others from offering their opinions.

The day after the assassination, U.S. attorney general Ramsey Clark held a press conference at the Justice Department and declared that there was "no evidence of conspiracy," despite the fact that the Los Angeles police had just put out an APB for a woman seen with the assailant before the shooting. In another story published in the *New York Times,* a Cuban refugee, Jose Duarte, who described himself as a former Cuban army officer, said he had encountered Sirhan Sirhan several weeks before in Hollywood, California. Duarte claimed that Sirhan had declared, "What we need in the United States is another Fidel Castro." According to Duarte, this statement led to a "scuffle."

A very different view of the crime came from Dr. Mohammad T. Mehdi, secretary-general of the Action Committee on American-Arab Relations in New York. The day after the murder Mehdi issued a statement that Sirhan may have been motivated by Robert Kennedy's assurance that if elected president he would honor the U.S. agreement to sell fifty Phantom jets to Israel. "It is this disrespect for the human Arab persons," said Dr. Mehdi, "which brings about this kind of violence."

Dr. Mehdi's statement was the first suggestion that the U.S. plan to sell jet planes to Israel, a deal negotiated by President Lyndon Johnson and Israeli prime minister Levi Eshkol in January of 1968, was the motivating factor in the murder of Robert Kennedy. In time this explanation would be embraced by the police, the prosecution, the defense, the press, the Arab community, the defendant, and the defendant's family. It was simple and easily understood, and it served the basic needs of almost everyone, as will be discussed. But there were serious problems with this explanation, problems that almost everyone was willing to ignore.

For example, if Sirhan murdered Robert Kennedy to make a political gesture on behalf of the dispossessed Palestinian Arabs, why didn't he shout "No bombers to Israel!" as he fired his gun? Why would he remain silent in police custody? Why would he withhold his identity? Having accomplished his task with no chance of escape, wouldn't he be eager to take credit for his deed and speak to the world about the injustices suffered by his people?

But for weeks after the shooting Sirhan did not announce any motive, political or personal. He never said meekly, much less with bravado, that he had killed Kennedy for the Arab cause. He did not deny the killing— he simply could not offer an explanation for it. In short, Sirhan did not act like a political assassin.

There is also a timing problem in the "jets-to-Israel" hypothesis. The official story was that on May 18 Sirhan saw Robert Kennedy on television promising to sell fifty jet planes to Israel. This, supposedly, so enraged Sirhan that he made up his mind to kill Kennedy and wrote, "RFK must die" in his notebook. This story has been told and retold many times. Those on Sirhan's defense team were as effective in propagating the tale as those on the prosecution. During his final argument, defense attorney Emile Berman said, "We come down to May 18 of 1968, and I told you about his blowing his stack when he heard this on television about the Phantom jets—pounding the TV, stalked to his room; he wrote and said and indicated that he, who had loved and admired Kennedy, had been betrayed; and he was outraged."

Defense psychiatrist Bernard Diamond also described in court the television show "in which Senator Kennedy gave his assurance . . . that if elected president he would see to it that the Israeli government received fifty bombers which had been promised to them."

The power and longevity of this story was evidenced in 1988, when Sirhan's then-attorney Luke McKissack gave his own rendition: "He felt after seeing Kennedy make the statement that he was gonna send . . . with the yarmulke on him in the temple . . . he was gonna send fifty Phantom jets to Israel, that was interpreted by Sirhan as basically sending planes to bombard and kill his own people."[1]

May 18 was a critical date in all this, because the incriminating notebook entry "RFK must die" bore that designation. If the date is correct, then the intent to murder had to exist at that time as well as the motive behind that intent. The difficulty here is that the documentary on Robert Kennedy that Sirhan watched on television was aired in Los Angeles on May 20, two days after the notebook entry. More important, it contained no references at all to sending jets to Israel.

The documentary is a relatively standard recapitulation of Senator Kennedy's political career. It reviews his tenure as U.S. attorney general, and touches on his relationship with President Kennedy and his ascent to the U.S. Senate. In searching for segments that might have disturbed Sirhan, one can find brief footage of Robert Kennedy as a reporter in Israel in 1948, "helping to celebrate their independence." Later, an announcer talks of Kennedy's desire to "play a role in the affairs of men and nations" as an Israeli flag is shown in the background. This imagery may well have angered Sirhan, but it could hardly be considered a catalyst for murder, and it is very different from the reported vision of Kennedy wearing a yarmulke in a temple and promising to send bombers.

Later Sirhan would say that he heard on the radio that Kennedy, while at some Zionist club in Beverly Hills, had promised to send fifty jet bombers to Israel. On May 20, Kennedy was at the Temple Isaiah in West Los Angeles. But his statements there were anything but inflammatory. He spoke mostly about a negotiated settlement between Israel and her Arab neighbors. When Kennedy did mention arms it was in response to the increased Soviet threat in the Mediterranean Sea. "We must assist with arms, if necessary, to meet the threat of massive Soviet military build-ups . . . But in the long run, an arms race helps no one, least of all the people of that region who have lived under war for two decades. What we need is an agreement . . . to defuse the Middle East and to stop on all sides further shipments . . . a small but important step toward peace in the world."

Kennedy also spoke of making the "desert bloom" by a peaceful sharing of the waters of the Jordan River. When someone asked where he stood on the city of Jerusalem, Kennedy sidestepped the question and did not take a pro-Israeli position. "I stand here," he said, "in Los Angeles."[2]

A week later, during his campaign against Eugene McCarthy in Oregon, Kennedy did voice his support for the Johnson-Eshkol agreement. Kennedy's comments were reported in a late-night AP news wire, so it is possible that a radio station picked up the story, but the senator's words were not mentioned in the Oregon newspapers, or those in Los Angeles and New York, until *after* the assassination.

Efforts to explain the May 18 "jets for Israel" non sequitur have created their own difficulties. In his 1982 book *American Assassins*, James W. Clarke attempts to solve the timing problem by postulating that Sirhan was set off on his murderous path in January 1968 when Kennedy, like many other political leaders, did voice support for the Johnson-Eshkol deal. To buttress this theory Clarke asserts that "on Friday, January 31, 1968, Sirhan scrawled what was the first series of trancelike notebook entries declaring repeatedly that 'RFK must die.' "[3]

Clark's assertion here is erroneous. The page he was referring to was not from Sirhan's notebook and was not written in 1968. It had been written by Sirhan in prison on Saturday, February 1, 1969, while under a hypnotic spell induced by defense psychiatrist Dr. Bernard Diamond. Diamond had asked Sirhan to write the date and Sirhan had written "Friday 31 January 689 Friday 31 January 69," the date of the day before the session.*

If Sirhan had harbored a death wish for Kennedy from January 1968, as Clark argues, then he certainly hid it well. In the dozens of police interviews conducted with virtually everyone who had contact with Sirhan during the year prior to the assassination, there emerged not a single instance of Sirhan having commented on Kennedy's support of Israel, on jet bombers, or on anything at all relating Kennedy to Jews, Israelis, or the Middle East. Moreover, nowhere in Sirhan's notebooks, before or after May 18, is there any

---

*It has also been suggested that perhaps on February 1, 1969, Sirhan, under hypnosis, was recalling the date and the first moments of his murderous resolve. In the context of Dr. Diamond's questions this seems very unlikely. Also, January 31, 1968, was a Wednesday.

mention of jet bombers for Israel. In addition, Sirhan has always maintained that until shortly before the murder he was an admirer of Kennedy.

In one of his jail cell interviews with prosecution psychiatrist Dr. Seymour Pollack, Sirhan is emphatic about this point.

"Now that was in May of '68, that you saw the television program, is that right?" asks Dr. Pollack.

"Right."

"He was already running in the primaries. Now you mean until that [TV documentary], up until that time, you were for Kennedy?"

"Hell, I was for him, sir."

The only testimony the prosecution was able to present regarding Sirhan's prior intent came from Alvin Clark, a Pasadena sanitation worker. Clark had collected trash on East Howard Street and over time had gotten to know Sirhan, because Sirhan had on occasion brought him coffee and snacks and then engaged him in conversation. Clark testified that on one of these occasions Sirhan had threatened to murder Robert Kennedy. On cross-examination Emile Berman seriously dented Clark's credibility by having him acknowledge that during an FBI interview he had said he did not want to take an oath when testifying at the trial because he was willing to say anything to see Sirhan convicted.

If Sirhan Sirhan was not motivated to murder by the U.S. plan to sell Phantom jets to Israel, when did those words enter his lexicon, and how did they get there?

On August 14 the accused assassin was interviewed by his attorney Russell Parsons and journalist Robert Blair Kaiser. It was the first of more than a dozen interviews Kaiser would conduct as a nominal defense investigator. As Kaiser reports in his book *"RFK Must Die!,"* during this session Sirhan talked about his reaction to the Robert Kennedy documentary. "I was pissed off," Sirhan said. "Those *must have been* my feelings. [Emphasis added.] Those were my feelings."[4]

In Sirhan's breast pocket during the interview was a *New York Times* article about the assassination, sent to him by John Lawrence, director of a New York City–based organization called FAIR—Federated Americans against Israeli Racism. The article quoted Lawrence as saying, "There are no tears in us for Robert Kennedy . . . the advocate of sending American jet bombers to Israel so Jews can kill more Arabs."[5]

Sirhan had received the clipping on Monday, June 10. It accompanied a letter by Lawrence, five dollars in cash, and three issues of *Insight,* the official newsletter of FAIR. In his letter Lawrence told Sirhan that he ought to be forgiven for his mistake, because he made it in the pursuit of justice. He also called Sirhan a soldier in the cause of justice for the Arab people.

Lawrence followed this with three telegrams on June 10, June 11, and June 13, each offering encouragement and advice to Sirhan. Sirhan replied by wire on June 13.

RESPECTED SIRS: GRATEFUL FOR MONEY ENJOYED "INSIGHT" PLEASE SEND MORE ISSUES ANXIOUS ABOUT MIDEAST REACTION. Sirhan. 718–486.

On June 14, John Lawrence responded to Sirhan with a long letter. In it he advised that Sirhan defend himself by putting American society and Robert Kennedy on trial for their sociopathic conduct. Lawrence warned Sirhan that the doctors who were examining him were working for and paid by the state. He advised against a psychiatric defense. If Sirhan pleaded insanity, he cautioned, all those who subsequently spoke out against the injustices suffered by the Palestinian people would also be judged insane.

Sirhan, understandably, was not receiving encouragement or support from many quarters. The little he did receive was from the Arab community, but that was conditional: Sirhan should behave like a loyal, although perhaps misguided, Arab nationalist.

"Every single Arab in America regrets the killing," explained Arab-American publisher Henry Awad to *New York Times* reporter Lacey Fosburgh. "But the trial will bring us a chance for publicity. We think it's the only way the United States will hear about the Arab cause."[6]

In his August 14 meeting with Parsons and Kaiser, the accused assassin cautiously began to do that. He wasn't very convincing. As Sirhan spoke about Kennedy's betrayal of the Arab people, Kaiser noted, "he didn't *sound* upset [emphasis Kaiser's]. His dislike of Kennedy—you could hardly call it so much as anger—seemed remote and detached."[7]

This was Sirhan's first attempt to give political coloration to the murder of Robert Kennedy. It is significant that at this moment he carried in his pocket the John Lawrence clipping linking Kennedy to the jets-for-Israel deal. Had this truly been Sirhan's motivation, it would hardly seem necessary to carry the *Times* article. On the other hand, if this were a new idea to Sirhan, then it would make sense that he might want to carry the clipping for reference and reassurance.

Sirhan's amnesia presents yet another difficulty for the question of motive. If the accused assassin was making a heroic gesture on behalf of his people, why would he not remember the crime or say he did not remember the crime, while at the same time not denying or challenging his guilt? Sirhan's lack of memory simply does not fit with the act as a political event. If one has no memory of planning to kill, then a subsequent offer of motive must be an after-the-fact rationalization. A careful examination of Sirhan's interviews with his lawyers and doctors exposes this process. These conversations do not show a politically motivated assassin, but, rather, a defendant who remains confused about what happened, and who adopts a particular motive as representing the least of the evils.

During December 1968, while others were on Christmas break, Robert Kaiser scheduled several private interviews with Sirhan. During these recorded sessions Sirhan was relatively relaxed and cooperative with the defense investigator. After some conversation about books Sirhan had in his cell—he had just finished Whittaker Chambers's *Witness,* and was in the middle of Victor Hugo's *Les Misérables*—Kaiser asked Sirhan about his father. Sirhan spoke about Bishara, but failed to acknowledge that his father had abandoned his wife and children. Kaiser pressed him on the point.

"What you are saying might be completely true," Sirhan replied, "but yet I was raised here. My whole mind is engulfed in the American way of life, American line of thinking, my mind operates American. Now my father . . . all this stuff is pretty well ingrained in him. And he is all Arab. One hundred percent Arab. Today he would be a complete stranger to me. His line of thought, his background and heritage are not mine. I don't think I could reconcile myself with him, you know, on a cultural basis."

Sirhan continued to explain his alienation. "I don't identify with the Arabs politically or any other way except for the fact that their blood flows in my veins. Their food I don't go for. Their clothing I don't dig. Their robes and all that bullshit. Their politics I can't understand and don't want to understand. Their religion? I'm a Christian. Their language I don't speak very well. Hell, I'm an American. That's the way I look at myself."[8]

For a man who is supposed to be the Arab avenger, this is a remarkable statement.

A little later Sirhan would say, "I'm not psychotic. I don't think I am. Except when it comes to Jews."

"I'll tell you something," said Kaiser. "Sometimes when we are talking about this . . . I feel you are putting me on. As if you are overplaying that."

"I could be sometimes," admitted Sirhan. "But it's in me."

"At times I think you are overdoing it."

"I could be. I could be. But I have to prove my point. That is my main weakness."

"You can't come across as one big mad-on against the Jews," replied Kaiser. "That's unbelievable."[9]

Kasier's conversations with Sirhan continued. To Sirhan's discomfort, the defense investigator attempted to pry into the prisoner's previous sex life. Sirhan resisted, but was more or less challenged into revealing that he had "gotten his share." He described to Kaiser several sexual encounters. These stories served only to reinforce Kaiser's notion that Sirhan had not had frequent or fulfilling sex.

"I don't want to talk about it . . . ," said Sirhan. "You know women, money and horses were my thing, but I still maintain this thing had a political motivation. There was no other . . . involving factor. And I will keep it political."[10]

Sirhan's sex life had already been probed by the psychologists, and Sirhan, understandably, found this scrutiny uncomfortable. In these situations the political motive seemed to serve as a defense against these threatening and distasteful inquiries.

For example, when Kaiser brought up Sirhan's difficulties with women, the defendant responded, "Don't talk about women to me."

Kaiser asked why.

"This is political," said Sirhan. "This is a politically motivated—" Sirhan then broke into a strange nervous laugh. "This is, heh heh, political, heh heh, politically motivated."[11]

Later Sirhan would assert, "If I had need of some sexual outlets, I'd go out and get a girl. I wouldn't go out and shoot that bastard."

"You weren't all tied up?" asked Kaiser.

"I *was* all tied up," answered Sirhan. "The Arab Israeli—"

"Well, you had a real burning gripe."

Sirhan, sounding confused, then replied in a manner quite unlike a political terrorist. "This is what puzzles me," he said. "I have had hatred, but not that much. Hatred was very foreign to me. That bothers me. I can't understand it."[12]

Sirhan's continued confusion about the crime was quite evident during his first full interview with attorney Grant Cooper in December 1968.

"One of the most important things in the world for a lawyer," began Cooper with his new client, "and more important for you, is that I get the complete truth. A lawyer's just got to have the truth—and that means the whole complete truth—because I can't operate any other way. . . . I am interested in when you first decided you were going to kill Kennedy, because it is written down in books and everything, and they have it, so you tell me. . . ."

"I honestly did not decide to do it, sir," replied Sirhan. "Objectively, I had no awareness of what I was doing that night. . . ."

"Well," said Cooper, "who do you think killed him?"

"Obviously I must have—but I have no exact—no objective of what I was doing."

Cooper was skeptical. He offered, instead, what had become the accepted motive. "As I view it," he told his client, "you heard Kennedy make a statement, in substance that he wanted to send these airplanes to Israel. This burned you up, and then you write down in the book 'Kennedy must go,' 'Kennedy must go,' or words to that effect."

To Cooper's chagrin Sirhan continued to maintain that he had no recollection of ever intending to murder Robert Kennedy. Cooper then asked Sirhan if he was angry at Kennedy when he went to see him at the Ambassador Hotel reception on June 2.

"No, I wasn't," said Sirhan.

"Why not?" asked Cooper incredulously.

"This is—well you have to hit me at the time. At the time I heard these things I was mad, but again sir, the madness, this feeling, this emotion or whatever had subsided . . . and that's why I thought I decided to like him again when I went down there to see him."[13]

In a subsequent session Grant Cooper presented Sirhan with photocopies of pages from his notebooks. Emile Berman and Robert Kaiser were also present. Cooper began reading randomly from the notebooks.

" 'Nasser is the greatest man who ever lived in this world. Nasser is the greatest man who ever lived in this world. Nasser is the greatest man who ever lived in this world. Lived. Lived. Lived.' What about that?"

"All this repetition!" said Sirhan, as though it were the first time he had seen the notebooks.

" 'Tonight. Tonight. Tonight. We. I must buy a new Mustang tonight. Tonight. Tonight. Tonight. Tonight. Meet me tonight.' "

"I must be psychotic," said Sirhan, laughing, but with no better explanation for the strange writing.

" 'Let us do it. Let us do it. Let us do it do it it it. Let us do it. Please pay to the order of. 50. 50. 50. 50,000. 5. 500,0000. Very good. Very good. One hundred thousand dollars.' "

"Whew!" exclaimed Sirhan.

"How much did you say you made a week?" asked Emile Berman.

"Seventy dollars a week," answered Sirhan, who had briefly made that much as a racehorse groom.

" 'Please pay to the order of Sirhan Sirhan the the the the amount of 15 15 15 15 death life 15. $15,000. Must die. Die. Die. Die. Dollar sign. Life and death.' "

"For Christ's sake," interrupted Berman. "Were you smoking hashish?" Berman had another question: "What kind of writing involves this constant repetition of a word?"

Sirhan had no answer. "That's what I've been wondering," he replied.[14] Once again, in the confidential company of his attorneys, Sirhan was more like a confused boy than a political assassin.

If Sirhan seemed unsuited for the role of political assassin in his sessions with Grant Cooper, he positively flunked the audition in his sessions with Dr. Seymour Pollack. Recall that Dr. Pollack was a renowned psychiatrist from the University of Southern California who had been brought into the case by the district attorney's office to provide the expertise needed to refute the defense's claim of diminished capacity. Pollack was given unprecedented access to Sirhan when Grant Cooper thought his input would help bring about a successful plea bargain for Sirhan.

Trial testimony, audiotapes, and documents released by the DA's office (in 1985–86) reveal that Pollack was not merely invited in for a supervised evaluation of the defendant. He got to work with Sirhan extensively. Pollack spent approximately forty hours in Sirhan's cell, in eight sessions lasting from one and a half hours to a marathon five and a half hours. At some of the sessions, Grant Cooper and Dr. Bernard Diamond, the defense psychiatrist, were present. At others, the prosecution psychiatrist had Sirhan to himself.

Pollack was aware of the conflicting nature of this role: "I'm doing my damnedest to bend over backwards to find something that would exonerate him, and I have to watch myself," he confided to Dr. Diamond. ". . . How the hell can I be so deceitful? Here I am the prosecution consultant, and yet at the same time—you get my point?"

Pollack's sessions with Sirhan raise serious questions as to the increasingly porous boundaries in this case between the prosecution and the defense, and also between the medical and the legal professions. As the audiotapes reveal, Pollack does not merely assess: he hypnotizes the prisoner, challenges him, and gives fairly impassioned minispeeches. Often he appears to be coaching a somewhat passive or reluctant Sirhan on his motive.

"I have a clear picture of what you did," lectures Pollack. "You were waiting for Kennedy. You were actively looking for him. . . . Apparently what was eating at you was these elections and how strongly you felt about the American political figures letting the Arab world down. . . . It isn't just letting the Arab world down, it's building up Israel."

Sirhan agrees and Pollack continues.

"It might not even have been just Kennedy [inaudible] so strong, if [Hubert] Humphrey were there, it might have been anybody else. Someone who was big, someone who was big, tough, somebody who was—it wasn't necessarily Kennedy—it could have been somebody else but someone who would still represent American policy that was pro-Israel. In fact, it—for example—might have been Humphrey. Because Humphrey was a person you didn't particularly like either."

Pollack then goes on to preview the upcoming trial for Sirhan in terms of its political theme:

"The trial is a trial in which you are sort of accusing America of . . . burying a million Arabs."

"In fact!" Sirhan seems pleased.

"And that's, that's, that's your—in a sense—that's your plea."

Sirhan says nothing and continues to listen to Pollack's sudden insight about the trial as a political showcase: "You see, if I, if I assume that this is so, that you really want the Arab—the world, not the Arab—want the world to see the Arab suffering, the Palestinian Arabs particularly, but all of the displaced Arabs . . . to see that American policy has helped [cause] that suffering."

That Sirhan had not acted like a political assassin before or after the murder didn't bother Dr. Pollack. These inconsistencies could be dismissed by viewing Sirhan as an amateur: "I don't really think you thought the whole thing out," Pollack says to Sirhan. "You certainly didn't work out a good way of killing him, in the sense that it was, uh, a good plan."

"That's what I don't understand," replies Sirhan. "If I wanted to kill a man, why would I have shot him right there where they could have choked the shit outta me?"

"It might be that you wanted to be caught, if you wanted the world to know it was an Arab who did it," answers Pollack, offering an escalated version of the alleged motive. There was nothing in Sirhan's behavior after the murder to warrant this opinion, and in his jail cell eight months later Sirhan wasn't buying it either.

"You don't think so?" asks Pollack.

"If I had wanted to kill him," says Sirhan, again, questioning whether he ever had planned to murder Robert Kennedy in the first place, "would I, sir, be so stupid as to leave that notebook there, waiting for those cops, sir, to pick it up?"

"It would seem not," Pollack agrees. "It would seem that if you planned to kill him you wouldn't leave things around."

"That's what puzzles me," says Sirhan.

"Only you're not a killer," says Pollack, returning to his earlier insight. "You see, a person who isn't a killer doesn't think about all those things. If I were to kill somebody, I could do something as stupid as that, too, and I'm not stupid either. And looking at it from your eyes, I don't think killing Kennedy was stupid. You see, I think Kennedy's assassination was a political assassination."

But Sirhan refused to fit neatly into Pollack's puzzle.

"I would love to die here right now," he says. "You don't have to take me to court, sir, and bring charges there."

"Hmm," replies Pollack, surprised.

"My own conscience doesn't agree with what I did."

"Your conscience?" says Pollack, taken aback. "In what way?"

"It's against my upbringing," answers Sirhan in a distressed tone. "My, my, my childhood, family church, prayers . . . the Bible and all this, sir. [The Sirhan family was Christian.] 'Thou shalt not kill.' Life is the thing, you know. Where would you be if you didn't have life? And here I go and splatter this guy's brains. It's just not me."

Dr. Pollack and Sirhan went around in circles for hours. Eventually

Pollack would throw up his hands and exclaim, "Ah, what a crazy mixed-up case!" But the doctor would overcome these feelings of confusion. On the witness stand two months later Seymour Pollack would turn on Sirhan in a most unexpected way.

In the trial of Sirhan Sirhan the political motive became an article of faith. Its disciples were drawn from those prosecuting Sirhan, and those most active in his defense—the Arab-American community. On June 11, Dr. M. T. Mehdi, secretary-general of the Action Committee on American-Arab Relations, wrote a letter to the *New York Times*. In the letter Mehdi once again mentioned the fifty jet bombers promised to Israel. "As we condemn Sirhan's act," he wrote, "we must [also] condemn the Zionist pressures which forced Senator Kennedy to support Israel wrongly against the Arabs. Senator Kennedy is in a very real sense an indirect victim of Zionism. The Senator was morally wrong; Sirhan was legally wrong."★

Later in the day Dr. Mehdi would tell newspaper reporters that he did not believe the assassination was an act of insanity, but that it was "a politically calculated thing." Sirhan, Mehdi said, "was not insane. Just as the man who decided to drop the A-bomb over Hiroshima was not insane."

Mehdi maintained that Sirhan's act "is not an ordinary case of murder, it is a political act and a political assassination. Hence traditional legal devices and legal remedies cannot adequately provide proper defense for the accused."

Mehdi's ideas about an unconventional defense had its proponent in defense consultant Abdeen Jabara. Recall that in October of 1968 attorney Russell Parsons met with Jabara in Chicago and agreed that some amount of Palestine history from the Arab point of view would make its way into the defense of Sirhan Sirhan.

The Parsons-Jabara arrangement went undisturbed until December, when attorney Emile Berman joined the defense team. Berman believed that emphasizing the accused's political motivation was not going to help Sirhan. At one meeting Berman voiced this reservation. "To put on Arabs as a counteroffensive in court," he said, "would be a very serious step."

Parsons didn't agree. "In the defense of diminished capacity," he replied, "damn near anything that influences a man is admissible."[15]

Parsons was technically correct. The defense of diminished capacity is

---

★Note: the continued identification of Sirhan's motive with Dr. Mehdi's words was demonstrated in 1994 when excerpts from Dr. Mehdi's letter were read at Sirhan's parole hearing as evidence of why he should not be released, as though Sirhan himself had written these words.

Senator Kennedy addresses his followers at the Ambassador Hotel after winning the California primary. *(Assassination Archives and Research Center [AARC], Washington, D.C.)*

The struggle to disarm Sirhan (profile visible in the center of melee): In the foreground is Los Angeles Rams tackle Roosevelt Grier, who recovered the revolver; on the extreme right (with only half his face showing) is hotel maître d' Karl Uecker, who has Sirhan in a headlock; and visible just behind Grier's head, looking directly at Sirhan, is writer George Plimpton. *(UPI/Corbis-Bettmann)*

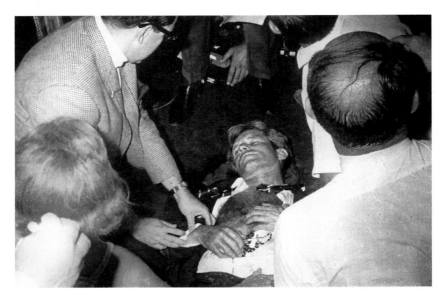

Clutching rosary beads given to him by busboy Juan Romero, Robert Kennedy lies wounded on the floor of the hotel pantry. His wife, Ethel, is at lower left. *(UPI/Corbis-Bettmann)*

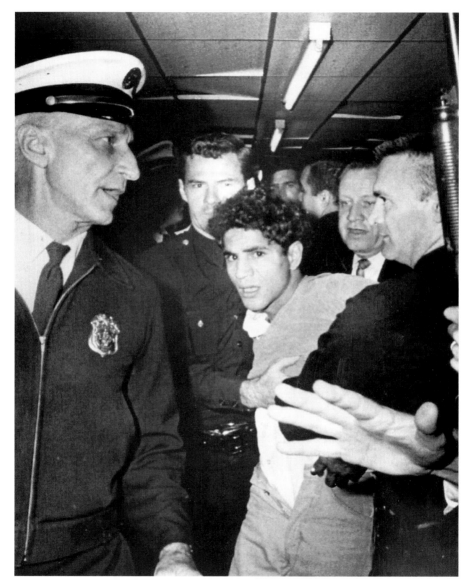

Sirhan Sirhan is taken into custody immediately after the shooting.
(UPI/Corbis-Bettmann)

L.A. coroner Thomas Noguchi points to two holes in the doorframe of the pantry doorway. *(University of Massachusetts, Dartmouth, Robert F. Kennedy Assassination Archives [UMDRFK])*

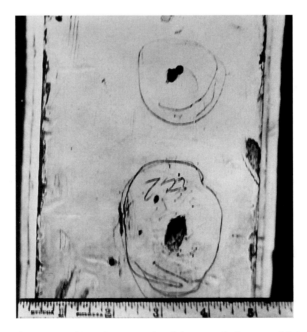

FBI photo close-up (released in 1975) of the two holes to which Noguchi was pointing. FBI caption reads: "Close up view of two bullet holes which is [sic] located in the center doorframe inside kitchen serving area and looking towards direction of back of stage." *(UMDRFK Archives)*

LAPD officers Charles Wright and Sergeant Robert Rozzi examine what appears to be a bullet in a pantry hallway doorframe. Years later, when asked how sure he was that the object in the hole was a bullet (on a scale of one to ten, with ten being a certainty), Wright responded, "as close to a ten as I'd ever want to go without pulling it out." *(UMDRFK Archives)*

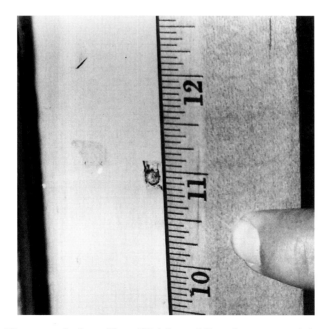

Close-up of what officers Wright and Rozzi were examining.
(Castellano-Nelson Collection, UMDRFK Archives)

LAPD photograph of police criminalist DeWayne Wolfer point-ing to an apparent bullet ricochet mark on pantry door hinge. *(UMDRFK Archives)*

FBI photograph (released in 1975) of this same hinge. FBI caption to photo describes "reported location of another bullet mark which struck hinge." *(UMDRFK Archives)*

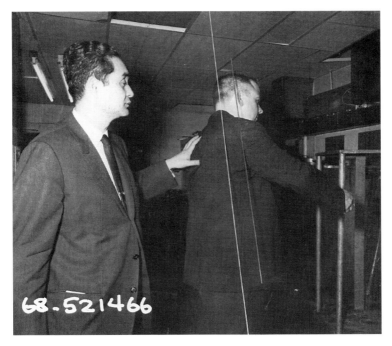

L.A. coroner Thomas Noguchi standing behind LAPD detective wearing Senator Kennedy's suit coat. Metal rod penetrating suit coat simulates the flight path of a bullet. According to the report of police criminalist DeWayne Wolfer, this bullet "passed through the right shoulder pad of Senator Kennedy's suit coat (never entered his body) and traveled upward striking victim Shrade in the forehead." *(Castellano-Nelson Collection, UMDRFK Archives)*

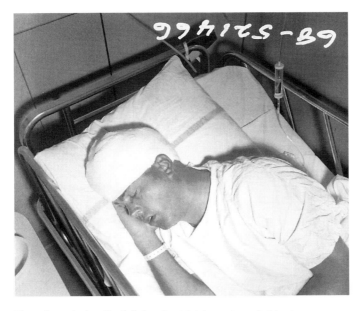

Shooting victim Paul Schrade. *(California State Archives)*

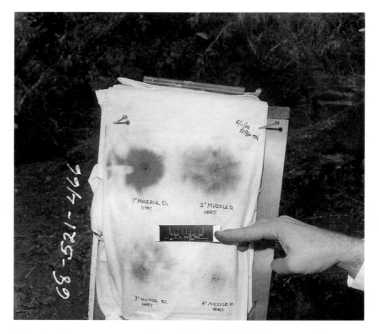

Muzzle distance test conducted by LAPD. This comparison test demonstrated that shots that hit Robert Kennedy were fired at point-blank range. *(UMDRFK Archives)*

Photo of Ambassador Hotel pantry where Robert Kennedy was shot. *(Castellano-Nelson Collection, UMDRFK Archives)*

Sirhan family in Palestine, 1946. *Standing, left to right:* Saidalla, Ayda, and Shariff. *Sitting:* Mary Sirhan holding nine-month-old Sirhan B. Sirhan, Munir (the first child to be named Munir, who would be killed during fighting in Jerusalem), Adel, and Bishara Sirhan. *(Rose Lynn Mangan Collection)*

Sirhan Sirhan during interview with Grant Cooper before his trial. *(Robert Blair Kaiser Collection, UMDRFK Archives)*

L.A. District Attorney Evelle Younger seated *(center)*, and flanked by Chief of Detectives Robert Houghton *(left)*, and U.S. Attorney Matthew Byrne *(right)*, introducing the team to prosecute Sirhan: *(standing, from left to right)* Lynn D. Compton, John E. Howard, and David N. Fitts. *(UPI/Corbis-Bettmann)*

Sirhan attorneys arrive at the Hall of Justice: *(left to right)* Russell Parsons, Grant B. Cooper, and Emile Zola Berman. *(UPI/Corbis-Bettmann)*

Superior Court Judge Herbert V. Walker. *(UPI/Corbis-Bettmann)*

Sandra Serrano on the back stairway of the Ambassador Hotel where she claimed to have encountered the woman in the polka-dot dress. *(California State Archives)*

LAPD photo of one of the polka-dot dresses used by the police for comparison in questioning witnesses Sandra Serrano and Vincent DiPierro. *(California State Archives)*

Kennedy campaign worker Valerie Shulte modeling the green dress with yellow shapes that she wore the night of the shooting. Both the defense and the prosecution would accept Shulte as the missing polka-dot-dress woman. *(California State Archives)*

Page from Sirhan's notebook dated May 18, 1968, where the writer speaks of his increasing "obsession" to eliminate Robert Kennedy. Passage repeats phrase "Robert Kennedy must be assassinated" fourteen times then ends with the sentence "I have never heard please pay to the order of of of of of of of of of of of this or that." *(California State Archives)*

Right: Page written by Sirhan while in prison under hypnosis, bearing controversial date "Friday 31, January 689." Sirhan writes "RFK must die" a dozen times, then writes that he doesn't know who killed Kennedy. When asked who he was with when Kennedy was killed he writes "girl the girl the girl." *(UMDRFK Archives)*

Two pages from Sirhan's notebook. (California State Archives)

Sirhan Sirhan with attorney Emile Berman during his trial.
(UPI/Corbis-Bettmann)

Gregory Stone, protegé of Allard Lowenstein. Researched and analyzed Robert Kennedy case for almost two decades. *(Jenny Stone)*

Paul Schrade and former congressman Allard Lowenstein at a New York press conference in 1974, where they publicly challenged the official version of the Robert Kennedy case. Lowenstein would be murdered in 1980. *(UPI/Corbis-Bettmann)*

Sirhan Sirhan speaking at his parole hearing in 1986.
(UPI/Corbis-Bettmann)

not automatically incompatible with a political motive. But Berman believed that a jury would only be able to understand one or the other. If the defense got the jury to accept Sirhan's political motivation, he reasoned, in the process they would reject diminished capacity.

The rift between Parsons and Berman over this issue was permanent, and the two-minded nature of the defense was evident throughout the trial. Grant Cooper may have felt uncomfortable introducing the Arab-Israeli conflict into the case, but he had little choice. The Arab community already had Sirhan's ear. Cooper tried to keep everybody happy.

"I won't exploit the Arab-Israeli problem," Cooper assured Berman, "unless and to the extent that it helps Sirhan."

"I am thinking," Cooper told Parsons, "about having an Arab observer here at the trial."[16]

But the friction continued. During a jail cell visit with Sirhan, Abdeen Jabara told the defendant that it was Emile Berman who was preventing the Arab-Israeli situation from coming out at the trial. Having rallied Sirhan to his cause, Jabara then invited Berman to have lunch. Robert Kaiser accompanied the two.

As Kaiser reports in *"RFK Must Die!,"* Jabara didn't touch his food. "This is a serious matter," he told Berman. Jabara then delivered a very well-spoken history of the Arab-Israeli conflict, beginning with Theodor Herzl and the foundation of the Zionist movement right up to the Arab defeat in the Six-Day War of 1967.

Berman was polite and receptive, but he wanted to know how the pieces fit. "The only question I have is how do we bring it home to Sirhan?" he asked. "The judge isn't going to let us present a history lesson in court, is he?"

"The conflict," said Jabara emphatically, "has to come into the trial."[17]

When the defense began to call its witnesses, Grant Cooper's Arab observer arrived in Los Angeles.

"If Your Honor please," said Cooper in court, "I would like to introduce Mr. Issa Nahkleh, who is a director of the Palestinian-Arab delegation to the United Nations. He is a member of the English bar, having been admitted at Lincoln's Inn and also a lawyer in Palestine, and I would move his admission in the case simply as an adviser for the period of time that he will be here."

"It is your desire?" Judge Walker asked Nahkleh.

"Yes."

"The motion will be granted and we are glad to have you here."

Ambassador Nahkleh would sit as an adviser to the defense for three weeks. He visited Sirhan in his cell. But, just as it had between Jabara and

Berman, animosity soon developed between Nahkleh and Berman. Berman had threatened to withdraw from the case if more political material were introduced. At a meeting of the defense attorneys Nahkleh spoke out; as leader of the nonvoting Palestinian UN delegation, he wanted more on the plight of the Palestinian refugees to "create a balance in the jurors' minds."

"Now lookit," said Cooper, trying to regain control.

"My friend Mr. Berman's objections," said Nahkleh, not ready to cede the floor, "were motivated by political reasons, not by a sincere desire to help your client. He threatened to withdraw from the case—"

"So did you, Mr. Nahkleh," interrupted Cooper. "This morning."

Berman, who had remained quiet, now spoke. "Political assassination," he said, "isn't exactly diminished capacity."

"Mr. Berman has stopped you from doing what you must," Nahkleh answered. "He's acting for political motivations."

"And you," Berman replied, "are sending Sirhan to the gas chamber."[18]

The standard way to make sense out of the Sirhan enigma—that promoted by the prosecution and the Arab community, and adopted by the defense attorneys, the press, and the public—is to accept Sirhan's assertions of political motivation and to disbelieve his professed lack of memory. Of all those connected to the case, only two—Robert Kaiser, and to a lesser extent, Dr. Bernard Diamond—understood Sirhan in reverse: giving credence to his lack of memory and disbelieving his political motive. While this reverse view needs additional clarification, it explains, far better than the official version, Sirhan's behavior before and after the shooting, as well as his words and actions once incarcerated.

It is important to understand that in the reverse model, Sirhan is not lying about his political motive. He awakens one morning to discover he has murdered an important political figure. He has no memory of the event or of planning the event. Why then did he do it? As much as anyone, Sirhan needed to answer that question.

Sirhan's choices were two: either he was crazy, or he murdered Robert Kennedy to defend his people. A third possibility, that he had been an involuntary dupe, was not seriously considered. When this possibility was suggested to him in his jail cell by Robert Kaiser, Sirhan rejected it. He had no memory of anyone bending his mind toward murder.

Though a finding of mental illness was within Sirhan's best interest in terms of escaping maximum punishment, Sirhan, without variation, rejected that idea. Throughout the trial he continually undermined his attorneys' efforts at establishing a psychiatric defense. Almost everyone noted that Sirhan seemed to favor the gas chamber over being judged insane.

Part of this rejection may have been cultural. Sirhan's brother Adel spoke to the authors about this in 1993. "In Arabic culture," he said, "there is a great stigma attached to mental illness. Not only is the person involved outcast, but also his family. Here it is a somewhat romanticized notion, but in the Middle East it is better to be a thief than to be thought of as crazy."

An example of this cultural bias can be seen in an incident that took place at the Hall of Justice. Sirhan's mother, Mary, was in an elevator and overheard defense attorney Emile Berman tell a reporter, "Oh, Sirhan is obviously mad. That notebook shows nothing but madness."

Berman, of course, was trying to demonstrate to anyone who would listen that the very strange writing in Sirhan's notebooks did not constitute legal premeditation. He was fighting for Sirhan's life. Mary Sirhan, however, would have none of it.

"What are you saying?" she demanded of Berman. "I don't like that. You cannot say that, that my boy is mad. What he did he did for his country."[19]

From Taibeh, on the West Bank, Sirhan's father echoed the same words. "If he did this," Bishara said, ". . . it was because he was doing something for his country. We know he is a hero."[20]

Sirhan's father had not always felt that way. The day after the murder he had said that news of the crime made him sick. "If my son has done this dirty thing," he proclaimed, "then let them hang him."[21]

Bishara Sirhan's change of outlook may be seen as parallel to that of his son. The political motive made the crime understandable and, within a certain context, even acceptable.

If one believes Sirhan, that he has no memory of the crime, then one must imagine the young immigrant waking to find himself in prison, not only the perpetrator of a foul murder, but the focus of an international debate on the injustices suffered by his people. Until this moment, his life had been one of unending failure and mediocrity. But now his likeness is on tens of thousands of Al Fatah posters; the ambassador of the Palestinian UN delegation attends his trial; he receives adoring letters from Palestinian girls. Is it so strange that this young man comes to embrace the political motive?

Through the careful examination of his words and behavior, it would appear that Sirhan adopted the political motive after the fact. As has been demonstrated in his conversations with his attorneys and doctors, Sirhan was quite puzzled by the crime. These private moments, not those when he was grandstanding before the public, are the clearest windows into the defendant's mind.

Sometimes the clue is in the phrasing of a statement. For example, when defense psychiatrist Dr. Bernard Diamond tries to persuade Sirhan that he is sick, Sirhan takes issue. He says he is not sick and doesn't want anyone to mess around with his mind or portray him as stupid. "I'd rather die," he says, "and *say* I killed that son of a bitch for my country, period [emphasis added]."[22]

A similar moment occurred in his cell in the presence of his attorneys when Sirhan confronted the fact that he might die for this crime. "Well," he said dispassionately, "if it is going to cost me my life, I want to help the Arabs."[23] This is not a statement a man would make if he had committed the capital offense to help the Arabs in the first place.

In another private conversation in his cell Sirhan was asked how he felt about being portrayed as a hero on an Al Fatah poster. Had he carried out a political murder on behalf of the Palestinians, Sirhan might have greeted such news with enthusiasm. Instead he replied, "The shot was expended, I might as well make the most of it."[24]

TEN

Sirhan Bishara Sirhan

✳ ✳ ✳

*Sirhan at all times stated he could not remember the killing nor
remember firing the shots. Because of my firm and conscientious
belief that Sirhan alone fired the shots . . . I advised Sirhan to testify
in substance that notwithstanding his lack of memory, that if
everyone said he did fire the shots he must have done so. Sirhan
followed my advice and so testified.*

—Grant Cooper, Sirhan defense attorney, 1972

T
HE AFFIRMATIVE DEFENSE of
Sirhan Sirhan began on Friday,
February 28. Grant Cooper's initial strategy was to present witnesses who
could enlighten the court about Sirhan's life, and, when possible, present
an Arab view of the Palestinian-Israeli conflict. Toward this end Mr. Baron
Serkess Nahas was called to the witness stand.

Mr. Nahas had been born in Jerusalem, where he lived until 1948. In
1949 he moved to Beirut, where he worked for the United States Information Service, and, following that, the United Nations agency that organized relief for the Palestinian refugees. Under Cooper's guidance Nahas
testified about conditions in Jerusalem at the time of the Sirhan family's
residence.

Following Nahas was Ziad Hashimeh. Hashimeh resided in Chicago,
but in 1949 his family and the Sirhans were two of nine families who shared
a house in the Old City of Jerusalem. Both families had been forced from
their original homes by the fighting between Arabs and Jews.

"Was it a very old house?" asked Grant Cooper.

"Well, I would say eight hundred years," answered Hashimeh, who then
described the privations suffered by those living there.

Hashimeh was born in 1944, the same year as Sirhan. The two boys
were friends. Hashimeh told the court that he frequently visited the single
room that sheltered the Sirhan family. He also described the violence that
Sirhan had received at the hands of his father.

"Did you ever see him strike Sirhan?" Cooper asked.

"Oh, yes, quite a few times."

"I take it because he was a bad boy, or something."

"Well, no. The husband, the man, was too emotional, you know. . . . Quite a bit of times he beat him."

"Did he strike him with his hands?"

"He used all sorts of sticks and hands."

Cooper asked Hashimeh if he remembered another time that he saw Sirhan crying.

"I was in the room and I heard him shouting, 'Mother, mother.' . . . The whole apartment they goes out and he was shaking, you know, like that, moving his body and he was crying, 'Hand, hand,' so we all had to go to the well."

"What did you see?"

"We saw hand in—"

"You mean a human hand?"

"A human hand."

"That was in the bucket?"

"In the bucket, yes."

Hashimeh remembered the young Sirhan as a "sensitive" boy who chastised him for telling a lie.

"He told me," Hashimeh recalled, " 'if you lie to people, you know, people are clever enough to lie back to you. . . . Do not lie.' "

Hashimeh also recalled a time when Sirhan talked him into coming to hear his mother lecture about religion.

"I am a Muslim and he is a Christian, and I said, 'I do not believe in religion, religion means nothing to me,' and then he said, 'You don't have to believe in religion, but you can believe in God. My mother is not speaking to people to make them follow a religion. She goes to make them follow God.' So I had a good feeling for those words, you know, so I went with him to his mother."

When Hashimeh stepped down from the witness stand, Grant Cooper introduced John T. Harris, an officer of the Pasadena School District, who testified about Sirhan's scholastic performance. Sirhan's grades in high school were mediocre.

During Harris's testimony Russell Parsons broke in and asked to speak to Judge Walker. "This morning he was wonderful," he said, speaking about Sirhan. "Since lunchtime he has been quite disturbed. For some reason he doesn't want this information that is going on to go into the Court. He has some objection to it, and he says he would like to talk to you in chambers."

"He will not talk to me in chambers," Walker insisted.

"I told him I didn't think it was possible," Parsons replied.

Grant Cooper then suggested that the jury be excused. "We might as well face this some time," he sighed. After the jury left he continued:

"Mr. Parsons just interrupted us quite properly to inform Your Honor that the defendant has objected to our calling this witness. . . . The defendant has objected to our calling approximately a dozen witnesses, whom we as lawyers all agree are relevant and proper to the issues in his best interest and for the defense. Nevertheless, he has indicated to us last week that he would forbid us to call those witnesses.

"Now I am informed—he informed me just before we started at two o'clock—that again he forbade us to call these witnesses whom in our judgment we deem proper. . . . Have I recited it correctly, Mr. Sirhan?"

"Yes, you have."

"There is something you want to say?" Judge Walker asked Sirhan.

"May I address the Court in chambers, sir?"

"No," replied Walker.

Since his youth Sirhan had suffered a nervous condition which made him tremble in difficult moments. Now, gripping his chair, he struggled to maintain control. "I, at this time, sir, withdraw my original plea of not guilty and submit the plea of guilty as charged on all counts. I also request that my counsel disassociate themselves from this case completely."

Judge Walker had been caught off guard: "Do I understand—stand up—do I understand that you want to plead guilty to murder in the first degree?"

"Yes, sir, I do."

"All right," queried Walker, "and what do you want to do about the penalty?"

"I will offer no defense whatsoever."

"The question is," repeated Walker, "what do you want to do about the penalty?"

"I will ask to be executed, sir."

At this the wire service reporters hurried for the courtroom door. Judge Walker appeared awkward as he sought to keep control of the proceedings.

"I know of nothing in the law that permits a defendant under any circumstances to enter a plea of guilty to murder of the first degree and ask for execution."

"Well, I have, sir," replied Sirhan.

"Well, now, just a minute. Why do you want to do this?"

"I believe, sir, that is my business, isn't it?"

"You just believe it is your business?" said Walker, searching for leverage.

"That is my prerogative."

"No it isn't," argued Walker. "Now when we come to accepting a plea, you have to give me a reason."

Thus challenged, Sirhan replied, "I killed Robert Kennedy willfully, premeditatively, with twenty years of malice aforethought: that is why."

"Well, the evidence has to be produced here in court," said Walker, appearing to invent new law. Normally a plea of guilty relieves the prosecution of proving anything. Certainly, the burden of proof does not fall on a defendant as a prerequisite for making a guilty plea.

"I withdraw all evidence, sir," said Sirhan.

"There is no such procedure."

"To hell with it."

Walker had heard enough. "Well, the Court will not accept the plea. Proceed with the trial. Let me give you to understand here and now that this Court will not put up with any more of your interrupting. You are to follow the advice of counsel and just sit down there. Any further interruptions by you in this trial will result in you being restrained. You understand that?"

"Sir?"

"I mean by that that you will have a face mask put on you which will prohibit you from talking and, further, your arms will be strapped to your chair and the trial will proceed. You understand that?"

"I understand. However, sir, I intend to defend myself *pro per*," said Sirhan, using the legal term for self-representation. "I don't want to be represented by these counsel."

"You have retained counsel," answered Walker. "Counsel is staying in the trial."

"What I have said, I don't want anyone to have a trial shoved down my throat, sir, and you are not going to shove it down my throat, sir, in any way you want."

"You say you want to go *pro per*?" asked Walker.

"Yes."

"What are the defenses; let me ask what are the elements of the crime of murder?"

"Sir, I don't know. I don't understand all of this legality. You let me—"

"I am conducting these proceedings, not you. What are the defenses to murder in the first degree?"

"I don't know."

"I find you are incapable of representing yourself. Sit down and keep quiet and, if not, I intend to keep you quiet."

"No, sir. I still maintain my original point. I plead guilty to murder and ask to be executed."

"I thought I made it clear. The Court will not accept the plea."

"I am sorry," answered Sirhan. "I will not accept it."

"The law tells me what I can do and cannot do. Now you understand from here on out you keep quiet, and if not, I will see to it that you are kept quiet."

"I am sorry, but my original position stands."

"Get the jury down."

"Why not let me go into chambers. I insist."

"You are not going to go in chambers. I let you go in there once and that was the beginning and the end. That procedure is over as far as I am concerned. We will proceed with the trial. Again, I will tell you to keep quiet and consult with your attorneys."

"Can I consult with them a minute?"

"We will proceed with the trial. Do you want to consult in the hold tank, Mr. Cooper?"

"Yes, Your Honor," Cooper replied. Judge Walker then called the afternoon recess.

What had caused this outburst? Why did Sirhan ask to be executed? Did he now suddenly remember the crime? Did he believe that his lawyers would not properly represent the Palestinian cause? Did he want to martyr himself in a more dramatic fashion? No, Sirhan sought to enter a plea of guilty because he was embarrassed at the thought that two young women would be called as witnesses.

"I told you not to bring those two girls in here," he screamed at his attorneys once they were in the holding cell. Sirhan had misidentified two women sitting in the courtroom as Gwen Gumm and Peggy Osterkamp, both of whom had been the subject of ramblings in his notebooks.[1] Gumm had been a fellow student at Pasadena Community College, while Osterkamp had worked at a horse farm where Sirhan was also employed.

Peggy Osterkamp's name appeared in the notebooks dozens of times. What would be labeled as page 31 was devoted entirely to her.

> P Peggy Osterkamp is I love you I love you sterkamp Miss Peggy
> P P P P I love you I love you . . . y y you P Miss Peggy Osterkamp
> Miss yo y you you you I your children Sol & Peggy I love you I
> your I I love love y y your children Sol & Peggy Peggy

Sirhan had not dated Peggy Osterkamp or Gwen Gumm. Neither woman had been any more than fleetingly aware of his existence. The public exposure of his notebooks had already caused Sirhan acute embarrassment, and having two women whom he fancied testify to the world that he meant nothing to them would have been the ultimate humiliation. To insure that this would not happen Sirhan was ready to fire his lawyers, plead guilty, and suffer the gas chamber.

When court resumed with the jury absent, Grant Cooper was the first to speak.

"Your Honor please. Since Your Honor declared the afternoon recess, we as counsel have conferred with our client in the holding cell and he has advised us definitely, positively, and unequivocally that he does not desire us to continue to represent him as counsel. I have conferred with my brethren of the defense, Mr. Parsons and Mr. Berman, and none of us have any desire to continue representing a client who does not desire our services.

"I think I should state this into the record historically," Cooper continued. "We were asked to represent him and each one of us has volunteered our services without compensation and we feel that with the work that each one of us has done, including two investigators who have worked long hours, month on month on end, we have prepared what we feel, based upon the facts and the law, is a legitimate defense of diminished responsibility."

Cooper told the court that Sirhan was quite capable of communicating with his attorneys; it was just a "violent difference of opinion as to how the defense should be conducted. Now all of us, having had some years at the bar in criminal cases, cannot allow a defendant to run the lawsuit and, so long as I am counsel, I am not going to let a client run the lawsuit. I am perfectly willing and we have done everything humanly possible to attempt to reason with him for the purpose of explaining what is in his best interests. . . . At this time, since the defendant does not desire us to represent him, we are perfectly willing, as a matter of fact I might say anxious, to withdraw from the case and let him either represent himself or be represented by other counsel.

"I want to hasten to add this: neither one of us wants to desert him. We are still willing, if Your Honor please, to represent him as conscientiously as we know how. With that I must leave it up to the court."

Judge Walker had already made up his mind.

"I know of no law that permits counsel to withdraw in the middle of proceedings except for good cause. I have examined the law and I don't feel that this situation is good cause. . . . He is incapable of representing himself. This is proven by the two questions I asked him. I will deny your motion to withdraw. . . . I think you have prepared a good defense, if not the only logical defense that could be presented."

"We are prepared to go forward."

"All right, we will proceed. Bring the jury down."

The afternoon session did not last long. Russell Parsons called Mary Sirhan. Dressed in a black suit, the diminutive Mrs. Sirhan walked bravely to the witness stand. She was in obvious distress, and the strain of the past year's events made her look older than her fifty-six years.

"Are you the mother of Sirhan Bishara Sirhan?" Parsons asked.

"Yes," answered Mrs. Sirhan in an unsteady voice.

"And when was he born?"

"He was born in 1944. March."

"March 1944?"

"Yes."

"And where was he born?"

"In the city of Jerusalem."

"And how long have you lived in Jerusalem before he was born?"

"Well, I'd say thousands of years. My family from generation to generation . . . The City of Peace."

"Is that what you called Jerusalem?"

"Yes," answered Mrs. Sirhan, crying now, "all over the whole world we call it the City of Peace. . . . Please don't mind if I look this way."

"If Your Honor please," interjected Grant Cooper, "may we approach the bench."

Cooper told Judge Walker that Sirhan's attempt to change his plea had shaken Mrs. Sirhan badly. He asked if the court could be recessed until Monday. Walker, sympathetic to Mrs. Sirhan's position, agreed.

On Sunday March 2, Grant Cooper took Ambassador Issa Nahkleh up to see Sirhan in an effort to get the defendant to cooperate once again with his lawyers. Nahkleh asked Sirhan what was troubling him. Sirhan replied that there were witnesses scheduled to testify that he did not want called. Nahkleh discovered that the witnesses most objectionable were the two girls Sirhan had mistakenly believed were present in the court Friday. He then asked Sirhan if those two were excluded would Sirhan reunite with his counsel? Sirhan agreed. Nahkleh then got Cooper to agree not to call the two women.[2] The courtroom crisis, sparked by adolescent embarrassment, not Middle East politics, was over.

On Monday, Mary Sirhan assumed the witness stand once again, followed by Adel, the defendant's brother. Each told the court what they could of Sirhan's life in Palestine and in the United States. Late in the day Grant Cooper called his next witness. Court clerk Alice Nishikawa administered the oath.

"Do you solemnly swear the testimony you are about to give in the cause now pending before this Court shall be the truth, the whole truth, and nothing but the truth, so help you God?"

"Yes, ma'am."

"Be seated. State your name, please."

"Sirhan Sirhan."

Trial testimony of a murder defendant carries with it some risk, because it leaves the witness open to cross-examination. In this case, since the defense had already conceded most of the facts, Grant Cooper felt there was little to lose. The jury, he reasoned, should see a human face on the accused.

Other than that, however, Cooper didn't appear to have a clear idea of what he was trying to accomplish with his client. And his client had some ideas of his own. As he had in February, Sirhan once again took the oath with his arm upraised and fist clenched.

"Mr. Sirhan," Cooper began. "It is alleged that on the fifth day of June 1968, you killed and murdered Senator Robert Francis Kennedy, a human being. Did you on or about that date shoot Senator Kennedy?"

"Yes, sir."

"Do you have any doubt but that you did it?"

"No, sir, I do not."

"Now, you were born in New Jerusalem on March 1944, and you moved to the Old City of Jerusalem within the walled city, sometime during the year 1948?"

"Yes."

"Do you, yourself, have any recollections of your childhood . . . ?"

"A little bit, yes."

"What do you remember?"

Sirhan's memories as a young boy were dominated by the brutal conflict in Palestine between the Arabs, the immigrating Jews, and the then-governing British. His young eyes saw the disembowelment of a man by a bomb, a group of Arabs blown apart while waiting for a bus, and, most traumatic, his older brother being crushed to death by a truck swerving to avoid sniper fire.

At that time the Sirhan family lived in a ground-floor apartment just outside Musrara, a mixed middle-class Arab and Jewish quarter. Sirhan's father, Bishara, a Greek Orthodox Arab from the nearby town of Taibeh, had a position with the British Mandate Government. But both the home and the job would be lost when Israel declared its independence in 1948, and the Arabs in their neighborhood were forced from their homes. What followed were eight difficult years as refugees.

After extended testimony on Sirhan's recollections of war-savaged Jerusalem, Grant Cooper changed venue.

"Now there came a time," he asked the defendant, "did there not, Sirhan, when the family decided to leave Old Jerusalem and come to the United States of America?"

"Yes, sir."

"What were your feelings about leaving?"

"I was very hesitant, sir. I didn't want to leave. I wanted to stay in my own country, sir, with my own people."

In 1956 the Sirhan family emigrated to the United States, sponsored by a California family Bishara had met in Jerusalem. The family traveled to California by rail and settled in Pasadena, but after seven months, Bishara returned to Taibeh. According to Mary Sirhan, her husband returned "because of his mother," who was old and ill. An alternate explanation was that Bishara simply abandoned his family, unable to adapt to the new American culture. Neither Mary nor Sirhan would ever see him again.

After Bishara left, Sirhan's older brother Adel became the primary breadwinner. Mary Sirhan had described it in court, "We were busy all the time trying to support the little ones and everything. It was really hard because father had left and we were alone in a strange country. We didn't know enough of the customs of the language enough, and we just tried our best to live and to do right."

Mrs. Sirhan finally landed a job at the Westminster Nursery School. At age thirteen Sirhan took on a paper route. He delivered the *Independent Star News* for four years, often delivering both the morning and evening editions. According to his mother he was proud of his economic contribution to the family. She got compliments on his work from neighbors who were customers.

Sirhan started his U.S. education in the sixth grade at Longfellow Elementary School. He especially liked geography and wrote that his occupational goal was to be a doctor. At John Muir High School, Sirhan studied history and government as well as Russian and German. He now thought about living life as a diplomat in the foreign service. But it was also at John Muir where Sirhan began to feel separate. He noticed that the popular kids were tall and blond, that they wore different clothes every day and had cars of their own.

In September of 1963 Sirhan enrolled in Pasadena Community College. His interests in government and foreign languages continued, and he joined the International Club (comprising 150 or so students interested in foreign affairs). But Sirhan's academic performance at Pasadena was poor. Soon, he was barely passing and sometimes failing his courses. According to his mother, the cause of his academic tailspin was the fatal illness of his sister Ayda. She was diagnosed as having leukemia in 1962 and became gradually worse until her death in 1965. Sirhan became preoccupied with the family tragedy. He dropped out of college after two years.

"Now after you were discharged or dismissed as a result of your poor grades and your absences," asked Grant Cooper, "what did you do then?"

"Having developed, sir," Sirhan replied, "a likeness [sic] for horses, and a love for horses, I decided to try to ride them, to become a jockey."

"I take it by this time, having flunked out, you gave up your ambition to be a diplomat?"

"I gave up my scholastic ambition completely, sir."

In 1966 Sirhan landed a job as an exercise boy at Granja Vista del Rio Ranch near Corona. He wanted to be a jockey. On the morning of September 25, several owners had gathered at Granja Vista to see their horses run on the training track. But the track was foggy and some owners backed out. A three-horse race then shaped up with Sirhan on a filly named Hy-Vera. At full gallop the horses disappeared into the fog and ran into the rail. Sirhan fell and was taken to Corona Community Hospital, where he was found to be intact, but he continued to complain of fuzzy vision and headaches. He sought the advice of at least eight medical doctors. None could relieve his pain.

"The eye kept bothering me," Sirhan recalled at his trial. He tried to return to work, and even summoned the courage to ride again. But his dream of being a jockey was finished. Sirhan would eventually receive $1,700 in workmen's compensation insurance. According to his friends and family, he became a different person—withdrawn and irritable.

Once again Sirhan redirected his energies. He became interested in the occult. When in court Grant Cooper asked how that came about, Sirhan responded:

"I have always asked the question myself, sir, 'What is this life about? What is this reality, this world?' I always wanted to know what was behind it."

Perhaps to fill the void created by his lost dream, and to overcome the physical pain that his numerous doctors could not abate, Sirhan fervently embraced the realm of the mind: self-hypnosis, mind control, mysticism. He practiced the mental projection of images and ideas. He frequented one Pasadena bookstore that specialized in the occult and got a part-time job at another. There he read books he could not afford to buy, books with titles like *The Laws of Mental Domination, Thought Power: Its Control and Culture,* and *Meditations on the Occult Life: The Hidden Power.*

Sirhan also joined the Rosicrucians, a self-described "ancient mystical order." In May 1968 he paid twenty dollars to join after seeing an ad in a newspaper. He then attended one meeting of the local "lodge." Sirhan participated in one of the evening's "experiments," an exercise in tactile, sensory perception, but he left immediately after the meeting was over. This fleeting, superficial contact with the Rosicrucians would be magnified to an event of great significance by his own attorneys and those prosecuting him.

Cooper next asked Sirhan about the day of the shooting.

"What were your plans for that Tuesday?"

"Well, Tuesday, sir, I planned to go to the races."

"What races were on?"

"At Hollywood Park."

Sirhan told Cooper that he had been going to the races for several weeks. Cooper asked how he had fared in the betting. Sirhan replied "good and bad," then conceded that he had lost more than he had won. Sirhan then told Cooper that he had looked at the racing entries in the newspaper and decided not to go to the track because he wasn't interested in any of the horses. It was then, he said, he decided to take his gun and go to a shooting range.

"All right, and then you drove where?"

"I drove to the San Gabriel Gun Club range."

Sirhan told Cooper that he had stayed the afternoon at the range, a fact borne out by a number of witnesses who saw him there. Sirhan reportedly left when the range closed at 5 P.M.

Sirhan said that he had planned to go to another Rosicrucian meeting scheduled for that evening, but as he looked through a newspaper as he was eating at Bob's Big Boy, he saw an advertisement for the "Miracle March for Israel," a parade on Wilshire Boulevard to celebrate the Israeli victory over the Arabs in the Six-Day War a year earlier. Sirhan told Cooper that just seeing the ad gave him "a burning feeling inside."

"What did you decide to do?"

"I commenced to go down to Wilshire Boulevard on Miracle Mile where they were having that parade."

In his anger Sirhan had failed to notice that the parade was scheduled for the following night. Instead of a parade, all Sirhan found was a storefront campaign party for U.S. senatorial candidate Thomas Kuchel. Sirhan stopped in and overheard that there were several larger parties going on at the Ambassador Hotel, a short distance away. He then made his way to the Ambassador.

Sirhan told the court that when he first entered the hotel, he noticed a sign for the Max Rafferty headquarters in the Venetian Room. Rafferty was the U.S. senator against whom Kuchel was running. Sirhan had attended classes in high school with Kathleen Rafferty, the senator's daughter, and he testified that he hung around the Rafferty party for about an hour hoping to spot Kathleen. During this time he said he consumed several Tom Collins drinks.

"Do you have any specific recollection of how many drinks you had?" Cooper asked the witness.

"No, sir, I don't."

"Do you know whether you had more than two?"

"I don't really know, sir."

Sirhan told Cooper that after an hour or so he left the Rafferty party and wandered around a bit.

"Now, at some point did you decide to go somewhere?"

"Yes, sir. I felt that I was quite high, and if I got any more drunk there was nobody with me to take care of me. So I decided to go home."

Sirhan then described walking back up Wilshire Boulevard to his car, getting in, and then deciding that he was too drunk to drive.

"What did you do then?"

"Then I decided, sir, to go back to the party and sober up, drink some coffee."

"Did you pick up your gun?"

"I don't remember, sir, if I did pick up my gun."

"As a result of what happened, you know you must have picked it up?"

"I must have, sir, but I don't remember picking it up."

"And where did you go when you got to the Ambassador?"

"I was in search of coffee, sir. I went in search of coffee. I tried to—I don't know where I found it, but eventually I found some coffee."

Sirhan described finding a large silver coffee urn and then meeting a dark-haired young woman and pouring coffee for her.

"Do you have any idea approximately how old she was?"

"About my age."

"A good-looking girl?"

"Beautiful."

"What happened next."

"I don't remember."

"What was the next thing you did?"

"The next thing I remember, sir, I was being choked."

"Do you remember anything between the time you had the coffee, anything?"

"No, sir. No, I don't remember."

"Now you have heard the testimony in here of at least a dozen witnesses . . . that you walked up to Senator Kennedy and put a gun toward his head, possibly within an inch or two, and you pulled the trigger and he eventually died?"

"Yes. I was told this. . . ."

"And you did kill him?"

"Yes, sir. I did."

"How do you account for all these circumstances?"

"Sir, I don't know."

After running through the events of the night of the murder, Grant Cooper asked Sirhan to explain what his feelings were toward President John Kennedy.

"I loved him, sir," Sirhan replied. "More than any American would have."

"Why?"

"Because just a few weeks before his assassination he was working, sir, with the leaders of the Arab government, the Arab countries, to bring a solution, sir, to the Palestinian refugee problem, and he promised these Arab leaders that he would do his utmost and his best to force or to put some pressure on Israel, sir, to comply with the 1948 United Nations Resolution, sir; to either repatriate those Arab refugees or give them back, give them the right to return to their homes. And when he was killed, sir, that never happened."

Cooper next asked Sirhan to relate to the court what he knew about the origins of the Palestinian conflict. Sirhan responded with a detailed account of the history of the region. He started with the 1897 conference in Switzerland that spawned the "Zionist movement." He explained how the politics of Palestine became polarized during the First World War, when, seeking help in its fight against Turkey, Great Britain made conflicting promises to both the Arabs and Jews in the region. He explained to the court how the 1917 Balfour Declaration pledged British support for a Jewish national home in Palestine, and how the British Mandate Government that followed facilitated the immigration of European Jews into the area.

Sirhan finished by providing some demographics for the court: the 1917 population of Palestine was, he said, "seven hundred thousand Palestinians . . . seventy thousand Christians, of whom I am one . . . and some fifty-six thousand Jews." By 1948, Sirhan asserted, the Jews numbered 650,000, and were militarily strong enough to declare themselves a separate nation and expel the native Palestinians.

When Sirhan was done with his history lesson, Grant Cooper changed the subject.

"Now, Sirhan," he said, "you had some notebooks."

A week earlier the prosecution had tried to introduce Sirhan's notebooks into evidence. As they approached the subject Sirhan started whispering loudly to Russell Parsons. "Those notebooks are private. They're my property. The police had no right to take them. They had no search warrant."

Since it was already late, Judge Walker adjourned for the day to avoid a scene. The next morning Grant Cooper entered Judge Walker's chambers accompanied by his client.

"Mr. Sirhan," Cooper scolded, "put out your cigarette, please. Court is in session. You wanted to make a statement?"

"Your Honor," began Sirhan, "if these notebooks are allowed in evidence, I will change my plea to guilty as charged. I will do so, sir, not so much that I want to be railroaded into the gas chamber, sir, but to deny you the pleasure, sir, of after convicting me turning around and telling the world: 'Well, I put that fellow in the gas chamber, but first I gave him a fair trial,' when you in fact, sir, will not have done so. The evidence, sir, that was taken from my home was illegally obtained, was stolen by the district attorney's people. They had no search warrant. I did not give them permission, sir, to do what they did to my home. My brother Adel had no permission to give them permission to enter my room and take what they took from my home, from my own room."

As has been demonstrated, Sirhan here was probably motivated more by the prospect of personal embarrassment than by juridical principle.

"Now Mr. Sirhan, let me tell you this," answered Judge Walker. "The Court has ruled on the admissibility of this evidence in court, and, if there is an error, the upper court can reverse this case. . . . You have got three counsel and they are running the lawsuit to your very best interest and there is no question in the Court's mind about that."

Sirhan reluctantly accepted the judge's view and Grant Cooper fought the notebooks in open court. As a result, only four of the most incriminating pages were entered into evidence. On Cooper's motion, several other pages containing angry rhetoric but no mention of Robert Kennedy were excluded as being inflammatory.

But now, with Sirhan on the witness stand, Grant Cooper had a different idea. He wanted to introduce all the remaining pages of the notebooks into evidence, so that the jury could better understand the portions they had already seen. "I am going to read them," Cooper said, "one page at a time."

Grant Cooper began by reading passages and then asking for comments from Sirhan. Some of the entries were clearly classroom notes, but many were not. There was a great deal of the material Sirhan could not explain. The best he could do was say that the handwriting appeared to be his. In some cases he could not even say that.

"Now, page thirteen, at the top," questioned Cooper. "Jockey, alcohol,' then 'alcohol' and then 'love love love love love love,' and this is in this space here and then there is 'feed, feed feed' and then 'Sirhan Sirhan' circled and then 'feed feed feed feed feed feed feed feed feed feed feed feed feed.' Do you know why you wrote that down and kept repeating feed, feed, feed?"

"No, I don't."

When Cooper got to page 15 he read the "RFK must die" passage. He went to the entry below it. "Do you remember writing this 'Please pay to the order of of of of of of of of of of of of this or that'?"

"No, sir," replied Sirhan, "I don't remember that."

"What significance does it have for you?"

"Nothing to me. I don't have a bank account. I don't understand it."

"Now let me ask you this. There is a date on there?"

"Yes, sir."

"May 18, nine forty-five A.M., and you recall what your feelings were about Robert F. Kennedy on or about May 18, which would be about three weeks roughly before June 5, approximately three weeks?"

"It could have been a time, sir, when he came out and said, when he said he would send fifty planes to Israel."

Cooper was now coloring in the official motive for the benefit of the jury. Sirhan cooperated in this effort, although his tentative answers reveal his uncertainty. Though no one appeared to notice, Sirhan correctly recalled that the television documentary did not mention any bombers to Israel. Still, the program had angered him.

"When I watched him on television, it burned me up, sir. And that is most likely, sir, the time I had written this."

"But you don't remember writing it?"

"I don't remember writing it."

From page 22, Cooper read another disturbing passage:

"The author expresses his wishes very bluntly to be recorded by history as the man who triggered off the last war. Life is ambivalence. Life is struggle. Life is wicked.

"If life is in any way other wise, I have honestly never seen it. I always seem to be on the losing, always the one exploited to the fullest."

"All of that is in your handwriting?"

"Yes, sir, it is."

"You wrote it?"

"I wrote it."

"Now what was on your mind when you wrote that?"

"I must have been a maniac at the time. I don't remember what was on my mind. . . ."

"That is what you said, isn't it?"

"That is what I said, but it's not me, sir. It's not Sirhan sitting right here who wrote that."

"Well, who wrote it?"

"I did."

"What do you mean, it isn't Sirhan writing this?"

"I can't explain."

On a subsequent page Cooper read the phrase: "Second group of American Sailors must be disposed of."

"What group of sailors did you have in mind?" Cooper asked.

"I don't know, sir, what group of sailors. I don't remember."

"Were there any group of sailors that you were angry at?"

"I am not mad at any sailors. I am not mad at any. I don't know."

"Do you have any idea why you wrote that there?"

"No, sir, I don't."

"Now you say here in the plural, 'We believe that we can effect such action and produce such results.' Was there somebody else that was going to join with you in doing what you wrote down there?"

"I did the writing myself, sir. I don't know who else it could be."

"Well, do you have any idea, did you have anyone with you as an accomplice?"

"No, I did not."

"Did anyone hire you?"

"No."

"What does that mean there, the 'we' that was in there?"

"I can't explain it. I have no explanation."

"That is an editorial 'we'?"

"It must be."

Cooper read Sirhan another passage: "Sirhan Sirhan, Jet Spec, please pay to the order of g Garner Ted Armstrong."

"Do you know who that is?"

"I don't know, sir."

"Do you know who Ted Armstrong is?"

"The only thing I can think of is the tire company."

"The tire company?"

Strangely, Sirhan Sirhan could not identify the then well known television evangelist whose name appeared in his notebook. But he did know who Jet Spec was. In fact the most enigmatic names in the notebooks, French Cargo, La Laguna Doll, King's Abbey, Jalousie, unrecognized by anyone else, were easily and willingly identified by Sirhan. They were racehorses.

Just as strange, there was a page of Arabic writing that Sirhan could not decipher. Issa Nahkleh, head of the Palestinian delgation to the UN, was called to the stand and read the page of what turned out to be gibberish. Once again Cooper had Sirhan admit his authorship.

"You wrote this, didn't you?" Cooper asked.

"Yes, sir, I did."

"Can't you read that? Or you just didn't want to make the effort?"

"No, I really couldn't read it."

"You couldn't read it?"

"No, sir."

Cooper continued, and again, the exchange between attorney and client was bizarre.

" 'Workers of the world unite. You have nothing to lose but your chains.' You wrote that, did you not?"

"It's my handwriting, yes."

"You believed that when you wrote it?"

"I must have, sir. At the time I wrote it. I don't feel so now."

"Why don't you feel that way now?"

"It sounds queer to me, it sounds queer to me."

"It sounds queer to you?"

"I don't remember writing it, but it is my handwriting, but I have actually no memory of writing it, sir. I don't have."

"Was there a time you felt that way?"

"There must have been at the time I wrote it, I must have felt that way."

"What caused you to feel that way?"

"I don't know."

But Grant Cooper had an explanation for the writing in Sirhan's notebooks. Holding up a magazine, he approached Sirhan.

"I show you a *Rosicrucian Digest* for May 1968. . . . Did you read this article on page one ninety-one?"

"Yes, sir, I did."

The article on page 191 was by Arthur J. Fettig. It was titled "Put It in Writing." Grant Cooper read the article to the jury:

> "Plan to dare something different—something exciting! Plan to become a success in some endeavor and be ready to jump barefoot into the excitement of living. But here's a word of advice: put it in writing! Put your plan, your goal, your idea in writing, and see how it suddenly catches fire. See how it gains momentum by the simple process of writing it down."

The author then quoted several people whom he termed "outstanding successes," such as bandleader Stan Kenton and Les "Jugger" Gervais, "one of the United States' finest professional archers," who attested to the power of putting one's goal down on paper. Cooper continued:

> "Try it. Pick a goal. Set a target date. Now start working to make it come true. But one more thing: BELIEVE—believe that it will come true! Start acting as if you are certain you will achieve your goal. . . . I DARE you to write it down!"

Cooper put down the magazine and approached Sirhan.

"Did you write these things down at the time you wrote them with the objective in mind of accomplishing your goal?"

"Yes, sir," answered Sirhan, "in reference to that, the assassination of Robert Kennedy."

Throughout the trial, Grant Cooper had demonstrated an incomplete knowledge of the physical facts of the murder. Some important evidence had clearly been hidden, and Cooper's late entry into the case did not aid his understanding. But Grant Cooper also had a poor understanding of his client.

When the two first met, Cooper asked Sirhan why he had committed the crime. When Sirhan answered he didn't know, Cooper offered his client the jets-to-Israel motive. At the trial Cooper presented that motive to the jury.

Cooper was particularly embarrassed by Sirhan's lack of memory. "I just don't know why he blanks out on so many things," the frustrated attorney told reporters during a recess. "We'd rather he remember everything that happened."[3] Cooper most of all wanted to keep his credibility with the court and public. He sought desperately to make sense out of the crime. But in this attempt, Cooper undermined the defense of diminished capacity.

By California law, if a defendant does not have the capacity to reflect maturely and meaningfully upon the gravity of the crime, he would be guilty of no more than second-degree murder. This was Cooper's chosen defense for Sirhan, and given the attorney's understanding of the case, it was the logical choice. The bizarre nature of the scribbling in Sirhan's notebooks—the sheer nonsense of much of it, the strange repetition, and Sirhan's apparent inability to remember the entries—certainly did not suggest mature and meaningful reflection. But by proposing that Sirhan's writings were an effort to bring into being his murderous intent, and getting Sirhan to agree to it (one wonders if the notebooks of Stan Kenton and Jugger Gervais looked anything like Sirhan's), Cooper simply handed the case to the prosecution.

Grant Cooper seemed oblivious to the fact that his examination of Sirhan was ripping apart the defense. Emile Berman was not. Promoting the political motive made no sense to him at all. "This is embarrassing to me," he said during a recess as he considered resigning from the case. "I thought we weren't going to make a political thing out of this. This makes it a political assassination, and that's no defense to murder."[4]

When prosecutor Lynn Compton initiated his cross-examination on Thursday, March 6, he questioned Sirhan about the anti–United States rhetoric in his notebooks:

"You don't deny that at some point in your career you felt very strongly about the overthrow of the United States government?"

"As I said, at that time, sir."

"At the time you wrote the material down?"

"Yes, sir, when I wrote it down and only at that time, sir. I don't remember entertaining it after or before. I don't even remember that itself right then."

Compton then went on to explore Sirhan's interest in the occult.

"Now, let me talk to you a minute about these studies of your books about how to improve your mind. When you read these things, you didn't really expect to acquire some supernatural power, did you?"

"Sir, that is what they claimed, sir, that you would."

"I know what they claim, but you didn't really expect to do that, did you?"

"You're wrong, sir. I did."

"You did?"

"Surely."

Compton's foray into the occult had a destination in the *Rosicrucian Digest* article that Grant Cooper had introduced the day before.

"You read in this book from the Rosicrucians that if you write things down and think about them enough it will help accomplish the goal, right?"

"That's what the book said, yes."

Sirhan, once again, appeared to be accepting the *Rosicrucian Digest* article as a possible explanation for the writings in his notebooks. All parties were apparently willing to overlook the fact that most of the strange writing in Sirhan's notebooks predated the article.

"So when you wrote down in your notebook 'Kennedy must die, Kennedy must die, Kennedy must die,' you were practicing the Rosicrucian approach?"

"I don't know what I was practicing, sir."

Compton would now lead Sirhan back to the well that Cooper had made him drink from the day before.

"Well, yesterday you remember what you said—your counsel said: 'Did you write these things down at the time you wrote them with the object in mind of accomplishing your goal?' and you said, 'Yes, sir, in reference to that, the assassination of Robert Kennedy.' "

"Do you remember telling us that yesterday? Yes or no?"

Compton had Sirhan read that portion of the trial transcript.

"Now is that what you told us yesterday?"

"Yes, sir."

Compton then questioned Sirhan regarding his purchase of the Iver Johnson Cadet pistol he had acquired in the winter of 1968 from his brother's friend.

"Did it look like a pretty good gun to you?"

"I thought it did, yes."

"You said you had shopped for guns in other places?"

"I didn't necessarily shop. I had looked at guns in other places, yes. . . ."

"Did you ever try to buy a gun in a gun store?"

"No, sir, I never had enough money to buy a gun from a gun store."

"As a matter of fact you knew they wouldn't sell you one, didn't you?"

"I did not know they would not sell me one."

"You knew that as an alien in fact you could not have one?"

"No, sir, I did not know that."

Compton then asked Sirhan about his practicing at the gun range. Did Sirhan remember signing his name at the registry?

"No, I don't remember exactly, sir—sir, you are asking me—this is just in the process—this is part of the process, sir. I don't exactly remember when I opened my gun and when I put in every bullet. Your asking me when I wrote my name, sir, is the same as asking me about every bullet that I put in that chamber. That's stupid."

"I confess at some times I do ask stupid questions."

"Yes, sir, you do."

"Thank you."

Compton next turned to Sirhan's conduct while in police custody the night of the murder.

"Everybody was very friendly?"

"They were extremely friendly, sir."

"Officer Jordan was a real nice guy?"

"He was."

"So he asked you what your name was, didn't he?"

"I don't remember if he did."

"You don't recall anybody asking you your name that night?"

"It was Mr. Howard asking me my name. Then he started with this 'If you say'—gave me those constitutional rights, whatever they were, and he said, 'If you give your name or say anything it can be used against you,' and I kept my mouth shut. . . ."

"Did you wonder why you were there?"

"The people said—and this Mr. Jordan was so friendly, sir, and at the time nothing was mentioned about the case. I didn't know what happened, sir."

"But you never were curious about why you were there, why you were handcuffed or why you were in the police station?"

"No, sir. I wasn't myself, sir. I didn't know what was going on."

"That is because you were still suffering from the effects of that liquor?"

"I don't know from the effects of what, sir. I was not myself, sir, as I am now."

"You were quite a bit different than you are now?"

"I must have been, otherwise I would have remembered all those things that happened, and what happened. . . ."

"Do you remember later on in that same conversation you said to Mr. Howard, 'I have been before a magistrate, have I, or have I not?' Mr. Howard said, 'No, you have not. You will be taken before a magistrate as soon as possible. Probably will be tried.' . . . You didn't ask Mr. Howard at that time, 'Tried for what?' did you?"

"I don't remember, sir, if I did or not."

Sirhan had not said, "Tried for what?" to Mr. Howard, but his question as to whether or not he had been before a magistrate was a clear indication that he was disoriented. He appeared to be normal, yet he did not know if he had been before a judge. What did this mean? Had Grant Cooper been running an aggressive defense, Mr. Howard would have been on the witness stand explaining what in Sirhan's behavior just hours after the murder had caused the assistant DA to repeatedly ask the prisoner if he knew where he was.

But since Cooper was embarrassed by Sirhan's lack of memory, he did not press the point. Nor was it necessary for the prosecution to explore the subject. They already had the defendant neatly packaged, as Mr. Compton's final exchanges with Sirhan demonstrate.

"Now, Mr. Sirhan, . . . you told us earlier this morning that as far as you were concerned you were willing to fight for the Arab cause, right?"

"Yes, sir. The Palestinian Arab cause."

"And do you think that the killing of Senator Robert Kennedy helped the Arab cause?"

"Sir, I'm not even aware that I killed Mr. Kennedy."

"Well, you know he's dead?"

"I know he's dead. I've been told that."

"In other words, the killing of Senator Kennedy would have only helped the Arab cause if you did it, right?"

"How do you mean that, sir? 'If I did it'?"

"Let me ask you this—again, I will repeat the question. Do you think that the killing of Senator Robert Kennedy by anybody helped the Arab cause?"

"I'm in no position, sir, to explain that. I am no political observer to say."

"There's no question in your mind but what you did it?"

"All the evidence has proved it. Your evidence."

"Are you glad he's dead?"

"No, sir, I'm not glad."

"Are you sorry?"

"I'm not sorry, but I'm not proud of it either."

"But you are not sorry?"

"No, sir, because I have no way of—no exact knowledge, sir, of having shot him."

"Well, the other day right here in this courtroom did you not say, 'I killed Robert Kennedy willfully, premeditatively, with twenty years of malice aforethought'—did you say that?"

"Yes, sir, I did."

Grant Cooper jumped to his feet. "If Your Honor please . . ."

Cooper began to object that Sirhan's statement had been made out of the presence of the jury and in a fit of anger directed at his own attorneys. Compton pointed out that the statement was made nevertheless and was admissible. Cooper then decided to bring out the circumstances of the statement on redirect examination, where Sirhan would explain to the court that twenty years earlier he was four years old and certainly not contemplating murdering Robert Kennedy.

"One last question, Mr. Sirhan," said Compton, continuing where he had left off. "You said you would be willing to do what you could to help the Arab cause and fight for it. Are you willing to die for it?"

"When did I say, sir, that I wanted to attempt to fight for the Arab cause?"

"This morning, I think—may I ask you again: Are you willing to fight for it?"

Sirhan Sirhan was now caught in a box that had been constructed with the encouragement of his Arab supporters, his family, and his attorneys. He would have to respond to Compton with the head of the Palestinian UN delegation present and millions of other Arabs observing from a distance.

"I am willing to fight for it," Sirhan answered.

"Are you willing to die for it?"

"I am willing to die for it."

In a handful of questions Buck Compton had summarized the prosecution case against Sirhan Sirhan. He was to be convicted and sentenced on the basis of his motive: political assassination. Despite the fact that the defendant professed no memory of the crime, Compton had gotten Sirhan to admit to the jury that he was willing to fight and die for the Arab cause. Nothing else needed to be said.

In putting Sirhan Sirhan on the witness stand, Grant Cooper had accepted the risk of cross-examination. Unfortunately for Sirhan, much of the damage done to the defense during his testimony was done by his own attorney. Cooper had actively promoted the political motive. He had tried to make sense out of Sirhan's strange writings by posing the bombers-to-Israel hypothesis. He had also tried to rationalize the notebooks by dragging out the article in the *Rosicrucian Digest.*

Sirhan's notebooks were quite clearly written in an abnormal state of mind. They should have represented very poor evidence of premeditation. But Cooper helped the prosecution skip over that difficulty by reducing the bizarre writing to some occult version of positive thinking. Thanks in great part to the defense attorney's efforts, the jury now had all the shorthand they needed. Sirhan had shot Senator Kennedy for advocating the sale of bombers to Israel; the writing in his notebooks was to strengthen his murderous resolve; he was willing to die for his cause. In such a syllogism the questions of guilt and punishment were already decided.

ELEVEN

Rorschach and Freud

✻　✻　✻

*In the amorphous smear of an inkblot, some people see castles,
animals, and a wide variety of other objects. Others impute vigorous
motion and life to the same stimulus. Still others see nothing. The
things people 'see' and don't 'see' have clinical significance for them.*

—Dr. Martin Schorr in a letter to defense attorney Russell Parsons

O N SUNDAY, MARCH 2, the doctors on the defense team again
met at Grant Cooper's office, this time to coordinate their trial testimony.
The defense that Cooper had selected for Sirhan, diminished capacity, was
a relatively new wrinkle in California criminal law. Cooper wanted to be
sure that everyone was up-to-date.

In the preceding decade decisions by the California Supreme Court had
dramatically modernized the intersection between law and psychiatry. Prior
to that the law had remained virtually unchanged for a century, its precedent
an 1843 case in which a man named Daniel M'Naghten murdered one
Edward Drummond, who happened to be secretary to the British prime
minister, Sir Robert Peel. At M'Naghten's trial the defense introduced
evidence of the accused's insanity, focusing on his obsession with certain
morbid delusions. Lord Chief Justice Tindal, in his charge to the jury, stated:
"[T]he question to be determined is whether at the time the act was committed, the prisoner had or had not the use of his understanding, so as to
know that he was doing a wrong or wicked act."

The jury returned a verdict of "not guilty, on the ground of insanity."

For one hundred years the knowledge of right and wrong, the
"M'Naghten Rule," was the test for insanity in criminal law. But modern
psychiatry eventually caught up with the concept, and by the 1950s and
1960s there was a string of cases in California which recognized gradations
in criminal responsibility. In two of the earliest cases, *People v. Wells* and
People v. Gorshen, Dr. Bernard Diamond, the psychiatrist that Grant Cooper
had selected to anchor the Sirhan team, testified as a witness for the defense.
In each case the defense was successful in establishing the relevance of the

defendant's state of mind or mental health to his formation of criminal intent.

In 1964 the California Supreme Court heard *People v. Wolff*. In this case a fifteen-year-old boy named Ronald Dennis Wolff had murdered his mother with an ax handle. There was evidence of both prior planning to the murder and evidence that Wolff understood his actions to be wrong, but he had also been diagnosed as "schizophrenic." In reviewing the case the California Supreme Court ruled:

> . . . there is no question that the defendant had the intent to kill; but . . . the true test must include consideration of the somewhat limited extent to which this defendant could maturely and meaningfully reflect upon the gravity of his contemplated act. . . . He knew the difference between right and wrong; he knew the intended act was wrong and nevertheless carried it out. But the extent of his understanding, reflection upon it and its consequences, with realization of the enormity of the evil, appears to have been materially . . . vague and detached.

The court reduced Wolff's conviction of first-degree murder to murder in the second degree, and in so doing redefined "premeditation" and established the defense of "diminished capacity."

In August of 1968, as Sirhan was awaiting trial, the California Supreme Court in *People v. Basett* reaffirmed the new boundaries of premeditation:

> Whatever that word may have signified prior to our *Wolff* decision, we there made it clear that the true test is not simply an adequate time to deliberate, or a manifest intent to kill, or even an abstract appearance of "rationality" in the defendant's planning, but rather the depth of his appreciation of the "enormity of the evil" he proposes to commit.

After reviewing the case law on diminished capacity for the doctors gathered in Grant Cooper's office, Emile Berman, who would conduct the questioning during this part of the trial, said that he wanted Dr. O. Roderick Richardson to lead off for the defense. Dr. Martin Schorr, however, insisted that he should testify first. Richardson voiced no preference. Seeking to keep peace, Berman changed his lineup.

Martin Schorr was a clinical psychologist who screened prison inmates for the county of San Diego. He was on the staff of a half dozen hospitals and clinics in Southern California, and was a member of numerous professional organizations, some arcane, including the Rorschach Exchange, the Society of Projective Techniques, and the Transactional Analysis Association. He had testified in court as an expert witness on numerous occasions, and had been invited into the case by Russell Parsons in June of the preceding year. All of this was told to the jury on Monday, March 10, by Dr. Schorr under defense counsel Berman's direction.

Dr. Schorr had examined Sirhan Sirhan in his cell on the thirteenth floor of the Hall of Justice on November 25 and 26. He had administered five tests: the Wechsler Adult Intelligence Scale (commonly known as the "IQ Test"), the Minnesota Multiphasic Personality Inventory (MMPI), the Thematic Apperception Test, the Bender-Gestalt Examination, and the Rorschach (inkblot) Examination. All of these tests, according to Schorr, were "projective," something he likened to "a mental X-ray," penetrating the "mask of sanity or conformity and getting down to the root feelings and attitudes of the true personality."

Dr. Schorr diagnosed Sirhan as being in "a paranoid psychosis, a paranoid state." He told the court that his tests revealed a man trapped in "a rigid, persistent, persuasive system of delusional false beliefs," with a personality structure that was in a "high degree of fragmentation." Later, under Berman's questioning, Schorr would agree that prior to the murder Sirhan was not able to "maturely and meaningfully reflect upon the gravity of his crime."

If Schorr had been able to say all of this in an hour or two, the defense might have benefited from his testimony. But the apparent defense strategy was to overwhelm the jury with expertise. Together, Berman and Schorr plodded through all of Schorr's tests, Sirhan's responses, how they were scored, what they meant.

"But this is most significant," said Schorr in the midst of one endless explanation. "Here we have forty-one percent—and the total here should always be under ten; less than ten. It's forty-one. So taking the upper limit of the norm, ten, forty-one is four times excessively wrong."

"Four times excessively what?" asked Berman.

"Wrong," replied Schorr. "Four times excessively abnormal. This is what I tried to say earlier; there are no right or wrong things; there are no good or bad. This is bad in terms of the norm, but it is not bad in and of itself; it depends on what kind of value you place on this kind of a personality profile. I haven't even given it a name yet."

As Schorr went on, the members of the jury heard all they cared to about the "psychodynamics of personality adjustment," "F percent columns," "projective psychodiagnostic techniques," "C primes," and "fantasy manifestations." At times Schorr's jargon confused his own lawyers as well as the presiding judge. Schorr said that during the murder he believed Sirhan was in a "dissociate state."

"Dis-associate?" Judge Walker asked

"Dissociate," Schorr answered.

"Dis–associate state?"

"Dissociate state."

"All right," said Walker, still baffled.

On Tuesday afternoon, after a tedious day and a half of charts, diagrams, and technical language, Assistant District Attorney John Howard began his cross-examination of Dr. Martin Schorr. Howard pressed Schorr on his definitions; he asked specific questions about the murder. When did Sirhan go into his dissociate state? What induced that state? At what moment did he emerge from it?

Under this questioning Schorr became uncomfortable. When Howard suggested he expand upon an answer, Schorr replied, "Well, I would rather get through and go home and get back to work." The doctor, it seemed, was beginning to lose his taste for the attention he had craved only days before.

Schorr sensed that he was being stalked, and his answers to Howard's questions were filled with qualifications, always leaving himself a route for retreat. When, on occasion, he was cornered, he would escape down a ladder of words, but at a cost. To the juror listening, Schorr's concepts and theories, difficult to understand to begin with, became less worthy as they changed contour according to the need of the moment. For example, Howard challenged Schorr on his split-personality model of Sirhan.

"Now are you telling us the Hyde and Jekyll Sirhan are the same?" he asked.

"The same person."

"The same personality?"

"The same personality structure."

"I got the impression yesterday they were different; have they merged together?"

"Maybe I better make that more correct. I didn't say that. The personality structure of this individual is essentially that of a paranoid state or paranoid psychosis, and the paranoid state itself doesn't matter whether he is in dissociate reaction or he is a paranoid psychotic, though psychotic disturbances, the paranoid state, personality structure, when in the dissociate reaction or not, it still is there."

When he came to questioning Schorr on his Rorschach Examination, Howard increased the pace. He was superbly prepared and at times seemed to demonstrate a better knowledge of Rorschach than did Schorr. Howard picked particular "inkblots" and asked Schorr how he had come to score them the way he did. Schorr stubbornly held to the idea that the test left little room for interpretation. "He makes his own diagnosis by the way he sees things," he said, referring to Sirhan.

"Well, Doctor," replied Howard, "I am suggesting you made the diagnosis, not he, so I am inquiring what you did." Howard's point was that there was considerable discretion in how a response was scored, yet if only one or two responses were scored differently, the results of the test would change dramatically because the base of the test was so small.

"If you get a different scoring or a different interpretation," insisted Schorr, "you are not going by Rorschach; you are developing something that has no correspondence with the reality of Rorschach."

"All right, Rorschach himself," challenged Howard. "Will you tell me in what book I can find that he ever suggested there was a scoring system for it?"

Schorr had to concede that the scoring systems for the examination had been developed by Rorschach apostles in more recent years, but, he added proudly, "I used the scoring system that is consonant with what is used in the state of California . . . only one of twenty-one possible scoring systems."

"Which one is it?"

"Klopfer."

Schorr might have thought it sounded impressive that there were twenty-one possible scoring systems, but the fact merely supported Howard's contention that the test demonstrated as much about the doctor as it did about the subject.

In the end Howard would catch Schorr in a trap the doctor had help set for himself. During cross-examination Schorr had asked to read his report on Sirhan written in December. He had spent days going over his test results for the jury, but hadn't had the chance to present his synthesis. Thinking that Schorr wanted only to read it to himself for reference, Howard produced the report. Once he began reading in open court, Fitts objected: "I thought the purpose of this was to refresh the witness's recollection."

"Yes," agreed Judge Walker, "you are not to read it."

Later Schorr would bring up the subject again: "I have to read the report in its entirety in order for the jury or for you to see—"

"I read it," said Howard, cutting him off.

"Well the jury hasn't heard it," Schorr countered.

"Fine. Can we do it my way?"

"Well, you're asking the questions."

"Fine. Would you like to read the report?"

"If you would like me to, yes."

"I don't want—"

"I would like to, yes."

"Would you? Fine."

At that point Grant Cooper jumped in: "I don't understand. Do you mean read it to himself or read it aloud?"

"I meant aloud," Schorr said, not waiting for Howard to answer. "I meant read it aloud. . . ."

"I'm not going to object," Cooper sighed, "if he wants to do it."

Howard then handed Schorr the report and asked him to read two paragraphs from page 3. Perhaps Howard sensed that this was the part Schorr was most eager to read, but when he handed Schorr the report those paragraphs had already been bracketed. Something was up. Schorr read the paragraphs.

> "By killing Kennedy, Sirhan kills his father, takes his father's place as the heir to his mother. The process of acting out this problem can only be achieved in a psychotic, insane state of mind. Essentially the more he railed and stormed, the more he withdrew into her protection.
>
> "He hated his father and feared him. He would never consciously entertain the idea of doing away with him, but somewhere along the line the protecting mother fails her son. The mother finally lets down the son. She whom he loved never kept her pledge, and now his pain has to be repaid with pain. Since the unconscious always demands maximum penalties, the pain has to be death. Sirhan's prime problem becomes a conflict between instinctual demand for his father's death and the realization through his conscience that killing his father is not socially acceptable. The only real solution is to look for a compromise. He does. He finds the symbolic replica of his father in the form of Kennedy, kills him and also removes the relationship that stands between him and his most precious possession, his mother's love."

As soon as Schorr finished, Howard approached and asked, "Who wrote that?"

"I did," Schorr replied.

The characterization of Sirhan's Oedipal manifestations was just the kind of thing the press was hungry for. At recess reporters crowded around Robert Kaiser. Hearing Kaiser give the text of the statement to the reporters, Mary Sirhan, who had been publicly humiliated by the language, approached the defense investigator. "I don't want that. I don't want that," she said. "It's all right if the prosecution gives that to the press, but I don't want you to do it." The prosecution, as it turned out, was only too happy for the press to possess the wording of Schorr's report.

On Monday morning Dr. Schorr was again on the witness stand, and John Howard sought to have the defense psychologist's December 16 report entered into evidence for the prosecution. Before there was time for Schorr to wonder what he was up to, Howard made another offering.

"Your Honor, here we have a book, *Casebook of a Crime Psychiatrist* by James A. Brussel, M. D., and may it be marked People's, next in order, 101."

Brussel's book was not a scholarly text about mental illness, but rather a recently published popular account of gruesome crimes committed by disturbed people. After considerable wrangling with the defense attorneys over how much of the book would be placed into evidence, Howard had Dr. Schorr read out loud a passage from Brussel's book taken from a chapter called "The Christmas Eve Killer":

> "And the more he stormed, the more the mother protected her boy and the more he withdrew into her protecting arms. The boy hated his father, yes—and more important feared him. Therefore, he would never entertain the idea of doing away with the man. . . . Then, somewhere along the line, the protecting mother may have 'failed' her boy. She whom he loved never kept her pledge and he began to feel that she really didn't love him. Pain had to be repaid with pain, and since the unconscious always demands the maximum, the pain had to be death.
>
> "Now his prime problem was the conflict between instinctual demand for her death and the realization, through his conscience, that killing one's mother is not socially acceptable. The only solution was to look for a compromise. He did. He found a symbolic replica of his mother, killed her, and took valuables that stood for her most precious possession—the thing she denied him, her love."[1]

The similarities of this passage to the one Dr. Schorr had read the previous week from his report were undeniable.

"At the time you prepared your report," questioned John Howard, "were you aware of a book called *Casebook of a Crime Psychiatrist* by James A. Brussel?"

"Oh yes," replied Schorr. "I read it."

"Doctor, you copied right out of this book, didn't you?"

"I took materials from this book that applied to the paranoid mechanism and I redesigned it to fit in with what I had already said."

Later Grant Cooper would say of this moment that he "could have crawled under a table."[2] Dr. Schorr was beyond help. He now had to play mouse to Howard's cat for as long as the prosecutor wanted the game to go on. And Howard was in no hurry. He had Schorr read other parts of his report and then had him read to the jury the corresponding sections from "The Christmas Eve Killer" or another chapter, "The Mad Bomber." Most of these were virtual matches.

Schorr was forced to admit over and over that he had "borrowed language" from Brussel, and that he had done so to extract the "psychological valuables."

"Doctor," Howard asked, "by the time you graduated from college did you know how to put quotation marks around or use footnotes to indicate that you had taken from another source?"

Schorr was left with no good answers. "I wanted to make a statement that one would not disbelieve," he said.

It was now March 18; Dr Schorr had taken the stand on March 10 only to numb the jury with a lengthy and pedantic presentation. After that, Howard had skillfully challenged the doctor's methodology. And now, Dr. Martin Schorr's summation of the defendant was shown to be plagiarized.

Bob Greene in *Newsday* described Schorr's last moments at court:

> Dr. Martin M. Schorr had the sick look of a man who has just taken a hard right to the belly yesterday when he stepped off the elevator on the first floor of the Hall of Justice at exactly 12:07 P.M.
>
> He is just getting used to contact lenses and had to tilt his head backwards to focus correctly before he started walking. A mob of interviewers tried to hold him back. But he kept shaking his head and broke into an awkward trot toward the street door.[3]

Throughout the trial the defense had offered little resistance to the prosecution's case. The promise was that they would fight on ground of their own choosing. This was the first engagement on that ground, and it was a rout.

The unenviable task of following Dr. Schorr onto the witness stand fell to Dr. Orville Roderick Richardson. Like Schorr, Richardson was a clinical psychologist, and, like Schorr, Richardson had conducted a number of tests upon Sirhan, including the Rorschach. After he was sworn in Richardson asked Grant Cooper if he could begin by reading his report.

"It was made by you?" asked Cooper, posing a question that would have seemed silly a few days earlier.

"Yes, it was."

"It is your work product?"

"Yes."

Richardson's report described "a very severe emotional and mental disturbance in a man of bright-normal to superior intellectual potential. He is well informed, shows a good vocabulary, and is capable under conditions of minimal stress of presenting himself in a logical, plausible fashion; however his personality is highly fragile . . . subject to episodes of acute and rapid deterioration." Richardson concluded that Sirhan "could not 'know' the difference between right and wrong, as nondisturbed individuals in this culture would judge this difference."

In presenting the results of his tests Richardson explained in half an afternoon what it took Dr. Schorr three times as long to cover. From his Wechsler Examination, Richardson reported a knowledgeable Sirhan, apparently in good contact with reality. "He says that yeast causes dough to rise by fermentation; he gives the population of the United States as two hundred fourteen million; he knows that there are one hundred senators; he says the main theme of the Book of Genesis is Creation; he knows that Homer wrote the *Iliad* . . . and so on."

In the "test of similarities," however, Richardson thought he detected a problem. To the question how a banana and an orange are alike Sirhan said, "You have to peel them before you eat them" instead of "They are fruit." He said, "A coat and a dress are alike because they are both worn," instead of, "They are clothing." He said, "An ax and a saw . . . cut wood" rather than "They are tools."

To Richardson these responses were "indicative of impairment, some fracture in his intellectual process." But to a member of the jury it may have seemed as though Dr. Richardson was reaching, for Sirhan's answers might well have been considered superior. That a saw and an ax both cut wood is a more distinguishing similarity than the fact that they are both tools. The same would be true of Sirhan's answer concerning the orange and the banana.

David Fitts directed the cross-examination of Richardson, and he began by asking the doctor whether he had an early opinion about Sirhan's psychological makeup, one that was formed before he had examined the defendant.

"Yes," said Richardson without the equivocation that was present in so many of Dr. Schorr's answers, "I think that there is no denying that the first thing that would pop to mind is a paranoid personality—to a psychologist. Since we know that assassins far back in the United States history are people who tend to be paranoid people, and this is what we read in our textbooks, and so the assumption is paranoid."

"Well, given that, it was impossible for you to give a blind test to Mr. Sirhan, isn't that true?"

Fitts then ran Richardson through his Rorschach Examination, exploiting the many differences between his conclusions and those of Dr. Schorr. Fitts pointed to the card where Sirhan saw a dove, and from which Dr. Schorr drew a "violent" inference, but Richardson did not. "He might be talking about some kind of total energy concept," explained Richardson, trying not to dispute the finding of a fellow clinician, ". . . what Klopfer called unmodified relative unsocialized intentional strive personality."

"Well most of the time doves symbolize peace," said Fitts, "isn't that what we are taught?"

"It means different things at different times in different contexts," said

Richardson, referring to the test scoring in general. "This is what we mean by the global integration of the Rorschach."

"Doctor for the sake of brevity, will you agree with me that the psychogram you have illustrated for us . . . doesn't seem to bear any superficial resemblence to the psychogram presented by Dr. Schorr?"

"I would say there are some differences," Richardson conceded after Cooper's objection had been overruled, "and those differences may be clinically significant."

Fitts's contention was that many of Sirhan's "abnormal" test responses might be completely normal if cross-cultural considerations were given weight. For example, seeing "a mosque" in one inkblot or a high number of "food responses" might be quite normal for one brought up in Jerusalem in a time of war and food shortage. Fitts also argued that many of Sirhan's "paranoid" responses might quite be reasonable given his present circumstance—incarceration with the knowledge that a great many people harbored malice toward him:

"Now, you have said that based on your diagnosis of him he was, among other things, suspicious, distrustful, felt hostile forces were working against him. . . . Now when you start giving these tests, how do you make allowances for the truth of some of these things which might otherwise be considered, let us say, paranoid characteristics?"

Fitts's question might have been applied to another set of strange responses recorded on Richardson's MMPI test. Sirhan answered "Yes" to the following assertions:

"Evil spirits possess me at times."

"I have had very peculiar and strange experiences."

"When I am with people, I am bothered by hearing very queer things."

"I believe I am being plotted against."

"I have strange and peculiar thoughts."

"I often feel as though things are not real."

"I have periods in which I carry on activities without knowing later what I have been doing."

Just as significantly, Sirhan gave no answer at all (that is, he did not answer "No") to the following:

"I see things or animals or people around me that others do not see."

"Someone has been trying to influence my mind."

"At one or more times in my life, I felt that someone was making me do things by hypnotizing me."

According to Richardson and standard MMPI analysis, these answers all indicate paranoia, yet never did Richardson or any other trial doctor consider a possible literal interpretation. Following the logic proposed by prosecutor David Fitts, if someone really had tried to manipulate Sirhan's mind, these responses wouldn't represent paranoia at all.

Fitts, of course, was not suggesting esoteric explanations, certainly not ones that pointed toward conspiracy. Over and over he offered common-sense rationales for Sirhan's test responses that Richardson had rated as abnormal. Richardson would acknowledge the logic in Fitts's scenarios, but then, like Schorr, he would take refuge in the strictures of the Rorschach scoring.

"Well I have difficulty sometimes with you, Doctor," Fitts said, finally losing patience. "I mean you admit that something I say is reasonable and logical, but then you go back to the books and the books tell you that . . . [it] is not right in this case. Is that right?"

"That's correct," replied Richardson. "Training in clinical psychology brings about a certain set of mind toward psychological data. . . . I think that your statements are quite reasonable from the layman's point of view, but not from the clinical psychologist's point of view."

Richardson had not been destroyed as a witness, but throughout the cross-examination Fitts had scored heavily. He made Richardson confess that he tended toward a diagnosis of paranoia before he ever saw Sirhan. Then he made Richardson concede significant differences in his test results from those of Dr. Schorr. Finally, he had gotten the doctor to separate psychology and common sense. In doing this Fitts had begun to frame in the mind of the jurors, in terms favorable to the prosecution, the choice they would ultimately have to make.

Following Richardson to the witness stand was psychiatrist Dr. Eric H. Marcus, who had been practicing medicine since 1960. Dr. Marcus had been appointed by Judge Alarcon several weeks after the murder to prepare a report on Sirhan's mental state for the defendant's then-court-appointed attorneys. Marcus had examined Sirhan four times between June and October; he had brought Dr. Richardson into the case, specifically to run tests upon Sirhan.

Dr. Marcus was familiar with the medical/legal intersection. In the year before the Sirhan trial, he had examined ninety accused criminals for the California Superior Court, making recommendations on insanity, diminished capacity, and competency to stand trial. He belonged to all the usual professional fraternities, and was the past president of the Southern California Society for Psychiatry and Law and the president-elect of the Medical-Legal Society of Southern California.

Under questioning by Grant Cooper, Marcus was quite willing to say that he had relied heavily on the tests and opinions of others in coming to his own diagnosis. On his extensive list of preparatory reading were two articles, one titled "Presidential Assassination Syndrome" and the other "The Psychiatry of Presidential Assassination." Marcus also told the court that he was present at the February 2 meeting in Cooper's office, attended by Drs. Schorr, Richardson, Diamond, and Pollack. "We reviewed each other's notes," he revealed, "we looked at each other's reports; I think we looked at some case law."

In gathering all this information Dr. Marcus formed a picture of an emotionally troubled, politically motivated assassin.

"In my opinion," he told the court, ". . . [Sirhan] was mentally disturbed and became increasingly more disturbed during the spring of last year. That is also noted in the psychological tests and I feel that his mental disturbances was relevant and directly related to his political views and his feelings about Robert Kennedy; I feel therefore that he could not meaningfully and maturely think and deliberate on his actions."

"Well now, Doctor," said Cooper, "let me ask you this. A person who is mentally ill, can he not plan?"

"Oh, yes," replied Dr. Marcus.

Cooper here appeared to be setting up to make the primary point for the defense—that a person can form an intent to murder (that is, he can plan the event in advance), but that does not, in itself, under California law, constitute premeditation. Premeditation has to include the capacity for mature and meaningful deliberation.

"And being a person who is mentally ill," Cooper continued, "can he form an intent to kill?"

"Yes."

"And being a person who is mentally ill, can he also entertain malice aforethought?"

"Yes."

"Now will you explain, Doctor, what you mean when you say that in your opinion the defendant could not?"

Could not what? Plan? Form intent? Entertain malice? Premeditate? The prosecution had taken every opportunity to argue that Sirhan had demonstrated some thought process before the murder. Thus, it was crucial for Cooper to separate the legal meaning of premeditation from the more popular concept of premeditation as thinking about something beforehand. He didn't.

In response Dr. Marcus tried to maintain momentum: "In my opinion Sirhan thought that he was more or less the savior of society. He was going to reorganize or at least destroy the current political leaders. . . . I don't feel he really was competent or capable of having malice within that technical sense."

"All right, now," said Cooper, seemingly still in a fog, and unable to formulate a clear question, "was his ability to plan and deliberate and the like?"

"I thought I covered that already," said Marcus no longer able to keep the ball in the air.

"You covered that in the first answer," Cooper conceded.

The moment was gone. Cooper had managed to throw around the terms "plan," "deliberate," "malice," and "premeditate" in a careless fashion, and, in so doing, had muddied the very issue that it was crucial for him to make clear.

That Dr. Marcus had relied so heavily on outside opinion in making his diagnosis of Sirhan might have made him vulnerable to cross-examination by David Fitts, but Marcus turned out to be a strong witness when under attack. He was not embarrassed to express an opinion, and he was quite willing to trade sarcastic remarks with the sharp-witted prosecutor. The energy of these exchanges was occasionally reinforced by the sound of thunder, as several fierce storms moved through downtown Los Angeles while Marcus testified. Three times the courtroom darkened, to become momentarily illuminated by the eerie glow of emergency lights.

Under Fitts's questioning Marcus described to the jury his vision of Sirhan's schizophrenia: "It is as if two people or two personalities exist in him at the same time; a sick personality and a healthy personality. These are not watertight compartments. Sometimes one part, the sick part, may take over; sometimes the healthy part takes over; sometimes they are both doing something at the same time."

Fitts tried to argue that this process might well describe any normal person under stress. He offered himself as an example of "an individual who generally tries to set the image in his household of a kind father, for instance. He puts up with the importunities of his children; he is vexed with them at times; he tries to be tolerant of them; and yet given a sort of a stress situation, such as perhaps having to work on a long trial, he blows up at the kids and does things for which he may be sorry later."

"No, that's not what schizophrenia means," answered Marcus. "What you are describing is sort of a middle-class neurotic phenomenon. 'Schizophrenic' . . . means there is something wrong with the way your brain operates. It's as if—using an analogy—you are using a telephone switchboard and the plugs were crisscrossed."

Fitts asked Dr. Marcus whether Sirhan could premeditate. Marcus replied that he could premeditate about some things but not about things concerning Sirhan's "mistaken political . . . aberrant beliefs."

"What was mistaken about Mr. Sirhan's political beliefs during this time?"

"Well I think one of his mistakes was assuming that he could start World War III. That was one mistake.

"He made some other mistakes," continued Marcus. "His mistake was that if he could assassinate President Johnson and the vice president and on down, that somehow he would make a new order of being in the world.''

Dr. Marcus might have included in his list of Sirhan's delusions the idea that murdering Robert Kennedy (whose views on the Arab-Israeli confrontation were hardly different from Johnson's, Humphrey's, or Nixon's) would benefit the Palestinian cause.

Fitts was determined to show that political assassination was on the fringe, but within the realm of sane activity: "Well, how about in Russia? Haven't we read . . . how every now and then they simply eliminate political leaders who are in opposition?"

"There's some question about the leaders, such as Stalin and others," replied Marcus with some humor. "Once you achieve a position of power you are considered sane by definition, since you run the show and you hire and fire the psychiatrists."

Fitts was looking to demonstrate that Sirhan was in a rational state before the murder took place and he had selected a passage from Sirhan's notebook to help him make his point.

"This particular page of the notebook that I am now about to show you"—Fitts held up a piece of paper and advanced toward the witness stand—"can I read it again to you? And ask you questions about it?" Fitts began to read the passage:

> "For a person to put his thoughts into words is a difficult task, if you remember that that person is a troglodyte who is therefore more physically inclined than his more urban contemporaries."

"That's pretty highfalutin language, isn't it, sir?" said Fitts after only one sentence.

"Well, what does 'highfalutin' mean?" replied Marcus. "It sounds crazy to me."

"It sounds crazy to you?" Fitts read on.

> "This American politician leads his people to any course that he wants them to—this is possible because the people lack the initiative or are indifferent to the actions of their leaders."

"Do I make sense?" asked the prosecutor, talking about the cohesion of Sirhan's prose.

"You make face-value sense, I'd say yes."

"There's nothing particularly psychotic or disturbed about that kind of statement, is there?"

"Well, statements aren't psychotic or disturbed," replied Dr. Marcus quickly, "only the people who make them."

"Their leaders say, 'You have the right to speak against your government and support its changeover—but remember through democratic means only—if otherwise we will blast the hell out of you and besides, you wouldn't want to do anything like that, it is stupid. Just let us run the country, hire our relatives to work for us and earn fat checks. We know what we are doing in Vietnam—we are keeping the economy going through our war spendings. We will keep busy here working on picayunish matters. To impress you all what we really want to do is' (excuse me) 'fuck you up, get fat and then quit.' "

"Well that's a criticism of our war policy in Vietnam, isn't it?" crowed Fitts.

"If you want to interpret it that way," replied Marcus, unimpressed.

"Well, that's the way to interpret it, isn't it?"

"Well that's one way."

"Would you interpret it another way, necessarily?"

"Yes."

"What? What is it? What is your other interpretation?"

"My interpretation is that this is the ramblings of an angry sick man."

"Why do you say this is rambling?"

"The grammar is off; it varies from rather erudite language to vulgarity; this isn't the type of thing you turn in in a political science course."

Fitts continued:

"My solution to this type of government, that is to do away with its leaders and declare anarchy the best form of government or no government."

"—another way of saying anarchy, I take it," said Fitts. "There is some material crossed out here. 'The President-elect is your best friend until he gets in power, then he'—some of this is a little difficult—'then he'—there's something crossed out." Fitts was apparently unfamiliar with how the quotation ended.

"It's interesting," said Marcus taking over: " 'is your most exploring fucker.' "

Fitts didn't like being pushed aside and began reading from the passage with a deliberate cadence that only served to emphasize the strange language: " 'Suck every drop of blood out of you, and if he doesn't like you, you're dead.'

"Well, now I will agree with you, sir," said David Fitts, no doubt wishing that he had never started with the notebook, "this is not the average composition that might be turned in to a high school English class. At the same time, the ideas expressed here are expressed by lots of people in criticizing government, are they not?"

" 'The President . . . sucks every drop of blood out until you're dead?' " asked Marcus incredulously. "These aren't political views."

Fitts was intent on demonstrating that Sirhan was in a normal state of mind when he was being interrogated after the murder, and he offered a quote: " 'I wish to abide by your first admonishment, sir,' he said to Lieutenant Jordan. Does that indicate sickness to you?"

"It indicates a very formal, stilted, legalistic frame of mind," replied Marcus, "which to me is a little inappropriate for somebody that you know has just committed the crime of the year."

Fitts, in trying to demonstrate Sirhan's mental cohesion before the murder, brought up Sirhan's story about going out to his car under the influence of alcohol. "He says, he thought he might not be in a condition to conduct a car carefully and he was worried about his failure to have insurance on the car. . . . Would you say that is showing a pretty good sign of social responsibility?"

"Well, again he is functioning on more or less one track at the same time," replied Marcus. "Part of his mind is saying, 'I better be careful I don't want to get a ticket for drunk driving,' and the other part of his mind is somewhere else, maybe planning an assassination at the same time."

"Now Sirhan told you, did he not, that at this time he didn't remember anything more until he was pinned to a table, is that right?"

"Yes, he told me that."

"You don't believe it, do you?"

"Yes, I believe it."

Fitts was now entering his endgame. If Sirhan were really suffering from amnesia, he asked Dr. Marcus, why didn't he show more concern or ask more questions of the police when he was in custody?

Marcus had no answer. A series of skillfully constructed questions by Fitts then forced the doctor to admit that he could not explain Sirhan's amnesia by way of schizophrenia, and that he could offer no good explanation for Sirhan's failure to inquire about his arrest.

"Then to go back to the question that I asked you earlier, when Mr. Sirhan claimed this amnesia in his interview with you, he was lying?"

"That's quite possible," conceded Marcus.

"I think that's all," concluded Fitts, quite satisfied.

Marcus's concession was another stunning setback for the defense. The trial of Sirhan, never a contest of facts, had become a contest of credibility. Were the doctors believable? Was Sirhan? Now one of Sirhan's chief defenders admitted that it was quite possible Sirhan was lying.

TWELVE

Hypnosis and Memory

✯ ✯ ✯

Let me specifically state that it was immediately apparent that Sirhan had been programmed. . . . His response to hypnosis was very different . . . strange, in many respects. And he showed this phenomenon of automatic writing, which is something that can be done only when one is pretty well trained.

—Dr. Bernard Diamond, chief psychiatrist for Sirhan's defense team, 1974

When Dr. Bernard Diamond arrived from San Francisco he was not pleased to learn that Dr. Eric Marcus had admitted in court that Sirhan might be lying about his loss of memory. Diamond, not Marcus, had been the one who had spent time probing this issue. Marcus, too, felt bad about the situation, and he apologized to Dr. Diamond when they met.

It was Emile Berman who called Bernard Diamond to the witness stand the following day, and Berman opened by having the doctor recite his academic credentials. Diamond had graduated from the University of California Medical School in 1939. He had served as a psychiatrist in the army in World War II. He had studied at the Neuropsychiatric Institute of the University of Michigan and at the San Francisco Analytic Institute. Most noteworthy, since 1964 Dr. Diamond had served on the faculty of the University of California, where he was a full professor in the law school, the medical school, and the school of criminology.

Bernard Diamond was at the very top of his profession. He was a former president of the San Francisco Analytic Institute, a member of the Committee on Psychiatry and Law of the American Psychiatric Association, and a fellow of the American Association for the Advancement of Science. He had served as a member of the California Commission on Insanity and Criminal Offenses; he had received the J. Elliot Royer Award for advancement of psychiatry and the Isaac Ray Award for achievement in psychiatry and law. The members of the jury might have been impressed by all this, but they weren't given the opportunity. Berman forgot to ask Diamond about his professional credentials.

"Now, then," said the attorney, unaware that he had already lost a wheel, "just tell us where your first examination [of Sirhan] was made and what it consisted of and what, if you are ready to state, what views you had at the time on your first examination."

It was a broad question and Dr. Diamond took advantage. He launched himself into a remarkable monologue which stretched over several days, rarely interrupted by Berman, during which Diamond told the rather extraordinary story of his encounters with Sirhan Sirhan.

Diamond's initial interview with Sirhan took place on December 23. He described Sirhan at that time as being "superficially cooperative."

"It seemed to me that he was more than willing to communicate to me that he had shot and killed Senator Kennedy; that he regarded Senator Kennedy as an enemy of his people, the Arab people; and that he committed this assassination because he felt it was necessary to prevent Kennedy from fulfilling a promise that Sirhan had heard, or thought that Kennedy had made over television in the previous month."

There was one part of Sirhan's story, however, that Diamond found most peculiar. "I readily observed that he did not describe to me spontaneously either the shooting or the notebook, and I questioned him about these, and he protested to me that he had no memory of the actual shooting and had no memory of the notebook itself."

Sirhan was able to relate to Diamond the chain of events that brought him to the Ambassador Hotel, but his memory stopped with his having coffee with a pretty girl. His recollections began again with his being choked after the shooting. Sirhan could remember being taken away in the police car, and being in a room in the police station with various officers talking to him. "Most of all he remembers," Diamond told the court, "and it became a kind of fixed obsession with him, it stood out like a beacon with him, the warning of the police officers initially that he didn't have to say anything, and anything he said would be held against him. . . . He described his state of mind at that time as being one of intense suspicion and that he was confused and he didn't know why he was there."

Besides Sirhan's strange lack of memory of the shooting itself, the other paramount mystery to Dr. Diamond was Sirhan's notebooks. "We talked about the notebooks on many occasions and at no time when he was awake and conscious did he say he had any inconsistent or different attitude about the notebooks, always the same, admitting they were his, but he has no memory of it."

Using photocopies Diamond and Sirhan would go over the notebooks page by page. "Some of the pages were dated and he would say, 'I can see the date, but I don't remember it; I know this is my writing.' But then he would point to some of the letters that were strange. . . . 'That's not the way I make that letter.' Then he would say, 'Do you think they have had a handwriting expert forge this for me?' And I did respond and say, 'No, I don't think they did.' And then he would say, 'Well, I must have written it.' "

Sirhan's lack of memory of the shooting and the notebooks was disturbing to Diamond. The explanation offered by the prosecution, that Sirhan was lying about this memory loss as some sort of defense ploy, made little sense given that he had admitted to the murder, offered a reason for committing it, and accepted the writing in the notebooks as his own. At that point there was no advantage to claiming a memory loss. This paradox led Diamond to attempt to probe Sirhan's mind in an effort to discover another answer. The method he used was hypnosis.

Diamond was somewhat apologetic in court about using hypnosis, claiming that in a more usual psychiatric relationship he would prefer to just talk to the patient, for hundreds of hours if necessary, to get the patient's mind to release its secrets. But here, time was in short supply.

"I don't go around hypnotizing people every time I see them in my private clinical practice," Diamond offered, "but under special circumstances of which there is a medical-legal situation, . . . you have to utilize some kind of shortcut."

Diamond told the court that he decided against using a lie detector because he had little faith in its accuracy. His favored tool would have been a "truth serum" like sodium Amytal, but, because of the slight medical risks involved, that had been ruled out.

Diamond was particularly anxious to make clear to the court that hypnosis is useful in overcoming unintentional mental blocks, but that it does not guarantee the truth or accuracy of what a person is saying. "Can a person tell lies under hypnosis?" Diamond asked for the benefit of the jury. "The answer is yes, they can. Hypnosis is especially valuable in overcoming unconscious resistance and unconscious evasions. It is much more valuable in doing this than it is in overcoming conscious intentional evasions and intentional lies."

Dr. Diamond hypnotized Sirhan by holding a coin about eight inches from his eyes and giving him repeated suggestions to go to sleep. To the doctor's surprise Sirhan went under quite quickly.

"Sirhan went into a sort of convulsive rage response in which his fists clenched, arms tightened up, and he got a most dramatic contorted rage expression on his face and sobbed. The tears poured down his face. For the first time I had a glimpse or image of a completely different Sirhan than I had previously observed. Never before had Sirhan shown any sign of what I would consider real emotional depth. Everything was a certain superciliousness, a certain superficiality; every other word was 'fuck' or 'shit' and it was a very coarse kind of clever, supercilious, smart-alecky type of approach without any depth to it."

Diamond decided to bring Sirhan back almost right away. "He wakes up kind of startled," he reported. "He looks around and is quite bewildered, obviously quite confused. It takes him a portion of a minute almost to reorient himself. He is immediately suspicious that somebody has done something to him, but he doesn't know what. . . . He would visibly shiver and complain of being cold."

The report of Sirhan being cold after hypnosis had its parallel during Sirhan's interview by the LAPD's Dr. Marcus Crahan the morning after the postmidnight assassination:

> SIRHAN: It's chilly.
> CRAHAN: You're cold?
> SIRHAN: Not cold.
> CRAHAN: Not cold, what do you mean?
> SIRHAN: No comment.
> CRAHAN: You mean you're having a chill?
> SIRHAN: I have a very mild one, yes.

If Diamond had made this connection, he didn't share it with the jury. What was significant to the doctor was Sirhan's posthypnotic attitude.

"He has no recollection of the hypnosis," Diamond told the court. "It is quite totally amnesic; and he denies that the hypnosis has worked. And each and every time that I have ever hypnotized Sirhan, no matter how long he has been asleep, he has denied that I have been successful and feels in some way that he has tricked me. . . . Now I was, of course, impressed with the similarity of his attitude about the hypnosis, hypnotic experience and his loss of memory as far as the shooting was concerned and his repudiation, shall we say, of the notebook."

On January 11 Diamond hypnotized Sirhan and questioned him about the murder of Robert Kennedy. He recounted this conversation for the benefit of the jury:

> "Sirhan, did anyone pay you to shoot Kennedy . . . ?"
> And he says, "No," so I asked, "Did the Arab government have anything to do with it, Sirhan?"
> And he says, "No" and I said, "Did you think this up all by yourself?"
> And he paused for about four seconds and then he said, "Yes," and it was clear and unequivocal. . . .
> "Are you the only person involved in the Kennedy shooting?"
> And he pauses a second or two and he says, "Yes."
> I repeat the "Yes."

"There was nobody involved at all; why did you shoot Kennedy?"

And he pauses, no answer, and I said, "Why did you shoot him, Sirhan?"

And he says, "The bombers."

I said, "What are the bombers, you mean the bombers to Israel?" And he says "Yes."

I said, "Why did you decide to shoot Kennedy?" And I repeated that several times because there was no response and finally he said, "I don't know."

The pauses that Dr. Diamond noted before some of Sirhan's answers are sometimes referred to as "blocking." This is an indication that the hypnotized subject may be giving a false response. Either by intention of the subject or through hypnotic instruction, the true answer is "blocked" and a substitute answer is offered in its place. The hesitation represents the time taken by this mental process.

Though Diamond drew no conclusions from these pauses, the prosecution, a little while later, referred to this "blocking" as evidence of Sirhan's insincerity. What the prosecution failed to mention was that this blocking occurred on questions where Sirhan was asked whether anyone else was involved in the crime. If these hesitations were blocking, then the implication is that Sirhan was lying about acting alone or was hypnotically influenced to say that he acted alone. The prosecution was surely not advocating either of these possibilities.

On January 26, Dr. Diamond, working with Dr. Pollack, attempted to take a hypnotized Sirhan, step by step, through the tragic events at the Ambassador Hotel. By any measure the taped session was bizarre. As the doctors attempt to move a hypnotized Sirhan toward a simulation of murder, Dr. Pollack tries to provoke his subject. "He can't send the bombers [to Israel]" he says. "You're not going to let him, are you Sirhan?" Sirhan just groans and breathes heavily. The session continues.

DIAMOND: Can you see Kennedy coming? . . . Now what do you see, Sirhan, you're back in the kitchen, now what do you see?

SIRHAN (under hypnosis, breathing heavily, whispers): You son of a bitch!

DIAMOND (ellipsis points indicate short pauses): You're talking to Kennedy now, huh? . . . He's coming. . . . Reach for your gun, Sirhan. Where is your gun? . . . Where is your gun? Reach for it. (Lots of heavy breathing by Sirhan). Reach for your gun . . . Sirhan! . . .

Take your gun out and shoot it. . . . Who are you shooting, Sirhan? . . . Who are you shooting? . . . You're shooting Kennedy now, huh?

In their efforts to get Sirhan to remember the murder, Diamond and Pollack became positively clumsy in their use of hypnosis. The session was not a skillful search for recollection; instead, it bordered on being a memory implant.

> POLLACK (speaking very slowly; ellipsis points indicate short pauses): Sirhan, you have wanted to remember the shooting of Kennedy. . . . You wanted to remember your shooting him. . . . Now you'll remember shooting him. . . . You'll remember taking the gun out, pulling the trigger again . . . and again . . . and again. . . . You'll remember all of it. . . . All of this will get clearer and clearer and you'll remember it all? . . . You'll remember it all.

But as the tape of the session reveals, the forces against Sirhan's remembering were so strong as to resist even this hypnotic suggestion. Diamond asks the now awake Sirhan where he kept his gun. A distressed Sirhan says that he can't remember.

> DIAMOND (getting annoyed): Five minutes ago, Sirhan, you showed me where the gun was. The gun was right here in your belt. . . . You showed us how, you reached for the gun and you showed us how you pulled the trigger. Try to remember.

Sirhan's performance in this hypnosis session was not illuminating. He had mostly sweated and groaned. But the doctors had seen him pull his trigger finger when they told him to shoot, and he had reached into his pants when they told him to reach for his gun. This was, at least, some new information. But Dr. Diamond was still troubled.

"A problem which still was unresolved as far as I was concerned," he told the jury, "was an explanation of the notebook. I felt very dissatisfied with Sirhan's explanations, which were essentially no explanation at all. He denied the notebooks in a very odd, peculiar kind of way. He admitted the notebooks were his, he admitted most of the time that the writing must be his, but he had no recollection about how it happened and couldn't give me an explanation as to how any part of the notebook came about . . . so it occurred to me that it was possible that at least parts of the notebook might have been written during one of those Rosicrucian correspondence exercises in front of the mirrors, and I decided to experiment with this."

On February 1, Bernard Diamond once again hypnotized Sirhan. Again, he invited Seymour Pollack to sit in on the session. As Diamond explained to the court, his primary problem in hypnotizing Sirhan was that Sirhan would go under too deeply, making it difficult to gain information from him. It was Diamond's idea to try to induce a light trance. To do this he counted backward from five rapidly, while trying to keep Sirhan alert. This seemed to have the effect of not hypnotizing Sirhan at all. As the exercise began Dr. Diamond concluded that Sirhan was "quite awake." He then provided Sirhan with a pencil and a piece of paper and commanded him to write his name.

"So he proceeded to write his name at the top of the page here, 'Sirhan B. Sirhan,' and then started to write it again, 'Sirhan B. Sirhan,' and by the time he finished the first line . . . it was quite evident that Sirhan had now sort of flipped automatically into a hypnotic trance.

"He continued to write his name, 'Sirhan B. Sirhan, Sirhan B. Sirhan,' and this sort of astonished me and I decided to just allow him to write. He wrote like a robot writes, in a stiff mechanical way, his eyes fixed to the paper, and writing mechanically, taking about thirty seconds to complete a line."

Diamond then told the jury how he asked Sirhan a series of questions concerning the murder:

"Is Kennedy dead?"
And he stared and he wrote "No, no, no."
"Is Kennedy alive?"
And I repeated that and he wrote "Yes, yes, yes," and that is an example, I might say, of the hypnosis that people, well, they sometimes don't say the truth, but they say what they feel inside of them . . .
"Does Kennedy talk to you?"
And he writes "No, no, no."
"Did anyone tell you to shoot Kennedy?"
And he writes "No, no, no."
"Did anyone give you money to shoot Kennedy?"
And he writes "No, no, no."
"Was anybody with you when you shot Kennedy?"
And he writes "No, no, no."
And then I say, "Who was with you when you shot Kennedy?"
Sometimes we ask them identical questions, but just in a little different form. . . .
He writes "Girl, the girl, the girl."
"Do you know the girl's name?" and he sort of groaned and I

say, "Write out the name of the girl." And there is no response and he just groans.

When Sirhan was asked to write about Robert Kennedy, his response was very similar to some of the entries found in his notebook:

"Robert F. Kennedy, Robert F. Kennedy, RFK, RFK, RFK, RFK must die, RFK must die, RFK must die, RFK must die, RFK must die, RFK must die, RFK must die, RFK must die, RFK must die."

In response to Diamond's questions, Sirhan told very much the same story he had told when conscious: he didn't intend to shoot Robert Kennedy; he had gone to the Ambassador Hotel by chance; no one had put him up to the job or helped him along the way. But when it came to the subject of his notebooks Sirhan appeared to confirm the very thing Diamond had suspected. The questions and answers went as follows:

"Is this crazy writing?"
"Yes, yes, yes, yes, yes, yes, yes, yes."
"Are you crazy?"
"No, no, no, no."
"Why are you writing crazy?"
"Practice, practice, practice, practice, practice."
"Practice for what?"
"Mind control, mind control, mind control, mind control."
"Who wrote your notebooks?"
"I, I, I, I, I."
"Were you hypnotized when you wrote the notebook?"
"Yes, yes, yes."
"Who hypnotized you when you wrote the notebook?"
"Mirror, mirror, my mirror, my mirror, my mirror, my mirror, my mirror."

The next experiment was to wake Sirhan up and see his reactions. Shown what he had written, Sirhan claimed it to be a foreign document.
"This is not Sirhan," he claimed.
When Diamond pointed out that maybe his notebooks were written the same way he replied, "Are you bugging me?"
"This is what made him feel crazy," Dr. Diamond told the court.
Though the doctor may have proved to his own satisfaction how the notebooks came into being, he still had questions. "It is customary to simplify the hypnotic procedure to give a posthypnotic suggestion as to how

they will be hypnotized the next time," Diamond testified. "Later developments showed that he learned this very well, which made me suspicious, because usually in my experience it is the exception rather than the rule that people pick this up so readily. It requires a certain kind of training period."

During Sirhan's next hypnotic session on February 8, Dr. Diamond ran another test on Sirhan.

"While he was asleep," Diamond told the court, "I told him that when he woke up, in a short while after he woke up, that I will take my handkerchief out of my pocket, which I did, and wipe my forehead, and that when I do that, that would be a signal for him to go over and ask the deputy sheriff what the weather is like outside.

"So then I woke him up and again he had no recollection of having been asleep, but after a few minutes of conversation I took out my handkerchief and he sort of looked around and he walked over and asked the sheriff about the weather.

"He wanted to know if it was raining so I told him, 'Sirhan, who told you to do that?' And he looked around and startled said, 'No one.'

"I said, 'Well, I told you to do that just five minutes ago when you were hypnotized. . . . '

"He said, I forgot his exact words but, 'You are bugging me; I thought up the question about the weather.' "

Sirhan continued to disbelieve Diamond, so the doctor offered to do another demonstration and tape-record the session for Sirhan's enlightenment. Robert Kaiser was in the room watching and gave the authors this description of what happened:

"Diamond put Sirhan under hypnosis and gave him a suggestion: 'Sirhan, when you awake you will feel normal, but when I take out my handkerchief you will climb the bars of your cell.' Ten minutes later Sirhan is climbing the bars like a monkey, and we look over and Diamond is blowing his nose. And he says, 'Sirhan, watcha doin' up there.' 'Oh I'm just getting some exercise.' Anyone in that situation will give a plausible explanation, but it won't be the right one; we all knew he'd been programmed."

This demonstration impressed Kaiser, who already had suspicions that perhaps Sirhan had been hypnotized by a third party and put up to the crime. Kaiser discussed this possibility with Diamond, but Diamond dismissed the whole idea as "a crackpot theory."[1] Diamond believed that Sirhan had performed the murder while in a trance all right; the trance explained so many of the outstanding questions of the case. But Diamond believed that the trance was self-induced, and as he delivered his summation in court, he tried to explain this concept to the jury.

"With absolutely no knowledge or awareness of what was actually happening in his Rosicrucian and occult experiments, [Sirhan] was gradually programming himself, exactly like a computer is programmed by its magnetic tape, programming himself for the coming assassination. In his unconscious mind there existed a plan for the total fulfillment of his sick, paranoid hatred of Kennedy and all who might want to help the Jews. In his conscious mind there was no awareness of such a plan or that he, Sirhan, was to be the instrument of assassination.

"But he was confused, bewildered, and partially intoxicated. The mirrors in the hotel lobby, the flashing lights, the general confusion—this was like pressing the button which starts the computer. He was back in his trances, his violent convulsive rages, the automatic writing, the pouring out of incoherent hatred, violence and assassination. Only this time it was for real and this time there was no pencil in his hand, this time there was only the loaded gun.

"I agree that this is an absurd and preposterous story, unlikely and incredible. I doubt Sirhan himself agrees with me as to how everything happened. Sirhan prefers to deny his mental illness, his psychological disintegration, his trances, his automatic writing and his automatic shooting. . . . Sirhan would rather believe that he is the fanatical martyr who by his noble act of self-sacrifice has saved his people and become a great hero. He claims to be ready to die in the gas chamber for the glory of the Arab people.

"However, I see Sirhan as small and helpless, pitifully ill, with a demented, psychotic rage, out of control of his own consciousness and his own actions, subject to bizarre dissociated trances in some of which he programmed himself to be the instrument of assassination, and then in an almost accidentally induced twilight state he actually executed the crime, knowing next to nothing as to what was happening. . . . I am satisfied that this is how Sirhan Bishara Sirhan came to kill Senator Robert F. Kennedy on June 5, 1968."

Dr. Diamond had taken the witness stand on Friday, March 21. It was the next Wednesday when prosecutor David Fitts began his cross-examination. Fitts wanted to dent Dr. Diamond's conclusion that Sirhan's mental problems began with his traumatic childhood in Jerusalem. To do so he challenged the testimony of Sirhan's mother, Mary.

"Don't you suppose," said the prosecutor to Diamond, "that Mrs. Sirhan, having her son in trouble, has some disposition to magnify the horrors of war and the effect on her son in hopes that they will have some impact on this jury and on your psychiatric opinion?"

"Sir," replied Diamond, "I don't think it is possible to magnify the fact of the horrors of war on children."

"Well, it depends, of course, on what they actually were, isn't that true?"

"I think I am familiar with war," said Dr. Diamond, "what the war conditions were. I went through five years of a world war and I have a family—for example, my daughter and granddaughter live in Israel and my son lives there, and I am fully aware of what conditions are. I don't feel they were exaggerated."

David Fitts, however, was most interested in attacking Sirhan's credibility. "The story that he gave you was obviously a structured one," he asserted to Dr. Diamond. ". . . Sirhan had access to newspapers, talked with his lawyers, talked with investigators, knew what he was accused of doing, knew that he was facing a trial for a capital offense. . . . He had adopted an attitude of what he was going to say and what he was not going to say."

"Well, no, that was the difficulty," replied Diamond, not giving ground. "He was talking in ways which to me seemed very strange. He was admitting information which certainly would not help him, and was concealing information which might help him; so there seems to be no logical rhyme or reason to his stories."

Undaunted, Fitts tried again. "Well isn't it rather usual for let us say just a sociopathic personality, a man who commits a crime and gets himself in jail, to concoct a story that might not please everybody, because he thinks it's the only way to help himself?"

"Sirhan had done just the opposite of that," Diamond protested. "He had concocted a story which couldn't possibly help him."

"In view of what? How couldn't help him?"

"Because Sirhan was quite prepared to admit to me or anybody who would ask him that he killed Senator Kennedy; that he hated Senator Kennedy; and that that he had done this to prevent Senator Kennedy from getting elected to the presidency and sending fifty bombers to Israel. This he would tell to anyone who would listen. This did not impress me as a sociopath who is inclined to help himself by concealing his crime. These are the things that he would talk about. What he wouldn't talk about were all these things which were related to his psychological state, and what I regarded as mental illness."

This was a pattern that Dr. Diamond recognized. In 1956 he had written an article on the subject titled "The Simulation of Sanity."[2] "Though most laypeople worry about whether a legal defendant is faking insanity," he said, summarizing his article, "it is my point that it is infinitely more often common that legal defendants fake sanity than they fake insanity."

This was not a concept that David Fitts was going to accept. He still wanted to show that Sirhan was covering up for a crime that he had planned in advance. "Did you know," he asked the witness, "that at some time after the death of Martin Luther King on a Wednesday, that Sirhan in a political discussion with a trash collector named Alvin Clark had said in substance, "Why are you going to vote for him? I am going to kill that

SOB," or words to that effect? Was that Sirhan in a dissociative state speaking or was that the usual Sirhan speaking?"

"I don't believe he said that, sir," Diamond answered.

"Well the witness testified to it from the stand," said Fitts, as though this would be the final proof.

"I think the witness was incorrect."

"Is that a polite word for saying that the witness was lying?"

"No," said Diamond, although Fitts had accurately characterized his response. "I prefer to believe Sirhan."

"Why do you prefer to believe Sirhan?"

"Because Sirhan's information is consistent with a large number of other things that he told me. This particular witness's story is not consistent. I think it is quite possible that the witness was not correct."

Fitts wasn't done with this point. "All right. You tell us, then, that he wanted to have himself pictured as a political assassin, that is one who had consciously decided to do it. Well, why do you suppose Sirhan would have quarreled with the testimony of Alvin Clark? Wouldn't that be right up his street?"

What Fitts seemed to be willing to overlook was that, up his street or not, perhaps Sirhan was angry at Clark, because he hadn't made any such threat in his presence. The police had been very quick to ascribe desire for attention to anyone who had testimony that they didn't agree with. They may have been less discriminating with Alvin Clark.

On June 5, the afternoon after the murder, the *Los Angeles Herald Examiner* published excerpts from an interview with Alvin Clark. In it the trash collector said that Sirhan was "very prejudiced against white people." Clark also said that Sirhan did not drink, never talked about girls, and "once told me he hated Kennedy." But, oddly, it was not reported that Clark said Sirhan had threatened to kill Kennedy.[3] Since Clark was apparently not shy about talking, the absent murder threat in his first rendition is reason to suspect that it was added afterward.

Even with Clark's tarnished testimony, the prosecution was severely lacking when it came to evidence of Sirhan's mature and meaningful deliberation, something they needed if Sirhan was to be convicted of first-degree murder. As a result the prosecutors focused on Sirhan's lack of memory: Make the jury believe this is the central question; get them to disbelieve Sirhan, and the case is won.

"Did Sirhan have true amnesia at the time he shot Kennedy?" Fitts asked Dr. Diamond.

"Yes, I think this was a true amnesia at the time he shot Kennedy."

"If Sirhan was truly forgetful of the incidents relative to the immediate killing of Senator Kennedy, should he not have inquired of the police why he was in custody and what he had done?"

This was a question that the prosecution asked over and over again. They seemed to be offering it to the jury as the key to understanding Sirhan's trickery. It was the question that Fitts had used to bully Dr. Marcus, but Dr. Diamond had some expertise in this area, and he wasn't about to be pushed around.

"That's not how dissociative states respond to police apprehension," he answered. "I have some familiarity with dissociative states as they are arrested and what happens to them, and they do not do, like in the Hollywood movies, look around with a blank expression on their faces and say, 'Where am I?'

"I have never seen an authentic case of amnesia or dissociation or hysteria or schizophrenia behave that way. That's Hollywood stuff. The typical kind of behavior is a sort of on-guard, cautious attitude of looking around, being very reserved; kind of looking around to see what people's reactions are; to kind of figure it out, being evasive, and sometimes very gradually, over a period of hours and hours and hours, a slow restoration to memory of kind of what is going on. From my study of Sirhan's behavior following his being taken to jail, I think it is very characteristic of this type of slow emergence from a state of dissociation."

Dr. Diamond was unlike the doctors who had testified before him. He had not tried to penetrate the mysteries of Sirhan with inkblots or personality exams. He focused, instead, on the facts of the case. He overcame his initial disbelief of Sirhan's claims of not remembering the shooting or the notebooks, and began to search for explanations. He had hypnotized Sirhan on eight occasions and made some interesting discoveries.

He discovered, first of all, that Sirhan was very easy to hypnotize. He discovered signs that Sirhan had been hypnotized before, perhaps many times. While Sirhan was under hypnosis Dr. Diamond had gotten him to write in a manner that was strangely similar to some of the writing in his notebook, and when he was awakened, Sirhan denied any familiarity with the work that he had just produced.

Diamond had also demonstrated that Sirhan was very susceptible to post-hypnotic suggestion. He had Sirhan do things in his normal awake state that he had been instructed to perform while under hypnosis, with no awareness that he had been programmed. He also noted that Sirhan, after he had been brought out of his trance, would shiver and complain of being cold. At the same time Sirhan would be confused and suspicious, with no memory of what had taken place, and a strong inclination not to believe that he had been asleep at all.

The prosecution maintained Sirhan's story was "concocted." Dr. Diamond's reasoning was the clearest response yet to that charge. It made no sense for Sirhan to be lying about his lack of memory, Diamond asserted, since he had already, very willingly, admitted all that could be damaging to him.

Dr. Diamond also presented a logical explanation for Sirhan's conduct in police custody. According to the doctor, the first thing Sirhan heard as he began to emerge from his trance was the police warning that anything he said would be used against him. From his professional experience Diamond also offered a more realistic view of how a person in such a situation would be likely to act, as opposed to the "Where am I?" stereotype being pushed forward by the prosecution.

All of this led Diamond to conclude that Sirhan had been in a hypnotic trance when he had murdered Robert Kennedy. But how did he get into that trance? Was there some outside direction? Diamond had repeatedly asked Sirhan this very question when he was under hypnosis. The answer was always negative. Diamond apparently attributed little significance to the "blocking" which seemed to occur whenever Sirhan was asked questions of this nature. As Robert Kaiser noted, Diamond did not seem inclined to favor conspiracy in any case.

But what would Dr. Diamond have concluded if he had known that there was a significant body of evidence that more than one gun was fired in the hotel pantry the night of the murder? What would he have thought if it were demonstrated to him that the wounds inflicted on Robert Kennedy appeared to come from a direction, range, and angle inconsistent with Sirhan's position relative to Kennedy? What would he have concluded if he had known that a number of apparently reliable witnesses had seen Sirhan with a mysterious woman before the murder, and that the police had used unsavory tactics to discourage or discredit these witnesses?

Dr. Diamond may well have reconsidered his conclusions had he known about this hidden information. Sirhan's apparent lack of memory and evidence of hypnotic trance are open to more sinister interpretation when laid beside evidence suggesting other participants. But Diamond was not aware of this evidence, due to the overzealous actions of some members of the police, and by the lack of diligence on the part of Sirhan's defense attorneys.

Unlike the attorneys at Sirhan's table, Dr. Diamond was not embarrassed by Sirhan's lack of memory. He sought to explain it, and, in the end, did so quite rationally by concluding that Sirhan had been in a trance. But without all the facts, and lacking the proper support from the defense attorneys, Diamond concluded that Sirhan unknowingly programmed himself to murder Robert Kennedy and unknowingly programmed himself to forget his crime—a feat regarded as next to impossible by leading experts in the field of hypnosis. His entire testimony teetered on this precarious point. Fitts was well aware of this, and although Diamond had probably bested the prosecutor in their major points of dispute, Fitts knew how to tip the wagon over with a carefully chosen last question.

"Doctor, in your summation which you read aloud you said, with reference now to the whole diagnosis I believe of Sirhan, you said, 'I agree that this is an absurd and preposterous story, unlikely and incredible.' You said that didn't you?"

"Yes, I did say it."

"Who were you agreeing with?"

"I agreed with the world."

"I think that's all I have."

The defense attorneys understood that Dr. Diamond's choice of words in his summation was damaging to his own conclusions. That evening, after Fitts had driven the point home again, it was decided that Diamond would prepare a statement in an effort to clarify to the jury what he meant by these words. He would read the statement in response to a question posed by Emile Berman the next day on redirect examination.

Although Dr. Diamond invested considerable time in formulating his answer, Emile Berman apparently did little to construct what should have been a very simple question. The following morning Berman read aloud Diamond's *entire* summation. When he was done he asked, "Now in that context, that is what you really referred to when you were on the witness stand?"

"Well, I am sorry, Mr. Berman," Diamond replied. "I'm not quite clear as to your question."

"What I am talking about is the sentence that says, 'I agree this is an absurd and preposterous story, unlikely and incredible.' That is what I am referring to."

Berman was performing poorly. He still hadn't asked a proper question. Diamond had no choice but to try to make sense out of it for him. He read the statement in which he admitted that the Sirhan case raised serious problems of clinical proof and credibility:

"When I first had personal contact with Sirhan I was prepared for the usual case of a paranoid fanatic who dreams of grand delusions—and that is what has been found to be so—I was not, however, prepared for what I discovered, these stirring instances of correspondence courses, hypnosis, dissociate trances, and mystical occultism . . . and that type of psychological thinking could have resulted in the death of Senator Kennedy that affected the destinies of the entire world."

Following Diamond's statement Berman fumbled about. He began to read a very long passage from the court transcript that appeared to have no bearing on what was being talked about and no point of its own. When he finished he said, "I don't know whether I have discussed this with you," and he began once again to read Dr. Diamond's entire summation. Once again the jury heard the words "I agree that this is an absurd and preposterous story." They then heard all the rest which had been read to them by Berman only a short time ago. Finally in frustration Fitts broke in. "If the Court please—"

"I am coming to my question," said Berman before Judge Walker could intervene. "What I want to know is when you started that to the extent I have read it, 'I would agree that this is an absurd and preposterous story, unlikely and incredible,' what were you referring to?"

Diamond was stunned. Clearly Berman had gotten lost in his notes and forgotten, just like Cooper had done with Dr. Marcus, that he had just asked that very question. Confusion prevailed.

"Objection," said Mr. Howard. "That has been asked and answered."

"What?" said Berman.

"It was asked and answered by the prosecution," said Judge Walker.

"I thought he started out this morning with a question from the same page," Howard corrected, "and an answer read that was prepared last night."

"I didn't know that the objection 'asked and answered' was a proper objection on cross-examination," offered Cooper.

"I don't think this is cross," said Howard.

"I mean redirect. Pardon me."

"Overruled!" said Walker.

Berman then asked Dr. Diamond a third time to explain why he characterized his explanation of the crime as "absurd and preposterous."

"Its unlikely nature, Mr. Berman," Diamond replied coolly, clearly not pleased by this latest gaffe by the defense attorney. "To me this is a script which would never be acceptable in a class B motion picture; and yet these are, I think, the realities of the psychiatric findings."

"If Your Honor please," said Berman. "We have concluded our redirect."

Bernard Diamond climbed down from the stand. He had been brought back to make a final impression on the jury, but whatever enlightenment the doctor was to impart was certainly overshadowed by Emile Berman's inept performance. This was not a good ending, particularly for someone who had been the defendant's most important witness.

THIRTEEN

Witness for the Prosecution

✴ ✴ ✴

From the beginning there was nothing old-fashioned about Sirhan Bishara Sirhan. As his lawyers painted him and as his own erratic courtroom behavior suggested, he was the quintessential contemporary assassin—a loner in the tradition of Lee Harvey Oswald and Richard Speck, a paranoid as loser playing out his psychic fantasies with real bullets.

—Martin Kasindorf in *Newsweek*

O N FRIDAY, MARCH 28, the prosecution began its rebuttal.

"With the Court's permission," announced John Howard, "the first order of business would center around bringing into this court, and asking permission to show, an approximately twelve-minute film taken at the speech of Senator Kennedy immediately preceding the assassination." Howard told the court that the purpose for showing the film would be to illustrate that nothing in Robert Kennedy's victory address could have triggered Sirhan's supposed dissociate state.

Grant Cooper frowned. Realizing that the film would only rekindle in the minds of the jurors the horror of the murder, he objected. The defense, he said, had not asserted that Sirhan had even heard Robert Kennedy's speech. Judge Walker quickly ruled in Cooper's favor, holding that the film's probative value was well exceeded by its "inflammatory" possibilities.

After Walker's denial, the prosecution called several witnesses. Adolph B. Melendres and Frank J. Patchett were both sergeants in the LAPD; George W. Murphy was an investigator for the district attorney's office. All three had spent time with Sirhan the morning after the murder, and they gave support to the prosecution's contention that Sirhan was in possession of all his faculties by variously describing their prisoner as intelligent, calm, coherent, lucid, and completely sober.

Later in the morning, Judge Walker interrupted the proceedings: "Ladies and gentlemen of the jury, I have the sad news to tell you—I have the sad news to tell you that President Eisenhower has died. . . . I am going to ask everybody to observe at this moment one minute of silence."

Dwight Eisenhower, in his retirement, had become a personification of the 1950s. He had led the nation in a world of new and fearsome perils—ICBMs, Quemoy and Matsu, the hydrogen bomb—but Eisenhower's America, with some exceptions, was confident and unified. In the decade since the general left office, however, deep divisions had developed along lines of generation and race. Images of this fracturing were present in the news every day, and they would soon appear at the Sirhan trial in the text of the final arguments.

The war in Vietnam was paramount, and the previous month had not been a good one. On March 7, it was reported that 453 Americans had lost their lives in the first week of a new push by the enemy. This exceeded American losses in the first week of the Tet offensive a year earlier.

Several weeks later tens of thousands of antiwar protestors marched up New York's Sixth Avenue chanting, "Stop the war in Vietnam" and "Bring the troops home." Many of the protestors wore arm bands that read "33,000," signifying the number of Americans already killed in the war. The actual figure that week was 33,641, which, for the first time, exceeded the American war dead in Korea.

Coalescing around war and race issues, disobedience was spreading across the nation, the host venues often being universities. In Boston four hundred police had to be called in to expel three hundred student protestors occupying administration buildings at Harvard. At Columbia, radical students seized university buildings, causing trapped professors to flee out windows. At Cornell, one hundred members of the university's Afro-American society took control of the student union building, where fighting broke out between the blacks and members of a prominent university fraternity.

In New Orleans a conflict of another sort was being fought. As Jim Garrison's prosecution of Clay Shaw for the murder of President Kennedy neared conclusion, attorney Dean Andrews was called to the stand. Andrews had originally claimed that a Clay Bertrand, a purported Shaw alias, had called after the assassination and asked him to defend Lee Harvey Oswald. Now on the witness stand, he maintained that no such thing had ever happened. Andrews claimed that he had made up the story while he was under sedation and the influence of drugs in a New Orleans hospital.

"So you deliberately lied to the Warren Commission?" challenged Assistant District Attorney James Alcock.

"I didn't deliberately lie," the short and overweight Andrews replied to the mirth of some onlookers. "My mouth got ahead of my brain. You can call it a lie if you want to, I call it huffin' and puffin'."[1]

In the end, the jury believed DA Jim Garrison was the one "huffin' and puffin'.'' In less than an hour they acquitted Clay Shaw. This, however, was not an end to the ugliness.

Garrison responded quickly to the verdict by filing perjury charges against Shaw and Andrews, claims which were ultimately dismissed as being "frivolous" and "vindictive." The district attorney also publicly charged that the case had been sabotaged, and that a member of the prosecution had been secretly slipping information to the opposition. In response to these new charges, the American Bar Association hinted that they might want to investigate Garrison's "motives."

One week after Clay Shaw's acquittal, another tangled case was brought to an adjudicated resolution. In Memphis, Tennessee, James Earl Ray pleaded guilty to the murder of Dr. Martin Luther King.

During the proceedings, both the prosecutor, P. M. Canale, and Ray's flamboyant lawyer, Percy Foreman, told the court that they possessed no evidence of conspiracy. "There have been rumors going around that Mr. James Earl Ray was a dupe, a fall guy, or a member of a conspiracy," said Mr. Canale. "We have no proof other than Dr. Martin Luther King was killed by James Earl Ray and James Earl Ray alone."[2]

In a stunning repudiation of this assertion, however, the confessed assassin stood up in court and declared that his plea of guilty did not mean that there was no conspiracy. Judge W. Preston Battle then asked Ray if he still wanted to plead guilty. Ray said yes. The proceedings ended with the judge sentencing Ray, as had been arranged, to ninety-nine-years in prison.

In an interview after Ray's sentencing Judge Battle admitted that he had been "puzzled" about many aspects of the case, but he defended his decision to accept Ray's plea. "I was convinced then and I am convinced now," he said, "that the trial would have muddied our understanding of the substantial evidence which established Ray as the killer."[3]

A week later the case took another strange turn. James Earl Ray wrote to Judge Battle from his prison cell in Nashville asking to have his plea bargain overturned. Ray had retained a new lawyer, J. B. Stoner, who quickly issued a statement saying that his client was innocent and was "pressured into a guilty plea."[4]

Battle would not have time to act on Ray's request. On Monday, March 31, he was found at his desk in Shelby County Criminal Court, dead of an apparent heart attack. The case was not reopened.

Those close to Dr. King also made statements pointing to conspiracy. Ralph Abernathy, King's successor at the Southern Christian Leadership Conference, asked for continued pressure upon the government "until justice is meted out to all of the perpetrators." The victim's widow, Coretta Scott King, agreed. "This plea of guilty," she said, "cannot be allowed to close the case or to end the search for the many fingers which helped pull the trigger."[5]

For several weeks unsettling stories from the other assassination trials were prominent in the news. Very often they were reported side by side with events from the Sirhan trial. Comparisons were inevitable. "The dissection of the tormented mind and soul of Sirhan Sirhan in Los Angeles," offered *Newsweek,* "stood in stark contrast to Ray's skittering moment on stage in Memphis."[6] As "Not another Dallas" had become a watchword during the police investigation of Robert Kennedy's murder, "Not another Memphis" or "Not another New Orleans" must have been in the minds of those conducting the trial for Senator Kennedy's accused killer.

The day Judge Battle died in his Memphis office, Dr. Seymour Pollack took the stand as the prosecution's principal rebuttal witness against Sirhan. Dr. Pollack had been brought into the case by the district attorney's office a few weeks after Robert Kennedy's murder, when it became apparent that Sirhan's defense options were mainly psychiatric. Pollack seemed an excellent choice. A forensic psychiatrist who headed the division of psychiatry and law at the University of Southern California, he was also a consultant for a number of state and county courts.

Recall that as part of Grant Cooper's strategy to gain a plea bargain, Pollack had been given unprecedented access to the defendant, and had interviewed Sirhan on eight occasions the last two weeks of January. Pollack had also attended the February 2 meeting in Grant Cooper's office. During that session Pollack maintained that he hadn't come to any conclusions on Sirhan's condition, but several days later he wrote a memo to District Attorney Younger filled with conclusions. In the letter to Younger, Pollack seemed to play both sides of the fence, but in the end he favored the idea that Sirhan was mentally ill and that this illness played a role in the assassination.

When the plea bargain failed, the district attorney's office was not altogether sure how much benefit Pollack would be as a prosecution witness. Would he be called to testify? On March 21, in open court, Grant Cooper asked John Howard what his intentions were.

"Are you going to call Dr. Pollack?"

"Yes," answered Howard.

"You are going to call him definitely?"

"Yes."

"The only reason I ask the question is that if you are not going to call him, we would call him. . . ."

Dr. Seymour Pollack, however, took the stand as a witness for the prosecution on March 28. A short man with a round, florid face, Pollack began, as he had done in the past, by seeming to argue both sides of the case.

"I consider Sirhan mentally disturbed," he told the court under Mr. Howard's direction, "but in summation I believe the assassination of Senator Robert Kennedy was triggered by political reasons."

A month earlier Emile Berman had entertained his colleagues with a parody of Pollack's two-faced diagnosis. "He can think pretty good about killing," chirped Berman, pretending to be Pollack, "but generally speaking he's a nut!"[7]

Now, on the witness stand, Pollack appeared to earn this derision once again. Much of what he said sounded contradictory. For example, Pollack said that Sirhan "has clinical signs and symptoms of psychosis. He has, for example, many delusions," but "there was nothing whatever that . . . indicated at any time that Sirhan was clinically psychotic," and "it's my belief that Sirhan's ideas, attitudes . . . were not evidence of psychotic delusional thinking."

According to Pollack, Sirhan committed murder for political reasons. "I believe that Sirhan focused on Senator Robert Kennedy as an individual who should die," he said in court, "not only because of the Kennedy promise to give Israel the jet bombers that would cause the death to thousands of Arabs, in Sirhan's opinion, but also because Sirhan wanted the world to see, he wanted the world to see how strongly our United States policy was in the pro-Israel-anti-Arab movement in the face of, in spite of our government's professed interest for the underdog, and world justice."

As reviewed in a previous chapter, during his eight sessions with Sirhan, Dr. Pollack engaged in a great deal of gratuitous coaching of the defendant regarding his motive. ("Apparently what was eating at you was these elections and how strongly you felt about the American political figures letting the Arab world down"; or "You really want the world to see the Arab suffering . . . to see that American policy has helped [cause] that suffering"; or "The trial is a trial in which you are sort of accusing America of . . . burying a million Arabs.") Dr. Pollack's courtroom explanation of Sirhan's motives resembled, strangely, not so much what Sirhan had said to Dr. Pollack, but what Dr. Pollack had said to Sirhan.

Although the initial phase of Pollack's testimony about Sirhan's diagnosis was, as expected, ambiguous, what followed was a surprising set of assertions about factual matters that were very unfavorable to the defendant.

Under Howard's questioning Pollack asserted that Sirhan had "little or no remorse" about killing Kennedy. He said he didn't believe Sirhan expected to be caught. He interpreted the struggle after the shooting as an attempt by Sirhan "to escape." He said that Sirhan had demonstrated reasonable foresight and planning before the murder, and that there was no evidence that Sirhan was in an "altered state" during the shooting. Pollack stated that the tapes of Sirhan in police custody demonstrated that Sirhan knew "what was going on." He asserted that he believed Sirhan was lying when he said he could not remember writing the notebooks and was lying when he said he could not remember the crime itself.

Pollack's assertions went well beyond the issue of whether Sirhan was mentally ill. They were inferences the doctor had made about matters of fact. Many of them not only contradicted the evidence of the case, they contradicted what Dr. Pollack knew or should have known from his own inquiry.

Concerning remorse, Sirhan had on numerous occasions expressed his distress over his alleged actions, to Dr. Pollack as well as to others. His taped confession to Pollack that the murder went against his conscience, that it violated the teachings of his childhood, family, and church, was a stunning personal moment.

"Where would you be if you didn't have life?" Sirhan inquired rhetorically. "And here I go and splatter this guy's brains. It's just not me."

Shortly thereafter Pollack mentioned to Sirhan that a number of other people were wounded during the shooting. "What did they do to me," Sirhan asked, "that they had to be hurt?"

Apparently, to Dr. Pollack, none of this counted as evidence of remorse.

Dr. Pollack also testified that he believed that Sirhan didn't expect to be caught. The doctor offered little to back up this idea, but if it were true, why would it be so? Perhaps Sirhan, contrary to Pollack's assertion of reasonable foresight and planning, was so deluded that he thought he could murder Kennedy in a crowded hotel and walk away, or perhaps he didn't expect to be murdering anyone. In any case, Dr. Pollack's assertion that Sirhan was "trying to escape" is unwarranted by the facts. Sirhan stepped forward and began firing. There was a struggle for his gun. There is no record of an attempt to escape.

Most damaging was Dr. Pollack's contention that Sirhan was faking his memory loss regarding the writing in his notebooks and the murder. "Sirhan's denial of recall of his written notes . . . ," said Pollack, "I interpret as an attempt to avoid some serious condition that would be attributed to his writings, that would be interpreted as evidence of planning, premeditation of killing Kennedy." Pollack saw the writings in Sirhan's notebooks as "attempts to strengthen his intention, to strengthen his courage, to strengthen his capability . . . ," the bizarre repetitions being, presumably, no more than additional evidence of Sirhan's reasonable foresight and planning.

At Pollack's suggestion that he was lying about his notebooks, Sirhan stood up.

"Your Honor, sir—"

"You sit down or I will do what I told you I was going to do," ordered Judge Walker, referring to his threat to have Sirhan put in leg irons and a leather mask. Walker called a recess and Sirhan was escorted toward the holding pen where Russell Parsons would try to calm him. Dave Smith of the *Los Angeles Times* was near the courtroom door as the group approached. "I don't like him calling me a fuckin' liar," he heard Sirhan say. Then Sirhan turned suddenly to face Pollack: "That son of a bitch."[8]

In the holding pen Russell Parsons rubbed water on Sirhan's forehead and neck. "That's the way you have to treat these agitated people," he told reporters.[9]

When court resumed a short time later Pollack continued his deconstruction of the defendant. This time there was no reaction from Sirhan, who was calm to the point of being oblivious, alternately trying on a pair of sunglasses and staring at the ceiling.

For the benefit of the jury Dr. Pollack labeled Sirhan's lack of memory as "conscious denial, . . . a particular method to avoid full legal repercussions." He said he found no evidence of any trance. "Had he been in an altered state of consciousness," the doctor testified, "he would have been perplexed when he awakened, . . . [and] he would have raised questions about where he was, what he was there for." This view mirrored the movie stereotype that Dr. Diamond had warned against and ignored Diamond's point that upon coming out of his trance Sirhan's first admonition from the police was to remain silent.

When Grant Cooper began his cross-examination of Seymour Pollack, he sought to exploit what seemed to be the weakest part of the doctor's testimony—his diagnosis.

"Now isn't it true," Cooper asked the witness, "that in your confidential report to Evelle Younger, the district attorney, on February 5, you diagnosed Sirhan Sirhan as suffering from a borderline schizophrenia, with paranoid and hysterical features? . . . Then you went further and said that you do believe he was clinically psychotic, isn't that right?"

"That is correct."

"Did you also believe he had been growing more disturbed for the last few years?"

"Yes."

"Now, was Sirhan Sirhan a psychotically disturbed individual?"

"I think that Sirhan Sirhan was a borderline psychotically disturbed individual."

"Borderline?"

"Borderline."

Cooper then read several paragraphs from Pollack's memorandum to Younger in which he described Sirhan as psychotic.

"Now was Sirhan a psychotic person?"

"Yes."

"This morning you told us he was not a pyschotic person, didn't you?"

"I said he was not clinically psychotic."

Pollack was caught in a web of his own words, and the more he struggled, the more tangled he became. His confident manner gave way to a frightened look. He nervously sipped water and tried to answer Grant Cooper.

"I said that Sirhan clinically had a paranoid personality; that he had, he was underneath, a psychotic personality."

"Underneath?"

"Underneath."

Cooper then began to cautiously chip away at Pollack's assertions about Sirhan. He asked Pollack if Sirhan's reputed hope of "a couple of years for killing a senator" represented mature and meaningful thinking.

"Not as mature or as meaningful as it should have been; as it could have been; yes I would agree very definitely it is immature thinking to a considerable degree."

But Pollack would go on to maintain that Sirhan did maturely deliberate.

"I said that mature deliberation in the sense that in contemplating the act of killing Senator Kennedy that Sirhan weighed in his mind, he considered it, he examined it, he evaluated it, the reasons for and against it, he considered it, he pondered it, he weighed the facts and arguments. . . . I am saying that Sirhan's decision was not hasty or rash, that the probable consequences of the degree and act were considered by him."

Recall that when Dr. Pollack was trying to convince Sirhan of his political motive during a jail-cell interview, he accounted for the defendant's irrational and apparently nonpolitical actions by saying, "I don't really think you thought the whole thing out." Now up on the witness stand Dr. Pollack was saying just the opposite. Sirhan not only thought the whole thing out, he carefully weighed the pros and cons as he planned the murder.

Grant Cooper should have never let Pollack get away with such a statement. This was the very crux of the case as Cooper had framed it. The defense attorney should have challenged the doctor to produce the evidence upon which he based his conclusion that Sirhan weighed, considered, examined, evaluated, and pondered the reasons for and against killing Robert Kennedy. What evidence did the doctor possess that such a rational process had taken place? But Cooper, seeming to follow a preset script, let the moment pass as he had so many others.

He asked Pollack if Sirhan's odd behavior during the police interrogation wasn't "out of keeping with the fact that he understood that he had shot a presidential candidate?"

"No, no. It was not out of keeping with that. He understood fully, I believe, and completely what he had done. . . . He was fully aware of where he was, what was going on and the circumstances. Even in our interview subsequently he made me fully aware—he made me to understand that he was aware of what was going on there."

"What did he say?"

"What did he say? He recalled his conversations with these people."

Pollack's assertion that Sirhan had revealed to him that he "was aware of what was going on" seemed to imply that Sirhan had revealed that he did indeed remember the shooting, yet Pollack's conclusion is merely his own inference. Sirhan had never claimed that he didn't remember the police interrogation—only that he couldn't remember the shooting. Cooper, however, once again failed to follow up and make this point clear to the jury. Instead he asked Pollack whether Sirhan's strange laughing was in keeping with the knowledge of having committed a great crime. This simply led to yet another of Pollack's unsupported assertions.

"His laughing? He was laughing in a very sardonic way about what he had done and how it was possible for him to have carried off this coup and to have killed a very important man." Again, nowhere in the police interrogation tapes does it appear that Sirhan is laughing about having killed a very important man.

Cooper wrestled Pollack for two full days. There were moments when it appeared the defense attorney was getting the best of the psychiatrist. He aptly demonstrated that Pollack was perfectly willing to play with words to the point of medical meaninglessness. But Cooper was never able to get the pin. He could not string together his winning points in a way the jury might comprehend. The majority of Pollack's unsupported assertions went unchallenged as the defense attorney attacked, instead, the doctor's diagnosis.

Pollack's gift to the prosecution was his commonsense view of Sirhan as a deceitful, clever, and scheming political assassin, who faked a memory loss as the foundation for his legal defense. The beauty of this model for a juror was its simplicity: "he's faking it, 'cause he wants to get off."

Looked at more closely, this vision of Sirhan makes little sense. If Sirhan were knowledgeable and clever enough to understand the legal ramifications of the "diminished capacity" defense in California and was already creating a false record starting with his police interrogation, why wouldn't he have done a better job? Why wouldn't he have faked waking up, or tried to fake insanity, a defense with the possibility of acquittal, rather than "diminished capacity," which would still most certainly mean life imprisonment? Every doctor who examined Sirhan agreed that he tried very hard to convince them that he was not crazy or mentally impaired. In the end Dr. Pollack seems to have succumbed to his frustration and prejudice in the case, and the defense attorneys simply did not have the energy or the vision to expose that prejudice.

Following Dr. Pollack, the prosecution continued its rebuttal by calling to the stand Dr. Leonard B. Olinger. Olinger was a private-practice psychologist who taught abnormal clinical psychology at USC.

In his classes at USC, Dr. Olinger instructed his students on "the ten precautions" that every clinician should observe in administering and evaluating psychological tests. Olinger brought these commandments to court in the form of an oversized chart, which was set up for the jury to see. Under John Howard's direction the doctor described the precautions—most were designed to inhibit the prejudice or preconceived notions of the tester from influencing the test results. Howard asked Olinger if he thought Dr. Schorr and Dr. Richardson had followed these precautions with Sirhan.

"Well, it seems to me," answered Olinger, "there's a great deal read into the data which really is not present in the data."

Attorney and witness then went step by step over all the tests administered by Drs. Schorr and Richardson. Olinger made a good case that the doctors found Sirhan to be sick because that is what they were looking to find. He offered numerous examples of test answers which the defense doctors scored as abnormal, but which, according to Olinger, were really just "commonsense responses."

As Dr. Olinger continued to ridicule the doctors who had testified for the defense, Sirhan smiled. He leaned over and told Russell Parsons he liked these guys the prosecution was bringing in. Sirhan liked having it said that his test responses were common sense. He liked it when the prosecution doctors said he was not sick, even though the testimony of these men might cost him his life.

Olinger's critique of Richardson and Schorr lasted almost the entire day. Douglas Robinson of the *New York Times* described the jury in the afternoon as "dazed as bees in smoke." "By now," Robinson reported, "no one on the jury should be unfamiliar with each and every ink blot in the Rorschach test or the enigmatic pictures in the Thematic Apperception Test."[10] Dave Smith of the *Los Angeles Times* made a similar observation:

> For more than a month, they have listened to such psychiatric verbal shorthand as C-prime response, small animal movement, inanimate movement, large human response, pure form response, large M and small fm, large F and little c and TH column. It is debatable how efficiently the jurors have been able to translate such arbitrary terms into their meaningful emotional equivalents. But the mere effort has extracted a toll that was apparent Monday as they listened to still more of the same with faces that ranged a gamut of expression from boredom to stupefaction.[11]

When it was time to cross-examine, Grant Cooper went right to work.

"Dr. Olinger, when were you engaged to make this evaluation?"

"I believe it was about a month or so ago."

"Who contacted you, Mr. Compton or Mr. Howard? Do you know who suggested your name to them?"

"I suggested my name to them."

"What?"

"I suggested my name to them."

"You suggested your name to them?"

"Yes."

Cooper then had Olinger review his charted precautions. He had the doctor repeat his belief that Drs. Schorr and Richardson had not been objective, that they had entered the case with preconceived notions. Then he brought the point full circle.

"Doctor, yesterday you were telling us what you taught your students in psychology, and see if I have this correct; maybe I don't use your exact words; but a psychologist should be objective in his approach?"

"Yes, sir."

"And he shouldn't have preconceived ideas or notions about the test materials or protocol . . . he should not consciously or unconsciously be swayed by knowledge of the patient or, in this case, knowledge that the subject was Sirhan?"

"That's correct."

"Now you have told us, Doctor, that you volunteered your services as consultant to the district attorney's office in this case?"

"Yes, sir."

"And I think, am I correct, that you heard some of Dr. Schorr's testimony and you didn't like what you heard, so you called the district attorney and told him you didn't like it?"

"That's not quite, exactly correct, sir."

"Well, you tell me."

"Some of the testimony that was reported to be given sounded as if it were unwarranted by the material that was being presented in support of it."

"All right. Had you ever seen any of the material?"

"No, sir, I had not."

"What had you read about the testimony of Dr. Schorr? Do you remember what? Was it a newspaper you read it in?"

"I don't believe I can recall where I read it."

"Did you hear it on the radio?"

"Probably."

"On television?"

"Probably."

"That was only a small part of his testimony, wasn't it?"

"Yes, sir."

"And from that small part that you read in the newspapers you felt that his testimony was—would you say unreliable?"

"Yes, sir."

"So feeling that it was unreliable you called the district attorney's office and volunteered your services?"

"Not quite."

"Well, you volunteered to help them?"

"Sort of."

"Is that right?"

"Sort of."

"Well, you volunteered to give them some advice?"

"Information."

"Information. All right. But you don't remember what you read. Do you remember what you read?"

"Not precisely."

"Do you remember the substance of what you read?"

"Only in a general way."

"Well, you had some preconceived ideas and notions, didn't you, before you called the district attorney?"

"Yes."

"Now isn't it a fact, Doctor, that you violated your ten commandments that you gave to your pupils?"

Grant Cooper was in rare form. He forced Dr. Olinger into a series of equivocations. He then made Olinger admit that his description of Sirhan as a "pseudoneurotic schizophrenic" was a diagnosis that was not in any of the psychological manuals. But, as well as Cooper was performing, the chief defense attorney was, unwittingly, doing the prosecution's chores.

As Cooper dismantled Olinger, the message to the jury was simple: here is yet another practitioner of mind medicine, and he is just as wordy and vain as the others. The prosecution could have introduced a dozen Olingers; Cooper could have butchered them all, and it still would have been to the prosecution's advantage.

In arguing "diminished capacity" Sirhan's lawyers forgot the basic elements of the defense. In a sense, they had set the clock back a hundred years and were operating in the old framework of the M'Naghten insanity rule: Was Sirhan crazy or was he not? Did he understand right from wrong? This was not the issue. The issue, under the defense of diminished capacity, was whether or not Sirhan was capable of mature and meaningful reflection upon the gravity of his alleged act.

The evidence on this point was clearly in Sirhan's favor. There were only fuzzy bits and pieces to suggest that Sirhan had thought about the murder beforehand, and no evidence at all that he had gone through any process of reflection. The principal evidence of Sirhan's prior intent appeared in his notebooks; but this, if anything, was evidence that he was not in a normal state of mind.

The primary strategy of Grant Cooper was to place the case in the hands of doctors who looked at Sirhan through the lens of psychological tests. On its face, this was a good plan. The professional qualifications of the doctors were impressive, and their opinions, even those brought in by the prosecution, were united on the fact that Sirhan was mentally ill. But when the psychological tests underlying the medical conclusions were successfully challenged, the doctors appeared foolish and fallible, and the case supporting Sirhan began to crumble.

Since there was little doubt in the public mind as to Sirhan's guilt, the most common characterization of the proceedings at this point was that psychiatry itself was on trial. "In the trial of Sirhan Sirhan there are two defendants," declared *Newsweek*. "The first, of course, is the 25-year-old Jordanian immigrant accused of murdering Sen. Robert Kennedy. The second is the clinical psychologist and his ability to diagnose diseases of the mind."[12]

The *National Review* took a similar but more critical position: "What was on trial in Los Angeles was not the defendant but the testimony of psychiatrists and psychologists, who would have us believe that every criminal is so sick as to deserve society's pity and succor rather than its punishment."[13]

But the most stunning indictment of the medical testimony would come after the trial from an unexpected source—a California prison psychologist. At the time he had encountered Sirhan on death row in San Quentin, Dr. Eduard Simson had been a practicing clinical psychologist for thirteen years. Simson had earned a B.A. at Stanford and an M.A. at New York University. He then received a postgraduate psychology degree from the University of Louisville and a Ph.D. (magna cum laude) from Heidelberg University. Simson had been a fellow of the British Royal Society of Health, the American Society for Clinical Hypnosis, and the International Council of Psychologists.

During the summer of 1969 Simson examined the incarcerated Sirhan on twenty occasions as part of his duties as senior psychologist at San Quentin, a position he had held for six years. He became suspicious when his diagnosis differed greatly from those of the trial doctors. "Nowhere in Sirhan's test responses," Simson claimed, "was I able to find evidence that he is a 'paranoid schizophrenic' or 'psychotic' as testified by the doctors at the trial. . . . [I] did not see any evidence of 'mental illness' in Sirhan in my extensive psychological testing, nor in his spontaneous behavior during the numerous hours we spent together."

Simson observed that Sirhan was highly intelligent, well oriented, and "an unusually good hypnotic subject." This was significant because, according to Simson, "psychotics . . . are among the poorest subjects for hypnosis" and "paranoid schizophrenics are almost impossible to hypnotize."

Simson came to believe that there was a mysterious truth to this case "which probably still lies very much concealed and unknown to the general public." To discover this truth, Simson believed, one would have to "unlock" Sirhan's mind. Dr. Simson thought he was on his way to accomplishing this task, but his visits with Sirhan were abruptly terminated in the autumn of 1969 by prison authorities, who did not approve of the psychologist's protracted interest in the convicted assassin. Four years later Simson felt compelled to sign a twenty-three-page affidavit explaining the conclusions he had reached during his sessions with Sirhan.

In the affidavit Simson said that the medical testimony at Sirhan's trial was shameful, "discrediting and embarrassing psychology and psychiatry as a profession."

"I am appalled at the conduct of the mental health professionals involved in this case," the doctor wrote, ". . . Assuming that Sirhan killed Robert F. Kennedy, an assumption the validity of which apparently no one seriously questioned, the mental health specialists saw their role primarily in proving what to them was a known fact, rather than discovering the truth." Simson claimed that the doctors merely worked backward from the assumed fact of political assassination to the "Freudian fantasies" of mental illness.

Simson was not afraid to say that many important questions about the case remained unanswered. He made note of the fact that the handwriting in Sirhan's notebooks differed, "often drastically," with the handwriting he observed in San Quentin. "Whether someone else wrote the notebooks or whether they were written under some special influence, such as hypnosis, is entirely unsolved. If someone hypnotized him when the notebooks were written, who was it? . . . Was [Sirhan] merely a double, a stand-in, sent there to draw attention? Was he at the scene to replace someone else? Did he actually kill Robert Kennedy? Whatever the full truth . . . might be, it still remains locked in Sirhan's mind and in other, still anonymous minds."

The last sentence in Simson's affidavit was blunt. "Sirhan's trial was, and will be remembered as," he boldly predicted, "the psychiatric blunder of the century."

FOURTEEN

The Verdict

✳ ✳ ✳

In the downtown coffee shops, in the drug stores along Sunset Strip
where girls in tight sweaters used to wait for screen tests, people said
this was the trial that Lee Harvey Oswald never had.

—Lacey Fosburgh in the *New York Times*

D R. LEONARD OLINGER was the last rebuttal witness to testify for the prosecution. After he stepped down, Judge Walker and the attorneys retired to discuss the instructions the judge would give to the jury after the prosecution and the defense had made their final arguments. Walker asked how long the summations would run.

"Mr. Fitts says 'two,' and I don't believe him," said John Howard, making mischief. "I hold with four hours."

"I tell you this," responded Walker, "I have no faith in estimates of attorneys on how long they are going to argue, because I did it myself and I got up there and fell in love with my own voice and I kept talking."

John Howard was right. David Fitts would speak the next day for more than four hours. He opened by describing how Sirhan approached Kennedy, drew his pistol, and fired eight shots.

> "In this case the People suggest to you that this cold and calculated decision to take the life of Robert F. Kennedy had been arrived at substantially in advance of the defendant's appearance at the Ambassador Hotel, and that the actual act of assassination was simply the culmination of a series of preparatory events, mental processes on the part of this defendant, which had been at work over a substantial period of time."

According to the prosecutor, a string of "uncontroverted facts" illustrated the defendant's nefarious intentions. Sirhan's "clandestine" purchase of his pistol from a friend was a "surreptitious transaction." In attending the June 2 Kennedy reception Sirhan was "casing the joint." Sirhan's "rapid fire" at the gun range was rehearsal for his deed. "The only people I know who are trained to engage in rapid fire," said Fitts, "are soldiers and policemen."

Fitts also drew meaning from the fact that Sirhan left his wallet and identification in his car.

> "I understand that burglars are in the habit of leaving their identification someplace else. Some of those who are caught unwittingly have had a wallet or something drop out of their pocket in places where they are not supposed to be. It's the sort of precaution which a reasonable assassin might take."

Fitts's argument here probably scored points with the jury, but the logic behind it was tortured. Keeping a wallet away from a crime scene might be rational behavior for a clandestine burglar; it hardly makes sense for one about to commit a murder for which apprehension is near certain.

At the suggestion that he had purposely hidden his wallet, Sirhan became agitated. "He's lying, he's lying, he's lying," he said to Russell Parsons, who was sitting next to him. Sirhan had not shouted these words, but Judge Walker was not going to risk another outburst. Walker called a recess and two security men escorted Sirhan from the court to a holding pen, where Russell Parsons tried to calm him down.

When court resumed, with Sirhan again present, David Fitts tried to make a connection between the Kennedy murder and the current unrest in the nation.

> "Mr. Sirhan, twenty-five years old, isn't the only young protestor in this country. A protest of the youth of this nation seems to be something that has been on the rise. I don't know, maybe it is just me and my time and my generation, but I view it with alarm. Maybe it was always that bad and I didn't know it, but things have happened in the last few years—they are alarming to me and I don't know what is going to happen if these people don't in time change some of their views which they have when they begin to take our places and run the affairs of this country. Just what kind of nation are we going to have? Well, obviously, Mr. Sirhan shares some of these views. They are not delusions."

Although the jury had been instructed to avoid news of the trial, they had not been sealed off from all outside information. They were well aware that there had been riots on several California university campuses. Much of this turmoil centered on the war in Vietnam, race issues, or what was called "the free speech movement." Dirty words spoken into public address systems, college students wearing cartridge belts—this was a rich emotional vein, and the prosecution was intent on tapping it.

The most recurrent theme for the prosecution was Sirhan's alleged play-acting. "Sirhan lied to us all," asserted Fitts, "and lied with a very logical reason and that is to avoid the full consequences of his act." Fitts described Sirhan's recollections as "pure rubbish" or "pure Sirhan," cleverly making the defendant's very name synonymous with prevarication.

> "His testimony, of course, is replete with what I would consider as lies, some of which are demonstrable, and some of which are not. But you will have observed that anything in this case, whether it be proven to your satisfaction or not, which would appear to indicate that this was a deliberate premeditated murder is denied by the defendant, regardless of what it is or who said it."

Fitts's assertion here simply isn't true. Sirhan readily admitted to things which didn't help his case. He admitted that he shot Robert Kennedy. He said he did so for political reasons. He admitted that the notebooks and writing were his, though he claimed to have no memory of making the entries. And even though the foundation of his defense was mental illness, Sirhan continually vexed his doctors and lawyers by vehemently maintaining that he was not mentally ill. But the prosecution would continue to insist that Sirhan lied at every opportunity, and was doing so for reasons of self-interest. In the continuing effort to discredit Sirhan, Fitts, incredibly, even attacked the defendant's professed motive.

"It is a rather common occurrence," he told the jury, "the more heinous the crime, the more likely it is that . . . one will fall back upon the defense that he did it for his country, which is, after all, all that is left. This is the entire Sirhan position."

Fitts, here, appears to be trying to tar Sirhan with Samuel Johnson's observation that "Patriotism is the last refuge of a scoundrel." He offers Sirhan's political explanation, which the prosecution was all too happy to accept on other occasions, as evidence of the defendant's perfidy—professed love of country masking an even uglier truth. But what could that truth be? If Sirhan didn't do it for his country, then why did he do it? For personal gain? Because he was crazy? Because he was put up to it? Certainly the prosecution was not embracing any of these explanations.

When it came time to review "the abstruse art" of clinical psychology, Fitts engaged in a little playacting of his own. Defense investigator Robert Kaiser in *"RFK Must Die!"* made the following observation: "Fitts had expressed himself with great erudition—he seemed to have an encyclopedic knowledge of classical music, Moorish architecture, modern linguistics, the history of art and Middle Eastern diplomacy, among other things—until the psychologists and psychiatrists appeared for the defense. Then Fitts was a dunderhead who had never heard of Mesmer, Freud or Rorschach, or, indeed, the defense of diminished responsibility in California."

Remaining in character for his summation, Fitts termed the medical testimony a "quagmire."

> "Frankly, it's some relief to me to know that the psychologists and the psychiatrists in this case do find him to be sick, because I can't imagine anybody in the Ambassador Hotel stepping from this tray rack with a .22 revolver in his hand and firing the shots into the head of Senator Kennedy . . . not being what I consider to be sick.
>
> "This is true, of course, for any number of serious or aggravated crimes. We do have criminal courts. Atrocious acts are committed. The jails are full of people who have committed atrocious acts—mutilation, rape, child molestation, murder for various reasons—and most of us, the normal—if there is such a thing—the relatively normal people find some way to refrain from doing these acts."

Fitts termed the testimony of Dr. Schorr "disgraceful." He savaged Schorr for his plagiarism, and for his highly interpretive Rorschach exam. He also faulted Schorr on the selection of cards offered for Sirhan's Thematic Apperception Test. "Not a single one of those cards is the kind which would appear to elicit the popular response of a happy tale," he said, preparing once again to champion the cause of common sense.

Fitts reviewed the cards one by one. "There's the slumped figure in an uncomfortable position with the back turned. Make a happy story out of that, if you will."

Or the woman on the bed:

"I look at that bed and it's only big enough for one person; that's one of those little ambiguities; but there she is with her breasts uncovered, a fully clad gentleman with his hands covering his eyes. Make a happy story about that, if you can."

When it came to Dr. Richardson, Fitts was more kind. "Let me say at the outset that I liked Dr. Richardson. He seemed to me very straightforward, and maybe a man that had played football at some time."

The prosecutor's most caustic remarks were reserved for Dr. Diamond. He ridiculed the idea that the lights and mirrors at the Ambassador Hotel put Sirhan into an unintentional trance which led to the killing of Robert Kennedy. To Fitts, the evidence for "this dissociate thing" was "flimsy," and he had a better explanation—Sirhan had been in custody a full six months and had "structured some sort of story which he hoped would in some measure exonerate him for the crime he knew full well he committed." This point of view conveniently ignores the fact that Sirhan's story remained virtually unchanged during his incarceration, something his attorneys would fail to bring up when it was their turn to speak.

Fitts referred to Dr. Diamond's hypnotic sessions with Sirhan as "séances." "What is the moral involved?" he asked the jury. "And what did we learn from it all?"

> "Dr. Diamond was very proud indeed of his hypnotic ability with Mr. Sirhan. It seemed to me with no point whatsoever he told us how Sirhan behaved like a monkey and crawled up the bars of his cage and went through a couple of other foolish things of that sort; one of them was an inquiry about the weather, was it raining outside and so forth. Well, so be it. . . . In any event, it is on this insubstantial edifice of fact that Dr. Diamond says Sirhan was in a dissociative state."

Fitts read once again Dr. Diamond's "absurd and preposterous" statement. "Well I can't improve on Dr. Diamond," said Fitts to the jury, although he had just spent a half an hour trying. "If that is what he thinks of this story and that's what he said about it, why need I say anything more? You understand it is impossible to have the last word on Dr. Diamond; so let him have the last word."

Without the assistance of notes and demonstrating an uncommon ability to put words and thoughts together in a compelling fashion, David Fitts had spoken for the entire morning and most of the afternoon. By any measure, his argument was a stunning success. Using logic, wit, and sarcasm, the prosecutor had taken the thin evidence of Sirhan's premeditation and made a convincing case that Sirhan had planned Robert Kennedy's murder in advance and was lying when he said he hadn't. Fitts conceded that Sirhan might be sick, but then made the point that anyone who commits a horrible crime must be sick. His final appeal to the jury was simple and direct.

> "No individual after mature and meaningful reflection would, as far as I can see, ever commit a deliberate and premeditated murder. And yet murder is commonplace in our society. What are we to do with the individuals who commit these crimes? . . . Every single one of us here, knowing the circumstances of the Kennedy assassination, knew that the individual who had done that was just something out of the ordinary—very out of the ordinary. We can live with that. We can live with that and have a trial for first-degree murder. . . .
>
> "Science has progressed to the point that we are on the verge of putting a man on the moon, an incredible feat. And yet, in terms of

judging human conduct . . . we seem to be back just where we were—twelve people in a box. Twelve representatives of society; judging human conduct as they deem best . . .

"That's your job.

"Thank you very much."

The jury had been given strong moral and emotional reasons to convict Sirhan Sirhan of first-degree murder. It was now up to Sirhan's lawyers to give them reasons to convict the defendant on a lesser charge. The following morning Russell Parsons rose for the defense. "If Your Honor please," he said, ". . . I might make a peculiar start here, but I think you will forgive me under the circumstances."

Parsons had decided to open his argument with a review of the Sirhan family history.

"The Sirhans were living in a nice home; she described it; no one has told you differently. There have been men in this courtroom from Palestine. She told you that they had a lovely home, the best of furniture; her husband was employed by the British with a good job. . . .

"All right, what happens? All of a sudden they had to give up their home, their home that had been their home for years. That is bound to have an effect on people, when you have to just pack up and leave."

Parsons had told the jury that he was not going to plead for sympathy— that he just wanted them to know the facts. But the defense attorney was appealing for sympathy. Worse still, this appeal was repellent in manner and tone.

"She told you about the toilets, the little holes in the pavement in this building; and it was borne out by the young Arab whom we brought here from Chicago. Fortunately, we were able to find him, and he came here and told about how the toilet conditions were such—I don't like to stress this—but it paints the picture of how these people lived; and when the toilets overflowed out into the street, then the authorities came by and cleaned it up. . . .

"She told you about the food; the Arab boy told you that the food they had, he told you about the margarine and someone suggested was it liquid, was it like Mazola?"

Russell Parsons spoke as though the jury couldn't help but make a meaningful connection between the Sirhan family's toilet or margarine conditions in Palestine and the shooting death of Robert Kennedy in Los Angeles. He continued to retell the Sirhan story.

> "He came to this country and he did pretty well. He did pretty well in school. . . . When the man from the school board was here and was pointing, pointing out the time he missed school, they never offered any evidence to you to judge why, when he had a sister lying there with an incurable disease. And he played hooky from school that he might tend the wants of the poor dying sister. You can't be very bad when you do that. . . .
>
> "Have you ever seen the Sun and Fun Candy Store in Palm Springs? She ran that, and so he loved her. Is he to be condemned?"

For loving his sister? Certainly not. But Sirhan was on trial for murdering Robert Kennedy, and Parsons, as the defense attorneys had been doing all along, was not dealing with the facts of the case: he was instead running frantically around the periphery.

Parsons did, however, take one stab at discussing the circumstances of the murder.

> "I think it has been said he fired the revolver eight times. Well, when a fellow who is as small as he is has got two great big burly ex–football players—one a champion of the world—admirable characters, but powerful—are lying on you trying to grab your hand and the gun is going back and forth, how can you say he shot it eight times? Nobody knows who pulled the trigger. Tell me—think it over—he's lying there and they are on top of him. Who pulled it? Are you sure? Some of you fellows when you're shaving all alone some morning, think that over."

In view of the substantial open issues of fact in this case—evidence of more bullets than Sirhan could have fired, wounds in Robert Kennedy inconsistent with his position relative to Sirhan, trajectory diagrams which defied the laws of Newton: issues which the defense attorneys could have explored if they had the will—it is pathetic to read this attempt to inject the idea that maybe Rafer Johnson really murdered Robert Kennedy. It is hard to imagine anyone taking a word of it seriously, before the shaving mirror or anywhere else. Its effect for Sirhan in the minds of the jurors could only have been negative.

Parsons followed this absurdity with another as he engaged in an odd moment of breast-beating. "The responsibility is clearly in the hands of we lawyers. If there was anything we didn't do, honest, I don't know what it was. We tried every way we could; we have sought advice; we have had it; we have had numerous lawyers. And to the credit of my profession, I thank God I am a lawyer."

Parsons here lays bare his self-absorption. To whom was he speaking? The press? Historians? These are words that one might utter after the case is lost. They are certainly not ideas which would inspire a jury to believe that the defense attorneys had confidence in their own presentation.

In another statement not likely to merit respect from the jury Parsons contended, incredibly, that there was "not one word" of evidence offered at the trial to refute the medical testimony of the defense witnesses. "I thought we did pretty well," he said, congratulating himself. "We brought these men from all over."

Douglas Robinson of the *New York Times* called Parsons's summation "impassioned, old-fashioned rhetoric."[1] This was a generous characterization for argument that was sloppy and crude. The edge of vulgarity in Parsons's speech, evident as he reviewed the list of doctors, did not appear to work in his favor. Of Dr. Schorr: "It only takes a seventy-cent phone call to find out whether anything he said was untrue." Of Dr. Georgene Seward, who had made a brief appearance for the defense: "Weren't you impressed with her, or am I some kind of sap?" Of Dr. Marcus: "Now here is a man appointed by the Court and is the Court powerless, do they have to appoint some nincompoop to guide the defense in one of the most important cases ever tried in the world?"

Parsons continued with his less than inspiring appeal: "Who else did we bring here? We brought the doctor from the University of California, one of the great institutions in America. It's had some rough days lately, but it's still a great institution. And he came here. . . . We picked the best men that we could find. Blame me if they weren't good enough."

In an odd effort to cultivate the sympathy of the jury, Parsons made mention of the multiple tragedies that had befallen the Kennedy family. "There isn't a man in America," he intoned gravely, "who shouldn't say a prayer for the remainder of that family—every night." Perhaps it was the defense attorney's overdramatic presentation that struck Sirhan, but at that delicate moment he let out a small laugh. Sirhan quickly covered his mouth with his hand, but he had been noticed.

Sirhan's dismal sense of occasion would be matched by that of his attorney, as Parsons finished his summation with a vision that could hardly be expected to warm the hearts of the jurors.

"I would like your verdict to spell in every hamlet on every desert in the Arab Republic; in Europe; that a man can get justice in America and that is neither life imprisonment or the death penalty, because this case doesn't warrant it—not for this sick wretch. No matter what he did. Think that over. . . .

"It's going to take a little courage to return a proper verdict in this case; a little courage to see that justice is done; but it should and must be done. It will go down in the history books.

"Thank you."

The court took a short recess; then Emile Berman stood up. "I do not intend to repeat any of the matters that were so broadly touched upon by Mr. Parsons," he assured the jury, "but I do want to talk to you specifically about a thing called trauma." For emphasis Berman spelled the word for the jury.

Berman then outlined what he called Sirhan's six major traumas, beginning with his abandonment by "dear, old ever-loving dad," to his humiliation at the Arab defeat in the Six-Day War of 1967. Contradicting his stated intentions, the defense attorney from New York covered much the same ground as his predecessor, and, in the end, he concluded that Sirhan "was just a sick little boy."

At the lunch recess Grant Cooper paid a visit to Sirhan. "Trust me," he said to his client. "You won't like what I say. But I'm trying to get second degree. Trust me."[2]

Back in court and standing before the jury, Cooper began by praising David Fitts for "one of the finest closing arguments for the prosecution that I have heard in my forty-one years at the bar." Then, as though he were trying to loosen the mood at a Rotary luncheon, he told a story of a boy who fell into a barrel of molasses. Mimicking the words of the sugar-coated youngster, Cooper invoked divine assistance. "Oh, Lord, make my tongue equal to this opportunity."

Grant Cooper's tongue had been equal to the task many times in the past. His defense of Dr. Bernard Finch and his mistress, Carole Tregoff, for murder was regarded as classic courtroom melodrama, as Cooper hung the jury with his stirring reenactment of Finch's supposed struggle to wrest the gun from his wife's hand before—as the story went—she shot herself. But here Cooper made it clear one last time that there was to be no contest of fact.

"We are not here to free a guilty man," he told the jury. "We tell you, as we always have, that he is guilty of having killed Senator Kennedy. . . . Whether Mr. Sirhan likes it or not; under the facts of this case he deserves to spend the rest of his life in the penitentiary." To this there was a barely audible moan of protest from Mary Sirhan sitting in the second row.

Cooper then engaged in a little pop psychology.

"There is a good Sirhan and a bad Sirhan and the bad Sirhan is very nasty . . . but I have learned to like him just as Mr. Parsons said he has learned to love him, and so I have learned to love him, the good Sirhan but not withstanding that we as lawyers owe the obligation to do what we think is right . . . and I, for one, am not going to ask you to do otherwise than bring in a verdict of guilty of murder in the second degree."

Cooper then launched himself into an elongated discussion of the concepts of law at play in the case and the instructions they would be getting shortly from Judge Walker. "Now what I am telling you is legalese," he said to the jury, "that's why I'm trying to explain it to you."

In the role of erudite uncle, Cooper reviewed the elements of murder, the difference between direct and circumstantial evidence, levels of culpability. He offered definitions of premeditation, malice, diminished capacity, and transferred intent, but he provided no insights or clever ways to think about these concepts. Instead he droned on, the molasses now clearly sticking to his tongue.

"The instructions with respect to harboring malice, there are two elements, ladies and gentlemen. First, if you find that he had diminished capacity to a substantial degree where it would affect his ability to premeditate and deliberate and reflect upon the gravity of the event or, second, you don't have to be satisfied with that; if you entertain a reasonable doubt as to whether he has substantially reduced mental capacity to the extent that it affected his ability to maturely and meaningfully deliberate and premeditate and reflect upon the gravity of the event, you could find him guilty of first-degree murder."

The mind-numbing legal lessons went on for the entire afternoon and a good portion of the next morning. Eventually Cooper began to talk about the case. He reviewed Sirhan's threats to Kennedy in his notebooks. "Is that mature thinking?" he asked. "Is that meaningful thinking?"

Cooper was eager for the jury to understand that first-degree murder was reserved for especially heinous crimes. He had one in mind.

"By a bad man I am talking about the kind of man who, we will say, just by way of example, who is married, married a long time and he meets some cute little chick younger than his wife and he falls for her and decides that he wants to go to Tahiti or someplace with this young girlfriend of his but he doesn't have enough money, so he takes out a life insurance policy on the wife for one hundred thousand dollars. That has happened. Then he and his girlfriend plan to kill and do away with his wife so that he can not only get her out of the way but get the one hundred thousand dollars and then live in luxury with his girlfriend of younger years.

". . . This is a bad individual."

Cooper then asked the jury to compare the wife killer with Sirhan.

"What was the motive? It wasn't for gain for him; political motive, yes; but something in his immature mind, because of illness that the psychiatrists and psychologists told you that he had, he believed that it was right; how stupid. He believed that he shouldn't be punished for it; how stupid. How immature."

Grant Cooper's instincts told him that Dr. Bernard Diamond had not endeared himself to the jury with his testimony. He understood that the jury was not likely to embrace the doctor's idea that Sirhan was in a trance, and he also realized that the prosecution had done a good job at casting Sirhan as a fake and a liar. Thus, as he concluded his four-hour argument, Cooper tried to put distance between himself and Dr. Diamond by attempting to refocus the jury onto a single point.

"I don't care whether he was in a hypnotic state at the time he fired the shot, or whether he was in a trance as Dr. Diamond said; this is beside the point. The question that you are here to determine is not what his condition was at the time he fired the shot, but whether he could maturely and meaningfully premeditate . . . whether or not the defendant had diminished capacity. That is the only issue you have before you. . . . I will now pass from our shoulders to yours the responsibility and the proper and intelligent fate of Sirhan Sirhan."

The following morning Lynn Compton would make the final argument on behalf of the prosecution. For only the second time in sixty days Mary Sirhan was not in court. Her son Adel explained that she did not want to hear what Mr. Compton was going to say.

"I will guarantee you this is not going to be a long or very profound dissertation on the principles of psychiatry or of the law," Compton began to the probable relief of the jury. "I am simply going to appeal to your common sense. . . . Now again, as I say, I'm not the most profound or articulate guy and I'm a little bit—oh—embarrassed, I guess it is, to stand up here and follow a Stanford man like Mr. Fitts, with his great command of the language and his great literary knowledge, and talk about a lot of things that I don't know about."

As if to emphasize his humble bloodline, Compton declined to stand at the podium as his predecessors had, but instead unbuttoned his suit jacket, sat down on the end of the prosecution table, and looked directly at the jury. With folksy charm, thick hands, and a large nose, visibly off center from a football injury, Compton, at least to some in the press, very effectively played the role of Spencer Tracy.

He was quick to compliment the efforts of the defense team. "They have done an outstanding, workmanlike job in seeing that the system works," he said in a slow drawl. "And the system has worked." The prosecutor's regard for the opposing attorneys was, most likely, genuine, but his words were also cleverly designed to take what respect they had earned with the jury and divert it from their client to his—the legal system itself.

Compton was also vocal in his approval for the police and the prosecution.

> "There were no secrets, no surprises, no sandbagging on our part. A public trial, so that the world, through the media of the people who came here as observers, could see and report to anyone who was interested everything that went on—no Star Chambers, no secrets—wide open for everybody to look at and criticize if they want; but there were no secrets."

Having praised both the prosecution and the defense, Compton turned his sights on the real villains of the trial, the men "whose profession is based on finding something wrong with people." The prosecutor did not try to hide his scorn for the doctors. "They are not going to come in," he assured the jury calmly, "and say nothing is wrong with Sirhan."

Compton then made a literary reference of his own. "At some time in my life I have heard that Charles Dickens once wrote a book," he said, "in which one of his characters said something about 'The law is an ass.' I think that's true and I'm a lawyer. I think the law became an ass the day it let psychiatrists get their hands on the law. . . . I say throw 'em out in one bag."

The scathing critique continued:

> "I can't for the life of me believe anyone can go back to June 5 and crawl inside his head and tell you what he was thinking about when he put that bullet in Senator Kennedy's head by showing him pictures of a kid with a violin or a man standing with his hands up to his face or a woman in a bed. . . .
>
> "I think it would be a frightening thing for the administration of criminal justice in this state if the decision of the magnitude of this case turned on whether or not he saw clowns playing pattycake or

whether they were kicking each other in the shins when he is shown some inkblot."

There were no outbursts from Sirhan as Compton spoke. Martin Kasindorf of *Newsweek* described the defendant as looking "unutterably sad, lonely and downcast, his pallid face cradled in his left hand, gazing at Compton like a bereft child."[3] The prosecutor turned to meet his eyes. "They like him, they say," he said with contempt, referring to Sirhan's lawyers. "I don't like him. I think he is a cunning vicious man."

"Mr. Cooper gives an example of what he thinks a bad guy is. Do you remember, the fellow who wanted to take his secretary and go to Tahiti and all that? . . . I submit to you that this nation could survive with two hundred bad guys like that carrying out their desires; there would be two hundred dead wives, which isn't good; but the nation would survive. But can the nation survive two hundred assassins like Sirhan? . . .

"I think it turns on this one question—the psychiatrists say if you hate a man a little bit and kill him, you are responsible and mature. But if you hate him a lot and kill him, you are not responsible and not mature.

"Ladies and gentlemen, in rendering a verdict of first-degree murder in this case, we ask you, don't put a premium on hate."

After lunch Judge Walker began his instructions to the jury. "In determining the guilt or innocence of the defendant you are to be governed solely by the evidence introduced in this trial and the law as stated to you by me. The law forbids you to be governed by mere sentiment, conjecture, sympathy, passion, prejudice, or public opinion." By three o'clock Walker was finished and the jury of seven men and five women was sent to the dingy, beige-colored conference room on the ninth floor of the Hall of Justice, just a floor above the small courtroom where, for the past two months, they had listened to the testimony of ninety witnesses.

The jury had been instructed to deliberate only during normal court hours. In the time they had left on Monday afternoon, they elected as foreman their best-educated member—Bruce D. Elliot, a computer analyst who held a Ph.D. degree.

The following day there was no word at all from the jury room, but on the second full day of deliberations the jurors sent a note to Judge Walker asking for clarification on the definition of second-degree murder. That same afternoon Russell Parsons managed to push himself back onto center stage when he told newsmen that Sirhan was expecting to be exchanged for some prisoner in an Arab country. Parsons said that a State Department "official" had discussed the idea with him a few months back. With nothing else to report, some newsmen began to write stories about the rumored exchange. Bob Greene of *Newsday* was one. Parsons told Greene that Issa Nahkleh, the Arab lawyer associated with the defense team, had gone to New York to discuss the possibility of this exchange with visiting King Hussein of Jordan.

"Why do you think he has been out there?" Parsons asked. "He hasn't been there for fun, you know. At first I was going to go to Jordan myself, but then we decided that this would be better." Greene asked whom the United States would want in an exchange. "I'm sure they have a lot of people we want," replied Parsons.[4]

Later it was discovered that Nahkleh never met with Hussein, and the government "official" who had supposedly started the whole thing was merely a translator, a former low-level employee of the State Department, who was accompanying a Lebanese businessman on a visit to Los Angeles. His comment to Parsons was that "such exchanges happen oftener than you think."[5]

The next morning at 10:47 A.M., three buzzes were heard on the signal system, indicating that a verdict had been reached. In less than half an hour all the principals were in court. Judge Walker asked jury foreman Bruce Elliott whether the jurors had reached a verdict.

"We have, Your Honor," replied Mr. Elliott.

The judge took six white forms from Elliot. He looked at them briefly and then glanced at the defendant as he handed them to the court clerk.

"We the jury find the defendant, Sirhan Bishara Sirhan," said Alice Nishikawa in a clear voice, "guilty of murder . . . in the first degree."

Sirhan, dressed in a light blue shirt with gray slacks, remained impassive as the verdict was read. The wire service reporters, on the other hand, moved quickly for the doors. Under California law the jury would now, in a separate hearing, have to decide between a sentence of life in prison or death. Judge Walker ordered the penalty trial to begin the following Monday, April 21.

The jury had deliberated for almost seventeen hours, delivering their verdict on the sixty-third day of the trial. When the panel was polled for the first time on Tuesday, eight jurors voted for the first-degree murder, two for second-degree, and two were undecided. Several hours later the vote was ten first-degree, two undecided. On Wednesday one of the undecideds, former alternate juror Ruth Stillman, twenty-six, an insurance adjuster, joined the majority. That left Susan J. Brumm, sixty-two, as the last holdout. During deliberations Brumm repeatedly referred to Sirhan as "that young kid," but Ms. Brumm changed her vote the following morning. Oddly, it was the fact that Sirhan had never been in trouble before that led her to conclude that he must have had the capacity to control himself.

Court was again in session the afternoon after the verdict (without the jury), as preparations were made for the penalty hearing. Grant Cooper put forth several "offers of proof" for Judge Walker's approval. The first was that Mr. Issa Nahkleh, the Palestinian U.N. representative, be permitted to give historical background to the Arab-Israeli conflict so that the jury might better understand Sirhan's mind. The second was that Evelle Younger, the district attorney, be called as a witness for the defense to testify that during the plea bargain he was in favor of recommending life in prison for Sirhan.

Cooper's third proposal was that the defense be permitted to introduce witnesses who would argue against the efficacy of the death penalty. Judge Walker didn't hesitate to deny this and the two preceding motions, holding that background on the Arab-Israeli conflict was irrelevant, that the negotiations during plea bargain were privileged, and that the death penalty was a debate topic more appropriate for the legislature.

At the penalty hearing on Monday morning Mary Sirhan was once again called as a witness. Robert Kaiser described the scene in *"RFK Must Die!"*:

> She rose from her seat in the second row, from which she had watched and wept through most of the trial, and marched bravely up to the stand with dignity, a diminutive homely woman in a light blue skirt and matching jacket, climbed into the jury box, adjusted the microphone on her bosom and moistened her lips. She frowned and blinked at Cooper from a face ravaged by tears enough for ten. She had buried eight of her thirteen children, lived through two wars, been abandoned by her husband. Now she was asked to testify at the death penalty hearing of her son, the assassin.[6]

"Mrs. Sirhan," asked Grant Cooper. "In his entire life, before the shooting, was Sirhan Sirhan ever at any time in any trouble with the law?"

"He has never been," she replied. "And that is not from me or from him. That is because I raised him up to the law of God and his love."

"Thank you, Mrs. Sirhan; I have no further questions."

It was the shortest penalty hearing in California history. In less than a minute it was time for final arguments to determine whether Sirhan would be sentenced to life in prison or death in the gas chamber at San Quentin. Assistant District Attorney John Howard spoke first.

"The only question now is the proper punishment for a political assassin in the United States," he began. ". . . If death is to be the reward for political aspiration, you will know your candidates as two-dimensional images on the television screen or as disembodied voices over the radio."

In the preceding weeks it had been reported widely in the newspapers that the prosecution was not going to seek the death penalty. Two weeks earlier, Buck Compton had told the press that very thing. "I think the public would be satisfied with a sentence of life," the deputy DA had said. But now, with the verdict of guilty in hand, John Howard seemed to be taking a hard line against Sirhan.

> "In resolving the question of this defendant's guilt you have found him lacking in honesty, in integrity, and even in the courage of his convictions. At the same time he obviously enjoyed the star status and the opportunity to engage in dramatic theatrics. . . . Perhaps you observed his reaction when Mr. Russell Parsons, in his address to you, urged in all sincerity that America pray for the ill-starred Kennedy family. . . .
>
> "This defendant will regard permission to live as a further triumph of imprisonment, for life imprisonment is an entry into a form of custodial society that can only suffer by the inclusion of this defendant. You may not be obliged to hear this defendant boast that he committed the crime of the century. Others will."

John Howard's speech was *genuine* "old-fashioned rhetoric," permitted in the final argument, and very effective. The prosecutor described a newspaper article he had read a few days earlier about the war in Vietnam. "Apparently it was a good week. Only two hundred and two Americans killed. The Sirhan trial dominated the paper and the front page. We have lavishly expended our resources for the sake of a cold-blooded political assassin, while content to send patriotic Americans to Vietnam with a seventy-dollar rifle and our best wishes."

In making his final appeal to the jury, the word "death" never passed John Howard's lips, but the meaning of his words was unmistakable. "Sirhan Sirhan was entitled to a fair trial, which each of you has now given to him. He has no special claim to further preservation. I would ask on behalf of the prosecution that each of you in your hearts have the courage of your conviction to write an end to this trial, and to apply the only proper penalty for political assassination in the United States of America."

Grant Cooper was stunned. He believed that the prosecution would not push for the death penalty, but John Howard had just done so, and in very harsh terms. It was now up to Cooper to raise the last voice in Sirhan's behalf.

> "Shortly after midnight on the morning of June the fifth a young vigorous senator fresh from his victory in the California primaries . . . met his untimely death . . . a victim of hate, hate generated in the bowels of war, a hate engendered at an early age in the child Sirhan,

hate that consumed a once healthy mind, hate that had reduced that mind to one described by the evidence as a substantial mental illness."

Cooper reminded the jury that they were gathered to decide the ultimate issue, "an issue which should be God's alone." The choice, said Cooper, was "whether Sirhan Sirhan end the rest of his natural life behind the bars of a penitentiary or shall he forfeit his life by inhaling the deadly fumes of cyanide gas . . . in the gruesome green room at San Quentin."

"Do you realize that yours is the power of discretion of a king?" Cooper continued, trying to increase the pressure. "A benevolent monarch or a despotic dictator? This is your awful power."

Cooper had never argued at a penalty hearing. He had built his reputation on hanging juries, and he knew now that he was looking for just a few jurors who would hold out against putting Sirhan to death. Most of his arguments were generic; many of his references were biblical.

"Remember—the taking of human life by the law also begets violence. 'Vengeance is mine, saith the Lord.'

". . . The Bible teaches us that love is reflected in love, but how many of us heed this biblical teaching? Instead it is hate, hate, hate, violence, violence, more violence; wars, wars, and more wars. When will we ever learn that love is truly reflected in love? . . . In the name of God, whence cometh all understanding, I appeal to your judgment; . . . let this circle of violence end here in this courtroom."

Cooper suggested that sparing Sirhan's life would be a "posthumous tribute to Senator Kennedy." He quoted Robert Kennedy on the night Martin Luther King was slain: " 'Whenever any American's life is taken by another unnecessarily, whether it is done in the name of the law or in defiance of the law . . . the whole nation is degraded.' "

Then in dramatic fashion Cooper turned toward the defendant.

"And now, Sirhan Sirhan—I have done all that I could do to the very best of my ability, for you and for the American system of justice, which I serve and revere.

"And to you Mary Sirhan, his mother, I say . . . 'May your prayers be answered.' "

Sirhan returned Grant Cooper's gaze without emotion. Mary Sirhan wept.

★　　★　　★

Almost exactly a week after it had retired to consider the verdict, the Sirhan jury found itself back in the ninth-floor conference room to decide the penalty. The first vote appeared to show a jury evenly divided—five jurors voted for death, three for life, with four undecided. But the jurors arguing for death were more tenacious and persuasive. By the next day the vote was nine for death, one for life, with two undecided. Soon only one juror, Alphonse Galindo, a Roman Catholic Mexican American, stood in the way of a unanimous verdict.

"What crime deserves capital punishment if not this one?" other jurors asked Galindo. Finally, Wednesday morning, after almost twelve hours of deliberation, Galindo changed his mind. "You've convinced me," he said. "Let's all go home."[7]

As the courtroom filled, Grant Cooper walked about in an agitated state. "I don't like it," he said to *Newsday* reporter Bob Greene. "I can feel a chill in my bones." Cooper then offered his analysis. "The weak ones crumbled, just like they did the first time around. They couldn't stand the pressure."[8]

It was 11:30. Sirhan calmly stared at the jurors as they filed into the courtroom. Some looked back; most avoided his gaze. Alice Nishikawa was handed the verdict. "We the jury," she read, "having found the defendant Sirhan Bishara Sirhan guilty of murder in the first degree, as charged in count one of the indictment, now fix the penalty at death."

After the jury was polled, Grant Cooper followed Sirhan out of the courtroom to the holding pen, where Cooper expressed his regret. "We did the best we could," he said, tears flowing from his eyes.

Moved by the emotion, Sirhan, in a momentary reversal of roles, sought to console his attorney. "Even Jesus Christ couldn't have saved me," he replied.[9]

Sirhan may have been right. During the trial, behind their poker faces, several jurors had developed an intense hostility toward the defendant.

"Sirhan is a conniving brat," said one juror to a newsman after the trial. Another juror, quoted anonymously, called Sirhan "an animal" and said someone ought "to cut a little piece out of him every day."[10]

Other statements by jurors were more reasoned. Many faulted the inability of the defense psychiatrists and psychologists to tell a convincing story. "Even the experts couldn't get together among themselves," said Benjamin Glick. "All those psychiatrists," added Albert Frederico, "they really had us all stirred up. It was confusing. It stunk."[11]

Glick, the owner of a women's clothes shop, was the only Jew on the jury panel. "It was a hell of a position," he admitted afterward, "and I thought I should bend over backwards to give him more of a break." Glick had been one of the original votes for life imprisonment. "But after viewing all the facts, I decided he deserved death for his dastardly crime."[12]

"One item that was very important was the idea that we should stand behind our laws," said George Stitzel, the pressman for the *Los Angeles Times,* an alternate juror, who had been placed on the panel the day closing arguments began. "There seems to be a tendency today not to do this, to be lax. As long as we have capital punishment, what other crime would justify the death penalty if this didn't?"[13]

Another juror echoed the same sentiment: "There is unrest all over the country and even now the students are rioting. We can't afford to have our leaders be in a position to be killed and I think we all hope this decision acts as a deterrent to others with the same idea."

George Broomis, a dark-haired man of Mexican descent, cast another of the original life votes for Sirhan. He had openly cried in the courtroom out of sympathy for Sirhan's position. "I know he premeditated the murder with malice," Broomis said to reporters, "but I still thought the death penalty was too harsh. Taking a man's life isn't exactly an easy thing to do. I had sympathy for Sirhan, but I tried to push it out of my mind. I'm a sentimental person and every time the tears came to my eyes I tried to stop them. Day after day, sitting there with him sitting in the chair in front of me, it was terrible. I tried not to look at him and I tried not to look at his mother, but they were always there and I couldn't help it. I hope what we did was right."[14]

After court adjourned, the jurors returned to the Biltmore Hotel, where they had been sequestered since they were chosen in mid-February. Douglas Robinson of the *New York Times* described the scene as they arrived at the hotel.

> As the jurors walked off a sheriff department bus, looking haggard and exhausted, a crowd of newsmen and spectators pressed around the security men guarding them. A number of persons in the throng applauded.
>
> The jurors, their heads down, ignored the applause.[15]

Once Sirhan's fate was cast, many of those who had hailed the jury's verdict the week before now felt uneasy. Writing in the *New York Times,* Tom Wicker voiced his distress: "This supposedly civilized nation is deliberately going to take the life of a distraught, displaced Arab boy who in some tortured shadow world of his own shot down Robert Kennedy."[16] Former Supreme Court justice Arthur J. Goldberg wrote a letter to Ronald Reagan asking the governor to commute Sirhan's sentence. Senator Edward Kennedy wrote a letter on behalf of Sirhan to District Attorney Evelle J. Younger.

Not all the reactions were negative. William F. Buckley, in the *National Review,* folded all the legal assistance and attention Sirhan had commanded into his newly promulgated "Law of Inverse Hazard for the Killing of Important People."[17]

Reaction in the Middle East was also strangely sanguine. The semiofficial Egyptian newspaper *El Ahram* noted that if Sirhan had been acquitted, "it would have meant the assassination was a rash act committed by an unbalanced person, therefore any political significance would have to be discounted." But as it was, the paper noted with apparent satisfaction, "murder in the first degree proved Sirhan was fully aware of his act."[18]

In an editorial, the *New York Times* expressed revulsion for the sentence passed upon Sirhan, calling it "a retreat to the law of the jungle." Nevertheless, like other journals, the newspaper's overall expressions about the trial were congratulatory:

> Justice was on trial with Sirhan B. Sirhan. Now . . . after a long and careful trial, it can be said that justice has been served. . . . The public at home and abroad may never know what goes on inside the twisted mind of an assassin. But at least, it has been able to see an open trial fairly conducted.[19]

PART II

The Secret Files

* * *

FIFTEEN

Disclosure

✳   ✳   ✳

*I do not know why those responsible for law enforcement in Los
Angeles decided to stonewall the RFK case. But once they had made
that decision, the rest followed: facts had to be concealed or distorted
and inconvenient evidence done away with; inoperative statements
had to be replaced by new statements, until they in turn became
inoperative; people raising awkward questions had to be
discredited, preferably as self-seeking or flaky.*

—Former New York congressman Allard Lowenstein (1977)

I N 1970, A book titled *Special Unit
Senator: The Investigation of the As-
sassination of Senator Robert F. Kennedy* was published by Random House.
The author was Robert A. Houghton, Chief of Detectives, LAPD. Special
Unit Senator was also the name of the elite task force set up by Chief
Houghton in June 1968 to investigate the Kennedy murder. Houghton's
book was coauthored by professional writer Theodore Taylor.

In the foreword, dated August 1, 1969, just three months after Sirhan's
trial, Houghton claimed that "the book . . . was written for the sole purpose
of acquainting the American public with the facts of the investigation, and
with the evidence, or lack of evidence, as it exists, of conspiracy in association with Senator Kennedy's assassination. *The material herein was drawn
from the files of the Los Angeles Police Department* [emphasis added]."

As a detective thriller, Houghton's book is in a class by itself—a genre
in which the police don't go out and catch the killers, but rather go out
and find there are no killers. Its most dramatic moment occurs when Sergeant Enrique Hernandez, using his polygraph machine, breaks witness Sandra Serrano, freeing the police from the obligation to find a possible
accomplice in the murder, the girl in the polka-dot dress.

Though Houghton's book praised the police investigation, confirmed
Sirhan's guilt, and discounted any notions of conspiracy, the office of the
district attorney was not pleased with the prospect of its publication. In a
memorandum to Assistant DA Joseph P. Busch, dated a month after

Houghton had written his foreword, Sirhan prosecutor John Howard informed Busch that he had reviewed Houghton's book for certain legalities, most specifically to determine if its publication would adversely affect the pending Sirhan appeal. Howard told Busch:

1. The publication will not affect the appeal.

2. Legal position of Chief Houghton in publishing same is questionable. . . .

3. It is ethically improper for Chief Houghton to benefit financially from the efforts and work product produced and paid for by LAPD.

Despite Howard's unofficial conclusions, no injunctive or disciplinary action was ever taken against Chief Houghton. Not addressed by Howard's memo was the issue of whether it was appropriate for Houghton and his coauthor, Theodore Taylor, to have access to the secret police files for the purpose of writing a book when these files were being denied to the public. This question would form the basis for a court battle in 1975.

In the summer 1973, Allard K. Lowenstein, a former New York congressman and a friend of Robert Kennedy, attended a meeting of people interested in the circumstances of Kennedy's death. Lowenstein had led the successful "Dump Johnson" movement in 1968, but in 1970, he had been gerrymandered out of his House seat. Even so, the former congressman was outspoken enough to merit inclusion on President Richard Nixon's secret enemies list.

At the meeting, which took place in the Los Angeles home of actor Robert Vaughn, Lowenstein was confronted with evidence that Robert Kennedy had not been murdered by Sirhan Sirhan acting alone. He was skeptical. "Nothing seemed clearer to me at the time," he recalled, "than the absurdity of this notion. Everyone had seen Sirhan shooting at Senator Kennedy."[1] Nevertheless, after examining the evidence, Lowenstein became convinced that there were serious outstanding questions, and that the refusal on the part of the Los Angeles police to open their files was a breach of public trust.

Lowenstein then fashioned an informal coalition to work for public disclosure. Among those who would soon join this effort were Robert Joling, president of the American Academy of Forensic Sciences; former Los Angeles deputy DA Vincent Bugliosi, who prosecuted Charles Manson; and Paul Schrade, the Kennedy friend and campaign aide wounded in the head at the Ambassador Hotel the night Kennedy was shot.

As part of his inquiry Lowenstein submitted a list of questions about the murder investigation to the LAPD chief, Edward Davis. Among other items, he inquired about the ceiling tiles and the doorframes taken from the Ambassador Hotel kitchen by the police. Though Davis promised to get back to Lowenstein, a reply never came. "The official response to my questions was as peculiar as the contradictions in the evidence," recalled Lowenstein. "Every official I saw at the DA's office was polite and talked about cooperation, but nobody did anything. . . . When a question was answered at all, the answer often turned out to be untrue—not marginally untrue, but enthusiastically, aggressively, and sometimes quite imaginatively untrue."[2]

In December 1974, Allard Lowenstein and Paul Schrade held a press conference at the Statler Hilton Hotel in New York, seeking to put pressure upon those holding the secret files. "I reject conspiracy theories until the evidence is in," said Schrade, "but we're asking questions and we want answers."[3]

Lowenstein was less cautious in his pronouncements. "I do not believe on the basis of the evidence in its present state," he said, "that Sirhan Sirhan is the murderer of Robert Kennedy." Lowenstein said that he had spoken recently with Sirhan's chief defense attorney, Grant Cooper, and that Cooper had made the stunning admission "that had he known during the trial what he has since learned, he would have conducted a different defense."[4]★

Just five days after the Schrade-Lowenstein press conference a secret seventy-six-page response to Lowenstein's inquiry was submitted to Assistant Chief of Police Daryl F. Gates. The cover sheet of the memo read:

> This separate addenda [sic] contains confidential information relative to the questions submitted by Allard Lowenstein. The information has not been revealed prior to this report and may conflict with previous statements made by the Chief of Police and other officials.
>
> Serious consideration should be given to the release of this information.

Gates heeded the warning; the information was not released. But although Daryl Gates could stonewall Allard Lowenstein, there were others to whom he had to answer. On August 21, 1975, the assistant chief of police was called before the Los Angeles City Council to explain the alleged disappearance of evidence from the Robert Kennedy case file. The issue had been raised by Councilman Zev Yaroslavsky, who had been disturbed

---

★Grant Cooper died in 1990. His widow, Phyllis, also an attorney, in an interview with the authors, maintained that her husband never had any second thoughts about the defense he provided for Sirhan. This leaves open the question of whether Cooper was patronizing Lowenstein or was reluctant to share his doubts with his wife.

by rumors that the doorframes and the ceiling tiles taken from the Ambassador Hotel were now either missing or destroyed.

"One would have thought," said Yaroslavsky to Gates before the meeting, "that after all of the problems with the John F. Kennedy assassination, the police department would be a little more sensitive to the preservation of evidence."[5]

When questioned about the missing ceiling panels at the hearing Gates replied:

> "They have absolutely no value whatsoever. All of the testing, the real important testing, as far as trajectory and the line of fire and the number of bullet holes, that was done prior to their removal [from the pantry]. . . . We made those tests and they showed absolutely nothing. They proved absolutely nothing. They did nothing so far as supporting the investigation or supporting the guilt or innocence of anyone."[6]

Gates went on to say that X rays of the ceiling panels had been made but that "the records of the X rays and the X rays themselves are not in existence." In addition Gates asserted that spectrographic analysis was also probably done by LAPD criminalist DeWayne Wolfer. "He [Wolfer] believes he did make a spectrographic analysis. Ordinarily he would not have conducted a spectrographic analysis, but because we were being so thorough, I think he did."[7]

Gates told the councilmen that the missing doorframes and the ceilings tiles were destroyed by the LAPD on June 27, 1969. If true, the destruction occurred only one month after the *Los Angeles Free Press* article by Lillian Castellano and Floyd Nelson citing evidence of extra bullets in the doorframes—and just three weeks after District Attorney Evelle Younger publicly promised full release of police files.

A week after Gates's revelations, Allard Lowenstein pointed out some contradictions in the police position regarding the missing items. In a letter to Samuel L. Williams, president of the Board of Police Commissioners, Lowenstein asserted:

> Assistant Police Chief Daryl Gates says that the ceiling panels were destroyed in June, 1969. Yet on October 11, 1971, a Police Department Board of Inquiry, in a report . . . described as a "reevaluation of the evidence," stated that "an inspection of the ceiling tiles removed from the pantry and a study of the schematic diagram showing the trajectory of the bullets fired by Sirhan refute the contention advanced by Mr. Harper [concerning a second gun].
>
> How were panels destroyed in June 1969, "reevaluated" in Oc-

tober, 1971? Did the . . . Board of Inquiry announce a "reevaluation" that had not in fact taken place? Mr. Gates now says that these panels "did nothing so far as supporting the investigation or supporting the guilt or innocence of anyone." But in October 1971, an inspection of these same panels was said to "refute" a challenge to the official version of the murder.

Speaking about the police commission's continued refusal to grant access to the investigation file, Lowenstein wrote: "Confidence will not be restored by invoking slogans about civil liberties to refuse reasonable requests designed to answer serious questions, while information leaks out piecemeal about the destruction of crucial evidence."[8]

Lowenstein had little confidence in the abilities of the police commission. Later he would publicly characterize its role in the disclosure process. "Whatever its motives," he wrote, "the commission has lent a kind of respectability to the cover-up, and it has done so with a clumsy arrogance that leads one to wonder if it took lessons from the Hapsburgs, who are said to have ruled Austria by tyranny tempered only by incompetence."[9]

While the controversy over the missing evidence continued to boil, several legal initiatives were begun in the California Superior Court. In one, Paul Schrade, as a victim of the crime, petitioned the court under the Public Records Act of California to open the files. Schrade was joined in this suit by CBS News. One of the petitioners' main arguments was that when Chief Robert Houghton wrote his book *Special Unit Senator,* his civilian coauthor, Theodore Taylor, had utilized the police files, which amounted to prior public disclosure. Thus, the petitioners asserted, they too should be granted access.

City attorneys weighed in with an impressive series of sworn affidavits from police officials, rebutting the petitioners' claims. Retired chief Edward Davis and acting chief Jack G. Collins provided statements, as did Houghton himself. To their knowledge, they said, the Robert Kennedy case file had been locked up at headquarters, with access provided only on a strict "need-to-know" basis.

As Houghton stated:

> "I did write a book with the assistance of Theodore Taylor. I had no recollection of having shown the ten-volume *Summary* [*Report*] to Taylor, but I did show Taylor some items and some material from LAPD files. Much of the material I showed Taylor was material used in the trial of Sirhan, or held by the district attorney. . . . At no time did Taylor ever come to Parker Center [LAPD headquarters] and go into the police investigative files."

On this part of the lawsuit Schrade and CBS lost. Presiding Judge Robert A. Wenke held that Taylor's access to the information did not constitute prior disclosure. The LAPD was permitted to keep the files secret.

A decade later Philip Melanson would interview writer Theodore Taylor, who, strangely, had not been called to testify in the 1975 court action. Taylor described to Melanson how he had come into possession of the police files. He related how he had picked up tapes and documents and transported them to his home, while the investigation was still ongoing: "My car was parked outside of Parker Center and I kept loading this crap in there. I don't know, the guy helped me with a cart; he had a big cart. And I thought, Jesus Christ, what really do I have here?"

Taylor related that he drove the files to his home and stored them in an office in his garage because there wasn't room in his study. Melanson asked Taylor how complete was the material turned over to him.

TAYLOR: I had access to some papers that I shouldn't have had access to. . . .

MELANSON: In what sense, since they were giving you most everything? What do you mean "you shouldn't have"?

TAYLOR: Well now, these papers were not involved, did not come from LAPD. They were FBI . . . Central Intelligence [CIA]. He [Houghton] said, "For Chrissakes, you know, you're looking at 'em and I'll give 'em to you for forty-eight hours and then you get 'em back up here and don't copy anything down from 'em."

MELANSON: That's an example of how much he turned over?

TAYLOR: He just turned over everything he had.[10]

The combined pressure of hearings before the police commission, the city council, and the California Superior Court prodded the district attorney's office to initiate a reinvestigation of their own. Acting district attorney John E. Howard appointed private attorney Thomas F. Kranz on August 14, 1975, as special counsel to "independently review all the previous evidence, transcripts, interviews, and documents relating to the Sirhan case, and make his own independent investigation into the assassination of Robert Kennedy."

A year and a half later a 135-page document titled *The Report of Thomas F. Kranz on the Assassination of Senator Robert F. Kennedy* was released to the public. In his opening remarks Kranz made it clear that the motivating force behind this new investigation was "not the validity of the verdict in the Sirhan case, but the erosion of public confidence in the system of justice in Los Angeles County due to the many questions that were continually being raised in the Sirhan matter." What seemed to escape Kranz was that this erosion of public confidence and the many questions being raised concerned the most fundamental conclusions of the police investigation. In characterizing these questions as "the orchestration of controversy," Kranz revealed a mind-set that was neither incisive nor open-minded. Though Kranz did briefly criticize criminalist DeWayne Wolfer for "sloppy" work, the report turned out to be an elaborate apology for the police.

In July 1977, Allard Lowenstein forwarded to the Los Angeles County Board of Supervisors a list of corrections to the *Kranz Report*. Lowenstein and his colleague, political scientist Gregory Stone, addressed seventy-five significant misrepresentations and errors contained in the report, inaccuracies which served to obscure important issues of fact.

According to the Lowenstein-Stone review, Kranz misrepresented key evidence regarding Kennedy's position in the pantry, the observed bullet holes in the pantry doorframe, the testimony of witness Sandra Serrano, and, on numerous occasions, the conclusions of the 1975 firearms panel, which refuted DeWayne Wolfer's trial testimony that victim bullets could be conclusively matched to Sirhan's gun. "A scientific ballistics hearing subsequently linked all the bullets to only one weapon," claimed Kranz in his report. This, as Lowenstein and Stone pointed out, was grossly inaccurate and represented either a failure to grasp the most elemental facts of the case or a serious disregard for the truth.

In concluding their review Lowenstein and Stone asserted:

> Whatever Mr. Kranz found or didn't find, his findings have not changed these facts:
>
> Law enforcement agencies violated for eight years their own promises that the investigation "work product" would be made available. They "lost" or destroyed key evidence and documentation, and suppressed the fact of this destruction. They opposed the firearms testing, which, when finally conducted, further discredited the official handling of physical evidence. They concealed the identities of police officers, misrepresented their observations, and then obstructed the effort to obtain statements or testimony from them. They have continually misstated basic facts and stonewalled legitimate inquiries.

In the foreword to his report Thomas Kranz asserted, "This report is my product and no changes in either content or substance have been made by any other persons." This may be an overstatement. Recently released documents from the district attorney's office, provided to the authors by Los Angeles attorney Marilyn Barrett, reveal that Kranz's vaunted independence as a special counsel was limited. In making the report, Kranz used the district attorney's top RFK case investigator, William R. Burnett. An undated memo from Kranz to Burnett states:

What I'd like to have you do is just take a look at this rough draft, it's pretty lengthy actually it's 19 tapes (sides). Give me your ideas when you have a chance. . . . Anyone in Tom McDonald's office can tell you where the rough draft copy is—I will talk to you next week. Thank you, Tom.

In the report, Thomas Kranz made particular efforts to dismiss speculation that there were bullets or bullet holes in the destroyed doorframes. He claimed to have interviewed "FBI investigators" who confirmed the fact that there were no such holes. But how thorough was his search?

In 1976 former FBI agent William Bailey, who had been at the Ambassador Hotel shortly after the shooting, swore an affidavit to former prosecutor Vincent Bugliosi that he had seen two bullet holes in the center divider between the pantry doors. In 1977 (the month is unclear), DA investigator William Burnett spoke to Bailey by telephone (an audiotape of this conversation was found in a closet of the DA's office in 1986). During the conversation Bailey made the same assertion to Burnett.

> BAILEY: There were at least two bullet holes in the center post, between the two swinging doors.
> BURNETT: You say at least two bullet holes. Now how do you base your determination that these were bullet holes?
> BAILEY: Let's put it this way, Bill. Short of actually taking the wood off myself and examining it, I would say that I'm reasonably certain they were bullet holes. I've seen bullet holes in wood before. I looked into these holes, they were definitely not nail holes. There appeared to be objects inside, imbedded inside. They were not nails.

Despite this conversation and despite the fact that Bailey had gone on record with this information the previous year and provided the name of another agent who could corroborate his observations, there is no mention of William Bailey in the supposedly comprehensive *Kranz Report*.

Also unanswered by the *Kranz Report* is an obvious question: Why was it necessary to spend public money and a year and a half to reinvestigate the Robert Kennedy murder, when the police had already produced, at considerable public expense, a more comprehensive 1,500-page *Summary Report*, which they were refusing to open for inspection? What was the purpose of such a report if it was not to be released? Knowing the controversy it was causing, why did the police department fight so hard to keep it secret?

Allard Lowenstein speculated on possible motives for the suppression of evidence in a 1977 article in *The Saturday Review*:

I do not know whether Sirhan acting alone murdered Robert Kennedy. I do know what happened when we tried to find out. Eventually, reluctantly, against all my instinct and wishes, I arrived at the melancholy thought that people who have nothing to hide do not lie, cheat, and smear to hide it.

It is possible that the small number of people in key places who have worked to head off inquiries and cover up facts have done so simply because their reputations or careers are at stake; but the fact that this is a possibility does not make it acceptable to allow the situation to rest as it is, for there are other possibilities, too.[11]

Three years later, on March 14, 1980, fifty-one-year-old Allard Lowenstein was murdered. Dennis Sweeney, a deranged former colleague in the civil rights movement of the 1960s, entered Lowenstein's law office in New York and shot him five times with a handgun. Some writers and researchers have suggested that Lowenstein's energetic efforts in the Robert Kennedy case were the reason behind the murder. Lowenstein's closest associate, Gregory Stone, remained agnostic about this theory. While aware that Lowenstein had made powerful enemies and was the subject of a thick CIA file, Stone was aware of no evidence of conspiracy. Nevertheless, he harbored doubts. "It's clear that Dennis Sweeney was a nut," he said some years later. "The only question is whether he was a handled nut."[12]

In 1983 Gregory Stone edited and published a book about his former colleague titled *Lowenstein: Acts of Courage and Belief* (Harcourt Brace Jovanovich). That same year, Stone met Philip Melanson, a professor of political science at the University of Massachusetts. Melanson had studied and written about political violence in the United States, and the two soon decided to continue the probe begun by Lowenstein. A year later, a formal request for release of the case files was made to the Los Angeles Police Commission by the newly endowed University of Massachusetts RFK Assassination Archives, of which Melanson was director. A group of nineteen journalists, academics, and political officials wrote letters supporting disclosure. These included RFK biographer and adviser Arthur Schlesinger, Jr., Massachusetts congressman Barney Frank, forensic scientist Dr. Cyril Wecht, and Kennedy Library archivist Henry Gwiazda. Several film industry people also wrote letters. Said historian Schlesinger: "There would seem no reason why, seventeen years after this tragic event, this information should still be withheld. The material is of indisputable historic significance. . . . Every consideration of scholarly and national interest calls for disclosure of all information related to Robert Kennedy's death."

The publicly stated rationale for keeping the files secret had always been murky. During hearings before the police commission in 1975, Chief Daryl

Gates claimed that release of the files would jeopardize rights to privacy. "There are still people who are living that I think would be harmed, seriously harmed," said Gates.[13] But whom was he referring to? If Sirhan alone had shot Robert Kennedy and the police had conducted an honest investigation, who could be harmed by release of the investigation files?

During a police commission hearing in February 1985, Commissioner Samuel Williams questioned Professor Melanson about the privacy issue.

"Can you tell me," he said emphatically, "that if someone was staying as a guest in the [Ambassador] hotel that night, and no one knew they were there, that information would not come out?"

So this was it? The investigation files in one of the most important political murders of the century were being withheld (at that point for seventeen years) because some politicians or private citizens might have been staying at the hotel with women who were not their wives? Melanson tried to sidestep the question.

"In past disclosures," he responded, "at both the state and federal level, rights to privacy have been protected by those agencies conducting the disclosure."

"Specifically, would that not come out?" Williams repeated.

"It may or may not," conceded Melanson. "There's no fixed standard."

In the end public pressure helped the commission overcome its concerns about secret hotel visits. At a highly charged hearing on July 30, 1985, it voted to release the LAPD's *Summary Report* first, then the main file. The commission's formal motion, however, left room for extreme censorship by promulgating the following "standard": ". . . remove items that are prohibited by law from being released, and those items which were to be held in confidence per agreements with other public agencies and information from informants; with due respect to issues of privacy and national security *and any other privileges not enumerated above* [emphasis added].

The motion carried no timetable. The petitioners were puzzled by the emphasis on national security in a domestic assassination which officially had no conspiracy dimension, foreign or domestic.

Chief Daryl Gates made a final pitch to the commission: release the file at a "future date certain" when no one could be harmed, but not now. Later in the hallway a reporter asked Gates what date he had in mind. "In the 1990s," he replied.

Despite his history of fierce resistance to opening the files, Daryl Gates, in a remarkable passage in his 1992 book *Chief: My Life in the LAPD,* credited himself with disclosure:

> By now, everyone was demanding to see our files. Personally, I had no objection to opening them up. The problem was, the files contained information given to us on a confidential basis. We had

all kinds of information from people who were around the senator, what they were doing, who they were with, *private* information. I didn't think we had any right to disregard a confidential relationship. This only added more fuel to the conspiracy theories. "If the police weren't hiding something, they'd let us into that file. So they're hiding something, they know there's a conspiracy, and that's why they won't give us that file."

Finally, I got so sick of this, I recommended the files be placed in the hands of our archivist, pointed out what we thought was confidential and let him worry what to do about it.[14]

After a year of foot-dragging and broken promises, the *Summary Report* was released by the police commission with great fanfare. Despite reminders from the prodisclosure group that the report was merely a secondhand summary of the primary case record and should have been released seventeen years earlier, the media bought the spin generated by the LAPD and the commission: that this was a landmark in public disclosure and would satisfactorily answer any reasonable questions regarding the case.

"Sirhan Acted Alone: Probe" was the UPI headline. The story went on to reveal that, after 5,500 hours of police work, the newly released report concluded "that most people making conspiracy charges were 'lying for one reason or another.' "

Despite the positive reviews, the value of the *Summary Report* had been greatly reduced by those who processed it for release. Taking full advantage of the police commission's guidelines, the report had been "redacted" (a favorite term among the commissioners) to the point where the name of almost every witness and investigating officer was deleted. Numerous paragraphs and pages were also blacked out. Researchers who wanted to know who said what to what investigator were completely stymied. Hope for any real revelations, and for holding the LAPD accountable, then rested in the release of the primary file. But how and when would that happen?

In 1986, in response to continued public pressure, Los Angeles mayor Tom Bradley appointed a distinguished committee of archivists, jurists, and professors to find a suitable repository for the LAPD files. Though not yet in the public domain, the investigation file—at least what remained of it—was out of the department's hands for the first time since it resided in writer Theodore Taylor's garage.

While the battle to open the LAPD files was being waged before the police commission in 1985, a separate attempt was launched to secure the case files of the FBI. A decade earlier the late Bernard Fensterwald, Washington attorney and assassination researcher, had used the Freedom of Information Act (FOIA) to obtain three thousand pages of RFK assassination documents and photos from the FBI, including the crucial photos of the holes in the pantry doorframe which the Bureau labeled "bullet holes."

While the documents pried free by Fensterwald provided important insights into the case, researchers were quite sure that the complete FBI file was many times larger. The difficulty in formulating any FOIA request resides in asking for files using the code names they are actually stored under. For example, a person might petition the FBI for its "Sirhan" file without knowing that the FBI's main file was stored under the the the name "KEN-SALT" (assault on Senator Kennedy). Without clues to a broader search the petitioner would get only what was in the requested file.

Under the direction of attorney Jim Lesar of Washington and cocounsel Lawrence Teeter of Los Angeles, Gregory Stone and Philip Melanson filed a seven-page request letter. It requested headquarters and field office files and asked that searches be conducted for a strange list of acronyms and rubrics. The outcome of this carefully designed, broad-spectrum search was 32,000 pages of previously unreleased documents—a tenfold increase on the 1975 release to Fensterwald.

Documents were processed in Washington, D.C., and shipped to the Robert F. Kennedy Assassination Archives in Massachusetts in batches of 1,500 to 2,500 pages. Some were heavily deleted. But the censorship of selected sentences, paragraphs, and pages was accompanied by a far more troublesome one: the name of every agent who worked on the case was blacked out. Lesar and Teeter immediately wrote to the Bureau requesting that the practice be halted and the names restored. They pointed out that in similar releases on the assassinations of President Kennedy and Dr. King, agents' names were not expunged. Why do so in the RFK case?

The Bureau refused the request, arguing that the agents' privacy out-weighed the value of historical research. The FBI did, however, offer to restore the name of any agent within the precise context in which it may have been previously disclosed. Thus, if the petitioners could provide documentation that an agent had conducted a particular interview, the Bureau would restore that agent's name to the released interview.

Stone and Melanson rejected this offer to give them what they already had and instead responded with a list of over one hundred agents who had worked on the case, garnered from books, newspapers, and previously re-leased documents. They argued that it was not a matter of privacy, since the identities of most agents were in the public record. The real issue was which agents did what, when, and how in this controversial investigation.

Five congressmen wrote FBI director William Webster and asked that the names not be deleted. In a written response Webster said: "The identities of remaining FBI and other law enforcement personnel are being withheld as disclosure would constitute an unwarranted invasion of their privacy. . . . Public identification could conceivably subject them to harassment or annoyance in the conduct of their official duties and in their private lives."

The dispute was taken to federal court (*Stone and Melanson v. Federal Bureau of Investigation*, No. 90–5065 D.C. Cir.). The case for disclosure seemed to the plaintiffs to be clear. Witnesses' names were not deleted. How could public servants accountable for their conduct have a more elevated right to privacy than witnesses? Lesar and Teeter argued that deletion of the names effectively insulated the Bureau from scrutiny of its performance in the case and all but precluded meaningful research by scholars and journalists.

The plaintiffs mustered nineteen supporting affidavits testifying to the importance of the names, the precedents for disclosing them, and the absence of any problems in previous releases of agents' names. These came from professors, reporters, authors who had written books about the Bureau, a former agent, and a former director of the Bureau's Freedom of Information Office.

Government lawyers produced no supporting affidavits. Although the FBI's major claim was that agents would be harassed, there was not a single statement documenting that this had ever occurred.

But in January 1989, federal judge Charles Richey issued a decision in favor of the FBI. He ruled that the agents involved "have a legitimate interest in preserving the secrecy of matters that conceivably could subject them to annoyance or harassment in either their official or private lives." Richey asserted that the passage of time had heightened the agents' legitimate expectation of privacy: they were *more* entitled to it now than in 1968. The judge ignored the augmented importance of the agents' names, given the issue of extra bullets and the conflict between FBI photos showing "bullet holes" and the LAPD's assertion that such holes did not exist.

On April 19, 1988, twenty years after the assassination, public disclosure of the primary case file was finally achieved. The panel appointed by Mayor Bradley had decided upon the California State Archives in Sacramento as the proper repository for the files. The archives were under the direction of state archivist John Burns, who oversaw the sorting and cataloging of the fifty thousand pages of material.

Under Burns's direction there was virtually no censorship. The names and most of the deleted passages were restored to the *Summary Report*. However, Burns and his staff could only disclose what they were given by the LAPD. During two decades of secrecy, key evidence and materials had been lost or destroyed. In a public report archivist Burns made note of these items:

Police admitted the destruction of the door jambs and ceiling tiles, removed from the crime scene. A .22 caliber projectile taken from

Sirhan pocket (evidence item #6) is also missing. 2410 photographs collected in the case were destroyed approximately 2 ½ months after the shooting. Archives photo indexes note that photos related to bullet fragments and shell casings, comparison tests, Kennedy clothing, gun firing tests, witness re-enactment of shooting, and tracing and location of bullets are absent from the file.

The press, which had been overly kind to the police two years earlier when the heavily edited *Summary Report* was released, now ran critical reports on the missing items. On *The ABC Evening News,* Peter Jennings spoke about the newly opened files saying they provided "some answers, and some more questions." A segment followed, reported by ABC correspondent Ken Kashiwahara:

> KASHIWAHARA: They are reminders of a national tragedy and controversy: 50,000 documents collected by the Los Angeles police after the murder of Robert Kennedy. . . . But the public release of the murder evidence has failed to answer questions about whether there was a *second* gunman because of evidence that is missing. State Archives officials say that a bullet taken from Sirhan's pocket is missing and that the police destroyed more than 2,400 photographs. Did Sirhan act alone?
>
> JOHN BURNS (CALIFORNIA STATE ARCHIVIST): I have gone through this material extensively but I can say that I *cannot* draw a firm conclusion.[15]

Although the doorframes and the ceiling tiles had been on record as being destroyed for over a decade, for many people this was the first notice. The police, on the other hand, were ready with their justifications. During an interview on Los Angeles television, retired Chief of Detectives Robert Houghton tried to explain the missing doorframes.

> "After the trial was over and I can't remember who it was came to me and asked me ah—whether or not it would be proper to destroy or get rid of those doorjambs. . . . And I presume they asked that the tile, about the tiles at the same time, to store them for . . . as we intended to do . . . in perpetuity, without taking up a lot of space. . . . So I told them if they had the adequate, ah, ah, evidence . . . from those doors . . . er, the doorjambs . . . ah, then go ahead and destroy them, as long as that evidence maintained in, was maintained in file; if anybody is, ah, curious about that they should go to the actual record where people, experts were testifying under oath, in my opinion."[16]

In a newspaper interview Houghton said that the idea that police had destroyed important evidence was "just crap." Speaking again about the possibility of bullet holes, he remarked, "There were holes all over the place, but not bullet holes. . . . Look, all you have to do is go to the trial testimony. . . . All this came out at the trial."[17] Houghton, of course, was incorrect: there was no testimony at the trial concerning any holes in the hotel pantry.

In a statement to UPI, former Los Angeles chief of police Edward Davis characterized the disclosure process. "It's like opening up a collection of pornography to a bunch of sex-hungry pornography addicts," he said. "They're going to fondle the gun, touch the wood, stick their fingers in the bullet holes."

As colorful as Davis's statement was, the former chief of police had apparently forgotten several facts: 1) "the wood," presumably the door-frames, had been secretly destroyed by the police twenty years earlier, and 2) according to the police, there were no bullet holes.

Although the "missing items" grabbed the headlines, the true significance of the file release was that for the first time it was possible to see if the official version of the crime was borne out by the physical evidence and the surviving interview transcripts. The reason for keeping the *Summary Report* secret quickly became clear. Now, for the first time, witnesses could be shown what it is the police asserted they had said. Some would forcefully deny making the statements. In other cases where the *Summary Report* asserted that a witness had admitted fabricating a story, all that could be found in the interview transcripts was the admission that the witness lacked an absolute certainty. In other instances where witnesses had changed their story, transcripts and tapes of those sessions revealed the extreme pressure to which these witnesses were subjected by police interrogators.

Over the next several years, as researchers sifted through the thousands of pages of documents and hundreds of audiotapes, it became clear that there had been many instances of misconduct by the police. As a result of these discoveries a working committee was formed under the banner of the Truth and Accountability Foundation, an organization founded by Gregory Stone. The committee (including Stone, Floyd Nelson, Paul Schrade, journalist Dan Moldea, and Philip Melanson) began to collate their research into the newly opened files.

But then tragedy struck. On a sunny afternoon in late January 1991, Gregory Stone drove to a local park, sat under a tree, and took his own life with a pistol. Unknown to most of those around him, Stone had been engaged in a losing battle against depression. The news of his death stunned his colleagues on the Robert Kennedy case. After a period of shock and reflection, a decision was made by the group to continue the work and proceed with a new legal initiative. A year later, on April 2, 1992, a petition, officially referred to as a "Request," was presented to the Los Angeles County Grand Jury by Paul Schrade, who had been wounded the night Kennedy was murdered, twenty-four years earlier.

The Request was a fifty-page document, supported by eight hundred pages of exhibits. It began:

> This Request to the Los Angeles County Grand Jury is being submitted because newly discovered evidence indicates that the Los Angeles Police Department ("LAPD") engaged in "willful and corrupt misconduct" in its investigation of the assassination of Senator Robert Kennedy. . . . This evidence shows that the LAPD was on notice of substantial evidence that at least one more gun was being fired at the same time that Sirhan was firing his gun, which evidence the LAPD decided to ignore. In addition, the evidence shows that the LAPD ignored material evidentiary leads, engaged in a concerted cover-up of its failures, and otherwise failed to conduct a thorough investigation of the crime.

The Request asserted that the LAPD's acts of misconduct included the destruction of evidence, the falsification of evidence, and the coercion of witnesses, which it described in its subsequent pages. The Request then asked the grand jury to appoint a special prosecutor to investigate the alleged acts of misconduct and to take action against those it found guilty of "obstruction of justice." It was signed by over fifty individuals and organizations, including the Southern California ACLU, actors Edward Asner and Martin Sheen, United Farm Workers president Cesar Chavez, former presidents of the American Academy of Forensic Sciences Dr. Robert Joling and Dr. Cyril Wecht, filmmaker Oliver Stone, former Senate Watergate Committee chief counsel Samuel Dash, author Norman Mailer, former RFK press secretary Frank Mankiewicz, historian Arthur Schlesinger, Jr., and Harvard law professor Gary Bellows.

In asserting its legal foundation the petition cited section 919c of the California Penal Code: "The grand jury shall inquire into the willful or corrupt misconduct in office of public officers of every description within the county." The petition maintained that its cause was timely under the rules of discovery because "decisive new evidence has been discovered in the LAPD's files on this case, which were released for public inspection only as recently as April 1988."

Official reaction to the Request was carefully muted. "This has been looked at a number of times before, and it hasn't resulted in anything different," said Chief of Police Daryl Gates, "so I am not going to comment on it."[18]

The timing of the submission was awkward. The sitting grand jury had only two months' tenure, not enough time to consider the document placed before them. Without recommendation it was passed on to the incoming jury. In the spring of the following year four members of the Criminal Justice Committee met with Paul Schrade and Marilyn Barrett, attorney for the petitioners. Both Schrade and Barrett left the meeting with the impression that the committee was interested in "doing something." What followed were several months of silence. Finally on June 22, 1993, more than a year after the submission of the petition, Marilyn Barrett received a letter of one sentence:

> With regard to your concerns about the Los Angeles Police Department's policies and procedures governing the safeguarding of evidence, the Criminal Justice Committee of the 1992–93 Los Angeles County Grand Jury has looked into the matter and has discussed it with the Los Angeles Police Department.
>
> John A. Grande, Foreperson

"Discussed it?" said a disappointed Paul Schrade in an incredulous moment. "We asked the grand jury to investigate the LAPD, not go have lunch with them."

Attempting to stimulate the grand jury into meeting its responsibilities, Barrett wrote back, thanking the jurors for their attention. She then asked if the jury would be good enough to answer several questions. Who were the LAPD officers the Criminal Justice Committee had met with? What actions did the grand jury or the LAPD take against officers accused of misconduct? If no action was taken, what was the reason? Did the grand jury analyze evidence that more than one gun was fired during the murder? If so, what were its findings? And so forth. "Responses to the foregoing questions," wrote Barrett, "will greatly help to assure the public that its very legitimate concerns have not been disregarded."

In a telephone call following her letter Marilyn Barrett was advised by John Grande that the 1992–93 grand jury would not have time to respond to her letter but would forward it along with the Request to the incoming jury for action. Later in the summer Barrett discovered that the Request had not been forwarded, but had been logged as "closed." In September she resubmitted the Request, reminding the grand jury that "the public's right to demand accountability is indisputable. Nevertheless [they have] yet to get a full accounting from the LAPD concerning its destruction of evidence (much of which was destroyed even before Sirhan Sirhan's criminal trial began or appeals from his conviction were heard)."

In February, Barrett received a letter stating that the material she had submitted had been already "thoroughly analyzed." The letter invited her to submit anything new she might have, but requested that she refrain from "reargument or reiteration." It was signed "Terry L. White, Grand Jury Legal Advisor." White was an employee of the district attorney's office.

In her reply a month later Barrett asserted, "There is simply no justification for the conclusion that the previously submitted information has already been appropriately handled. The obligation of the Grand Jury . . . remains unfulfilled." Barrett then questioned the involvement of Terry White. "In view of Mr. White's employment in the DA's office, any participation whatsoever by him in your deliberations on this case would be a clear violation of the conflict of interest rules."

Barrett then accepted the invitation to submit new material. Over the preceding months she had gained access to files in the district attorney's office concerning the Robert Kennedy case, files which had not been made public previously. "In reviewing the DA's files," she wrote, "I found a number of documents that suggest the DA's office itself was involved in covering up an inadequate investigation by the LAPD and its own office." What followed were nine single-spaced, typed pages summarizing additional evidence of official wrongdoing.

In early May, Barrett got a phone call from the chairperson of what was now called the Criminal Justice Systems Committee, inviting her and Paul Schrade to meet with the committee in private. The meeting took place on May 10 at the County Courthouse. Both Barrett and Schrade were immediately impressed with the caliber of jurors and their apparent interest in the subject. Then the bad news. The jurors informed the petitioners that they had no power to investigate any action without prior approval of the district attorney.

Schrade and Barrett were shocked. "That, of course, is not our reading of the statute," Barrett commented later. "I believe they were being honest with us. I just think that's what they were told." The remaining discussion centered upon recommendations the grand jury could make to safeguard evidence in the future. Schrade and Barrett left. After more than two years, the effort to hold the LAPD accountable for its actions by going through proper legal channels was finished.

The sting of this final setback had barely had time to sink in when, the next morning in the *Los Angeles Times,* a column by Bill Boyarsky attacked outright the grand jury system.

> The Los Angeles County Grand Jury is supposed to be the people's watchdog, exposing corruption and inefficiency in government. . . . As anyone familiar with the process knows, that isn't the way it works. . . . Smart politicians have long been aware of the situation. So when reporters uncover waste or dirty dealings, the pols immediately turn the matter over to the grand jury. They do this

knowing the panel will never have the time to investigate. It's like dumping a potential scandal into a bottomless pit.

Boyarsky, it turns out, had been approached by two jurors from the 1992–93 grand jury, Don Dodd and Richard Mankiewicz, who a year earlier had been on the committee which met with Schrade and Barrett. Their complaints were now printed in Boyarsky's column. "It is our view that it is a mistake for anyone to serve on the Los Angeles County Grand Jury," the two reported. "One cannot escape the conclusion that grand juries are merely meant to give the appearance of citizen watchdogs, but are prevented from acting as such."

In a telephone interview with the authors Mankiewicz told why he thought the grand jury system was so ineffective. "Because you are all twenty-three virgins," he explained, "it takes you months to figure out what you are supposed to be doing." Mankiewicz remembered the Request and the presentation made by Schrade and Barrett, but indicated that there simply was not the time or the resources for the jury to act independently. "If powerful people want something covered up, it will be covered up," he said. "And the grand jury can't do anything about it. By the end of our term we realized that the grand jury as now constituted is useless except as a flunky for the district attorney."

SIXTEEN

Prison and Parole

✻ ✻ ✻

*Sirhan is a political assassin. His murder of Senator Kennedy was
an act intended to kill more than a man or woman. It was different.
It was an act intended to kill a living and vital part of our
democratic and representative government.*

—Los Angeles district attorney John Van de Kamp, 1981

O N NOVEMBER 13, 1970, while
Sirhan Sirhan was occupying a cell
on San Quentin's death row, a legal appeal on his behalf by attorney Luke
McKissack was filed with the Supreme Court of California. Two years
earlier Grant Cooper had considered McKissack, then in his mid–twenties,
for the position of interim attorney in the original trial, but had decided
instead upon the more tread-worn Russell Parsons. After the trial, with
Cooper, Berman, and Parsons no longer actively involved, McKissack had
assumed the position of lead attorney.

The appeal brief, eight hundred pages in length, contained eighteen
formal arguments questioning the adequacy of Sirhan's trial. Many of the
points had been argued by the trial attorneys. There were objections to
the court's rejection of the original plea bargain agreement, objections to
the legality of the seizure of evidence from Sirhan's home, objections concerning the makeup of the grand jury and the trial jury, and an assertion
that Sirhan didn't have the capacity to maturely and meaningfully reflect
upon the gravity of his crime.

Prior to his assumption of the Sirhan appeal, McKissack's most well
known clients were Black Panthers Angela Davis and Elmer Pratt. Davis
had been accused of providing guns for a deadly courtroom escape attempt
in San Rafael. Pratt had been accused of murder in Los Angeles. (Davis
would be subsequently acquitted, Pratt convicted.) With Sirhan Sirhan
added to this list, McKissack became the object of abnormal scrutiny by
Los Angeles authorities, and a number of unflattering memos about him
circulated. One, written to Los Angeles district attorney Joe Busch on June

3, 1971, stamped "CONFIDENTIAL," asserted that "according to a confidential source (so far proven to be reliable), McKissack and friends are actively participating in various Panther (Pratt faction) criminal plots. . . . Over the past four months we have received information from several sources which describe criminal conduct on the part of Luke McKissack."

The following month another memo written to DA Busch by Richard Hecht, head of the Organized Crime and Pornography Division, alleged that "a Black Panther working in the Clerk's Office had assisted another person in switching bullets which were part of the Sirhan evidence" and that this person "still has a friend in the Clerk's Office involved in altering and/or changing the Sirhan exhibits." The motive for the Black Panthers to alter evidence in the Sirhan case now had a rationale, however strange: McKissack represented both.

Another document in the files of the DA's office was a bizarre, unsigned spiderweb diagram. It showed the purported nefarious interlocking relationships of people involved in either the Sirhan appeal or the challenge to the competency and integrity of LAPD criminalist DeWayne Wolfer. In this diagram McKissack was identified as a "communist" who had "past felony involvement, including conspiracy murders + cocaine to panther in court." McKissack's co-attorney in the appeal, George Shibley, was also designated "communist." So was attorney Barbara Blehr, who had mounted the public challenge to DeWayne Wolfer's promotion to chief forensic chemist.

The claims of criminal misconduct on the part of Luke McKissack were baseless, as were the claims against Shibley and Blehr. They are perhaps best understood as representative of the siege mentality then rampant in Los Angeles law enforcement, part of a general strategy to discredit anyone involved in left-wing politics or who questioned the official version of the Robert Kennedy murder. Although a grand jury was convened to hear complaints against the County Clerk's Office for mismanaging access to the Sirhan exhibits, no charges were ever filed.

On February 18, 1972, the California Supreme Court ruled by a vote of 6 to 1 that the death penalty as practiced in California violated the state constitution's prohibition against cruel and unusual punishment. "We have concluded that capital punishment is impermissibly cruel," said the court. "It degrades and dehumanizes all who participate in its process." In its decision the court held that the cruelty of the punishment "lies not only in the execution itself and the pain incident thereto, but also in the dehumanizing effects of the lengthy imprisonment prior to execution."

The day the court's decision was announced, a picture of a broadly smiling Mary Sirhan dominated the front page of the *Los Angeles Times*. Out of the 104 persons on death row in California, Sirhan Sirhan had become the poster boy for the abolition of the death penalty.

"This is the happiest day of my life," Mrs. Sirhan was quoted as saying. "I just knelt on my knees and prayed and thanked God for what He did and the mercy He had."[1] The *Los Angeles Times* praised the new ruling as "a decision of persuasive clarity and wisdom."[2]

Reaction by public officials was less enthusiastic. Sirhan's prosecutor, Evelle J. Younger, now attorney general of the state of California, called the new ruling "ill-advised" and suggested several remedies, including a state constitutional amendment. The attorney general argued that the court was applying its own definition of cruelty and not that of society. He also voiced contempt for the court's ruling that long delays in carrying out the death sentence were a determining factor, citing "the procrastination which this court has built into our system of criminal justice."[3]

Four months later, on June 16, the California Supreme Court denied Sirhan's appeal, filed two years earlier by Luke McKissack, and upheld his conviction for the murder of Robert Kennedy. At the same time, in accordance with their ruling in February, the court reduced Sirhan's sentence to life in prison. This action was reinforced two weeks later when the United States Supreme Court, by a ruling of 5 to 4, struck down as "cruel and unusual" the death penalty laws as then written in most states.

In December of 1974 former congressman Allard Lowenstein, a friend of Robert Kennedy who had begun his own investigation into the murder, petitioned Los Angeles district attorney Joseph Busch to reopen the Sirhan case. Lowenstein cited three reasons to reopen the investigation.

> Evidence which indicates that at least nine bullets were fired during the assassination, and Sirhan's gun held only eight.
>
> Evidence which showed the gun to have been fired inches from Senator Kennedy's head, and witnesses said Sirhan never got that close.
>
> Ballistics which indicated a television news producer wounded during the shooting was shot by a gun other than the one which killed Senator Kennedy.[4]

Joseph Busch rejected Lowenstein's plea, saying that these questions were answered during the original investigation conducted by the police. He added that he would be more inclined to open the case if the request came directly from Sirhan's attorney.

Four weeks later such a request came, not to DA Busch, but to the

California Supreme Court. It came in the form of a writ of error coram nobis. The writ differed from the appeal filed previously on Sirhan's behalf because, as the appeal was unable to do, the writ requested the high court to consider evidence in the Sirhan case beyond the trial record. Attorney Godfrey Isaac, who had drawn up the fifty-five-page document, claimed to newsmen that the new evidence "tended to show that Senator Robert Kennedy was not killed by bullets from Sirhan's gun." He went on to assert that this evidence had been "deliberately, intentionally and willingly suppressed by the prosecution and their agents."[5]

The following month, the California high court turned down, without comment, Isaac's attempt to reopen the case. In reaction to the decision Sirhan's attorney said he believed that the evidence presented in the writ "showed scientifically that Sirhan could not have committed this act . . . It is difficult to accept, as final, a determination made without a court hearing."[6]

Despite the failure of Isaac's writ, the winds of change continued to blow favorably for Sirhan in 1975. As a result of a quickly growing prison population and the increased practice of sentencing criminals to open-ended and widely varying prison terms, a movement developed in California to institute more uniformity and certainty into the sentencing and parole policies. A motion was introduced into the state legislature to end indeterminate sentencing; several lawsuits challenged the prolonged incarceration of inmates. Thus in March 1975, in response to this pressure, the nine-member California Adult Authority instituted a new set of guidelines, establishing a fixed range of sentences for each type of crime. These guidelines were also to be applied to men already in prison serving indeterminate sentences, giving them "a date certain" when they could expect to be released. Among the reasons stated for this new policy was the tendency of the system to hold men who had committed highly publicized crimes much longer than those who had committed more egregious but less noted ones.

Pursuant to this new policy, on May 20, 1975, a three-member panel of the Adult Authority interviewed Sirhan over a two-day period. They then granted him a parole date of February 23, 1986. Questioned by the press, the chairman of the Adult Authority, Ray K. Procunier, praised the decision of the panel. "I'm proud as hell that [they] didn't search for some bogus reason to deny him [Sirhan] or refer it to someone else," he said. "It would have been simple to rationalize, to do the popular thing and avoid the issue . . . This should prove we don't have any political prisoners."[7]

Citing figures which showed that men convicted of first-degree murder "have been going out, on the average, in about 11 years," state prison official Philip Guthrie also defended the 1986 date, which would have given

Sirhan almost eighteen years of time served. "He's at the top of the range for most inmates," Guthrie said. "The Adult Authority didn't choose to deny him or go beyond the range because they figured the guy had been well-behaved and it would be difficult to say that because of who he killed he was going to do more time."[8]

In the same way he had played a symbolic role when the death penalty was abolished, it was inevitable that Sirhan would become the focus for the debate on the new parole policy. News of his parole date, still a decade away, made front-page headlines. The *Los Angeles Times* published a cartoon showing a smiling Sirhan sitting in his cell marking off the days till his release.[9]

There was also published in the *Times* an impassioned protest of Sirhan's parole date by State Treasurer Jesse Unruh, who had helped rescue Sirhan from a violent crowd the night of the murder:

> Sirhan did not commit "just another murder." The record clearly indicates he planned and carried out a political assassination. The .22 caliber bullets which he fired into Robert Kennedy did far more than kill Rose Kennedy's third son; they wiped out the votes of 1.4 million Californians cast just hours before. These shots also destroyed the hopes of millions of other Americans, let alone of other peoples around the world.
>
> The act was treason—and its perpetrator should be treated as a traitor as well as a murderer.[10]

Unruh's missive brought a flood of letters. Most were outspoken in their desire to have Sirhan's parole date revoked. Some, however, took issue with Unruh's logic:

> Unruh notes Kennedy's 1.4 million votes; suppose he'd only received half as many? Twice as many? Does the value of Kennedy's life or the length of Sirhan's term go up or down accordingly? Suppose the personal loss to me of my girlfriend . . . would be greater than the loss of a local politician. Yes, we must protect our politicians, but who are they? Is Bob Dylan included?[11]

Following his receipt of a parole date, Sirhan was transferred from San Quentin, where he had been residing on death row, to Soledad. There, though still in a special protected unit, he would have more contact with other prisoners. Shortly thereafter the Los Angeles district attorney's office began to hear from prisoners who claimed to have exclusive information about Sirhan.

One of these was Daniel T. Estrada, who was in San Quentin with

Sirhan from 1972 to 1973. In his audiotaped interview with the DA's chief investigator on the RFK case, William Burnett, Estrada claimed to have occupied the cell next to the convicted assassin for seven months. Estrada told Burnett that he had information that Sirhan had been behind the prison murder of an inmate named Ronald Woods. The reason? According to Estrada, Sirhan had told Woods that "there were more people involved" in the Kennedy assassination. Thus Woods had to be silenced.

In 1977 Carmen Falzone, a recently released inmate who had been with Sirhan in Soledad, also approached investigator Burnett with a story. Falzone claimed that he was recruited by Sirhan to help in a plan with Sirhan's brothers to steal plutonium and smuggle it to Libyan leader Mu'ammar Gadhafi. During the taped session with Burnett, Falzone reported that Sirhan told him: "I did it by myself," referring to the murder of Robert Kennedy. Then, according to Falzone, Sirhan reenacted the crime. "Oh, he showed me how he brought the gun up with his left hand, 'cause I stopped him. I goes, 'Whoa—you're left-handed?' He says, 'I can shoot with either hand.' That's a direct quote."

Falzone then described how worked up Sirhan got over this piece of theater. "He was enraged," says Falzone. "Always obscenities. The word Kennedy and fuck were synonymous."

Daniel Estrada had miscalculated. The DA's office wasn't interested in stories about a conspiracy to murder Robert Kennedy. But Carmen Falzone's tale had allure. Here Sirhan is both a lone assassin and a dangerous conspiratorial terrorist.

As the tape of his meeting with the DA's investigator reveals, Falzone finds a willing ear for his story. The former inmate agrees to follow additional leads in the Libyan plot, so long as he is compensated "for expenses." He then comes up with another condition. "I do not want to be under the jurisdiction of a parole office," he says, "where somebody can pull a couple of strings and find out where the fuck I live."

"If you come forward," Burnett responds, "you wanna pull a vanishing act on us and disappear out of sight?"

"After it's over; yes, I do."

In 1978 *Playboy* magazine would run the story of the Libyan plutonium plot in an article titled "Inside Sirhan." A full-page drawing of Sirhan's face accompanied the story, with a keyhole drawn in place of the mouth, implying that *Playboy* had finally been able to unlock the hidden thoughts of "America's most secretive assassin." The article claimed that while at Soledad Sirhan had formed "an intimate bond of trust with a cellmate who, for the first time, reveals the twisted mind of Robert Kennedy's killer."

The "cellmate" who had sold the story to *Playboy* was Carmen Falzone, who might better have been described as a fellow inmate, since Sirhan did not share his cell with anyone. In the article Falzone was described as a "master criminal" who specialized in "sophisticated con jobs." "The first couple of months," Falzone said of his relationship with Sirhan, "I thought he was kinda neat, and he thought I was kinda neat. He knew who I was— the superburglar on the tier—and I knew who he was. I was attracted to him, sure: He has an aura of power around him. . . . I was curious; I wanted to get into his pants. It was a challenge."

Falzone described Sirhan to *Playboy* as "the perfect terrorist," who, with "hate oozing out of him," had confessed to Falzone that he made up his "psycho act" and "all that trance and hypnosis stuff." (For the record, Sirhan has always denied that he was psychotic and has never claimed that he was hypnotized.) Falzone intimated that Sirhan was receiving messages from Mu'ammar Gadhafi through Sirhan's brother Adel.

Falzone then went on to describe the Libyan plot: First, Falzone would make parole. Then, once on the outside, he would smuggle a saw, some amphetamines, and a radio transmitter to Sirhan concealed in a canned ham at Christmas. Finally, the day of the escape would come. Sirhan would ingest the pills, saw the bars on his windows, and climb down to a roof below. He would then radio Falzone, who would appear in a helicopter which, using a cargo net, would pluck Sirhan off the roof.

Where would they go? According to Falzone he would stash Sirhan in a specially equipped tractor-trailer rig and then hide him on the nation's interstate highway system. "I'd have a radio scanner, TV monitors, living space, the works in the truck," reported Falzone.

And the nuclear material for Gadhafi? Falzone reported that Sirhan wanted "50 tactical nuclear weapons."

How would these be obtained? "I could probably go onto a SAC base," said Falzone, "meet some people, force some favors, then fly in a cargo plane or roll in the right vehicle, all with the right looking people, and hand them some dummy papers, then drink a cup of coffee while they load what I want for me. . . . I tell you the guy had it all figured out."

As reported by *Playboy,* Falzone was so disturbed by this plan that he decided to go to the DA, because he was hoping they would "do something about the potential danger." *Playboy* then quoted a "spokesman" for the district attorney's office who said, "We asked Mr. Falzone to take a polygraph examination and he passed the polygraph on the stories Sirhan supposedly told him."[12]

As bizarre and patently unlikely as it was, the Libyan plutonium story would surface again three years later, this time in a petition submitted to the Board of Prison Terms (the new name for the California Adult Authority) by Los Angeles County district attorney John Van de Kamp. His petition sought a hearing to rescind Sirhan's scheduled parole, arguing that Sirhan should not be released "because political assassination tears at the very fabric of a democratic society." Among the witnesses Van de Kamp proposed to bring before the board was Carmen Falzone.

The petition apparently had great meaning to Van de Kamp, because he delivered it in person to Sacramento, whereupon he held a press conference. He held another the same day when he returned to Los Angeles. The *Los Angeles Times,* which supported Van de Kamp's position editorially, had the good sense to describe the district attorney as "an unannounced candidate for state attorney general."

Van de Kamp's petition alleged that Carmen Falzone had revealed to authorities "some rather startling facts about Sirhan." It then reviewed the plot to steal nuclear material and send it to Gadhafi. The story, as it was intended, made headlines in the California newspapers. The *Los Angeles Times* reported that Van de Kamp said that Falzone passed a lie detector test regarding his statements.[13]

In addition to Falzone, Van de Kamp had several other witnesses with stories to tell about Sirhan. One was Philip C. Clark, a former inmate at San Quentin, who was prepared to say that Sirhan had told him he was a member of the Black September cell of the Palestine Liberation Organization, and had been assigned to murder Edward Kennedy, Ronald Reagan, and former secretary of defense Robert McNamara. A third story revealed in Van de Kamp's petition was from an inmate named Lawrence Eugene Wilson, who had been convicted of murdering a man while committing a robbery at a motel. Wilson told authorities that he had had a conversation with Sirhan the previous year. The alleged conversation was printed in the newspapers:

> WILSON: I wonder, if Ted Kennedy were to become President, if he would be assassinated, because of what happened to his two brothers?
>
> SIRHAN: I know he would be. If I get out of here in 1984 and he's still President, I'll do it myself.
>
> WILSON: Haven't you done enough time?
>
> SIRHAN: Well, I've got a commitment to certain things and my commitment is that I've got to take care of business.[14]

Several days after John Van de Kamp's petition was filed, the California Board of Prison Terms released documents which disputed the district attorney's portrayal of Sirhan as a self-proclaimed terrorist. In these documents prison officer J. V. Billman was quoted as saying, "I believe Lawrence Wilson's account to be a malicious fabrication. I have never known Sirhan to discuss any aspect of this case with anyone."[15]

Van de Kamp's campaign against parole spurred a flurry of local comment on his petition, most of it favorable. A few letters to the *Times* protested the district attorney's motives and logic. One writer asked: "Does our esteemed DA feel that the punishment should fit the victim rather than the crime?"[16]

Another commented: "Van de Kamp said, 'My position is that a political assassination should not be compared with an average murder because it tears at the very fabric of a democratic society.' Average murder? What is the definition of an average murder? Each and every murder, regardless of a victim's name or reputation, tears at the very fabric of a democratic society."[17]

Van de Kamp's initiative resulted in a hearing before the Board of Prison Terms in late April 1982. About a week before the hearing an article by staff writer Bill Farr appeared in the *Los Angeles Times* alleging that Lawrence Eugene Wilson was now suspected of forging the name of author Joseph Wambaugh on a letter to the parole board urging his release. The very next day another article written by Farr appeared with the headline "FBI Hunting Witness in Sirhan Case." The story read:

> Carmen Falzone, a former prison inmate scheduled to be a key witness in Dist. Atty. John Van de Kamp's effort to keep Sirhan Sirhan behind bars, is now a fugitive being sought by the FBI.
>
> The FBI confirmed Thursday that a warrant charging Falzone with interstate transportation of stolen property has been issued by the bureau's Salt Lake City office.
>
> The charge stems from the theft of a $750,000 coin collection from safe deposit boxes in a Salt Lake City bank.[18]

The Farr story then quoted state Board of Prison Terms chairman Raymond C. Brown. "Falzone is still on the list of witnesses for the Sirhan hearing later this month," he said, "but under the circumstances, it is unlikely that he will show up." Five years after his negotiations with deputy DA Bill Burnett, Carmen Falzone had finally pulled off his vanishing act.

Neither Carmen Falzone nor Philip Clark testified at Sirhan's parole hearing. James Park, a former associate warden at San Quentin, testified that he doubted very much whether Clark, who was not on death row, could have possibly penetrated that area to talk with Sirhan about Black September assassination plots as he had claimed.

Lawrence Wilson did attend the hearing, despite the bad press regarding his veracity. He took the stand and, with Sirhan glaring at him, retold the story of Sirhan threatening the life of Senator Edward Kennedy. Sirhan's attorney, Luke McKissack, pressed Wilson on several fronts. He asked Wilson about another case where he had come forward with information on a fellow prisoner and then flunked a lie detector test. He asked Wilson about the letter with the forged signature of author Joseph Wambaugh. Wilson denied writing or forging the letter but refused to answer any further questions, saying, "I don't wish to discuss that at great length because there is a possible criminal action and a civil matter involved."[19]

McKissack subsequently called several fellow inmates from Soledad. Robert William Bell, who was in prison serving a sentence for burglary, testified that he had been solicited by Lawrence Wilson to corroborate Wilson's claim that Sirhan had threatened the life of Senator Edward Kennedy.

"I went along at first," said Bell, "and agreed that I would say I overheard Sirhan make that Kennedy death threat to Larry Wilson. But I always intended to come here to tell the truth, that it didn't really happen. . . . It's all through the system that Larry Wilson is lying about the [Sirhan] matter."[20]

Thomas Nicochea, another resident of Soledad, testified that Wilson approached him with a proposal to lie about the supposed Sirhan conversation, but that he turned Wilson down immediately. Another prisoner, William Kogan, also testified against Wilson, calling him "an opportunist."[21]

Wilson's credibility was further damaged when the parole board's chief investigator, Richard Washington, Jr., testified to a series of incidents on record which demonstrated "the pattern of deceit Wilson has employed to gain his ends, including trying to blame his own father for the murder he committed."[22]

With three of John Van de Kamp's principal witnesses discredited, the hearings went forward with great emphasis now placed on two threatening letters Sirhan had written while in prison. In one, Sirhan had threatened Soledad correctional officer Vern Smith in 1975 for failing to provide him with medical attention to a painful dental problem. The other was written from San Quentin in 1971 to Sirhan's attorney Grant Cooper, and began "Hey Punk!" In it Sirhan threatened the life of defense investigator Robert Kaiser "if he continues to talk about me like he's been doing on radio and TV. . . ." It ended: "Don't forget [Cooper], you son-of-a-bitch, you are the one who cost me my life."

After thirty-two witnesses over a two-week period, Deputy District Attorney Larry Trapp rose to offer a summation for his boss, John Van de Kamp. "Mr. Sirhan will boldly tell you he has been punished enough and suggest to you that he has paid his debt to society," said Trapp. "But Sirhan, who took it upon himself to rewrite history, is like a debtor who is bankrupt. He can never repay the debt."

Trapp argued that to let the parole date stand "means we in California will risk sending a message to every misfit, fanatic and political crusader that assassination in this state is worth only 13 years."[23]

When Luke McKissack rose for Sirhan he pointed out that if paroled on schedule in 1984 (the date advanced two years for good behavior) Sirhan would have served sixteen years, more time than many murderers who had committed more egregious and aggravated crimes. McKissack then reminded the board that Sirhan's treatment should not depend upon "who the victim was and his stature in society."[24]

Following these summations Sirhan rose and read a statement in which he expressed remorse for the death of Robert Kennedy, denied having made any death threats against Edward Kennedy, and characterized the threatening letters he wrote in the early 1970s as "regrettable" expressions of frustration.

Three weeks later the three-member hearing panel revoked Sirhan's scheduled parole date, saying that in the fourteen years since he assassinated Senator Kennedy he had demonstrated "a pattern of threatening behavior." In making its determination the panel requested a psychiatric evaluation of Sirhan, expressing concern with his "loner status," a concern which appeared to ignore the repeated attempts by unscrupulous inmates to use their contact with Sirhan to fabricate incriminating stories about him, often with what appeared to be official encouragement. The decision stated that "this panel is not impressed with the apologies offered by Sirhan. . . . [His] threats and conduct do not indicate the prisoner has made a substantial change for the better."[25]

At a press conference after the decision DA Van de Kamp told reporters, "We are pleased with the decision because it is the right decision. The people of this country and, indeed, the people of the world, can collectively heave a sigh of relief that Sirhan will remain in prison."[26]

Five months later John Van de Kamp would be elected attorney general of California.

In 1982, the same year Sirhan's parole date was revoked, Princeton University Press published *American Assassins*, a book by Professor James W. Clarke. The book was a study of this nation's best-known political assassins (not all of whom succeeded in killing their intended victims).

Clarke began his section on Sirhan by asserting that of the sixteen assassins studied, Sirhan "stands out as possibly the shrewdest, most devious and remorseless of the lot . . . no other assassin, with the possible exceptions of John Wilkes Booth and Carl Weiss, hated his victim more."

Clarke claimed to see in Sirhan's strange notebooks "the efforts of a determined assassin to prepare himself psychologically for the assassination as well as for his anticipated capture and defense." He cited the Carmen Falzone article in *Playboy* magazine to show that Sirhan was still hopeful that "Arab terrorists would be successful in arranging the circumstances for his release." He compared Sirhan to the Black September terrorists who murdered the Israeli Olympic athletes in Munich in 1972.

Clarke's portrait of Sirhan was harsh, but also conventional. It did not take into account great bodies of information not consonant with its conclusions. For example, a review of Sirhan's interviews with his doctors and lawyers reveals that he is noteworthy for his *lack* of hatred for his victim. His notebooks hardly constitute a shrewd posture for his legal defense, and other than that he has Arab origins and has voiced anti-Israeli sentiments, he has remarkably little in common with Black September. Nevertheless, Clarke's book would become the unofficial manifesto for those opposing parole for Sirhan.

When Sirhan returned before the Board of Prison Terms in 1985, he was accompanied by the psychiatric report that the board had asked for when it revoked his parole. In the report, prepared by prison staff psychiatrist Dr. Philip S. Hicks, Sirhan was described as "an exemplary inmate . . . a man who is in good contact with reality . . . a pleasant, cooperative person [who] demonstrates maturity and good judgment concerning his situation."

Hicks found Sirhan to be "of above average intelligence, intellectually curious [with] a remarkably good memory for detail." He concluded: "There appears to be no psychiatric contraindication to parole consideration. He has no demonstrable predilection toward violence at this time."[27]

The report was presented to a three-member panel of the Board of Prison Terms, consisting of Raymond Jaurequi, Joseph Aceto, and chairman Rudolf Castro. Because the previous parole hearing in 1982 had generated so much public interest, the hearing in 1985 was also well covered by the press. While not allowed into the hearing room itself, the newsmen were allowed to view the proceedings from a separate room via closed-circuit TV. After hearing appeals for justice from Sirhan's attorney, Luke McKissack, who maintained that Sirhan had already paid his debt and was no longer a threat to society, and from Deputy DA Larry Trapp, who maintained that a message had to be sent that political assassination would not be tolerated in California, the board asked that the hearing room be cleared so they could deliberate. The closed-circuit TV monitor was turned off.

After an hour or so, panel chairman Rudolf Castro appeared in person before the newsmen to announce that Sirhan was once again to be denied parole.

"How long did you deliberate?" asked one of the newsmen.

"About forty-five minutes," replied Castro.

The newsmen then informed Castro that they knew this to be a lie, because while the TV monitor had been turned off, the sound monitor had not. The newsmen asserted that the board had deliberated no more than three minutes and much of that was horseplay and dirty jokes. At that point Castro announced, "On the advice of counsel I am curtailing further discussion on this."

An edited transcript of what the newsmen heard was printed in the *Los Angeles Times:*

> CASTRO: For the record the time is 2:40. Prisoner will leave first. (*Pause, footsteps, papers being shuffled.*)
> JAUREQUI: Is it all right if I kiss you on the forehead? (Interrupted at the end by someone.)
> VOICE: (*Spanish vulgarity for sexual intercourse.*)
> VOICE: (*Inaudible words*) . . . somebody kissing him in the bucket.
> VOICE: He kissed you why can't I?
> CASTRO: (*Spanish vulgarity.*)
> JAUREQUI: (*Spanish vulgarity.*) Get the bum to do it.
> CASTRO: (*Spanish vulgarity.*)
> JAUREQUI: (*Spanish vulgarity.*) He kissed you in the elevator.[28]

After what Luke McKissack estimated was one minute and forty seconds of discussion, Rudolf Castro then enumerated the reasons why Sirhan would be denied parole: "the lack of sufficient programming, the crime itself, the need for in-depth diagnostic evaluation. Agree?"

Moments later, speaking about transferring Sirhan to another prison, one of the board members said, "We'll send his ass down there for as long as possible."

Then a few minutes later a panel member said, "Let's make sure the sound is off."

"Oh, hey," replied Castro, "that is very important."

"Terrific," said another panelist to general laughter. "The whole world will know."[29]

Sirhan's attorney, Luke McKissack, quickly criticized "the atmosphere of frivolity" in the deliberations as heard by the attending press, saying that "American justice is now on trial."[30]

In Sacramento, William Elliot, head of the state Board of Prison Terms, responded: "At this point, we don't perceive what happened in the deliberations to be a fatal flaw to the hearing. They may have come quickly to a decision, but then they really took quite a bit of time to deal with all of the ramifications and the setting up of Sirhan's future programming."[31]

Parole hearings for Sirhan Sirhan would take place in 1986, 1987, 1989, and 1990. The transcripts of these proceedings are very similar. Luke McKissack would point to evidence that Sirhan was suitable for parole. Sirhan would express remorse. Deputy DA Lawrence Trapp would speak of the heinous nature of the murder. And the hearing panel, in denying parole, would utter words about crimes against democracy.

In 1992 Sirhan was scheduled for another hearing at his new home at Corcoran State Prison. In a chamber outside the hearing room the escorting prison officials told Sirhan that he could only enter the hearing room if he were wearing chains and manacles. Sirhan refused to be so attired. The hearing went on without him or his attorney. He was again denied parole.

Although Sirhan's refusal to attend his 1992 parole hearing in chains was not reported in the news, another hearing that same year did make big headlines. This was a reversal hearing in Los Angeles Superior Court on behalf of Clarence Chance and Benny Powell. Both men had been convicted of the 1973 murder of a Los Angeles County Sheriff's deputy. They had been in prison for more than seventeen years, but had consistently maintained their innocence.

At the hearing before Judge Florence Cooper, the attorneys for Chance and Powell introduced statements by the two witnesses at the original murder trial, teenage girls at the time, that they had been intimidated and coerced by the police to change their statements to implicate Chance and Powell. The attorneys were also able to demonstrate that Chance was in custody at the time of the shooting and could not possibly have committed the murder.

At the original 1975 murder trial, both girls had given their now admitted false testimony against Chance and Powell. But the case against the defendants was still weak, so the prosecutors introduced another witness who testified that Benny Powell had bragged to him in prison that he had indeed murdered the sheriff's deputy. The witness swore that he was telling the truth and had received no incentives to make these statements. This witness was Lawrence Eugene Wilson, the same man who authorities would bring forward at Sirhan's 1982 parole hearing, to swear that Sirhan intended to murder Senator Edward Kennedy if he were released on parole.

At the 1992 reversal hearing Sandra Smith, the attorney representing Benny Powell, would say that Eugene Wilson "lied with the knowlege of the officers who investigated the case." The attorneys then introduced evidence that the police had concealed the fact that Wilson had earlier implicated two other men in the crime, concealed evidence that Wilson had failed two polygraph tests concerning his statements about Powell, and that in return for his testimony Wilson had received a three-room prison "suite" where he was allowed private conjugal visits. "Wilson graduated from this case to go on to commit other fraudulent acts," said Smith, referring to his testimony at Sirhan's parole hearing as fraudulent."

The Los Angeles DA's office did not oppose the release of Chance and Powell, saying that Wilson's testimony at the original murder trial was tainted, although that fact was unknown at the time to the prosecutors.

At the conclusion of the hearing, Judge Florence Cooper released both Chance and Powell saying that the police conduct in the case was "reprehensible." LAPD Chief Daryl Gates, however, continued to defend the actions of the officers involved. "No one was framed at any time," he said. "The detectives were persistent in seeking the truth." Gates attributed any shortcomings in the case to "procedural error."

By December 1994, when Sirhan was scheduled for his next hearing, the rules at Corcoran Prison had changed. Sirhan was escorted into the hearing room without chains and seated at a table before the three-man Board of Prison Terms panel. Also at the table was Lawrence Teeter, a criminal defense lawyer who also specializes in environmental and civil rights litigation. Teeter had recently replaced Luke McKissack as Sirhan's attorney of record.

The proceedings, which were televised live by *Court TV,* began with Board of Prison Terms commissioner Steve Baker reading a short history of the crime. The commissioners then reviewed Sirhan's conduct in prison. It was noted that Sirhan had been discipline-free for twenty years. It was also revealed that Sirhan had maintained a 4.0 average in his academic studies, which had been discontinued. A letter was read in which Sirhan was offered a job by family friend Rose Lynn Mangan if he were to be released on parole.

When the commissioners were finished, Deputy District Attorney Lawrence Trapp was introduced. Trapp, as he had done since 1980, spoke on behalf of the Los Angeles district attorney's office. He cited "three major factors" in support of the DA's position that Sirhan should not be given parole.

"The first factor is the extraordinary degree of violence associated with this criminal event. The second factor was the extraordinary degree of planning over an extended period of time, as well as Sirhan's relative calmness immediately following the criminal activity. And finally and the factor most interesting to me is the almost unparalleled degree of heartlessness and remorselessness towards the inmate's victim, this, again, over a long period of time."

As evidence of Sirhan's "lengthy planning period" Trapp asserted:

"On January 9, 1968, Robert Kennedy proposed the sale of jets to Israel. This was reported the next day in the *New York Times*. Later that same month, on January 31, 1968 we find the very first entry in Sirhan's now famous notebooks, 'RFK MUST DIE.' This sentence is repeated over and over and over again on this page and is followed by the question and answer 'Who killed Kennedy?' 'I don't know, I don't know.' "

Trapp's assertion here simply parroted the error in James W. Clarke's book *American Assassins*. The document Trapp was referring to was written by Sirhan while under hypnosis in Februrary 1969, eight months *after* Robert Kennedy had been murdered.

In offering other examples of Sirhan's nefarious intent Trapp recited to the parole board Sirhan's "rapid fire" at the shooting range, his failure to carry a wallet to the scene of the crime, and his calm demeanor during the shooting. "Finally," asserted Trapp, "in case any doubt remains as to Sirhan's intent all along, during the course of the trial Sirhan asserted, 'I killed Robert Kennedy, willfully, premeditatively, with twenty years of malice aforethought.' Nevertheless, despite his courtroom assertion Sirhan through the years has continued to attempt to mitigate his responsibility for his crime by claiming diminished capacity and even amnesia for the events surrounding the assassination."

"The issue before us today," answered Lawrence Teeter, when it was his turn to speak, "is the question of whether Mr. Sirhan's release would present an unreasonable risk to society. That's the issue and that's the only issue." Teeter went on to quote excerpts from various psychological reports done on Sirhan within the past decade.

1986 report by Dr. Philip S. Hicks: "This individual appears to be genuinely rehabilitated since incarceration, and demonstrates no evidence of current fanaticism or proneness towards violence. He appears to be an excellent candidate for parole."

1986 report by Dr. Robert Dry: "I believe this man has made a considerable personal change. . . . His potential for violence is very low. . . . I would recommend that Mr. Sirhan continue in his present program but with an early discharge being seriously considered."

1989 report by Dr. Clyde Martin: "During observation in the institution the inmate has psychiatrically improved moderately and in a less controlled setting such as a return to the community the inmate is likely to hold any present gains. . . . At this time his potential for violence is less than that of the average inmate."

1990 report by Dr. Douglas A. Farr: "If he is paroled he should be able to maintain his maturation in terms of his personality. He appears to have considerable family support and should be able to parole in the United States without undue difficulty."

After he had read the excerpts from the medical reports, Teeter changed tactics. "Mr. Trapp remarks that Mr. Sirhan shot Robert Kennedy from nearly point-blank range," he asserted. "Now . . . the autopsy report states very clearly that the gun that fired the shots that struck Robert Kennedy, was either in contact with or no more than one inch away when the fatal shot was fired. . . . The problem is that no witnesses have testified that he ever got that close—"

"Excuse me, Counselor," interrupted Commissioner Baker. "Are you going to readjudicate this case? I'm not going to allow you to do that."

"No, but I think I am entitled—"

"No, you're entitled to speak to the suitability of parole of Mr. Sirhan. We're not going to retry the case. If you want to retry the case, file an appeal and go through the courts."

Despite Baker's objections, Teeter was determined to go on record that there were major evidentiary questions still open in the case.

"No, I understand," he replied to Baker. "I was simply trying to direct myself to what I consider an important factual inaccuracy in the board's file about the circumstances under which the crime took place. This is a telling inaccuracy because if the witnesses place the gun as far away as they did, then it would be physically impossible for Mr. Sirhan to have fired the shots that killed Robert Kennedy."

"It's not relevant to this hearing."

"I understand your position. But I did want to address that one comment in the board's file." Teeter went on to question Trapp's use of the Sirhan "twenty years of malice aforethought" comment, slipping in that Sirhan's trial attorney Grant Cooper never contested the fact of whether or not Sirhan actually committed the murder. Teeter next attacked the parole board's repeated allusions to Sirhan's inability to remember the crime as evidence of his lack of remorse. "Lack of recollection of what he is supposed to have done does not equate with lack of remorse," Teeter said. "He has again and again at hearings over the years spoken in very moving terms about how tragic these events were and about how he wishes they hadn't happened and how sorry he is that they did happen."

Teeter went on: "There has been great discussion today from the district attorney's office about these notebooks, and I mentioned that Mr. Sirhan did not remember writing them. He also advised the psychiatrist, the defense psychiatrist, that some of the writing didn't look like his. The issue, characteristically, wasn't explored by his attorneys at his trial."

"And it won't be explored here today either, Counselor," interjected Commissioner Baker.

"I understand, I just want to mention that the authenticity of the notebooks was never explored."

Teeter then reviewed Sirhan's suitability for parole. "Is this man a danger to the community? Well, the psychiatric reports say he's not. His behavior says that he is not. His plans for the future say that he is not. His lack of any criminal history except for this offense says that he is not. His expressions of remorse say that he is not. And again I would like to emphasize the question of whether Mr. Sirhan actually killed Robert Kennedy was never proven. . . . It was not proven by the district attorney's office because they didn't have to. Mr. Sirhan's lawyers just gave it away and rested upon a mental defense."

In concluding his remarks Teeter deftly held off censure while taking one more swipe at the conduct of Sirhan's trial. "You're absolutely correct," he asserted. "This board is not authorized to set aside someone's conviction because of constitutional violations, because of the ineffective assistance of counsel, because of newly discovered evidence, because the police destroyed evidence that would demonstrate his innocence; you are not authorized to grant any of that relief. But I think it is very clear you are authorized to grant one form of relief, which is to authorize his release on parole and I would ask you to do that at this time. . . . Thank you."

Sirhan was then asked if he had any comments. He didn't seem to be prepared to speak. In a disjointed way he told the panel that he had expressed remorse for the crime over the years. "People should not kill, period," he concluded.

After a thirty-minute break the members of the parole board returned to the room. Commissioner Steve Baker read a statement "concluding that the prisoner is not suitable for parole and would pose an unreasonable risk of danger to society and a threat to public safety if released from prison. Offense was carried out in an especially atrocious, cruel, and callous manner. Offense was carried out in a dispassionate and calculated manner. Multiple victims were attacked and injured, killed, in this or separate incidences. The prisoner has progressed in a limited manner while incarcerated, and has failed to develop a marketable skill that can be put to use upon release. . . . Parole is denied for two years."

Several hours after the parole hearing Lawrence Teeter, unfettered by any rules of discourse, spoke freely to the authors.

"At every parole hearing, the same words are spoken. 'Sirhan cannot be let go because we have to send a message that assassins are dealt with severely in California.' The truth is that in this case, the police covered the tracks of the real assassins. Evidence was destroyed, witnesses were intimidated, and files were kept secret. Because of this, they must demonize Sirhan. If Sirhan is not the monster they make him out to be, then they will have to answer real questions about this case.

"I have no doubt Sirhan is an innocent man," Teeter continued. "The evidence shows that he was unconscious at the time of the shooting, and I believe that this unconsciousness was the result of sophisticated hypnosis. If this is so, then Sirhan is a victim of this crime and not a perpetrator. He is kept in prison because, out of sight and out of mind, it is far easier to limit public interest in the sinister events that led to his conviction."

The next day in the *New York Times* there was a story on the difficulties encountered by televangelist Jim Bakker in expelling newsmen from his front lawn following his release from prison. There was another story concerning Paula Jones, who had accused President Bill Clinton of sexual misconduct. Jones, it was reported, was having legal difficulties with *Penthouse* magazine. Despite the fact that the day before, for the first time in twenty years, an attorney for Sirhan Sirhan had asserted in a legal forum that important evidence in the Robert Kennedy murder had been suppressed, there was no story on the Sirhan parole hearing.

The Phantom Photographs

✻ ✻ ✻

"I saw Robert Kennedy. He was turning to the left and to the right.
He was shaking hands with people and speaking with the kitchen
help in Spanish. I could hear him talking and then there was a
tremendous amount of noise, people yelling, balloons popping, things
like that. He suddenly sort of stiffened and then twisted and fell to
the ground. Fell out of the frame."
"And you were snapping pictures throughout this time?"
"Yes."

—Scott Enyart, answering the questions of attorney
Louis Miller during deposition in 1995

O N T H E M O R N I N G of July 2, 1996,
attorney Christine Harwell stood
up in Los Angeles County superior court to deliver her opening statement
in a lawsuit which had its beginnings the night Robert Kennedy was murdered. Ms. Harwell represented Jamie Scott Enyart, who was suing the city
of Los Angeles for not returning photographs he took at the Ambassador
Hotel the evening of the assassination.

Scott Enyart was fifteen years old in 1968. He had gone to the primary-
night celebration at the Ambassador with several friends, equipped with a
camera and an unauthorized press pass. As Robert Kennedy spoke to his
supporters in the Embassy Room, Enyart took photographs from in front
of the stage. What happened next is in dispute, but Enyart claims that after
the speech he followed Kennedy into the hotel pantry.

"The evidence from the police department's own records will show,"
said Ms. Harwell to the jury, "that Mr. Enyart stood on a steam table above
the crowd immediately behind the senator taking pictures of the assassination in progress, that he was the *only* photographer to take pictures at
that time. We will prove that had Mr. Enyart's negatives been available for
use in the investigation and trial of Sirhan B. Sirhan . . . many questions
that plague us today would have been answered about whether or not
someone else may have shot off guns at the same time."

In 1968 Christine Harwell had worked for the Los Angeles police as a clerk, hoping that their regulations barring women from becoming police officers would change. They didn't, and Harwell left the department to study law.* Now, at age forty-seven, she would castigate her former employer in front of the jury, saying that the most crucial pictures taken by her client were either lost or "destroyed to hide what they showed . . . to keep the LAPD from being embarrassed for doing a one-sided job and hiding evidence in one of the three major political assassinations of the century."

On May 26, 1988, just a month after the LAPD's files on the Robert Kennedy assassination had been made public, thirty-five-year-old Scott Enyart wrote to Los Angeles chief of police Daryl Gates.

> Dear Chief Gates,
> My name is Jamie Scott Enyart and I was present the tragic evening Senator Robert Kennedy was assassinated. I was 15 years old and taking photographs for a school assignment when this tragedy occurred. After your men arrived I was taken as a witness to Rampart Station where I described what happened and volunteered my film for use in the investigation. Now, twenty years later, I understand the files are open and I had hoped, by writing to you, I could now have my film back.

Enyart said he was enclosing "Xeroxes of my pictures your detectives gave me years ago" to help in locating his film. He told Gates that he wished to express his appreciation for his efforts "to rid our city of violent crime, drugs and gang activity." He enclosed an envelope so that Gates might return autographed photos of himself for Enyart's two children who "consider officers of your department as friends and role models."

A month later Enyart received back a letter from Chief Gates saying that "everything that was in possession of the Los Angeles Police Department concerning the Kennedy investigation has been delivered to the custody of the State of California." He provided Enyart with the name and telephone number of state archivist Laren Metzer, who had already agreed to help Enyart look for his film. Gates thanked Enyart for his "assistance and cooperation in the Kennedy investigation" and enclosed two autographed photographs of himself.

Enyart then wrote to the State Archives, enclosing the same photocopies

---

*Harwell would go on to become a U.S. District Court staff attorney for nine years, before joining the law firm headed by Alvin Greenwald, a successful and respected business attorney, who was also Scott Enyart's father-in-law.

he had sent to Gates and requesting that, if possible, his film be located. On October 11, Laren Metzer replied on behalf of chief archivist, John Burns: they had been unable to locate any photographs or film that matched the photocopies sent by Enyart. "I can only conclude," wrote Metzer, "that your photographs were among the 2,400 images destroyed by LAPD in August 1968."

That photographic prints were burned by the LAPD is not in question. A property report dated August 21, 1968, says that two police officers took "2410 S.U.S. Unit photographs without code numbers to County General Hospital and deposited these photos in the hospital incinerator and witnessed their destruction." The police maintain that all photos burned were duplicates, however, no records were kept of what was destroyed.* At the same time, there is no evidence that Scott Enyart's photographs were among those burned. Nevertheless, the failure of his photographs to appear once the files were opened angered Enyart.

A year later, in August 1989, Scott Enyart filed suit against the City of Los Angeles seeking two million dollars in damages for the loss or destruction of his photographs.[1] Enyart claimed that the night of the assassination that he had shot three, 36-exposure rolls of film, which he said had been taken from him by the police. He claimed that several months after the murder he was able to recover from the police only eighteen prints and no negatives.

The city responded by claiming that Enyart's suit was not timely and therefore was barred by the statute of limitations. The court agreed and the case was dismissed. Enyart appealed. In December 1993, the California Court of Appeals overturned the lower court's decision, citing the years of police secrecy. "The [LAPD's] own actions for over 20 years prevented [Enyart] from obtaining his property or any information about its status or existence," ruled the court. "The order of dismissal is reversed."

With the case back on the calendar, the city began to organize its resources for the fight against Scott Enyart. Although his office had 358 attorneys on staff, City Attorney James Hahn retained Louis "Skip" Miller of the law firm Christensen, White, Miller, Fink, Jacobs, Glaser & Shapiro to handle the Enyart case.

Christensen, White had been one of the law firms hired by Los Angeles the previous year to defend councilman Nate Holden against charges of sexual harassment. The firm received a reported $800,000 for its successful defense, and the money spent on Holden's defense became

---

*An August 20, 1968, memo from Captain Hugh Brown, second in command at SUS, to Chief Robert Houghton described the extensive search for five lost photographs. It then set forth procedures for cataloging all case photos, even those of "no value," procedures designed to "prevent incidents of this nature in the future." The burning of the unrecorded 2,400 photos occurred the day after the date on this memo.

a page-one story in the *Los Angeles Times*. According to the *Times,* the contract for Christensen, White allowed the city to be billed $250 an hour for a partner, $175 an hour for an associate attorney, and $70 an hour for a paralegal.

The Christensen, White partner who had defended the Holden lawsuit was Skip Miller. His assumption of the Enyart case stimulated another protest in the *Los Angeles Times*. "Why," asked columnist Bill Boyarsky, "is Los Angeles paying $225 an hour to Miller, a Century City courtroom star, instead of letting a deputy city attorney do the job for about a quarter of the cost? Is it because the city is trying to cover up failures in the Kennedy investigation, as Enyart charges?"[2]

City Attorney Hahn answered that Miller was brought into the case to combat any latent perception that there was "a giant conspiracy" responsible for the murder of Robert Kennedy. "It is important to emphasize," said Hahn, "the credibility of the Los Angeles Police Department."[3] Boyarsky then concluded that Miller was hired because the case was "too big for the city and the LAPD to lose."

With the outside law firm in place, trial preparations moved forward. Motions for discovery were filed, depositions taken, and a new search for Scott Enyart's missing photographs begun. Then, an unexpected discovery. In August 1995, attorneys for the city found photos and negatives in the state archives that seemed to match those that Scott Enyart had received back from the police in 1968. The pictures had been booked and filed under the name of George Ross Clayton, and there was only one set of negatives with 30 images. Clayton could not be located, but from what could be deduced from the original 1968 police reports, there appeared to be a legitimate question as to whether Clayton had been the source of the film.

Scott Enyart and his attorney Christine Harwell traveled to Sacramento to inspect the new discovery. Although the images there appeared to match most of the photographs he had received back from the police, Enyart claimed that there was some mistake. The film found at the archives was Ilford brand, 125 ASA, while Enyart claimed that the night of the California primary he had been using Kodak, Tri-X, 400 ASA.

Enyart suggested that if the images were indeed his, then some sort of forgery must have taken place. He would testify at his trial that he noticed enhanced contrast in the images, which suggested to him a generational copying from the original negatives. He also noted that the single roll of film in the archives appeared to include images from all three of the rolls he said he had shot. He said that some of the photographs appeared to be out of sequence. And there were no photographs at all from inside the pantry.

With the authenticity of the discovered film now challenged, superior court judge Emilie Elias★ ordered the negatives delivered from Sacramento to the court in Los Angeles where they could be used as evidence in the trial and be examined by photographic experts for both the plaintiff and the defense. On January 12, 1996, just a month before the scheduled start of the trial, courier George Philip Gebhardt flew from Sacramento to Los Angeles. In his locked briefcase was a folder containing the negatives.

When he arrived in Los Angeles Gebhardt went to the Midway Rent-A-Car agency where he picked up a white Mazda sedan, which he had reserved. On Century Boulevard just outside the airport, the courier stopped for a red light. According to his videotaped testimony in court (Gebhardt had suffered a heart attack shortly after this incident and testified from his hospital bed), a red car pulled up next to him and a Hispanic man got out and began to bang on his own car for no apparent reason. A block later the white Mazda was making a dull thumping noise. Gebhardt pulled over, got out to inspect and found that his right rear tire was slashed. When he got back into his car, the briefcase with the negatives was gone.

With the most important piece of evidence now stolen, the trial was postponed. The rising intrigue, however, found a forum in the media. In a story printed in the *Los Angeles Times,* Enyart's attorney Alvin Greenwald hinted at conspiracy. "Somebody, for some reason," he said, "is making sure those photos do not reach public view."[4]

"What happened here," responded attorney Skip Miller in the same story, "is just a petty theft. A run of bad luck."

The television show *Unsolved Mysteries* was quick to broadcast a story on the Enyart case. During that program a photograph was displayed, which was said to be new evidence. It was from *The Last Campaign,* a book by Bill Eppridge and Hays Gorey, documenting Robert Kennedy's 1968 quest for the presidential nomination. The book included ten photographs Eppridge had shot in the chaotic hotel pantry after the attack upon Robert Kennedy. In the selected print, a young man with a camera could be seen in the background, standing on a table, taking photographs. The young man was said to be Scott Enyart.

Court TV, which was hoping to televise the upcoming trial, then ran a story of its own. In the nationally televised segment, Assistant City Attorney Edmund Fimbres commented on Enyart's claim that he took important photographs of Kennedy being shot. "It's just a fish story," he said with disdain. "Over the years the fish has gotten bigger."

★   ★   ★

★Emilie Elias is a court-appointed jurist, empowered to preside at trials. Her official title is commissioner. She has the powers of a judge and will be referred to as a judge in these pages.

In the last week of June 1996, jury selection for the Enyart trial finally got underway. The jury pool was a varied mix of mostly working-class Angelenos. Attorney Skip Miller, intent on finding out which panelists believed that President John Kennedy had been murdered by conspiracy, repeatedly screened the candidates by asking, "Did you enjoy Oliver Stone's movie *JFK*, or did you find it long and tedious?" Panelists who enjoyed the movie were not likely to become jurors.

Not to be outdone, and understanding this to be a case about the value of photographs, the plaintiffs had their own cinematic litmus: "What did you think about *The Bridges of Madison County?*"

As the jury was being selected, Judge Emilie Elias denied Court TV's request to televise the trial. The decision was made without formal comment, but it was understood that the judge was concerned that the presence of television cameras would serve to sensationalize the trial and distract the jury.

In his opening statement to the jury Skip Miller likened the case to a "Sherlock Holmes mystery." "This is an interesting case," he said. "I think you'll enjoy it. Contrary to all the discussion in voir dire it really isn't about the assassination, it isn't about wilful and intentional manipulation of evidence. For pete's sake, who would want to do that?"

According to Skip Miller, Scott Enyart's claim that he took important photographs in the hotel pantry was just "wishful thinking." He said that the reason Enyart had no access to the investigation files for twenty years was that the police had to "protect confidential informants." He told the jurors that they would have to decide for themselves whether or not the recent theft of the negatives was "part of the Evil Empire's twenty-eight year plot."

During his statement Miller only occasionally glanced at his notes for reference. He spoke with confidence and moved easily about the courtroom in something that resembled a prowl. He was smartly dressed and looked younger than his forty-nine years.

Miller told the jury that there were two key questions: Did Scott Enyart take three rolls of film as he claimed or just one roll? Was Scott Enyart was in the hotel pantry when the shots were fired, or was he still in the Embassy Room? Miller promised to prove that Enyart took only one roll of film and was not in the pantry. He offered Enyart's own words as proof. "In his own statement to police that night there's no mention of pantry. I read that statement over a dozen times. . . . There's not a word in there that's spelled P-A-N-T-R-Y."

After Miller finished speaking, the plaintiffs called their first witness, Jamie Scott Enyart. Dressed in a rumpled linen suit, the tall, attractive, slightly gaunt-looking Enyart took the witness stand. In answer to his attorneys' questions, Enyart began to tell his story. He related how at a young age he had become interested in photography. Later he would tell the jury about Scott Enyart Studios, the professional photography business he had run for almost twenty years. This was important, because his lawyers wanted to demonstrate that at the time of the murder, Enyart had the skills to take good photographs under difficult circumstances and would be using the proper camera and film to do so.

Enyart would go on to relate events the night Robert Kennedy was shot. He told how he had brought his camera to the Ambassador Hotel so that he could take pictures for his high school newspaper. He said he was in the company of two friends and that they all had arrived at the hotel at around six in the evening.

Enyart told the court how later in the evening he had managed to get to within five feet of the podium from where he was able to take pictures of Kennedy's victory address. After the speech, Enyart said, he anticipated Kennedy's move to the Colonial Room and using a side exit in the Embassy Room managed to intercept Kennedy as he walked down the narrow hallway behind the stage. Enyart said he stepped in behind Kennedy and followed him into the pantry hoping to get some candid shots.

"As I got into the pantry I was about ten feet behind him [Kennedy]," Enyart told the authors in 1992, "continuing to take pictures as he began to shake hands with people. All of a sudden I saw him drop from the frame. He fell. And I continued taking pictures. I backed up, jumped up on a table. Everyone in front of me had been shot and fell and I jumped up to get out of the way."

Enyart said he continued to take photos for a brief time. Then he stopped.

"Once I realized what happened, particularly when Ethel Kennedy came into the room five months pregnant, kneels down next to her husband and says, 'Please, leave us alone.' I couldn't take pictures anymore. The rest of the press behaved like animals. They just crawled all over the place. They blocked the doors, the ambulance attendants couldn't get in, so they could bring in more lights and get more footage of this poor man dying on the floor with his wife next to him."

Enyart said he made his way back out into the Embassy Room. When he tried to leave the hotel about a half an hour later, however, he said he was surrounded by police officers who took his film. In Enyart's deposition, Skip Miller asked the witness about this exchange.

"When you say the film was confiscated, in other words, it was demanded and seized?"

"It was taken at gunpoint."

"Taken at gun point?"

"That's correct."

"Was the gun pointed at you?"

"That's correct."

"Did you resist? Is that why the gun was pointed at you?"

"I was running away from what I thought were evil people which turned out to be two detectives in suits. . . ."

"And how did the guns get drawn?"

"At the main entrance to the Ambassador Hotel there are two glass electric doors. I waited until the doors were closing and I ran out as they were closing which put some distance between myself and these two gentlemen. At that point I was blinded by lights. I was grabbed. I was put down on my face on the red carpet. My camera was taken, my wallet was taken, my pockets were emptied. . . . I looked up and saw guns pointed at me, at which point they basically saw that they had a kid and did not abuse me."

Enyart said he was then placed in a squad car and was questioned by two detectives who sat on either side of him. Miller asked what the detectives wanted to know. Enyart responded that they wanted to know whether or not he had seen the shooter.

"What did you say in response to the question?"

"I said, I don't know. I said I was taking pictures at the time and maybe—I said I couldn't tell without looking at the pictures."

"So you didn't have a view of the shooter . . . ?"

"At the time I would not have known who the shooter was. I saw Robert Kennedy and I saw a number of people through the viewfinder as I was taking these pictures. I saw Robert Kennedy fall as he was shot. Whether or not in those photographs you would see Sirhan who was in front of him because I was behind him. I cannot tell without seeing those photographs. . . ."

"Would you agree with me that since you weren't called as a witness that the police and the prosecutor concluded that you could not give eyewitness testimony as to the Kennedy shooter?"

"Objection!" said Christine Harwell. "This witness cannot testify as to what others conclude."

"I'll rephrase the question. Will you agree with me that you were not an eyewitness to the Kennedy shooting?"

"No, I will not."

"Did you actually see Sirhan shoot Robert Kennedy?"

"I saw Robert Kennedy being shot and falling. Sirhan was in front of him and shorter than him so, no, I did not see Sirhan in front of him, but I did see Robert Kennedy during the shooting."

"This is difficult. I am just trying to find out if you are a witness to a murder. . . . I know you say you were there. I know you say you saw Kennedy get shot. . . . Did you see Sirhan shoot Kennedy?"

"Objection! It assumes facts not in evidence."

After his film and camera had been taken from him, Enyart said he was driven to the back of the hotel where he was put into a holding room. Later he was transferred to Rampart Station by jailbus. There at around six in the morning he was briefly interviewed by the police.

On the second day of the trial, in a hushed courtroom, an audiotape of Scott Enyart's police interview was played for the jury.

"I'm Sergeant McGann from Homicide Division, Scott. I understand you took some pictures, did you?"

"Yes."

"—of the shooter—of the suspect doing the shooting?"

"I'm not exactly sure. I was about four feet from the stage while Mr. Kennedy was speaking and after he stopped speaking and began to walk off the stage, the crowd started to clear; so I immediately headed for the door. . . ."

"Were you in the Embassy Room?"

"Embassy Room. . . . Right about here," said Enyart apparently pointing to a small layout of the hotel the interviewing officers had for this purpose.

"Okay, and he left this way?"

"Yes, he left this way and I left this way. I got to about here and the crowd was going toward him, like they always do, to shake his hand and everything; so I figured I can catch some good pictures. So there was a table here about three-and-a-half feet tall, I'd say, so I got up on it so I was above everyone and I was going to—and then the shots started to be fired and I took pictures and kept taking pictures."

"While all the shots were being fired?"

"While the shots were being fired, maybe a little afterward. I'm not exactly sure. I couldn't tell. I can only tell by the pictures."

"This was down a hallway, more or less, you were shooting?"

"No. Can I—I'll show you."

"Uh huh [yes]. Let's use this one here [apparently referring to a sketch of the hotel floorplan]."

The next exchange contained pauses as Enyart could be heard drawing upon the floorplan.

"Here was a bar and here was this table. I was right here and I headed over to here, got to about here. And Mr. Kennedy walked off the stage and got to about here. I got up on the table and was above and I took pictures down at it—and a friend of mine was there, too, taking pictures, and I'm sure he has some pictures. I can get in touch with him."

"What is his name?"

"Brent Gold. . . ."

"Okay. So that's about all you can tell us, then, about this thing. Did you see the suspect that did the shooting?"

"Couldn't exactly say, 'cause, no, I don't believe I saw the suspect."

"You were just taking pictures of everything and everybody?"

"Yeah. And I took a picture of a boy come running back. His face was bleeding rather bad and he came running back. I got a picture of that. There are miscellaneous pictures on the roll. . . . Do you want a description of the film so you'll know how to process it?"

"No, they'll send it down to the lab and take care of it."

"Will I get the film back?"

"Might get the prints or the negatives. I don't know. We—"

" 'Cause it was kind of important to me."

The officers then gave Enyart a card.

"Give us a call and we'll let you know."

As Skip Miller had said in his opening remarks, whether or not Scott Enyart was in the pantry when the shooting occurred was the pivotal issue. And what Enyart told the police the night of the murder about his whereabouts would have to be considered strong evidence of where he had actually been. If he didn't place himself in the pantry, then the historic and forensic value of whatever photographs he took would be next to nothing. If he did place himself in the pantry, then it would be strong evidence in his favor, because he had no reason to lie—the police already had his film. The frustrating reality for both sides was that Enyart's murder-night interview can bear either interpretation: that he was in the pantry or that he wasn't.

Miller's assertion to the jury, that the word *pantry* does not occur in the interview, is correct. This, in itself, has little meaning because the night of the shooting, few people besides hotel personnel were referring to the narrow room next to the kitchen as the pantry. Most intriguing is that as the tape plays one can hear Enyart drawing a map of his movements for the detectives. "I was right here, and I headed over to here, got to about here and Mr. Kennedy walked off the stage and got to here." The map that Enyart drew was not found in the LAPD's released files.

Thus the question remains, what map did Enyart draw? He was asked whether he had seen the suspect who did the shooting. That would tend to support his claim that he had drawn a route into the pantry. More important, the police reports of Enyart's interview also tend to support his claim. A file card describing the taped interview bearing the names "Calkin/ McGann" states about Enyart: "Was in kitchen when Kennedy came in, climbed on table to take pictures, heard shots, kept taking pictures. Did not see suspect." An interview report written out by officer T. J. Miller reads: "Was in Embassy Rm taking pictures of speech. Kennedy left podium subj went to hallway outside kitchen. Got up on table to take pictures. Subj believe[s] at that time he may have gotten pictures of shooting. Subj turned undeveloped pictures over to police.''

Scott Enyart claims that in the months following Robert Kennedy's murder he tried a number of times to recover his photographs from the police. Finally, on one visit to police headquarters, he was brought to a room where photographs were locked away. The young man watched as several envelopes were removed from a steel cabinet.

"I was not allowed to look at my photographs," Enyart recalled to the authors. "They took this stack of prints, and one of the detectives shuffled through them and separated them into two piles. He gave me the photographs from one roll of film—everything leading up to the assassination—and then some pictures I had taken after the assassination. What he didn't give me, were the pictures that I took in the pantry."

Under direct examination Scott Enyart was a compelling witness. He spoke with confidence and certainty about his missing photos. He demonstrated an advanced knowledge of photography. He spoke in great detail about the night of the assassination.

Enyart also identified himself in two photographs taken in the hotel pantry after the shooting. One was the Bill Eppridge photo which had appeared on *Unsolved Mysteries*. That photo had been taken perhaps several minutes after the shooting. Another photograph by amatuer photographer Richard Harrison, taken during the struggle for Sirhan's gun (and thus less than a minute after the shooting), recorded a shadowy figure apparently standing on the table where Enyart said he was. Positive identification was impossible, but Enyart claimed that the figure was wearing a sport jacket like the one he had worn and appeared to be in a stance consistent with the taking of photographs.

After a week of direct testimony, Skip Miller began his cross-examination of Scott Enyart. He showed visible disdain for the witness, and his questions were often tinted with sarcasm. Miller attacked on all fronts. He paid particular attention to Enyart's detailed description of the events in the pantry.

"Has your memory improved over the years?" asked Miller.

Enyart responded that certain things leave a strong imprint in the mind. "My first child was born nineteen years ago," he said, "and I can remember that as though it happened yesterday."

Miller then took portions of Enyart's story and found passages in books and articles that described them in a similar way, suggesting that Enyart's memories had been pasted together after the fact, from secondary sources. Enyart had in court told of Robert Kennedy lying on the floor with a ''halo of blood" spreading from his head. Miller read a description of the murder which used that very image. Enyart claimed he had not read the passage.

"So the word 'halo' occurred to you?" challenged Miller. "Came out of your head?"

"I was raised Roman Catholic," Enyart responded. "The word 'halo' was very familiar to me."

Miller asked Scott Enyart about his attempt to market a book titled *A Witness to History* and a proposed screenplay with the same title. Both were to feature Scott Enyart's story and his photographs. Miller read a portion of a letter Enyart had written to his agent in June of 1991 where Enyart referred to the ongoing lawsuit against the city as enhancing the value of the proposed project by providing a focus for public interest in his story. "Isn't it a fact," asked Miller, "that you were marketing this story as part of an effort to advance this lawsuit?"

On Thursday, July 11, Miller would interrupt his cross-examination of Enyart to introduce a witness for the defense, photographer Bill Eppridge. Still a working photojournalist, Eppridge was on his way to Atlanta to photograph the Olympic games for *Sports Illustrated*. From the witness stand he told the jury of the events the night of the murder, when he had been taking photographs for *Life* magazine. The courtroom became still as he recounted how he entered the pantry moments after the shooting to first find Paul Schrade and then Robert Kennedy lying on the floor.

Miller then showed Eppridge an enlarged version of his photo with the young man on the table in the background.

"Do you recognize this photograph?" asked Miller.

"Yes," answered Eppridge. "I took that photograph."

"Do you know who this person is up on the table?"

"Yes. That's Harry Benson."

Harry Benson was a photojournalist from Great Britain. He had been Bill Eppridge's friend and rival, and Eppridge made it clear that there was no question in his mind that the young man in the photograph was Benson. Upon resuming the witness stand Scott Enyart would tell the jury that after hearing Bill Eppridge's testimony, he had changed his mind and was now willing to accept that the young man in the photo was not Scott Enyart. Later Harry Benson would appear in court. Even after twenty-eight years, the image of the young man, which had only born a generic likeness to Scott Enyart, bore an undeniable resemblance to Benson.

After Bill Eppridge, Miller resumed his examination of Enyart. He introduced into evidence a portion of Theodore Charach's 1973 film documentary *The Second Gun,* in which Charach spoke to a young Scott Enyart in 1969 or 1970. (This would be the only segment of the documentary that the jury would see. Over the objections of Enyart's attorneys, Judge Elias refused to allow the jury to see other portions of the documentary that explored allegations of conspiracy in the Robert Kennedy murder.) A video monitor was wheeled into place and the Enyart segment was shown.

In the interview Scott Enyart talked about going to the Ambassador Hotel with his friends and then taking photographs. "I shot a thirty-six exposure roll of film," Enyart said on camera, "and I got twenty-six prints back. I definitely feel there are some missing." The video went on to display the Enyart prints.

"Now Mr. Enyart," said Miller when the video was done. "Last year in deposition you said you received back from the police eighteen prints, is that not so?'

"Yes."

"And in court a few days ago you said you got back twenty prints?"

"Yes.

"Can you tell me, Mr. Enyart, why in the video we just saw you say you received back twenty-six prints?"

Enyart was forced to say that over the years he must have "misplaced" some of the pictures given back to him by the police.

It was a devastating day for Scott Enyart. Bill Eppridge's repudiation of his claim to be the young man on the table wasn't fatal to his case, because the picture had been taken some minutes after the shooting, at a time when Enyart may have already been off the table. But the Eppridge testimony had been dramatic, and the best interpretation for the plaintiff was that Scott Enyart had been mistaken or perhaps reckless with the evidence.

The Charach video was also very damaging. As the documentary would reveal, there were at least twenty-six prints provided to Charach by Enyart, and presumably at least twenty-six prints provided to Enyart by the police. Where were they now? If the photos were so important to Enyart, how were they lost? Enyart said that they had been kept in different envelopes over the years and "shuffled" around. It wasn't much of an answer from a plaintiff whose trademark until this day had been care and precision. Now, either Enyart had misstated the evidence or he had been careless with the very pictures he was accusing the LAPD of losing.

There were other problems. Skip Miller was quick to point out that during the video Enyart had not mentioned being in the pantry, or seeing Kennedy fall. Enyart responded that he had told Charach those things and that he had no say in what appeared on the documentary. Miller asserted that during the video Enyart had not said anything about taking three rolls of film. Enyart answered that he had been only speaking about the crucial second roll of film which had been shot in the pantry.

* * *

As the trial progressed Judge Elias made it clear that she intended to limit the scope of the case. "We are not trying conspiracy or retrying Sirhan Sirhan," she said. "We are not here to try whether there were two gunmen." But the Enyart lawsuit and the Kennedy murder shared a common border, and one that was not easy to fence or patrol. Despite efforts to assure otherwise, the haunting underlying theme of the two-month trial became the assassination of Robert Kennedy.

The defense attorneys, understandably, did not want the assassination to enter the case for fear it would prejudice the jury against the city and the police. The plaintiff's attorneys wanted certain questions about the murder brought into evidence because they felt it demonstrated possible motive for the loss or destruction of Scott Enyart's photographs. The sharpest battles in the case were fought on this terrain.

When the plaintiffs called former L.A. County Coroner Thomas Noguchi, Skip Miller objected.

"I don't have an understanding as to what he could possibly testify to."

"Yes, you do," replied Judge Elias.

"I don't. I'm not just saying that. I don't."

"We went through this." The judge sighed. "It's a question of, if Mr. Enyart shot photographs of Mr. Kennedy as he was falling, what would have, from Dr. Noguchi's analysis, what would have been in the view."

Dr. Noguchi would go on to testify as he had twenty-eight years earlier at Sirhan's trial, that the gun that killed Robert Kennedy had been fired from within a few inches of Kennedy's head.

Although there are no known photographs of the shooting in the pantry as it was taking place, the belief that the event was captured on film has endured in the public mind. Stories in the press and statements by various officials have helped perpetuate this myth. One story in the *Los Angeles Times* stated, "The shooting of Kennedy, recorded on television film and by still cameras, occurred in the pantry just off the Ambassador's main ballroom floor."[5] In 1975 a police spokesman defended the police investigation by saying, "We think that Sirhan Sirhan killed this guy because we got it on TV."[6]

But no pictures of the murder of Robert Kennedy have ever emerged. Thus, if Scott Enyart's alleged pantry photos actually captured Robert Kennedy at the time he was assaulted, their commercial and forensic value would be considerable: Robert Kennedy was shot at point blank range and photographs taken at that moment might very well capture the gun or the gunman or both. Such a circumstance might also represent a motive for their disappearance. These were considerations that the plaintiff's lawyers were eager to impress upon the jury.

The level of care demonstrated by the police concerning the evidence was also an issue that the plaintiffs wished to bring out. Toward this end, they subpoenaed Philip Melanson, who, as director of the RFK Assassination Archives at the University of Massachusetts, was granted the status of expert witness. Melanson testified that he had found "glaring inaccuracies" in the LAPD *Summary Report*, and that in the report there was little "that threatened anyone's privacy," or that justified the twenty years of secrecy. He also spoke about a "pattern whereby some of the least important, most trivial material seems to have been carefully preserved without problem, whereas other categories . . . some of the most central and most controversial—were missing."

Paul Schrade, the campaign aide who was wounded at the Ambassador Hotel, was also called to testify. Under the direction of Christine Harwell, Schrade spoke about the efforts to get the police to open their files. Harwell asked Schrade about a meeting that he and former congressman Allard Lowenstein had with police chief Ed Davis in 1974.

"Did you make a request of Chief Davis to give you further access to the LAPD records and photographs?"

"Yes. He said that we should submit questions to him in writing and to Sam Williams, president of the police commission, which we did."

"And did you get an answer to your questions?"

"Never."

Schrade went on to say that the reason given to him for continued secrecy was to keep the files away from "kooks and profiteers." Harwell asked if he had made other attempts to open the files.

"In 1986 we had made another effort to get information from the police files, and Chief Gates was sitting with the police commission at the LAPD headquarters for this hearing. I put in front of him the police department photos simulating the shot that went through Robert Kennedy's jacket into my head . . . I told him, 'These photographs show that shot, based upon a rod going through two holes in Kennedy's coat, that shot was directed toward the ceiling. How could that have gone into my head? I'm not that tall.' "

"And what did Police Chief Gates do?"

"He just sat there stonefaced. I asked him three times. He refused to answer me."

Following Schrade, journalist Theodore Charach was called to the witness stand. Like Schrade, Charach had also been present at the Ambassador Hotel the night of the murder. It was Charach's documentary that the defense had used the week before to cast doubt upon Scott Enyart's story. Now, however, Charach bolstered the plaintiff's case by testifying that he had seen Scott Enyart up on the table in the pantry when he entered the room shortly after the shooting. Then, in an embarrassing moment for the plaintiffs, Charach also asserted he recognized Scott Enyart in the Eppridge photograph, which had previously been shown to be—even to Enyart's satisfaction—a picture of Harry Benson.

After Charach stepped down, Rose Lynn Mangan, a case researcher and friend of the Sirhan family, was called. She testified that while doing research at the state archives she discovered that the evidence log numbers, #24 & #25, assigned to the disputed and newly discovered "Clayton" film (the prints and negatives found in the state archives that matched those returned to Scott Enyart in 1968) were also the same numbers originally assigned to the bullet fragments taken from Robert Kennedy's head. The evidence log numbers for the bullet fragments were then imperfectly erased and written over to become #26 & #27. That the disputed and now missing negatives at the center of the Enyart trial had at some time shared evidence log numbers with the bullet fragments that killed Robert Kennedy was, indeed, disturbing. But its meaning was unclear.

Another alumnus of the Sirhan trial, retired police officer Frank Patchett, was called as a witness by the plaintiffs. In charge of case preparation for Special Unit Senator, Patchett was the liaison between the police and the district attorney's office. In this capacity, he had the primary responsibility for determining who was placed upon the official list of witnesses in the pantry at the time of the shooting.

Patchett's testimony was consistent and believable, but the former police sergeant could not explain why Scott Enyart had not been reinterviewed in light of the police reports that he had possibly taken photographs of the murder. Under Christine Harwell's questioning, Patchett admitted that he had no recollection of seeing any police reports about Scott Enyart or any memory of eliminating him from the pantry list. "Why Mr. Enyart does not appear on the list of people in the pantry, I cannot tell you," said Patchett. "But I can guarantee you that at the time there was a good reason, and what that was I don't know."

As Scott Enyart had testified, he had gone to the Ambassador Hotel on primary night with a friend named Brent Gold. Both young men had brought cameras and they had spent much of the evening in each other's company. But Brent Gold was not called as a witness by the attorneys for Scott Enyart; he was called by the city.

Gold, now a psychotherapist by profession, testified that Enyart and he had been "best of friends" while they had been in junior high school and had shared an interest in photography. Gold said that he had no knowledge of what kind of film Enyart shot the night of the murder, nor how many rolls of film Enyart had brought with him, but he also said that both of them frequently used the inexpensive Ilford brand hand-loaded film. This was significant because the negatives found at the California State Archives were Ilford, but Enyart was claiming that he had used factory-packaged Kodak film the night Robert Kennedy was shot.

As photographs taken that night reveal, both Brent Gold and Scott Enyart were in front of the stage, close to each other, when Robert Kennedy was speaking. Defense attorney Skip Miller asked Gold to describe where he went after Kennedy's speech had ended.

"I simply walked out to the front," said Gold, "to the lobby."

"Which way did Scott Enyart go?"

"We were together."

"Did you walk together?"

"Yes."

"Did either you or Mr. Enyart attempt to fight against the crowd and go in the direction of the podium?"

"No."

Gold testified that both he and Enyart were in the hotel lobby just outside of the Embassy Room when they heard the first screams and commotion indicating something was wrong inside. According to Gold, both of them went back into the Embassy Room to see what had happened and became separated.

Miller then asked Gold if they had ever subsequently talked about what had happened at the hotel. Gold said they had.

"Until the lawsuit was filed, did Mr. Enyart ever tell you that he had been in the pantry and took the only pictures in the world of Senator Kennedy being shot?"

"No," answered Gold. "He never said that he had taken pictures of Senator Kennedy being shot."

Gold would go on to say that after high school he and Scott Enyart had encountered each other only a few times at social gatherings. Then in 1992 Gold saw Enyart being interviewed on TV, claiming that he had been in the pantry during the murder. Gold said he called Enyart on the telephone because he was "fearful" that he was going to get himself into trouble, "because I knew where we were. I knew we were both outside in the lobby area when Kennedy was shot and he wasn't in the pantry."

"And what did Mr. Enyart say?" asked Miller.

"He said that wasn't his recollection of the event."

Upon cross-examination Scott Enyart's attorneys were able to show that Brent Gold's memory was not crisp, continually chasing Gold back to his notes to refresh his recollection about events in the past. They also elicited from Mr. Gold that he had spent more than twenty hours with police detectives and lawyers for the city.

"Did you enjoy participating with the LAPD," Gold was asked, "the detectives and talking about the events and meeting with them at Parker Center and going out to the hotel? Did you enjoy that?"

"This entire process has been extremely painful and upsetting to me," responded Gold. "I would never want to speak out against a friend, especially a friend of thirty years. No, it has not been fun."

Enyart's lawyers did what they could do, but the problem remained. Scott Enyart had said one thing, and his former friend Brent Gold had said something quite different. Who was telling the truth, and who would the jury believe?

While the movies talked about during jury selection were *JFK* and *The Bridges of Madison County*, the true cinematic antecedent of the Enyart trial was Michelangelo Antonioni's *Blow Up*. In this 1960s classic, a series of apparently innocent photographs are enlarged and enhanced until the image of a murder weapon emerges from obscure shadows. But murder scene photographs by Scott Enyart or anyone else were not at the trial, and the negatives found at the state archives were also missing, so they couldn't be analyzed to see if some sort of forgery had taken place. But when certain photographs at the trial were enlarged, the resulting images didn't support Scott Enyart's assertions.

The Bill Eppridge photo, when enlarged, showed a young man who didn't look particularly like Scott Enyart. Moreover, a blow-up of one of the "Clayton" prints solved another mystery. Earlier in the trial Enyart had suggested that the print seemed to be out of sequence because it appeared to be shot before Kennedy had even taken the stage. But the enlarged print produced by the defense attorneys revealed the obscure but unmistakable image of shooting victim Irwin Stroll being carried out into the Embassy Room. Thus, the "Clayton" prints were not out of sequence as Enyart had suggested.

After five weeks of bruising, often acrimonious, conflict in court, Christine Harwell, representing Scott Enyart, stood once again in front of the jury. By California law the plaintiffs in a civil lawsuit speak first in final argument, the defendants respond, and then the plaintiffs speak again.

With a stern look on her face Harwell began by praising the competence of attorney Skip Miller, calling him "a very skilled attorney, a very clever attorney." She then went on to describe ways in which she thought Miller had been clever. She pointed to his representation that Scott Enyart had not spoken the word *pantry* in his police interview, even though few people were using that word the night of the murder. She scorned Miller's attempt to cast Enyart's financial stake in his photographs as a motive for fabrication. She noted Miller's attempt to discredit Enyart's account of the murder by finding other, similar descriptions. She mentioned the "halo" of blood. "Of course, had Scott Enyart described Kennedy's head resting in a "pool" of blood, she said, "no doubt Mr. Miller could have found another reference somewhere else which used that term."

Harwell went on to speak about Skip Miller's literal reading of the transcript of Enyart's police interview. "Of course, reading the transcript of the interview and listening to the interview are two very different things," said Harwell. "When we listened to the tape we heard a young man drawing a map of where he had been. We hear a police officer asking Mr. Enyart if he had seen or photographed the shooter. Why would the police ask Scott Enyart if he had seen the shooter if Scott Enyart had drawn them a diagram that hadn't even put him in the pantry? Why would the police report of this interview assert that Scott Enyart had said he was in the pantry, if it had been their understanding that Scott had only been in the Embassy Room?"

Harwell then set forth for the jury the list of strange anomalies in the case: Enyart having his film taken from him at gunpoint, his not receiving back his negatives, his not being reinterviewed or included on the list of pantry witnesses, no film being on file under his name, the failure of his interview to appear in the *Summary Report*, and the theft of the newly found negatives. "Are all of these occurrences just coincidence?" asked Harwell. "Innocent mistakes? I don't think so. I think what we see here is a consistent and deliberate attempt to erase Scott Enyart and his photographs from the record of this case."

Harwell told the jury that pressing a civil suit is a very expensive proposition, that the lawsuit against the city had placed a tremendous burden upon the Enyart family. "Do you really think Scott Enyart would have put himself and his family through this terrible ordeal if he were missing just a couple of photos? If he hadn't really been in the pantry at the time of the murder? If he hadn't been outraged at his treatment at the hands of the police?"

As she closed her remarks Harwell wanted the jury to understand that the cost to the Enyart family was not just financial. "The LAPD has put Mr. Enyart through a degrading process and tried to make him out to be a profiteer. You know that is not so. All we ask for is justice."

Christine Harwell had made a forceful appeal on behalf of her client. The atmosphere in the courtroom was charged. As Skip Miller began his argument he attempted to reduce the pressure.

"This is a case about Mr. Enyart's photographs," he reminded the jury. "It is not a kick in the door, send a message to the police, kind of case."

Miller said that Enyart's claim against the city was one fabricated with "smoke and mirrors." He replayed the Enyart segment of the Charach documentary, and reminded the jury that on the video Enyart had not claimed to have shot three rolls of film or even to have been in the pantry. He said that Enyart had come forward now because he had a motive.

Miller said that Enyart's motive could be found in a letter to his agent where he talked about promoting the proposed screenplay of his story.

"There's nothing wrong with him trying to break into Hollywood, sell his screenplay. Go for it. All the luck in the world. But don't come into court, spin a yarn, and try to get a jury to conclude that you are a 'witness to history.' That was the title of his proposed story. But he wasn't a witness to anything. And it's not right for him to come to court and ask you to help him sell his property to Hollywood."

Speaking of the police handling of the evidence in the RFK case, Miller said, "They were doing their job and they did it right." He called the theft of the negatives outside the L.A. airport a "snafu." "If you believe that we had something to do with that," he said, challenging the jury, "then you believe in the tooth fairy."

Miller then recalled the descriptive language in Scott Enyart's story. "I submit to you, ladies and gentlemen, that all the colorful detail that he told to you he got from books, he got from videos, he got from movies, he got from other sources after the fact."

Miller ended his summation to the jury by saying that Scott Enyart had been trying to "pull a fast one." "He doesn't deserve a dime," said the attorney, his emotional level rising. "I think he's dishonored the court process. I think he's dishonored the memory of that night by trying to profit from it. This case is all about profit, personal gain, self-promotion, and greed. Just say no."

Skip Miller sat down; Christine Harwell rose again. The defense attorney's accusations had reddened her face. Abandoning her notes she spoke in an uncharacteristic angry voice.

"Mr. Miller has said that Scott Enyart was not a witness to anything," she said to the jury. "Well just ask yourself. Why was he apprehended? Why was he interviewed? Why was his film immediately developed? Why is there no diagram? Why is there no receipt? Why is there no logging? Why is there no booking? No followup report? No indexing?"

Harwell then made reference to the seven years she had been working on the lawsuit. "I have spent a lot of time on this case," she said in a more measured tone. "I care and believe in my client. I think that you know the truth. That Mr. Enyart took those pictures, he didn't get them back, and they have never been produced to him. It's up to you to determine what that is worth."

The following day Judge Emilie Elias gave her instructions to the jury. She instructed them that in a civil suit a plaintiff did not have to prove his case "beyond a reaonable doubt," but only by "a preponderance of the evidence." She reminded them that only nine of the twelve jurors had to agree to decide any issue and that the number of witnesses testifying on any fact was less important than the "convincing force of the evidence."

Because the trial had taken weeks longer than anticipated it had been assumed that the jury was fatigued and eager to go home. A quick verdict was expected. It didn't come. Rumors of discord in the deliberations began to leak out, and day after day, no verdict arrived. Soon the rumor spread that the jury was deadlocked 8–4. But which way? Only nine votes were necessary to bring forth a verdict, but whose side did they favor?

After two weeks of jury deliberations a crisis developed: jury foreman Robert Pinger, a high school history teacher, announced that he had to leave the jury to ready himself for the coming school year. He then filed with the court a statement, outlining his frustrations with the deliberation process and alleging "misconduct" on the part of several jurors. After Pinger's final day with the jury, but before he had been officially released and replaced by an alternate, attorney Skip Miller obtained a detailed statement from him as to what had occurred in the jury room. Upon learning this, Judge Elias exchanged harsh words with the defense attorney.

"Mr. Miller, I can't think of anything more inappropriate than you having talked to a juror in the middle of deliberations. . . . I think it's outrageous."

"I don't agree at all, Your Honor. I think I had an obligation to do it. It was entirely appropriate, this juror was released from jury duty."

"No, he wasn't. If you really want to know, he wasn't. He was told not to speak to anyone and you contacted him. . . ."

"Instead of being angry at me, which frankly shocks me, it just shocks me that the court could be angry at me, instead of being angry at me I would think this court would be upset, angry, and concerned about what was going on inside the jury room. . . . I did nothing wrong. For this court to get upset with me, I don't understand it. Where are you coming from, Your Honor? Where, I mean, are we talking about justice? Fairness?"

"Mr. Miller, I've heard enough."

"Excuse me, Your Honor, I take this whole thing very seriously."

"Mr. Miller, why don't you wait until more reporters come and you can make your comments then."

"Excuse me, Your Honor? I don't understand that kind of a comment."

"It was inappropriate and I shouldn't have said it—I was outraged that you would do this and—"

"You were outraged? You're not upset about what was gong on for the last two weeks in your courtroom, Your Honor?"

"Mr. Miller, I'm very upset about your behavior and if you don't stay quiet I'm going to start a contempt hearing. Okay? That's how upset I am."

Conversation between Miller and Elias returned to normal, and Miller was not cited for contempt. Miller's strident words in this exchange would be a clue to the verdict to come. On Thursday August 22, after three weeks of deliberation, the jury awarded Scott Enyart $450,600* for the loss of his photographs. "This case had a lot of potential for things going wrong," lamented City Attorney James Hahn weeks before the verdict was in.[7] Now, from the city's point of view, the prophecy had come true. Others didn't see it that way. "We definitely thought the city and police screwed up all the way through," said jury foreman Dorsey Caldwell.[8]

The verdict had not been unanimous. The final vote had been 9 to 3, the minimum necessary for a judgment. And even that was shaded by a cloud. Ex-jury foreman Robert Pinger later would tell the authors that he believed the verdict in the Enyart case had more to do with "anti-civic-authority sentiment" on the part of some jurors than it did with the evidence of the case.

As would be expected the heavy judgment in Scott Enyart's favor released strong emotions on both sides. Enyart, of course, was elated. In the hall outside of the courtroom he characterized his battle with the police as "David versus Goliath." "I'm thrilled," he told newsmen, "but I would much rather have my three rolls of film."[9]

The defense team tried to avoid the newsmen, but their frustration with the verdict was evident. "Absurd in the extreme" was Skip Miller's comment. He also privately promised the Enyart lawyers that their client would "never see a dime" of the award, alluding to the probability of appeal.

On October 15, attorneys representing the City of Los Angeles filed a series of motions before Judge Elias. In one, the city asked the judge to declare a mistrial.

The grounds for the motion were multiple. The city charged that a new trial should be granted because Scott Enyart's lawyers were "allowed to present witnesses who misled and inflamed the jury with allegations of a purported conspiracy and cover-up by the LAPD, resulting in a jury poisoned by speculation as to a possible conspiracy to assassinate Senator Robert F. Kennedy." The city also alleged "serious misconduct" on the part of the jury. In making this charge the city presented the declarations of five former jury members. According to the motion, these declarations revealed that "certain jurors threatened and abused other members of the jury in what can only be characterized as a war of attrition, in derogation of the law."

Conversations with the city's attorneys revealed that they believed that "jury misconduct" was their most powerful argument. "There was talk in the jury room," said Assistant City Attorney Ed Fimbres, "like 'Everybody knows that the man screws over the people. Everybody knows that the LAPD doesn't know how to take care of evidence. Everybody knows that

---

*On September 18 the plaintiffs were awarded an additional $175,000 in interest which brought the total judgement to $625,600.

there was a conspiracy that killed the Kennedys.' All that kind of stuff. It wasn't part of the evidence, and yet it was discussed in the jury room. It was highly improper."

Attorneys for Scott Enyart were, of course, less judgmental. "There is conduct here," said Christine Harwell, "that is viewed as improper by some and proper by others, and that's just the nature of the process."

Judge Emilie Elias apparently agreed. On November 22 she denied the defense motions for a new trial. After the ruling Assistant City Attorney Fimbres seemed disappointed and perplexed. "We thought we put on a very compelling case," he said. "It was just a very, very strange trial."

Strange indeed. With missing photographs, stolen evidence, and sharply conflicting testimony, the Enyart trial served to rekindle the many frustrations felt by both sides in the smoldering twenty-eight-year debate over Robert Kennedy's murder. What else it accomplished was unclear. For some observers the large verdict in Enyart's favor was the spanking the Los Angeles Police deserved for their inadequate and secretive handling of the Robert Kennedy murder investigation. For others, Enyart's suit against the city represented the perfect example of how evidence can be distorted to further the interests of "kooks and profiteers."

Both views are parochial. Despite the large verdict in his favor, Enyart's claim to have taken important pictures of Robert Kennedy's murder seemed more in doubt after the trial than before it began. Conversely, even if it could be proven that Enyart didn't take photos of Robert Kennedy as he was murdered, that wouldn't dispell the many other disturbing questions still open in the case.

In the last week of December the City of Los Angeles brought the verdict in the Scott Enyart lawsuit to the Appellate Court of California, 2nd District.

Epilogue

✳ ✳ ✳

. . . The atrocities we [Americans] commit trouble so little our official self-righteousness, our invincible conviction of our moral infallibility.

—Arthur Schlesinger, Jr., speaking at a commencement ceremony the day after Robert Kennedy was shot

In the autumn of 1993, William Klaber interviewed Sirhan Sirhan in prison on two occasions. The following is a brief portrait of Sirhan based on those interviews.

AN HOUR NORTH of Bakersfield, amid endless acres of cotton, Corcoran State Prison rises from the dusty plains like a fortress from the future. Dozens of one-hundred-foot steel poles housing high-powered lights protrude from the facility like spines of a sea urchin, and on the perimeter, two fourteen-foot-high cyclone fences topped with tightly coiled, stainless-steel razor wire straddle a twenty-foot alleyway, which, in turn, is guarded by gun towers at regular intervals. This is where California keeps its high profile security risks. Juan Corona and Charles Manson are here. So is Sirhan Bishara Sirhan.

Upon entering the prison one must surrender all portable possessions—wallet, keys, coins, belt—but once you are scanned and frisked, the walk to the visiting room is undramatic. There are no echoing footsteps, no reverberations from closing steel doors. The visiting room itself, with painted cement block walls and asphalt tiles underfoot, resembles an immaculately kept truck-stop cafeteria, complete with microwave for heating single-serving cans of what is normally thought of as children's lunch food. In one corner a thin man in blue prison fatigues lightly strokes the head of an overweight woman with a tired look on her face. In another, a Hispanic prisoner with tattoos on his biceps sits with his wife and three children.

Dressed in jeans, sneakers, and a light blue work shirt Sirhan Sirhan enters the room. An awkward smile betrays his initial discomfort. He greets his visitors, and then embraces his brother Adel.

Sirhan asks about the fires that have been raging in the hills near the family's home in Pasadena. Adel replies that there has been heavy damage in nearby Altadena, but only drifting smoke in their neighborhood, except that the strong winds that preceded the fires brought down the large eucalyptus tree near the house.

"Really," Sirhan says, "the whole thing?"

"No, about half. But it landed right on the fence in the side yard."

Sirhan shakes his head in dismay, but, despite the sad nature of the story, news of a tree that he has not seen for twenty-six years seems to give him fresh energy.

Corcoran has been Sirhan's home since 1992. He says it is more pleasant than Soledad or San Quentin, where he had spent the majority of his years without freedom. To the uninitiated, however, the prison's galvanized perimeter would seem to fence a bleak emotional landscape.

"The worst part is the monotony," says Sirhan, trying to describe life at Corcoran. "A bell rings, you get up. Another rings, you eat. And every day is exactly the same."

While extended imprisonment can smother a man's soul, it can also, in a perverse way, be kind to his body. In some manner this may be true of Sirhan. Though he is over fifty, Sirhan has no age lines on his face. There are just the slightest traces of gray in his hair. If he were wearing it differently, were his hair standing up on his head, then he would look remarkably like the Sirhan who was on the front page of every daily newspaper in the country the day after Robert Kennedy was shot.

But despite this resemblance to a known villain, it is difficult to escape the feeling that, as the most enigmatic man behind bars in America today, Sirhan Sirhan has been miscast. He is bright-eyed, considerate, well-spoken, and has the sly little smile of everybody's kid brother. His manners and conversation appear to lack calculation, and there is a charming boyishness about him, though he is intellectually inclined and conversant in world affairs. Yet dark mysteries, undiminished by the passage of time, still cling to this man, the most immediate being that he has been in jail for almost his entire adult life for a crime he claims he has no memory of committing.

To visit Sirhan as a journalist is difficult. One needs the prisoner's cooperation, his family's cooperation, and the often complicated approval of the prison authorities, who are strict, perhaps obstructionist, when it comes to granting access to high-profile prisoners. Over the last twenty-five years, only a handful of people have been able to see Sirhan in this manner.

To gain access to Sirhan as a visitor, as we were doing, is less complicated.★ Sirhan's cooperation and that of his family are still needed, but the
prison requirements are merely generic. In addition, a visitor can spend the
whole day with the prisoner while a journalist is usually restricted to a one-
hour interview.

A visitor, however, can bring nothing into the prison, including any
kind of recording device. No video cameras, no tape recorders, no pens,
pencils, or writing pads. Once inside, pencils, about two inches in length,
are available as well as scraps of paper. But the pencils, dull to begin with,
quickly become unusable. Employing the lip of an opened soda can, Adel
does his best to sharpen them as the conversations proceed.

A handsome man at age fifty-seven, Adel Sirhan is the third oldest of
the five Sirhan brothers. Living in the same house that the family owned
when Robert Kennedy was murdered, Adel takes care of his mother, Mary,
and manages what there is of Sirhan's affairs. In years gone by, Adel sang
and played the *oud* at the Ali Baba and other Arabic night clubs, and around
his eyes are the crinkled vestiges of good times and late nights. These days,
however, Adel works evenings in a bookstore, and there is little in the way
of time or money to devote to pursuits beyond the necessary. He survives,
he tells me, "with a faith in God and a sense of the absurd."

Over the next six hours there is, of course, mixed in with the serious
talk, a great deal of casual conversation—sports, gossip, current events. The
other opportunity for needed breaks is provided by the vending machines
in the corner. Snack food wrappers soon litter our table. Sirhan pays particular attention to a Mounds Bar he had purchased, eating it slowly, one
small piece at a time. "It's a delicacy," he says in subtle mockery of his
living situation, explaining that inside at the commissary, which he can visit
twice a month, there is available without variation only Snickers and Pay
Day.

On a normal day Sirhan is awakened at 5:30, and after breakfast he begins
his duties cleaning in the prison for which he is paid $18 a month. Sirhan's
cell, which he occupies by himself, is about 8 × 10 feet in dimension, with
floors, walls, and ceilings of unpainted cement, and a five-inch slit for a
window. This cell is part of what is called a Protective Housing Unit, which
Sirhan shares with just thirty-seven other inmates, who are presumed to
require special security either because of the nature of the crime they committed, or, more usually, because they have something to fear from other
prisoners.

During our conversations Sirhan describes the staff at Corcoran as "professional," and their relationship with the inmates as "symbiotic." How

---

★During this visit I was accompanied by Adel Sirhan, case researcher and family friend,
Rose Lynn Mangan, and journalist Dan Moldea.

many other prisoners in his block would make that observation is unclear, but Sirhan is the only prisoner in the unit to opt for a radio instead of a television in his cell. "TV is pretty boring," he says. "It's just the same stupid jokes and phony laughter." Sirhan mostly tunes his radio to KVPR, the National Public Radio affiliate out of Fresno. He enjoys listening to ethnic music and the evening news program "All Things Considered." The news of the Palestinian/Israeli peace accord he regards as stunning. "Really, I never thought I'd live to see this," he says. It's his brightest and most animated comment of the day.

In his off hours Sirhan likes to jog and lift weights. Though he stands five foot four and weighs 140, he claims he can bench press three hundred pounds, though he is at first reluctant to tell me this for fear people will think he is a brute. Sirhan says he gets along "well enough" with the other prisoners, but he has no friends. Sirhan must keep his distance. Because of who he is, some prisoner is always willing to sell stories or make deals with authorities based on new information they say Sirhan has told them in confidence.

Even though the event is decades old, when the conversation turns to his trial, Sirhan's emotions begin to surface.

"All this talk about killing my father and marrying my mother," he says, "it was ridiculous. It was insulting. I protested."

During his trial Sirhan did frequently object to Grant Cooper's handling of his defense. In response, Sirhan claims that Cooper would remind him how much per hour his time was worth on the open market. "I had the best criminal lawyer in California," Sirhan says ironically. "He knew all the tricks of the trade. Unfortunately, he used them all on me."

This view on Sirhan's part is, perhaps, a bit self-serving. As is documented, Grant Cooper and Sirhan Sirhan did not relate well to each other. Cooper openly admitted that he didn't understand Sirhan. Sirhan tried several times to have Cooper dismissed. But Sirhan could hardly be said to have offered Cooper constructive assistance. At the time of the trial Sirhan's dissatisfactions had little to do with his attorney's failure to explore the physical facts of the case. Sirhan was as blind in this direction as Cooper. Nevertheless, as Sirhan sits in prison several decades later, his resentment, justified or not, is still apparent.

As we begin a reconstruction of his movements on the day of the assassination, Sirhan offers his own version of unkind fate. "If the horses had been running that night," he says, "I would have been down at the track." In place of playing the horses, Sirhan claims he went downtown to observe a parade celebrating the one-year anniversary of the Israeli victory in the Six Day War.

"I'm not sure if I was just going to watch or heckle or what, but I wasn't going down there to shoot anybody, I know that."

But Sirhan had misread the advertisement and the parade was to be held the following night, so, as the story goes, he found his way to the Ambassador Hotel where several election night parties were underway. While there he consumed four Tom Collinses which, he says, "I drank like lemonade." The drinks made him sleepy, so Sirhan says he left the Ambassador and went to his two-tone Desoto parked on New Hampshire Street. Sirhan has stated in the past that he must have picked up his gun during this visit to his car.

"Do you have a memory of actually getting your gun?" I ask.

"Well, no. I must have. Pollack [the prosecution psychiatrist] told me that."

"Do you remember being in your car?"

Sirhan scrunches his face, trying. "Well, I remember walking up a hill."

Sirhan says he was too drunk to drive home, so he returned to the Ambassador where he became intrigued by a teletype machine. "It didn't seem real, a typewriter that was typing with nobody there."[1]*

After that Sirhan remembers having coffee with a pretty girl, bright lights, mirrors and then . . . nothing . . . until he is being beaten and choked by an enraged mob.

"Do you have any vague recollections at all of the event?" I ask. "Anything, even dreamlike?"

"I'm sorry," Sirhan says. "I just don't have any mental images of shooting Robert Kennedy. Clearly, I was there. I just can't remember."

A major purpose of the prison interview was to come to some judgment as to Sirhan's sincerity. A tour of duty in the Bronx criminal courts had taught me never to confuse mild manners or good elocution with innocence.[2] I had reviewed the audiotapes of Sirhan's police interviews and the recorded conversations with his attorneys and psychiatrists. I had found nothing to indicate that Sirhan's lack of memory had been fabricated, but I now was looking for anything that might indicate deception. During our time together I found nothing false in Sirhan's words, mannerisms, or demeanor.

But the things Sirhan does recall are open to question. His recollections are a little like an old family story, remembered more from its retelling than from the actual event. In attempting to recall things that took place twenty-six years ago, Sirhan is covering ground that has been walked on so many times that no original footprints remain.

Nevertheless, it was hard to resist the temptation to probe further.

---

*Mary Grohs, a teletype operator that night, confirms this part of his story. "He came over to my machine and started staring at it," she told defense investigator Robert Blair Kaiser, for his book *"RFK Must Die!,"* "just staring. I'll never forget his eyes. I asked him what he wanted. He didn't answer. He just kept staring. I asked him again. No answer. . . . He just kept staring."

"What about the girl?"

"She was very pretty," Sirhan says, "with brown hair."

"What was she wearing?"

"Forget about polka dots," he says smiling, aware of the controversy, but unwilling to add to it. "I don't remember anything about what she was wearing."

When we begin to talk about his parole situation, Sirhan becomes agitated. His anger is apparent yet he struggles to control himself. He knows that any ill-considered comment will be used against him in his next hearing and all those that follow.

Sirhan tells me the story of his first parole hearing at Corcoran in 1992. Moments before he was to be led into the hearing room he was approached by an escort officer, who told him he could only go in if he were wearing manacles and chains. Sirhan refused and he was led away, his next parole hearing to be in two years. There is no doubt in Sirhan's mind that he did the right thing. "What board," he asks, "is going to believe that I'm ready for the outside if I'm brought in tied up like an animal?"

Sirhan has come to expect disappointment at his parole hearings. "I come before the board, I have done well in school, my record is good, but they say I need more psychological tests. Two years later I have the tests, the tests say I'm fine, but then the board wants me to go through an AA program. I haven't had a drink in twenty-six years, but I go through the AA program and I come back two years later, but now they say they want to see my job offers. Job offers? Just what's supposed to be on my resume?"

Sirhan believes that he has not received impartial treatment from the parole board. "There are many people who have committed worse crimes, whom I have seen come and go," he says. "The whole thing has just become political." He pauses and then tags on a strange afterthought. "It's like we're still living under George III."

The discussion then returns to the assassination and the discovery of Sirhan's notebook, surely one of the most bizarre pieces of evidence ever introduced at a trial to prove the requisite state of mind for first-degree murder. What is Sirhan's explanation?

"I believe the notebook is mine," he says. "I just don't remember writing those things."

Does he have any memory of being angry at Robert Kennedy?

"I had a lot of affection for Bobby Kennedy," he answers, "but I felt ambivalent. I saw him as a caring, gentle person who stood up for the downtrodden, the blacks, the Latinos, but it hurt that he wouldn't stand up for everybody."

Of course, talk of motive by Sirhan must be viewed with great caution. If he is telling the truth that he has no memory of planning to shoot Robert

Kennedy, then discussion of motive on his part must be after-the-fact rationalization. I point this out to him.

"I'm aware of that," Sirhan replies. "I'm just trying to explain what must have been propelling me forward. But, honestly, I don't know. Clearly I was there, but still it's a mystery, because I really don't have it in me to kill anyone—drunk or not. That's what I don't understand."

A little while later he would say, "I must have known about the jets,"* but his words lack conviction.

In the space of twenty minutes Sirhan has just demonstrated the strange duality of mind that he has consistently maintained for twenty-six years. On the one hand, he doesn't remember planning to kill Robert Kennedy and can't imagine performing the act, on the other, he believes that he murdered Robert Kennedy because he was a threat to the Palestinians. Which is the real Sirhan?

For most people this has not been a difficult question. When I posed it to Manuel Pena, the former police lieutenant who helped prepare the Sirhan case for trial, he didn't hesitate. "If they ever parole Sirhan," he said, "I'll make you a bet right now that within months he's gonna jump and he'll be over there with Abu Nidal and he will be a prize, prize terrorist. He'll be doing Allah's work, which is 'Kill more whities.' "

When I reminded Pena that Sirhan is a Christian, he replied, "Yeah, but it's still the same."

Pena's view, sincerely held, is similar to that of many law enforcement officers and parole board members. It runs counter to the police investigation, which found no ties between Sirhan and any terrorist group. Sirhan barely had what could be described as a passive political life, much less an active or violent one.

In our conversations Sirhan was also remarkably nonassertive. Although he knew I was a journalist, at no time did he ever argue or hint that he might be innocent. Though he is aware that such ideas have been advanced, Sirhan never promoted the notion that perhaps he had been manipulated by others. His recounting of events, the ones he could remember, seemed straightforward.

Through the involvement of researcher Rose Lynn Mangan, Sirhan has become aware in recent years of some of the evidentiary conundrums in his case. But unlike other prisoners convicted of capital crimes, he is hardly an expert. At one point when we begin a discussion about the ballistic evidence he stops the talk with a gesture. "You must understand," he says

---

*Sirhan here is referring to the Johnson/Eschol agreement for the United States to send fifty jet planes to Israel. As described in Chapter 9, the "jets to Israel" motive became accepted by all parties to the trial.

apologetically, "you know much more about this than I do. I don't spend my time thinking about these things. If I did I would surely go crazy."

Although he seemed grateful for the company, it was becoming apparent that, for Sirhan, having visitors was stressful. He was being forced to think about things that happened many years ago, things he doesn't normally think about, things he can't change.

"I wish I had just gone up and shook his hand," he says, speaking of Robert Kennedy. "If I could bring him back to life, of course, I would do it. If I could go back and trade my life for his, I would do that too—he was the father of eleven children. But none of us have that power."

I ask Sirhan what he would like to do if he were released.

"Live a quiet life somewhere," he answers. "Help people if I could."

What kinds of things would he find enjoyable?

"I'd like to walk down a street," he says, "say hello to someone, go into a store, buy a quart of milk."

As we prepare to leave the prison, the pencils are returned, the candy wrappers are gathered. Sirhan and Adel embrace once more. There is a weary look on Adel's face not apparent before. Sirhan, in contrast, seems more lively.

"So am I the great devil you were expecting to meet?" he asks in parting.

"All that and worse," I answer to his mirth. But the jest, as intended, avoids the question. What Sirhan is really seeking is a new verdict, and, in truth, it is hard to know what to think. Evidence suggests the presence of a second gun, but there are no accomplices in Sirhan's memory. Reliable witnesses saw Sirhan with a woman, but he says he was alone the night of the murder. Sirhan claims not to have planned to shoot Robert Kennedy, yet he offers a motive for doing so. At times it's as though his mind is a hall of mirrors in which every image is a reflection of another, making him a most awkward protagonist. Nothing in Sirhan's youth appears to lead to the most pivotal moment of his life. Nothing of significance happens to him after that moment. And the moment itself is invisible to him.

Sirhan's public persona is a blank sheet upon which investigators, pros-ecutors, psychiatrists, con artists, parole officers, assassination buffs, and journalists get to paint a picture. Communist, terrorist, political martyr, psycho-killer, innocent dupe, robot assassin—Sirhan's tragedy is that he is exactly whomever we wish him to be: a stand-in for random societal vio-lence, unpunished terrorism, or the dark forces suspected of murdering a generation of this nation's most charismatic leaders. He cannot be let go, because the political cost would be to appear to appease these evils or rec-ognize their existence. Meanwhile, what's left of a human being approaches his ten thousandth day in prison, retribution for an act of violence that has never been adequately explained.

Notes

✻ ✻ ✻

Preface

1. Allard Lowenstein, "Robert F. Kennedy and Power in America," 1977 essay published posthumously in *Lowenstein: Acts of Congress and Belief*, edited by Gregory Stone and Douglas Lowenstein (New York: Harcourt Brace Jovanovich, 1983), 317.

Chapter 1: The Ambassador Hotel

1. Sirhan (John Doe) interrogation tape, June 5, 1968, LAPD # 28918.

2. Jesse Unruh, trial testimony, February 14, 1969, p. 3267 trial transcript.

3. Lisa Urso, interview with Philip H. Melanson, October 30, 1987, San Diego, Calif.

4. LAPD witness interview tape, George Plimpton, June 5, 1968, CSA-K19.

5. Dan E. Moldea, *The Killing of Robert F. Kennedy* (New York: W. W. Norton, 1995), 47–48.

6. Sirhan (John Doe) interrogation tape, June 5, 1968, LAPD # 28976

7. LAPD witness interview tape, Vincent DiPierro, June 5, 1968, CSA-K5.

8. Sirhan (John Doe) interrogation tape, June 5, 1968, LAPD # 28917.

9. "Reagan Scoring Courts, Links Shooting to Permissive Attitude," *New York Times*, June 6, 1968, p. 29.

10. Robert Blair Kaiser, *"RFK Must Die!"* (New York: Dutton, 1970), 97.

11. Gladwin Hill, "Woman Is Sought in Kennedy Death," *New York Times*, June 7, 1968, p. 22.

12. "Spectacle of Justice," editorial, *New York Times*, June 10, 1968, p. 44. Note: Despite his nominal Democratic affiliation, Mayor Yorty had supported Richard Nixon against John Kennedy in 1960. In 1968 he was supporting Nixon again. He even had presidential ambitions of his own. In 1972 he announced his candidacy but was soundly defeated in the New Hampshire primary. Shortly thereafter he joined the Republican Party.

13. Tom Buckley, "Yorty Defends Disclosure from Suspect's Notes," *New York Times*, June 7, 1968, p. 26.

14. Gladwin Hill, "Sirhan Said to Reject Offers of Two Defenders," *New York Times*, June 12, 1968, p. 32.

15. James Reston, "Violence Threatening Modern Public Order," *New York Times*, June 6, 1968, p. 20.

16. John Kenneth Galbraith, "Violence Commission Criticized," *New York Times*, June 10, 1968, p. 52.

17. "Gallup Poll Finds Public in Favor of Gun Controls," *New York Times*, June 9, 1968, p. 5.

18. Jack Gould, "TV: Truman Capote Defines His Concept of Justice," *New York Times*, June 15, 1968, p. 71.

19. "Yevtushenko: 'You Shoot at Yourself, America,' " *New York Times*, June 8, 1968, p. 15.

Chapter 2: The Summer of '68

1. Dial Torgerson, "Sirhan Hires New Defense Attorney," *Los Angeles Times*, June 20, 1968, p. 28
2. Ibid.
3. Ron Einstoss, "Sirhan Enters Not Guilty Plea," *Los Angeles Times*, August 3, 1968, part 1, p. 3.
4. Summary of the Los Angeles Police Department Investigation of the Senator Robert F. Kennedy Assassination (Summary Report). (1968), 1422.
5. Russell Parsons, interview by Betsy Langman, audiotape, Los Angeles, 1974.
6. Lacey Fosburgh, "Sirhan Trial Judge," *New York Times*, April 12, 1969, p. 16.
7. "Sirhan Prosecutor Urges Easing of News Restrictions," Associated Press, October 25, 1968, p 38.
8. Robert Blair Kaiser, *"RFK Must Die!"* (New York: Dutton, 1970), 327.

Chapter 3: Voir Dire

1. Gene Blake and Howard Hertel, "U.S. Probes Alleged Transcript Bribe in Friars Club Trial," *Los Angeles Times*, December 3, 1968, p. 3.
2. Gene Blake and Howard Hertel, "Cooper Ordered to Answer Friars Transcript Quiz," *Los Angeles Times*, January 8, 1969, p. 1.
3. Gene Blake, "Five Found Guilty in Friars Club Card Cheating Conspiracy," *Los Angeles Times*, December 3, 1968, p. 1.
4. Gene Blake and Howard Hertel, "4 in Friars Club Case Get 4- to 6-Year Terms," *Los Angeles Times*, February 4, 1969, part 2, p. 1.
5. Ovid Demaris, *The Last Mafiosi* (New York: Bantam, 1981), 252–58.
6. Douglas Kneeland, "Woman Is Barred from Sirhan Jury," *New York Times*, January 18, 1969, p. 25.
7. Robert Blair Kaiser, "Conversations in Jail with Sirhan," *Life*, January 17, 1969, pp. 21–25.
8. Dave Smith, "Sirhan Jury Selected," *Los Angeles Times*, January 25, 1969, part 2, p. 1.
9. Ibid.
10. William Tuohy, "New Palestine Liberation Chief Vows to Escalate 'Revolution,' " *Los Angeles Times*, February 5, 1969, part 1, p. 1.
11. Carl Greenberg, "Reagan Calls Campus Violence Part of Plot to Destroy Nation," *Los Angeles Times*, February 8, 1969, part 1, p. 1.

Chapter 4: The Judge's Chambers

1. Ralph Blumenfeld, "New Questions: The Death of RFK," *New York Post*, May 23, 1975.
2. Dr. Orville Roderick Richardson and Dr. Eric Marcus had been been appointed by the court. Dr. Martin Schorr and Dr. Bernard Diamond had been retained by the defense. Dr. Seymour Pollack had been retained by the prosecution.
3. Robert Blair Kaiser, *"RFK Must Die!"* (New York: Dutton, 1970), 370–72.
4. Bob Greene, *Newsday*, February 12, 1969.
5. Kaiser, 309.
6. Ibid., 319.
7. Ibid., 379.
8. Ibid., 381.
9. Grant Cooper, in taped interview with journalist Betsy Langman, Los Angeles, 1973.
10. John Seigenthaler, *A Search for Justice* (Nashville: Aurora Publishers, 1971), 219.

Chapter 5: Doorframes and Dish Trays

1. Allard Lowenstein, "Suppressed Evidence of More Than One Assassin?" *Saturday Review*, Feb. 19, 1977.
2. Al Stump, "Daily Drama Unfolds in the Sirhan Trial," *Los Angeles Herald Examiner*, February 16, 1969, p. A7.
3. As recalled to Rose Lynn Mangan by Grant Cooper in 1969; further supported by written report of police telephone interview of Grant Cooper by Lt. Booth on June 8, 1971, in which Cooper summarized to Booth this conversation with Harper.
4. DeWayne Wolfer in deposition for defamation lawsuit filed by Wolfer against Los Angeles attorney Barbara Blehr, September 1971.
5. Dr. Thomas T. Noguchi in written statement given to Vincent Bugliosi, Los Angeles, December 1, 1975.
6. Robert Rozzi in written statement given to Vincent Bugliosi, Los Angeles, November 15, 1975.
7. Dan E. Moldea, *The Killing of Robert F. Kennedy* (New York: W. W. Norton, 1995) 240.
8. Robert Weidrich, "Felt Him Fire His Gun, Hotel Worker Says," *Chicago Tribune*, June 6, 1968.
9. Dion Morrow, attorney for the City of Los Angeles, "Officer Ordered Items Destroyed," *Santa Monica Evening Outlook*, August 21, 1975.
10. Evelle Younger, legal brief in response to Paul Schrade lawsuit before Judge Wenke, Superior Court (December 1975).
11. Moldea, 234.
12. Ibid., 245.
13. Ibid., 245.
14. Ibid., 259–260.
15. Wolfer, Blehr deposition, 1971.
16. Karl Uecker, interviewed by John Burns, California State archivist, taped in Sacramento, April 13, 1990.
17. Report of Joseph Busch, district attorney (1971), p. 70.
18. Trial transcript, pp. 3967–68.

Chapter 6: The Criminalist

1. Thomas T. Noguchi with Joseph DiMona, *Coroner* (New York: Simon and Schuster, 1983), 104.
2. Written statement of Karl Uecker, given to Allard K. Lowenstein in Dusseldorf, Germany, February 20, 1975.
3. Ralph Blumenfeld, "New Questions: The Death of RFK," *New York Post Magazine*, May 23, 1975.
4. Martin Patrusky in affidavit given to Vincent T. Bugliosi, Los Angeles, December 12, 1975.
5. Blumenfeld.
6. Sir Gerald Burrard, *The Identification of Firearms and Forensic Ballistics* (New York: A.S. Barnes, 1962), 154–155.
7. Lowell Bradford, 1974, cited in *Kranz Report*, p. 44.
8. Dave Smith, "Sirhan Case—Was There a 2nd Gunman?" *Los Angeles Times*, August 16, 1971, part 1, p. 1.
9. Dinko J. Bozanich, Deputy District Attorney, *Memorandum to Joseph P. Busch, District Attorney* (July 30, 1974), p. 23.
10. Ibid. 11.
11. Ibid. 21.
12. Ibid. 18.
13. Ibid. 39.
14. Charach and Harper have always maintained that they never tampered with any Sirhan exhibits.

15. Bozanich, 4.

16. Gregory Stone, *RFK Manuscript* (1983) unpublished, Chapter 5, "Firearms, Wolfer and the Forensic Panel," p. 39.

17. Ibid.

18. Gene Blake, "Criminalist Gave False Testimony Court Decides," *Los Angeles Times*, December 5, 1975, pp. 3, 25.

19. *The Report of Thomas F. Kranz on the Assassination of Robert F. Kennedy* (March 1977), p. 63.

20. Ibid.

21. Ibid.

22. Myrna Oliver, "LAPD Suspends Forensic Chemist," *Los Angeles Times*, May 31, 1980, pp. 1, 29.

Chapter 7: Missing Persons

1. Theodore Charach, *The Second Gun* (1971), film documentary.

2. Dave Smith, "Sirhan Case—Was There a 2nd Gunman?" *Los Angeles Times*, August 16, 1971, part 1, p. 1.

3. Ibid.

4. Charach.

5. The LAPD *Summary Report* summarizes over 1,400 witness interviews. Many of these interviews were of little or no consequence. Certainly any witness allegedly near the scene of the shooting was supposed to be in this report.

6. Jerry Cohen, "23-Man Task Force Selected to Probe Kennedy Murder," *Los Angeles Times*, June 14, 1968, p. 8.

7. Robert Houghton and Theodore Taylor, *Special Unit Senator* (New York: Random House, 1970), 302.

8. Lacey Fosburgh, "Rumors Dispelled in Trial of Sirhan," *New York Times*, February 28, 1969, 14.

9. Grant Cooper, *Declaration to the Los Angeles Superior Court*, May 22, 1969, copy of which is Exhibit VI in *Writ of Habeas Corpus on Behalf of Sirhan Sirhan, Trial Case #233421*, May 6, 1993, filed by Adel Sirhan and Rose Lynn Mangan.

Chapter 8: The Spotted Ghost

1. Discrepancy between court testimony and grand jury testimony brought to the attention of authors by Rose Lynn Mangan.

2. Robert A. Houghton and Theodore Taylor, *Special Unit Senator* (New York: Random House, 1970), 120.

3. Jerry Cohen, "Police Halt Hunt for Mystery Girl," *Los Angeles Times*, June 22, 1968, p. 1.

4. Houghton and Taylor, 126.

5. Robert Blair Kaiser, *"RFK Must Die!"* (New York: Dutton, 1970), 255.

6. "Eye of the Hurricane," *Newsweek*, March 3, 1969, 24.

7. Jonn Christian and William Turner, *The Assassination of Robert Kennedy* (New York: Thunder's Mouth Press, 1993), 82–83.

Chapter 9: Malice Aforethought

1. Luke McKissack to radio interviewer Carol Hemingway, broadcast KPFK, Los Angeles, April 22, 1988.

2. Robert Kennedy at Temple Isaiah, May 20, 1968 *Los Angeles Times*, May 21, 1968.

3. James W. Clarke, *American Assassins* (Princeton, N.J.: Princeton University Press, 1982), 87–88.

4. Robert Blair Kaiser, *"RFK Must Die!"* (New York: Dutton, 1970), 420.

5. "Notebook Found in Sirhan Home," *New York Times*, June 6, 1968, p. 1.

6. Lacey Fosburgh, "Sirhan Trial," *New York Times,* January 19, 1969, p. E4.

7. Kaiser, 188.

8. Ibid., 275–76.

9. Ibid., 277.

10. Ibid., 280.

11. Ibid., 273.

12. Ibid., 288.

13. Ibid., 248–54.

14. Ibid., 324–27.

15. Ibid., 257.

16. Ibid.

17. Ibid., 320.

18. Ibid., 425.

19. Ibid., 422.

20. Dave Smith, "Sirhan Trial Opens," *Los Angeles Times,* January 8, 1969, p. 22.

21. Terrence Smith, "Father of Suspect 'Sickened' by News," *New York Times,* June 6, 1968, p. 1.

22. Kaiser, 345.

23. Ibid., 230.

24. Ibid., 466.

Chapter 10: Sirhan Bishara Sirhan

1. Robert Blair Kaiser, *"RFK Must Die!"* (New York: Dutton, 1970), 406.

2. Ibid, 415–16.

3. Al Stump, "Sirhan Memory 'Failing,' " *Los Angeles Herald Examiner,* March 7, 1969.

4. Kaiser, 421.

Chapter 11: Rorschach and Freud

1. James A. Brussell, *A Casebook of a Crime Psychiatrist* (New York: Bernard Geis Associates, 1968).

2. John Seigenthaler, *A Search for Justice* (Nashville: Aurora Publishers, 1971), 369.

3. Bob Greene, *Newsday,* March 19, 1969.

Chapter 12: Hypnosis and Memory

1. Robert Blair Kaiser, *"RFK Must Die!"* (New York: Dutton, 1970), 536.

2. Bernard Diamond, "The Simulation of Sanity," *Journal of Social Therapy* (1956).

3. "Friends Describe Sirhan," *Los Angeles Herald Examiner,* June 5, 1968.

Chapter 13: Witness for the Prosecution

1. Martin Waldron, "Lawyer Testifies He Made Up Story," *New York Times,* February 26, 1969, p. 16.

2. Martin Waldron, "Ray Admits Guilt," *New York Times,* March 11, 1969, p. 9.

3. "Judge Preston Battle Dies," *New York Times,* April 1, 1969, p. 47.

4. "Ray Changes His Mind," *Newsweek,* March 31, 1969, p. 29.

5. John Herbers, "US Will Continue Its Inquiry on Ray," *New York Times,* March 11, 1969, p. 1.

6. "Ray: 99 Years—and a Victory," *Newsweek,* March 24, 1969, p. 32.

7. Robert Blair Kaiser, *"RFK Must Die!"* (New York: Dutton, 1970), 415.

8. Dave Smith, *Los Angeles Times,* April 2, 1969.

9. Ibid.

10. Douglas Robinson, "Sirhan Jury Told Test Scores Err," *New York Times,* April 8, 1969, p. 7.

11. Dave Smith, "Psychiatrist's Testimony Sends Sirhan into Rage," *Los Angeles Times*, April 9, 1969, part 2, p. 1.

12. "Test Case," *Newsweek*, April 7, 1969, p. 94.

13. "Psychiatry on Trial," *National Review*, May 6, 1969, p. 427.

Chapter 14: The Verdict

1. Douglas Robinson, "Sirhan Called a 'Little Sick Boy,' " *New York Times*, April 11, 1969, p. 26.

2. Robert Blair Kaiser, *"RFK Must Die!"* (New York: Dutton, 1970), 486.

3. Martin Kasindorf, "Verdict on Sirhan," *Newsweek*, April 28, 1969, 41.

4. Kaiser, 496.

5. Douglas Robinson, "Sirhan Jury Asks for Clarification," *New York Times*, April 17, 1969, p. 21.

6. Kaiser, 502.

7. Martin Kasindorf, "The Jury vs Sirhan," *Newsweek*, May 5, 1969, 35.

8. Kaiser, 509.

9. Douglas Robinson, "Sentenced to Die," *New York Times*, April 24, 1969, p. 1.

10. Kasindorf, "The Jury vs Sirhan," 34.

11. Ibid.

12. Lacey Fosburgh, "Sirhan Jurors Reveal That 'Law and Order' Was Major Consideration," *New York Times*, April 25, 1969, p. 50.

13. Robinson, "Sentenced to Die," 29.

14. Fosburgh, 50.

15. Robinson, "Sentenced to Die," 29.

16. Tom Wicker, "In the Nation: Sam Yorty and Sirhan B. Sirhan," *New York Times*, June 3, 1969, p. 46.

17. William F. Buckley, "Reflections on the Sirhan Trial," *National Review*, March 11, 1969, 247.

18. "Egyptian Paper Describes Sirhan Case as Political," *New York Times*, April 21, 1969, p. 17.

19. "The Sirhan Verdict," *New York Times*, April 18, 1969, p. 42.

Chapter 15: Disclosure

1. Allard K. Lowenstein, "Suppressed Evidence of More Than One Assassin?" *Saturday Review*, February 19, 1977, p. 6.

2. Ibid., 9.

3. John M. Crewdson, "Lowenstein Says Year's Study of Evidence Shows Sirhan Was Not Assassin of Kennedy," *New York Times*, December 16, 1974, p. 29.

4. Ibid.

5. William Farr, "Some Material on Kennedy Destroyed," *Los Angeles Times*, August 22, 1975, p. 3.

6. Ibid.

7. Ibid.

8. Allard Lowenstein; letter to Samuel L. Williams, August 27, 1975.

9. Lowenstein, "Suppressed Evidence," p. 11.

10. Philip Melanson interview with Theodore Taylor (1986).

11. Lowenstein, "Suppressed Evidence," p. 12.

12. Gregory Stone, personal communication to Philip Melanson (1985).

13. David Freed, "Police Told to Disclose Summary of RFK Case," *Los Angeles Times*, July 31, 1985, part 2, p. 3.

14. Daryl Gates, *Chief: My Life in the LAPD* (New York: Bantam, 1992), 152.

15. *ABC News with Peter Jennings*, April 19, 1988.

16. Robert A. Houghton, remarks broadcast on KTTV, June 6, 1988.

17. Lance Williams, "Prober Insists Purged RFK Evidence Useless," *San Francisco Examiner*, April 1988.

18. Andrea Ford, "Investigation Urged in LAPD's Handling of Kennedy Slaying," *Los Angeles Times*, April 3, 1992, B3.

Chapter 16: Prison and Parole

1. Gene Blake, "California to Seek Rehearing of Court's Death Penalty Ban," *Los Angeles Times*, February 19, 1972, part 1, p. 1.
2. "The Death Penalty Overruled," editorial, *Los Angeles Times*, February 21, 1972, part 2, p. 1.
3. Gene Blake, "High Court Gets Younger Petition on Death Penalty," *Los Angeles Times*, March 4, 1972, part 2, p. 1.
4. "Sirhan Case Rejected," *Los Angeles Times*, December 17, 1974, part 2, p. 4.
5. Robert Kistler, "High Court Rejects Sirhan Plea," *Los Angeles Times*, February 14, 1975, part 1, p. 30.
6. Ibid.
7. William Endicott, "Panel Went by Book on Sirhan Parole," *Los Angeles Times*, May 22, 1975, part 1, p. 32.
8. Ibid.
9. CONRAD cartoon, *Los Angeles Times*, May 22, 1975, part 2, p. 7.
10. Jesse Unruh, "Unruh Calls Sirhan a Traitor," *Los Angeles Times*, June 6, 1975, part 2, p. 7.
11. Tom Wheeler, letter to editor, *Los Angeles Times*, June 17, 1975, part 2, p. 6.
12. James McKinley, "Inside Sirhan," *Playboy*, April 1978, 96–98, 206–14.
13. Bill Farr, "Sirhan Threat to Kill Ted Kennedy Told," *Los Angeles Times*, August 13, 1981, part 1, p. 1.
14. Ibid. p. 28.
15. "New Testimony Disputes DA's View of Sirhan," *Los Angeles Times*, November 25, 1981, part 1, p. 14.
16. Raul Rodriguez, letter to editor, *Los Angeles Times*, June 8, 1981, part 2, p. 8.
17. Kathy McNelis, letter to editor, *Los Angeles Times*, June 8, 1981, part 2, p. 8.
18. Bill Farr, "FBI Hunts Witness in Sirhan Case," *Los Angeles Times*, April 16, 1982, part 2, p. 1.
19. Bill Farr, "Killer Tells of Sirhan Threat on Ted Kennedy," *Los Angeles Times*, April 27, 1982, part 1, p. 23.
20. Bill Farr, "Witness: Hidden Razor Blades Found," *Los Angeles Times*, May 3, 1982, part 1, p. 3.
21. Bill Farr, "Testimony on Sirhan Threats Challenged," *Los Angeles Times*, April 28, 1982, part 1, p. 3.
22. Ibid.
23. Bill Farr, "Sirhan Plea for Parole Invokes Kennedy Name," *Los Angeles Times*, May 11, 1982, part 1, p. 17.
24. Ibid.
25. Bill Farr, "Sirhan's 1984 Parole Date Revoked; Threats Cited," *Los Angeles Times*, May 22, 1982, part 1, p. 1.
26. Ibid. p. 28.
27. Bill Farr, "Psychiatric Test Shows Sirhan as a Model Inmate," *Los Angeles Times*, June 26, 1985, part 2, p. 1.
28. John Kendall, "Sirhan Attorney Assails Parole Unit," *Los Angeles Times*, August 21, 1985, part 1, p. 3.
29. Ibid. p. 28.
30. Ibid. p. 3.
31. Ibid. p. 28.

Chapter 17: The Phantom Photographs

1. *Jamie Scott Enyart v. March Fong Eu, #C734190.* March Fong Eu is the Secretary of State of California and was severed as a defendant in the case.
2. Bill Boyarsky, "The Spin," *Los Angeles Times*, July 9, 1996, B1.

3. Ibid.

4. Emi Endo and Eric Malnic, "Kennedy Photo Mystery Deepens," *Los Angeles Times*, January 18, 1996, B1.

5. "Had No Choice," *Los Angeles Times*, May 22, 1975, p. 32.

6. Ralph Blumenfeld, "The Death of RFK," *New York Post*, May 23, 1975,

7. Boyarsky, "The Spin," B1.

8. Carla Rivera, "Man Wins Battle," *Los Angeles Times*, August 23, 1996, B3.

9. David Bloom and Janet Gilmore, "Photographer Awarded $450,600," *Daily News*, August 23, 1996, p. 14.

Epilogue

1. Robert Blair Kaiser, *"RFK Must Die!"* (New York: Dutton, 1970), 531–532.

2. In 1969 author William Klaber worked on a sentencing project for the Vera Institute of Justice in the criminal courts of Bronx, New York.

Index

✽ ✽ ✽